HOW TO SOLVE IT
BY COMPUTER

Prentice-Hall International
Series in Computer Science

C.A.R. Hoare, Series Editor

Published

HOW TO SOLVE IT
BY COMPUTER

by

R. G. DROMEY

Department of Computing Science
The University of Wollongong

Prentice/Hall International

ENGLEWOOD CLIFFS, NEW JERSEY   LONDON   NEW DELHI

SINGAPORE   SYDNEY   TOKYO   TORONTO   WELLINGTON

Library of Congress Cataloging in Publication Data

DROMEY, R. G.,   1946–
   How to Solve it by Computer.

   Bibliography: p.
   Includes index
   1. Mathematics—Data processing
2.   Problem solving—Data processing
2.   Electronic digital computers—Programming
   I. Title.
QA76.95.D76   519.4   81-19164
ISBN 0-13-433995-9   AACR2
ISBN 0-13-434001-9 (pbk.)

British Library Cataloging in Publication Data

DROMEY, R. G.
   How to Solve it by Computer.

   1. Algorithms
   I. Title
511'.8   QA9.58
ISBN 0-13-433995-9
ISBN 0-13-434001-9 (pbk)

© 1982 by PRENTICE-HALL INTERNATIONAL, INC., London

© 1982 by PRENTICE-HALL INC., Englewood Cliffs, N.J. 07632

ISBN 0-13-433995-9
ISBN 0-13-434001-9 (PBK)

PRENTICE-HALL INTERNATIONAL, INC., *London*
PRENTICE-HALL OF AUSTRALIA PTY. LTD., *Sydney*
PRENTICE-HALL CANADA, INC., *Toronto*
PRENTICE-HALL OF INDIA PRIVATE LTD., *New Delhi*
PRENTICE-HALL OF JAPAN, INC., *Tokyo*
PRENTICE-HALL OF SOUTHEAST ASIA PTE., LTD., *Singapore*
PRENTICE-HALL, INC., *Englewood Cliffs, New Jersey*
WHITEHALL BOOKS LIMITED, *Wellington, New Zealand*

Printed in the United States of America

10 9 8 7 6 5 4 3

This book is dedicated to
George Polya

We learn most when
We have to invent

Piaget

We learn most when
We have to invent

Piaget

CONTENTS

PREFACE

The inspiration for this book has come from the classic work of Polya on general and mathematical problem-solving. As in mathematics, many beginners in computing science stumble not because they have difficulty with learning a programming language but rather because they are ill-prepared to handle the problem-solving aspects of the discipline. Unfortunately, the school system seems to concentrate on training people to answer questions and remember facts but not to really *solve* problems.

In response to this situation, it was felt there was a definite need for a book written in the spirit of Polya's work, but translated into the computing science context. Much of Polya's work is relevant in the new context but, with computing problems, because of their general requirements for iterative or recursive solutions, another dimension is added to the problem-solving process.

If we can develop problem-solving skills and couple them with top-down design principles, we are well on the way to becoming competent at algorithm design and program implementation. Emphasis in the book has been placed on presenting strategies that we might employ to "*discover*" efficient, well-structured computer algorithms. Throughout, a conscious effort has been made to convey something of the flavor of either a personal dialogue or an instructor–student dialogue that might take place in the solution of a problem. This style of presentation coupled with a carefully chosen set of examples, should make the book attractive to a wide range of readers.

The student embarking on a first course in Pascal should find that the material provides a lot of useful guidance in separating the tasks of learning how to develop computer algorithms and of then implementing them in a programming language like Pascal. Too often, the end is confused with the means. A good way to work with the book for self-study is to read only as much as you need to get started on a problem. Then, when you have developed your own solution, compare it with the one given and consciously reflect on the strategies that were helpful or hindersome in tackling the problem. As Yohe[†] has rightly pointed out "programming [computer problem-solving] is an art [and] as in all art forms, each individual must develop a style which seems natural and genuine."

Instructors should also find the style of presentation very useful as lecture material as it can be used to provide the cues for a balanced amount of instructor–class dialogue. The author has found students receptive and responsive to lectures presented in this style.

The home-computer hobbyist wishing to develop his or her problem-solving and programming skills without any formal lectures should find the completeness of presentation of the various algorithms a very valuable supplement to any introductory Pascal text. It is hoped that even some of the more advanced algorithms have been rendered more accessible to beginners than is usually the case.

The material presented, although elementary for the most part, con-tains some examples and topics which should be of sufficient interest and challenge to spark, in the beginning student, the enthusiasm for computing that we so often see in students who have begun to master their subject. Readers are urged not to accept passively the algorithm solutions given. Wherever it is possible and practical, the reader should strive for his or her own simpler or better algorithms. As always, the limitations of space have meant that some topics and examples of importance have either had to be omitted or limited in scope. To some degree the discussions and supplemen-tary problems that accompany each algorithm are intended to compensate for this. The problem sets have been carefully designed to test, reinforce, and extend the reader's understanding of the strategies and concepts presented. Readers are therefore strongly urged to attempt a considerable proportion of these problems.

Each chapter starts off with a discussion of relatively simple, graded examples, that are usually related in some fairly direct way. Towards the middle and end of each chapter, the examples are somewhat more involved. A good way to work with the book is to only consider the more fundamental algorithms in each chapter at a first reading. This should allow the necessary build-up of background needed to study in detail some of the more advanced algorithms at a later stage.

The chapters are approximately ordered in increasing order of concep-tual difficulty as usually experienced by students. The first chapter intro-

[†] J. M. Yohe, "An overview of programming practices", *Comp. Surv.*, **6**, 221–46 (1974).

duces the core aspects of computer problem-solving and algorithm design. At a first reading the last half of the chapter can be skimmed through. Where possible, the ideas are reinforced with examples. The problem-solving discussion tries to come to grips with the sort of things we can do when we are *stuck* with a problem. The important topic of program verification is presented in a way that should be relatively easy for the reader to grasp and apply at least to simple algorithms. Examples are used to convey something of the flavor of a probabilistic analysis of an algorithm.

The second chapter concentrates on developing the skill for formulating iterative solutions to problems—a skill we are likely to have had little experience with before an encounter with computers. Several problems are also considered which should allow us to come to a practical understanding of how computers represent and manipulate information. The problem of conversion from one representation to another is also addressed. The algorithms in this chapter are all treated as if we were faced with the task of discovering them for the first time. Since our aim is to foster skill in computer problem-solving, this method of presentation would seem to be appropriate from a pedagogical standpoint. Algorithms in the other chapters are also discussed in this style.

In the third chapter, we consider a number of problems that have their origin in number theory. These algorithms require an extension of the iterative techniques developed in the first chapter. Because of their nature, most of these problems can be solved in a number of ways and can differ widely in their computational cost. Confronting the question of efficiency adds an extra dimension to the problem-solving process. We set out to "discover" these algorithms as if for the first time.

Array-processing algorithms are considered in detail in Chapter 4. Facility with the use of arrays needs to be developed as soon as we have understood and are able to use iteration in the development of algorithms. Arrays, when coupled with iteration, provide us with a very powerful means of performing computations on collections of data that share some common attribute. Strategies for the efficient processing of array information raise some interesting problem-solving issues. The algorithms discussed are intended to address at least some of the more important of these issues.

Once arrays and iteration have been covered, we have the necessary tools to consider merging, sorting and searching algorithms. These topics are discussed in Chapter 5. The need to organize and subsequently efficiently search large volumes of information is central in computing science. A number of the most well-known internal sorting and searching algorithms are considered. An attempt is made to provide the settings that would allow us to "discover" these algorithms.

The sixth chapter on text and string processing represents a diversion from the earlier emphasis on "numeric" computing. The nature and organization of character information raises some important new problem-solving issues. The demands for efficiency once again lead to the consideration of some interesting algorithms that are very different from those reviewed in earlier chapters. The algorithms in this chapter emphasize the need to develop the skill of recognizing the essentials of a problem without being confused or misled by extraneous detail. "Discovering" some of these algorithms provides an interesting test-bed for us to apply some of the problem-solving skills we should have absorbed after covering the first five chapters.

Chapter 7 is devoted to the fundamental algorithms for maintaining and searching the primary dynamic data structures (i.e. stacks, queues, lists, and binary trees). The issues in this chapter arise mostly at the implementation level and with the use of pointers.

In the final chapter, the topic of recursion is introduced. A recursive call is presented as an extension of the conventional subprocedure call. The simplest form of recursion, linear recursion, is only briefly treated because the view is taken that there are almost always simple iterative schemes that can be found for performing what amounts to linear recursion. Furthermore, linear recursion does little to either convey anything of the power of recursion or to really deepen our understanding of the mechanism. The same cannot usually be said for problems involving either binary recursion or the more general non-linear recursion. Algorithms that belong to both these classes are discussed in detail, with special emphasis being placed on recognizing their underlying similarities and deepening our understanding of recursion mechanisms.

As a concluding remark about the book, if the author were to hope that this work may achieve anything, it would be that it stimulated students and others to embark on a journey of discovering things for themselves!

A SUGGESTION FOR INSTRUCTORS

"...any idea or problem or body of knowledge can be presented in a form simple enough so that any particular learner can understand it in a recognizable form."

—Bruner.

In comparison with most other human intellectual activities, computing is in its infancy despite the progress we seem to have made in such a short time. Because the demand for computers and people with computing skills is so great in our rapidly changing world, we have not had time to sit back and reflect on the best way to convey the "computing concept" on a wide scale. In time, computing will mature and evolve as a well-understood discipline with clear and well-defined methods for introducing the subject to beginners—but that is in the future. For the present, because we are not in this happy situation, it is most prudent to look to other mature disciplines for guidance on how we should introduce computing to beginners. Assuming we want to have the highest possible success rate in introducing computing to students (a situation which clearly at present does not prevail) and that we want to teach computing on the widest possible scale, then the most obvious discipline to turn to is that of *learning to read and write*.

Educators have mastered the process of teaching people to read and write to the extent that these skills are able to be transmitted on a very wide scale, efficiently, and with a very high rate of success. Putting aside the various methods within the learning-to-read-and-write discipline we see that there are some fundamental principles acknowledged by all methods that are highly relevant to teaching computing.

In teaching people to read and write a very substantial time (years in fact) is devoted to reading. Only after such preparation is it considered appropriate that they should attempt to write stories or essays, or books, etc. In fact, even before people attempt to learn to read they undergo several years of listening to language, speaking, and being "read to". Clearly, in learning a language, the ultimate goal is to be able to verbalize and write fluently in that language. Similarly in computing the goal is to be able to program (or design and implement algorithms) effectively. In learning to read and write it has long been recognized that reading is easier and that it must precede writing by a considerable margin of time to allow the assimilation of enough models and constructs of text to make writing possible.

In teaching computing we seem to have overlooked or neglected what corresponds to the reading stage in the process of learning to read and write. To put it strongly, asking people to design and write programs early on in their computing experience is like expecting that they be able to competently write essays *before* they have learned to read or even to write short sentences—it is expecting just too much of a lot of people. It also probably explains why many otherwise very able people just don't get started in computing.

What we are therefore proposing is that in teaching computing we should draw as much as we can from the learning-to-read-and-write analogy. This means that we must be able to provide the beginning student with his or her "reading experience" in computing before embarking on the more difficult computer problem-solving tasks which require considerably more creative effort, discipline, and technical skill.

At this point it is important to recognize that the "reading experience" cannot be gained by sitting down with a book of programs and attempting to "read" them. The problem with this approach is that program instructions as written on a piece of paper are a *static* representation of a computer algorithm. As such they do not very fluently convey anything of the dynamic aspect of computer algorithms and programs.

It can be argued that it is important to have a clear and in-depth understanding of the dynamic character of programs before attempting algorithm design and program implementation. What is needed is a practical and economical method of giving students their "reading experience" in computing. To gain this experience the students need to "see" programs written in a high level language executing. Traditionally, all the student sees is the output printed on the terminal or line printer and prompts by the program when it requires input from the terminal. This level of "seeing" a program execute is unsatisfactory for beginners because it conveys very little about the program's flow of control or about the effects of individual and groups of program statements. What we need is much more explicit demonstrations of what is happening in a program that causes it to produce the outputs that it does. A far more transparent way to do this is to place before the student on a terminal the text of the program being executed and then to trace the execution on the displayed program while at the same time dynamically updating on the screen the changes in program variables as they are made and related to steps in the displayed program. This dynamic method of studying algorithms can greatly assist the student in acquiring a level of understanding necessary to design and implement his or her own algorithms.

The facilities and software tools needed to adequately demonstrate execution of a program in this way are relatively economical to provide. All that is needed is a terminal with cursor addressing facilities and a *small set of software tools* (several hundred lines of code) that can be inserted into the program being studied to make its execution "visible" on the screen. Only one procedure call per statement of the program being studied is needed to operate it in a visible mode (this software is available from the author). The display software is transparent to the user. The appropriate tools allow us to see a program execute in single-step mode while monitoring the changes in variables as they are dynamically displayed on the screen. The student can cause the program to execute the next statement at each stage by simply pressing a single key (e.g. the RETURN) on the terminal.

As an example, the screen layout for "visible" execution of a selection sorting procedure in Pascal is as illustrated in Fig. 1. The next statement to be executed at each stage is tracked by having an arrow that can be moved from statement to statement on the procedure text displayed on the screen. A more complete description of the software is given elsewhere.[†]

---

† R. G. Dromey, *Before Programming—On Teaching Introductory Computing*, Technical Report No. 81/6, Dept. of Computing Science, University of Wollongong (1981).

```
procedure selectionsort(a:nelements; n:integer);
var i {index for sorted part}, j {index for unsorted part},
    p {position of minimum}, min {minimum in unsorted part}: integer;

begin
    for i := 1 to n−1 do
        begin
            min := a[i];
            p := i;
            for j := i+1 to n do
                if a[ j] < min then
                    begin
                        min := a[ j];
                        p := j
                    end;
            a[p] := a[i];
            a[i] := min
        end
end
```

i : [1] $a[i]$: [12]

j : [2] $a[j]$: [4]

p : [1] $a[p]$: [12]

n : [8] min : [4]

[7] →

array: 12   4   56   67   9   23   45
                    i j

condition: $a[j] < min$: [true]

Fig. 1   Screen layout for visible program execution.

The cause-and-effect nature of what is displayed when executing programs in this manner (automatic single-step mode) can accomplish a number of things.

(1) Most importantly, it provides a good understanding of the dynamic nature of algorithms—an essential prerequisite if students are to later design and implement their own algorithms.

(2) It gives a deep insight into the basic laws of composition of computer algorithms (sequence, selection, iteration, and modularity).

(3) It is a useful vehicle for helping students to learn various programming constructs. Actually observing constructs being used within different programming contexts and linking these constructs to changes in the values of variables and conditions gives the student the necessary concrete demonstrations that will enable him or her to master the use of these constructs.

(4) It conveys in a very vivid fashion the workings of a particular algorithm. For example, the selection sort algorithm when visibly executed conveys the difficult concept of how we can have one loop executing within another loop. It also highlights the difference between subscripted variables and subscripts.

(5) It also provides an ideal tool for teaching students debugging techniques. That is, programs with logical bugs can be implemented and the student asked to diagnose the problem after studying the program in visible execution mode.

Visible program execution has the added advantage of being ideally suited for use in the lecture room, classroom, or library. Most terminals have the capability of video output which can be connected to a video recorder. Using these facilities it is very easy and cheap to monitor and record the visible program execution of a variety of programs for later use on video monitors in the classroom or library. This gives us a teaching aid far superior to handwritten blackboard examples when lecturing about algorithms in the classroom. We have recorded and used a number of programs in this way.

We can take the visible mode of program execution a step further by making it more *active* with respect to the student. At each step in the program's execution we can ask the student to supply the appropriate value of the variable or condition etc. How this works can be best illustrated by referring back to the figure. The arrow is indicating that the 7th statement (i.e. $p := j$) is the next one to be executed. What the software can do is move the cursor to the "p" box on the screen and indicate to the student that he must supply the appropriate value for p (in this case 2) before the program will continue. If the user enters the wrong value the word ERROR will flash in the p-box. This will be followed by a flashing of the INPUT sign to prompt the user to again try to enter the proper p value. If the user gets it wrong twice the software flashes VALUE in the p-box and then supplies the user with the correct value, switches from interactive to automatic single step mode, and moves to the next program statement to be executed.

Using a visible program in interactive single-step mode can in a very direct way reinforce the student's comprehension of how a program really works and what individual program statements accomplish. At the same time it can give the student very positive and direct feedback when he gets something wrong.

What we are therefore advocating is that students be given *considerable* exposure to visible "program-reading" in both the modes described as a preparatory step to considering the problem-solving aspect of computer algorithm design. Exposure to visible program execution (VPE) should be accompanied by a study of the basic laws of composition of computer algorithms (sequence, selection, iteration and modularity) including how these laws of form relate to the way programs are executed. Concurrently, a study should also be made of the syntax of the programming language being read.

ACKNOWLEDGEMENTS

The inspiration for the approach taken in this book grew out of an admiration for George Polya's classic works on problem-solving. During the summer and autumn of 1980, I had the pleasure of spending a number of afternoons chatting with Professor and Mrs. Polya.

The influence of Polya's work and that of the pioneers of the discipline of computing science, E. W. Dijkstra, R. W. Floyd, C. A. R. Hoare, D. E. Knuth, and N. Wirth, is freely acknowledged. There is also a strong influence of Jeff Rohl's work in the last chapter on recursion.

I sincerely appreciate the guidance and encouragement given to me by Professor Hoare, Henry Hirschberg, Ron Decent, and my reviewers.

I am also grateful to the University of Wollongong and Stanford University for the use of their facilities.

A number of people have generously given helpful comments and support during the preparation of the manuscript. I would particularly like to thank Tom Bailey, Miranda Baker, Harold Brown, Bruce Buchanan, Ann Cartwright, John Farmer, Tony Guttman, Joan Hutchinson, Leanne Koring, Donald Knuth, Rosalyn Maloney, Richard Miller, Ross Nealon, Jurg Nievergelt, Richard Patis, Ian Pirie, Juris Reinfelds, Tom Richards, Michael Shepanksi, Stanley Smerin and Natesa Sridharan and my students at Wollongong.

The understanding and encouragement throughout this whole project that I have received from my wife Aziza is deeply appreciated.

Finally, I wish to extend my deepest gratitude to Bronwyn James for her loyalty and untiring and able support in the preparation and typing of the manuscript.

Chapter 1
INTRODUCTION TO COMPUTER PROBLEM-SOLVING

1.1   INTRODUCTION

Computer problem-solving can be summed up in one word—it is *demanding*! It is an intricate process requiring much thought, careful planning, logical precision, persistence, and attention to detail. At the same time it can be a challenging, exciting, and satisfying experience with considerable room for personal creativity and expression. If computer problem-solving is approached in this spirit then the chances of success are greatly amplified. In the discussion which follows in this introductory chapter we will attempt to lay the foundations for our study of computer problem-solving.

1.1.1   Programs and algorithms

The vehicle for the computer solution to a problem is a set of explicit and unambiguous instructions expressed in a programming language. This set of instructions is called a *program*. A program may also be thought of as an *algorithm* expressed in a programming language. An algorithm therefore corresponds to a solution to a problem that is *independent* of any programming language.

To obtain the computer solution to a problem once we have the program we usually have to supply the program with *input* or data. The program then takes this input and manipulates it according to its instructions and eventually produces an *output* which represents the computer solution to the problem. The realization of the computer output is but the last step in a very long chain of events that have led up to the computer solution to the problem.

Our goal in this work is to study in depth the process of algorithm design with particular emphasis on the problem-solving aspects of the task. There are many definitions of an algorithm. The following definition is appropriate in computing science. An *algorithm* consists of a set of explicit and unambiguous finite steps which, when carried out for a given set of initial conditions, produce the corresponding output and terminate in a finite time.

1.1.2 Requirements for solving problems by computer

From time to time in our everyday activities, we employ algorithms to solve problems. For example, to look up someone's telephone number in a telephone directory we need to employ an algorithm. Tasks such as this are usually performed automatically without any thought to the complex underlying mechanism needed to effectively conduct the search. It therefore comes as somewhat of a surprise to us when developing computer algorithms that the solution must be specified with such logical precision and in such detail. After studying even a small sample of computer problems it soon becomes obvious that the conscious *depth of understanding* needed to design effective computer algorithms is far greater than we are likely to encounter in almost any other problem-solving situation.

Let us reflect for a moment on the telephone directory look-up problem. A telephone directory quite often contains hundreds of thousands of names and telephone numbers yet we have little trouble finding the desired telephone number we are seeking. We might therefore ask why do we have so little difficulty with a problem of seemingly great size? The answer is simple. We quite naturally take advantage of the order in the directory to quickly eliminate large sections of the list and home in on the desired name and number. We would never contemplate looking up the telephone number of J. R. Nash by starting at page 1 and examining each name in turn until we finally come to Nash's name and telephone number. Nor are we likely to contemplate looking up the name of the person whose number is 2987533. To conduct such a search, there is no way in which we can take advantage of the order in the directory and so we are faced with the prospect of doing a number-by-number search starting at page 1. If, on the other hand, we had a list of telephone numbers and names ordered by telephone number rather than name, the task would be straightforward. What these examples serve to emphasize is the important influence of the data organization on the performance of algorithms. Only when a data structure is symbiotically linked with an algorithm can we expect high performance. Before considering these and other aspects of algorithm design we need to address the topic of problem-solving in some detail.

1.2 THE PROBLEM-SOLVING ASPECT

It is widely recognized that problem-solving is a creative process which largely defies systematization and mechanization. This may not sound very encouraging to the would-be problem-solver. To balance this, most people, during their schooling, acquire at least a modest set of problem-solving skills which they may or may not be aware of.

Even if one is not naturally skilled at problem-solving there are a number of steps that can be taken to raise the level of one's performance. It is not implied or intended that the suggestions in what follows are in any way a recipe for problem-solving. The plain fact of the matter is that there is no universal method. Different strategies appear to work for different people.

Within this context, then, where can we begin to say anything useful about computer problem-solving? We must start from the premise that computer problem-solving is about understanding.

1.2.1 Problem definition phase

Success in solving any problem is only possible after we have made the effort to come to terms with or understand the problem at hand. We cannot hope to make useful progress in solving a problem until we fully understand what it is we are trying to solve. This preliminary investigation may be thought of as the *problem definition phase*. In other words, what we must do during this phase is work out *what must be done* rather than *how to do it*. That is, we must try to extract from the problem statement (which is often quite imprecise and maybe even ambiguous) a set of precisely defined tasks. Inexperienced problem-solvers too often gallop ahead with how they are going to solve the problem only to find that they are either solving the wrong problem or they are solving just a very special case of what is actually required. In short, a lot of care should be taken in working out precisely what must be done. The development of algorithms for finding the square root (algorithm 3.1) and the greatest common divisor (algorithm 3.3) are good illustrations of how important it is to carefully define the problem. Then, from the definitions, we are led in a natural way to algorithm designs for these two problems.

1.2.2 Getting started on a problem

There are many ways to solve most problems and also many solutions to most problems. This situation does not make the job of problem-solving easy. When confronted with many possible lines of attack it is usually difficult to recognize quickly which paths are likely to be fruitless and which paths may be productive.

Perhaps the more common situation for people just starting to come to grips with the computer solution to problems is that they just do not have any idea where to start on the problem, even after the problem definition phase. When confronted with this situation, what can we do? A block often occurs at this point because people become concerned with details of the implementation *before* they have completely understood or worked out an implementation-independent solution. The best advice here is not to be too concerned about detail. That can come later when the complexity of the problem as a whole has been brought under control. The old computer proverb[†] which says "the sooner you start coding your program the longer it is going to take" is usually painfully true.

1.2.3 The use of specific examples

A useful strategy when we are stuck is to use some props or heuristics (i.e. rules of thumb) to try to get a start with the problem. An approach that often allows us to make a start on a problem is to pick a specific example of the general problem we wish to solve and try to work out the mechanism that will allow us to solve this particular problem (e.g. if you want to find the maximum in a set of numbers, choose a particular set of numbers and work out the mechanism for finding the maximum in this set—see for example algorithm 4.3). It is usually much easier to work out the details of a solution to a specific problem because the relationship between the mechanism and the particular problem is more clearly defined. Furthermore, a specific problem often forces us to focus on details that are not so apparent when the problem is considered abstractly. Geometrical or schematic diagrams representing certain aspects of the problem can be usefully employed in many instances (see, for example, algorithm 3.3).

This approach of focusing on a particular problem can often give us the foothold we need for making a start on the solution to the general problem. The method should, however, not be abused. It is very easy to fall into the trap of thinking that the solution to a specific problem or a specific class of problems is also a solution to the general problem. Sometimes this happens but we should always be very wary of making such an assumption.

Ideally, the specifications for our particular problem need to be examined very carefully to try to establish whether or not the proposed algorithm can meet those requirements. If the full specifications are difficult to formulate sometimes a well-chosen set of test cases can give us a degree of

---

† H. F. Ledgard, *Programming Proverbs*, Hayden, Rochelle Park, N.J., 1975.

confidence in the generality of our solution. However, nothing less than a complete proof of correctness of our algorithm is entirely satisfactory. We will discuss this matter in more detail a little later.

1.2.4 Similarities among problems

We have already seen that one way to make a start on a problem is by considering a specific example. Another thing that we should always try to do is bring as much past experience as possible to bear on the current problem. In this respect it is important to see if there are any similarities between the current problem and other problems that we have solved or we have seen solved. Once we have had a little experience in computer problem-solving it is unlikely that a new problem will be completely divorced from other problems we have seen. A good habit therefore is to always make an effort to be aware of the similarities among problems. The more experience one has the more/tools and techniques one can bring to bear in tackling a given problem. The contribution of experience to our ability to solve problems is not always helpful. In fact, sometimes it blocks us from discovering a desirable or better solution to a problem. A classic case of experience blocking progress was Einstein's discovery of relativity. For a considerable time before Einstein made his discovery the scientists of the day had the necessary facts that could have led them to relativity but it is almost certain that their experience blocked them from even contemplating such a proposal—Newton's theory was correct and that was all there was to it! On this point it is therefore probably best to place only cautious reliance on past experience. In trying to get a better solution to a problem, sometimes too much study of the existing solution or a similar problem forces us down the same reasoning path (which may not be the best) and to the same dead end. In trying to get a better solution to a problem, it is usually wise, in the first instance at least, to try to *independently* solve the problem. We then give ourselves a better chance of not falling into the same traps as our predecessors. In the final analysis, every problem must be considered on its merits.

A skill that it is important to try to develop in problem-solving is the ability to view a problem from a variety of angles. One must be able to metaphorically turn a problem upside down, inside out, sideways, backwards, forwards and so on. Once one has developed this skill it should be possible to get started on any problem.

1.2.5 Working backwards from the solution

There are still other things we can try when we do not know where to start on a problem. We can, for example, in some cases assume that we already have the solution to the problem and then try to work backwards to the starting conditions. Even a guess at the solution to the problem may be enough to give us a foothold to start on the problem. (See, for example, the square root problem—algorithm 3.1). Whatever attempts that we make to get started on a problem we should write down as we go along the various steps and explorations made. This can be important in allowing us to systematize our investigations and avoid duplication of effort. Another practice that helps us develop our problem-solving skills is, once we have solved a problem, to consciously reflect back on the way we went about discovering the solution. This can help us significantly. The most crucial thing of all in developing problem-solving skills is practice. Piaget summed this up very nicely with the statement that "we learn most when we have to invent."

1.2.6   General problem-solving strategies

There are a number of general and powerful computational strategies that are repeatedly used in various guises in computing science. Often it is possible to phrase a problem in terms of one of these strategies and achieve very considerable gains in computational efficiency.

Probably the most widely known and most often used of these principles is the *divide-and-conquer* strategy. The basic idea with divide-and-conquer is to divide the original problem into two or more subproblems which can hopefully be solved more efficiently by the same technique. If it is possible to proceed with this splitting into smaller and smaller subproblems we will eventually reach the stage where the subproblems are small enough to be solved without further splitting. This way of breaking down the solution to a problem has found wide application in particular with sorting, selection, and searching algorithms. We will see later in Chapter 5 when we consider the binary search algorithm how applying this strategy to an ordered data set results in an algorithm that needs to make only $\log_2 n$ rather than n comparisons to locate a given item in an ordered list n elements long. When this principle is used in sorting algorithms, the number of comparisons can be reduced from the order of n^2 steps to $n \log_2 n$ steps, a substantial gain particularly for large n. The same idea can be applied to file comparison and in many other instances to give substantial gains in computational efficiency. It is not absolutely necessary for divide-and-conquer to always exactly halve the problem size. The algorithm used in Chapter 4 to find the kth smallest element repeatedly reduces the size of the problem. Although it does not divide the problem in half at each step it has very good average performance.

It is also possible to apply the divide-and-conquer strategy essentially in reverse to some problems. The resulting *binary doubling strategy* can give the same sort of gains in computational efficiency. We will consider in Chapter 3 how this complementary technique can be used to advantage to raise a number to a large power and to calculate the nth Fibonacci number. With this doubling strategy we need to express the next term n to be computed in terms of the current term which is usually a function of $n/2$ in order to avoid the need to generate intermediate terms.

Another general problem-solving strategy that we will briefly consider is that of *dynamic programming*. This method is used most often when we have to build up a solution to a problem via a sequence of intermediate steps. The monotone subsequence problem in Chapter 4 uses a variant of the dynamic programming method. This method relies on the idea that a good solution to a large problem can sometimes be built up from good or optimal solutions to smaller problems. This type of strategy is particularly relevant for many optimization problems that one frequently encounters in operations research. The techniques of *greedy search*, *backtracking* and *branch-and-bound* evaluations are all variations on the basic dynamic programming idea. They all tend to guide a computation in such a way that the minimum amount of effort is expended on exploring solutions that have been established to be suboptimal. There are still other general computational strategies that we could consider but because they are usually associated with more advanced algorithms we will not proceed further in this direction.

1.3   TOP-DOWN DESIGN

The primary goal in computer problem-solving is an algorithm which is capable of being implemented as a correct and efficient computer program. In our discussion leading up to the consideration of algorithm design we have been mostly concerned with the very broad aspects of problem-solving. We now need to consider those aspects of problem-solving and algorithm design which are closer to the algorithm implementation.

Once we have defined the problem to be solved and we have at least a vague idea of how to solve it, we can begin to bring to bear powerful techniques for designing algorithms. The key to being able to successfully design algorithms lies in being able to manage the inherent complexity of most problems that require computer solution. People as problem-solvers are only able to focus on, and comprehend at one time, a very limited span of logic or instructions. A technique for algorithm design that tries to accommodate this human limitation is known as *top-down design* or *stepwise refinement*.

Top-down design is a strategy that we can apply to take the solution of a computer problem from a vague outline to a precisely defined algorithm and program implementation. Top-down design provides us with a way of handling the inherent logical complexity and detail frequently encountered in computer algorithms. It allows us to build our solutions to a problem in a stepwise fashion. In this way, specific and complex details of the implementation are encountered only at the stage when we have done sufficient groundwork on the overall structure and relationships among the various parts of the problem.

1.3.1 Breaking a problem into subproblems

Before we can apply top-down design to a problem we must first do the problem-solving groundwork that gives us at least the broadest of outlines of a solution. Sometimes this might demand a lengthy and creative investigation into the problem while at other times the problem description may in itself provide the necessary starting point for top-down design. The general outline may consist of a single statement or a set of statements. Top-down design suggests that we take the general statements that we have about the solution, one at a time, and break them down into a set of more precisely defined subtasks. These subtasks should more accurately describe how the final goal is to be reached. With each splitting of a task into subtasks it is essential that the way in which the subtasks need to interact with each other be precisely defined. Only in this way is it possible to preserve the overall structure of the solution to the problem. Preservation of the overall structure in the solution to a problem is important both for making the algorithm comprehensible and also for making it possible to prove the correctness of the solution. The process of repeatedly breaking a task down into subtasks and then each subtask into still smaller subtasks must continue until we eventually end up with subtasks that can be implemented as program statements. For most algorithms we only need to go down to two or three levels although obviously for large software projects this is not true. The larger and more complex the problem, the more it will need to be broken down to be made tractable. A schematic breakdown of a problem is shown in Fig. 1.1.

The process of breaking down the solution to a problem into subtasks in the manner described results in an implementable set of subtasks that fit quite naturally into block-structured languages like Pascal and Algol. There can therefore be a smooth and natural interface between the stepwise-refined algorithm and the final program implementation—a highly desirable situation for keeping the implementation task as simple as possible.

1.3.2 Choice of a suitable data structure

One of the most important decisions we have to make in formulating computer solutions to problems is the choice of appropriate data structures.

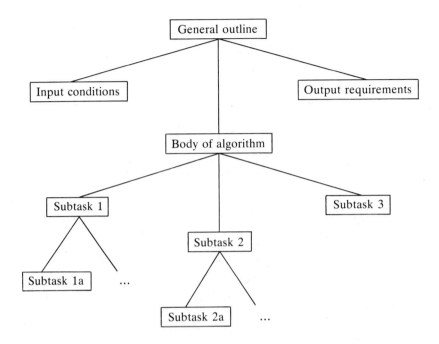

Fig. 1.1 Schematic breakdown of a problem into subtasks as employed in top-down design.

All programs operate on data and consequently the way the data is organized can have a profound effect on every aspect of the final solution. In particular, an inappropriate choice of data structure often leads to clumsy, inefficient, and difficult implementations. On the other hand, an appropriate choice usually leads to a simple, transparent, and efficient implementation.

There is no hard and fast rule that tells us at what stage in the development of an algorithm we need to make decisions about the associated data structures. With some problems the data structure may need to be considered at the very outset of our problem-solving explorations before the top-down design, while in other problems it may be postponed until we are well advanced with the details of the implementation. In other cases still, it can be refined as the algorithm is developed.

The key to effectively solving many problems really comes down to making appropriate choices about the associated data structures. Data structures and algorithms are usually intimately linked to one another. A small change in data organization can have a significant influence on the algorithm required to solve the problem. It is not easy to formulate any generally applicable rules that say for this class of problem this choice of data structure is appropriate. Unfortunately with regard to data structures each problem must be considered on its merits.

The sort of things we must however be aware of in setting up data structures are such questions as:

(1)   How can intermediate results be arranged to allow fast access to information that will reduce the amount of computation required at a later stage?

(2)   Can the data structure be easily searched?

(3)   Can the data structure be easily updated?

(4)   Does the data structure provide a way of recovering an earlier state in the computation?

(5)   Does the data structure involve the excessive use of storage?

(6)   Is it possible to impose some data structure on a problem that is not initially apparent?

(7)   Can the problem be formulated in terms of one of the common data structures (e.g. array, set, queue, stack, tree, graph, list)?

These considerations are seemingly general but they give the flavor of the sort of things we need to be asking as we proceed with the development of an algorithm.

1.3.3   Construction of loops

In moving from general statements about the implementation towards subtasks that can be realized as computations, almost invariably we are led to a series of iterative constructs, or loops, and structures that are conditionally executed. These structures, together with input/output statements, computable expressions, and assignments, make up the heart of program implementations.

At the time when a subtask has been refined to something that can be realized as an iterative construct, we can make the task of implementing the loop easier by being aware of the essential structure of all loops. To construct any loop we must take into account three things, the initial conditions that need to apply *before* the loop begins to execute, *the invariant relation* that must apply after each iteration of the loop, and the conditions under which the iterative process must *terminate*.

In constructing loops people often have trouble in getting the initial conditions correct and in getting the loop to execute the right number of times rather than one too few or one too many times. For most problems there is a straightforward process that can be applied to avoid these errors.

1.3.4 Establishing initial conditions for loops

To establish the initial conditions for a loop, a usually effective strategy is to set the loop variables to the values that they would have to assume in order to solve the *smallest* problem associated with the loop. Typically the number of iterations n that must be made by a loop are in the range $0 \leqslant i \leqslant n$. The smallest problem usually corresponds to the case where i either equals 0 or i equals 1. Algorithms 2.2. and 4.3 illustrate both these situations. To bring this point home let us suppose that we wish to sum a set of numbers in an array using an iterative construct. The loop variables are i the array and loop index, and s the variable for accumulating the sum of the array elements.

The smallest problem in this case corresponds to the sum of zero numbers. The sum of zero numbers is zero and so the initial values of i and s must be:

$$\left. \begin{array}{l} i := 0 \\ s := 0 \end{array} \right\} \quad \text{solution for } n = 0$$

1.3.5 Finding the iterative construct

Once we have the conditions for solving the smallest problem the next step is to try to extend it to the next smallest problem (in this case when $i = 1$). That is we want to build on the solution to the problem for $i = 0$ to get the solution for $i = 1$.

The solution for $n = 1$ is:

$$\left. \begin{array}{l} i := 1 \\ s := a[1] \end{array} \right\} \quad \text{solution for } n = 1$$

This solution for $n = 1$ can be built from the solution for $n = 0$ using the values for i and s when $n = 0$ and the two expressions

$$\left. \begin{array}{l} i := i+1 \\ s := s+a[i] \end{array} \right\} \quad \text{generalized solution for } n > 0$$

The same two steps can be used to extend the solution from when $n = 1$ to when $n = 2$ and so on. These two steps will in general extend the solution from the $(i-1)^{th}$ case to the ith case (where $i \geq 1$). They can therefore be used as the basis of our iterative construct for solving the problem for $n \geq 1$.

$$
\left.
\begin{array}{l}
i := 0; \\
s := 0;
\end{array}
\right\}
\begin{array}{l}
\text{initialization conditions} \\
\text{for loop and solution to} \\
\text{summing problem when } n = 0
\end{array}
\left.
\begin{array}{l}
\\
\\
\end{array}
\right.
$$

while $i<n$ **do**		solution to summation
begin	solution of the	problem for $n \geq 0$
$i := i+1$;	array summation	
$s := s+a[i]$	problem for $n \geq 1$	
end		

The process we have gone through to construct the loop is very similar to that of mathematical induction. We will consider these ideas more closely when proof of correctness and invariant relations are discussed.

The other consideration for constructing loops is concerned with the setting up of the termination conditions.

1.3.6 Termination of loops

There are a number of ways in which loops can be terminated. In general the termination conditions are dictated by the nature of the problem. The simplest condition for terminating a loop occurs when it is known in advance how many iterations need to be made. In these circumstances we can use directly the termination facilities built into programming languages. For example in Pascal the **for**-loop can be used for such computations:

```
for i := 1 to n do
    begin
        ⋮
    end
```

This loop terminates unconditionally after n iterations.

A second way in which loops can terminate is when some conditional expression becomes false. An example is:

```
while (x>0) and (x<10) do
    begin
        ⋮
    end
```

With loops of this type it cannot be directly determined in advance how many iterations there will be before the loop will terminate. In fact there is no guarantee that loops of this type will terminate at all. In these circumstances the responsibility for making sure that the loop will terminate rests with the algorithm designer. If the model for the computation is straightforward it may be a simple matter to guarantee termination (e.g. in our example above if x is changed with each iteration in either a monotonically increasing or decreasing fashion, then eventually the conditional expression $(x>0)$ **and** $(x<10)$ will become false. There are loops of this kind where it is very difficult to prove that termination is guaranteed. Algorithm 3.1 (for computing square roots) contains a loop that is typical for this type of termination.

Yet another way in which termination of a loop can be set up is by forcing the condition under which the loop will continue to iterate to become false. This approach to termination can be very useful for simplifying the test that must be made with each iteration. An example best illustrates this method of loop termination. Suppose we wish to establish that an array of n elements is in strictly ascending order (i.e. $a[1]<a[2]<\cdots<a[n]$). To do this we can use the following instructions:

$$a[n+1] := a[n];$$
$$i := 1;$$
$$\textbf{while } a[i]<a[i+1] \textbf{ do } i := i+1$$

If n was assigned the value 5 and the data set was 2, 3, 5, 11, 14, then the first assignment prior to the loop would result in the array configuration below:

$a[1]$	$a[2]$	$\cdots$		$a[n]$	$a[n+1]$
2	3	5	11	14	14

The two 14s guarantee that the test $a[i]<a[i+1]$ will be false when $i=n$ and so the loop will terminate correctly when $i=n$ if not before.

The general rule for using this method of termination is to arrange the data at the end of the array so that it will force the conditional expression for the loop to become false. If we were not to use this device for loop termination in this situation our only alternative would be a loop implementation that uses two tests e.g.

$$i := 2;$$
$$\textbf{while } (a[i-1]<a[i]) \textbf{ and } (i<n) \textbf{ do } i := i+1$$

We have now completed an examination of the most common ways in which loops are terminated.

1.4   IMPLEMENTATION OF ALGORITHMS

The implementation of an algorithm that has been properly designed in a top-down fashion should be an almost mechanical process. There are, however, a number of points that should be remembered.

If an algorithm has been properly designed the path of execution should flow in a straight line from top to bottom. It is important that the program implementation adheres to this top-to-bottom rule. Programs (and subprograms) implemented in this way are usually much easier to understand and debug. They are also usually much easier to modify should the need arise because the relationships between various parts of the program are much more apparent.

1.4.1   Use of procedures to emphasize modularity

To assist with both the development of the implementation and the readability of the main program it is usually helpful to modularize the program along the lines that follow naturally from the top-down design. This practice allows us to implement a set of independent procedures to perform specific and well-defined tasks. For example, if as part of an algorithm it is required to sort an array, then a specific independent procedure should be used for the sort. In applying modularization in an implementation one thing to watch is that the process is not taken too far, to a point at which the implementation again becomes difficult to read because of the fragmentation. When it is necessary to implement somewhat larger software projects a good strategy is to first complete the overall design in a top-down fashion. The mechanism for the main program can then be implemented with calls to the various procedures that will be needed in the final implementation. In the first phase of the implementation, before we have implemented any of the procedures, we can just place a write statement in the skeleton procedures which simply writes out the procedure's name when it is called; for example,

```
procedure sort;
begin
    writeln('sort called')
end
```

This practice allows us to test the mechanism of the main program at an early stage and implement and test the procedures one by one. When a new procedure has been implemented we simply substitute it for its "dummy" procedure.

1.4.2 Choice of variable names

Another implementation detail that can make programs more meaningful and easier to understand is to choose appropriate variable and constant names. For example, if we have to make manipulations on days of the week we are much better off using the variable *day* rather than the single letter *a* or some other variable. This practice tends to make programs much more self-documenting. In addition, each variable should only have *one* role in a given program. A clear definition of all variables and constants at the start of each procedure can also be very helpful.

1.4.3 Documentation of programs

Another useful documenting practice that can be employed in Pascal in particular is to associate a brief but accurate comment with each **begin** statement used. This is appropriate because **begin** statements usually signal that some modular part of the computation is about to follow. A related part of program documentation is the information that the program presents to the user during the execution phase. A good programming practice is to always write programs so that they can be executed and used by other people unfamiliar with the workings and input requirements of the program. This means that the program must specify during execution exactly what responses (and their format) it requires from the user. Considerable care should be taken to avoid ambiguities in these specifications. They should be concise but accurately specify what is required. Also the program should "catch" incorrect responses to its requests and inform the user in an appropriate manner.

1.4.4 Debugging programs

In implementing an algorithm it is always necessary to carry out a number of tests to ensure that the program is behaving correctly according to its specifications. Even with small programs it is likely that there will be logical errors that do not show up in the compilation phase.

To make the task of detecting logical errors somewhat easier it is a good idea to build into the program a set of statements that will print out information at strategic points in the computation. These statements that print out additional information to the desired output can be made conditionally executable. If we do this then the need to remove these statements at the time when we are satisfied with the program becomes unnecessary. The simplest way to implement this debugging tool is to have a Boolean variable (e.g. *debug*) which is set to true when the verbose debugging output for the program is required. Each debugging output can then be parenthesized in the following way:

```
if debug then
   begin
      writeln(...)
         ⋮
   end
```

The actual task of trying to find logical errors in programs can be a very testing and frustrating experience. There are no foolproof methods for debugging but there are some steps we can take to ease the burden of the process. Probably the best advice is to always work the program through by hand *before* ever attempting to execute it. If done systematically and thoroughly this should catch most errors. A way to do this is to check each module or isolated task one by one for typical input conditions.

The simplest way to do this is to draw up a two-dimensional table consisting of steps executed against all the variables used in the section of program under consideration. We must then execute the statements in the section one by one and update our table of variables as each variable is changed. If the process we are modelling is a loop it is usually only necessary to check the first couple of iterations and the last couple of iterations before termination.

As an example of this, consider the table we could draw up for the binary search procedure (algorithm 5.7).

The essential steps in the procedure are:

```
lower := 1; upper := n;
while lower<upper do
   begin
      middle := (lower+upper) div 2;
      if x>a[middle] then
         lower := middle+1
      else
         upper := middle
   end;
   found := (x = a[lower])
```

For the search value x and the array $a[1..n]$ where $x = 44$ and $n = 15$ we may have:

Initial
configuration

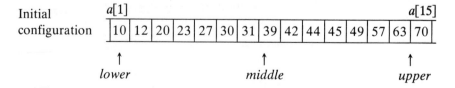

a[1]   a[15]

| 10 | 12 | 20 | 23 | 27 | 30 | 31 | 39 | 42 | 44 | 45 | 49 | 57 | 63 | 70 |

↑   ↑   ↑
lower   *middle*   *upper*

Then the associated execution table is given by Table 1.1.

Table 1.1   Stepwise execution table for binary search.

Iteration no.	lower	middle	upper	lower < upper	a[middle]	x > a[middle]
Initially	1	—	15	true	—	—
1	9	8	15	true	39	true
2	9	12	12	true	49	false
3	9	10	10	true	44	false
4	10	9	10	false	42	true

NOTE: The values of variables associated with each iteration apply *after* the iteration has been completed.

If we get to the stage where our program is executing but producing incorrect results (e.g. it might be a sort routine that places most, but not all, elements in order) the best idea is to first use a debugging trace to print out strategic information. The next step is to follow the program through by hand in a stepwise fashion checking against the computer's debugging output as we go. Whenever we embark on a debugging procedure of this kind we should be careful to ensure that we follow in a straight line along the path of execution. It is usually a wasted effort to assume that some things work and only start a systematic study of the algorithm halfway through the execution path. A good rule to follow when debugging is not to assume anything.

1.4.5   Program testing

In attempting to test whether or not a program will handle all variations of the problem it was designed to solve we must make every effort to be sure that it will cope with the limiting and unusual cases. Some of the things we might check are whether the program solves the smallest possible problem, whether it handles the case when all data values are the same, and so on. Unusual cases like these are usually the ones that can cause a program to falter.

As an example, consider the testing we would need for the binary search algorithm (i.e. algorithm 5.7). Appropriate data sets and tests are given in Table 1.2.

It is often not possible or necessary to write programs that handle all input conditions that may be supplied for a given problem. Wherever possible programs should be accompanied by input and output assertions as described in the section on program verification. Although it is not always practical to implement programs that can handle all possible input conditions we should always strive to build into a program mechanisms that allow it to gracefully and informatively respond to the user when it receives input conditions it was not designed to handle.

Table 1.2   Appropriate data sets for testing binary search algorithm

Test	Search value(s) x	Sample data		
(i) Will the algorithm handle the search of array of one element?	0, 1, 2	$a[1]=1$		$n=1$
(ii) Will it handle the case where all array values are equal?	0, 1, 2	$a[1]=1$ $a[2]=1$	...	$a[n]=1$
(iii) Will it handle the case where the element sought equals the *first* value in the array?	1	$a[1]=1$ $a[2]=2$	...	$a[n]=n$
(iv) Will it handle the case where the value sought equals the *last* value in the array?	n	$a[1]=1$ $a[2]=2$	...	$a[n]=n$
(v) Will it handle the case where the value sought is *less than* the *first* element in the array?	0	$a[1]=1$ $a[2]=2$	...	$a[n]=n$
(vi) Will it handle the case where the value sought is *greater than* the *last* value in the array?	$n+1$	$a[1]=1$ $a[2]=2$	...	$a[n]=n$
(vii) Will it handle the case where the value sought is at an *even* array location?	2	$a[1]=1$ $a[2]=2$	...	$a[n]=n$
(viii) Will it handle the case where the value sought is at an *odd* array location?	3	$a[1]=1$ $a[2]=2$	...	$a[n]=n$
(ix) Will it handle the case where the value sought is absent but within the range of array values?	5	$a[1]=2$ $a[2]=4$	...	$a[n]=2n$

The last statement should not, however, be taken to mean that we should only design algorithms to solve specific problems. This approach should be far from our goal. Almost without exception we should design algorithms to be very general so that they will handle a whole class of problems rather than just one specific case. The latter approach of writing programs for specific cases usually, in the long run, amounts to a lot of wasted effort and time. It is far better to do a thorough job in the first place and produce a program that will solve a wide range of problems. This brings us to a bad practice that beginning programmers (and some others) often adopt. The practice referred to is that of using fixed constants where variables should be used. For example, we should not use statements of the form

while $i<100$ **do**

The 100 should always be replaced by a variable, i.e.

while $i<n$ **do**

A good rule to follow is that fixed numeric constants should only be used in programs for things like the number of months in a year, and so on. Pascal provides for the use of constant declarations.

The considerations we have made concerning the implementation of algorithms leads us to other very important topics concerning just what we mean by a good solution to a problem and, secondly, the question of what actually constitutes a correct program.

1.5 PROGRAM VERIFICATION

The cost of development of computing software has become a major expense in the application of computers. Experience in working with computer systems has led to the observation that generally more than half of all programming effort and resources is spent in correcting errors in programs and carrying out modification of programs. As larger and more complex programs are developed, both these tasks become harder and more time-consuming. In some specialized military, space, and medical applications, program correctness can be a matter of life and death. This suggests two things. Firstly, that considerable savings in the time for program modification should be possible if more care is put into the creation of clearly written code at the time of program development. We have already seen that top-down design can serve as a very useful aid in the writing of programs that are readable and able to be understood at both superficial and detailed levels of implementaion.

The other problem of being able to develop correct as well as clear code also requires the application of a systematic procedure. Proving even simple programs correct turns out to be a far from easy task. It is not simply a matter of testing a program's behavior under the influence of a variety of input conditions to prove its correctness. This approach to demonstrating a program's correctness may, in some cases, show up errors but it cannot guarantee their absence. It is this weakness in such an approach that makes it necessary to resort to a method of program verification that is based on sound mathematical principles.

Program verification refers to the application of mathematical proof techniques to establish that the results obtained by the execution of a program with arbitrary inputs are in accord with formally defined output specifications.

Although we have only now come to consider this aspect of algorithm design, it is not meant to imply that this process should be carried out after the complete development of the algorithm. In fact, a far better strategy is to develop the proof in a top-down fashion along with the top-down development of the algorithm. That is, we start out by proving the correctness of the very basic structure of the algorithm at an abstract or superficial level. Then as abstract tasks are replaced by more specific mechanisms, it is necessary to ensure that these refinements do not alter the correctness of the more abstract level. This process is repeated until we get down to the specific program steps.

1.5.1 Computer model for program execution

To pursue this goal of program verification, we must fully appreciate what happens when a program is executed under the influence of given input conditions. What is important in this respect is the execution path that is followed for the given input conditions. A program may have a variety of execution paths leading to successful termination. For a given set of input conditions *only one* of these paths will be followed (although obviously some paths may share common subpaths for different inputs). The written algorithm implementation therefore defines a whole set of execution paths. The progress of a computation from specific input conditions through to termination can be thought of as a sequence of transitions from one *computation state* to another. Each state, including the initial state, is defined by the values of *all* variables at the corresponding point in time. A *state transition* and progress towards completion is made by changing the value of a variable followed by a transfer of control to the next instruction on the current execution path. As well as instructions that change the computation state there are also other instructions that simply make tests on the current state. These tests are used to bring about a change in the sequential flow of execution. This model for program execution provides us with a foundation on which to construct correctness proofs of algorithms.

1.5.2 Input and output assertions

The very first step that needs to be taken in order to prove a program correct is to provide a formal statement of its specifications in terms of the variables that it employs. The formal statement has two parts, an input assertion and an output assertion which can be expressed in logic notation as predicates that describe the state of the executing program's variables. The *input assertion* should specify any constraints that have been placed on the values of the input variables used by the program (e.g. an input variable d may play the role of a divisor in the program. Clearly d cannot have the value 0. The input assertion is therefore $d <> 0$). When there are no restrictions on the values of the input variables the input assertion is given the logical value *true*. The *output assertion* must specify symbolically the results that the program is expected to produce for input data that satisfies the input assertion (e.g. if a program is designed to calculate the quotient q and remainder r resulting from the division of x by y then the output assertion can be written as:

$$(x = q*y+r)\wedge(r<y)$$

where the symbol "$\wedge$" represents the logical connective "**and**".

1.5.3 Implications and symbolic execution

The problem of actually verifying a program can be formulated as a set of implications which must be shown to be logically true. These implications have the general form:

$$P \supset Q$$

where the logical connective "$\supset$" is read as "implies". P is termed the *assumption* and Q the *conclusion*. The associated truth table defining implication is given in Table 1.3.

Table 1.3 Truth table defining implication

P	Q	$P \supset Q$
true	*true*	*true*
true	*false*	*false*
false	*true*	*true*
false	*false*	*true*

In order to show that these implications or propositions are logically true, it is necessary to take into account the effects of executing the program for arbitrary inputs that satisfy the input assertion. A relatively straightforward way to do this is to use the technique of *symbolic execution*. With symbolic execution, *all* input data values are replaced by symbolic values and all arithmetic operations on numbers translate into algebraic manipulation of symbolic expressions. As an example, consider the following program segment labelled with input and output assertions:

A $readln(x,y)$;
    {**assert**: *true*}
    $x := x-y$;
    $y := x+y$;
    $x := y-x$

B   {**assert** $x = y0 \wedge y = x0$}
    where $x0$ and $y0$ refer to the initial values of x and y respectively.

Table 1.4   Normal and symbolic execution for exchange mechanism

Step	Normal execution	Symbolic execution
	input values: $x = 3$ $y = 1$	input values: $x = \alpha$ $y = \beta$
1	$x := x-y \Rightarrow x = 3-1 = 2$	$x := x-y \Rightarrow x = \alpha - \beta$
2	$y := x+y \Rightarrow y = 2+1 = 3$	$y := x+y \Rightarrow y = (\alpha-\beta)+\beta = \alpha$
3	$x := y-x \Rightarrow x = 3-2 = 1$	$x := y-x \Rightarrow x = ((\alpha-\beta)+\beta)-(\alpha-\beta) = \beta$

Both normal execution and symbolic execution, shown in Table 1.4, indicate that the values of x and y are exchanged.

Symbolic execution enables us to transform the verification procedure into proving that the input assertion with symbolic values substituted for all input variables implies the output assertion with final symbolic values substituted for all variables. A proposition phrased in this way is referred to as a *verification condition* (*VC*) over the program segment from the input assertion to the output assertion.

To proceed with the verification procedure it is usually necessary to set up a number of intermediate verification conditions between the input and output assertions. Taken to the limit this involves carrying out the verification procedure statement by statement. For practical purposes it is, however, usually sufficient to only consider verification conditions for blocks of a program as marked by straight-line segments, branching segments, and loop segments. We will adopt the convention that $VC(A-B)$ refers to the verification condition over the program segment from A to B. We will now consider the verification of each of these basic segment types in turn.

1.5.4   Verification of straight-line program segments

The best way to illustrate the verification procedure is by example. Our exchange mechanism mentioned above will serve as an example of a straight-line program segment.

The verification condition for this program segment is:

$$VC(A-B): \textit{true} \supset \{x = y0 \land y = x0\}$$

On substitution of the initial and final values of all variables, we get:

$$VC(A-B): \textit{true} \supset ((\alpha-\beta)+\beta)-(\alpha-\beta)) = \beta \land (\alpha-\beta)+\beta) = \alpha$$

The conclusion part of the verification condition can be simplified to yield $\beta = \beta$ and $\alpha = \alpha$ which is clearly true and so the implication is true.

1.5.5 Verification of program segments with branches

To handle program segments that contain branches it is necessary to set up and prove verification conditions for each branch separately. As an example, consider the following program segment that ensures that x is less than or equal to y.

```
      readln(x,y);
 A   {assert P_A: true}
      if x>y then
          begin
              t := x;
              x := y;
              y := t
          end
 B   {assert P_B: ((x<=y)∧(x = x0∧y = y0))∨(x = y0∧y = x0)}
```

In general, the propositions that must be proved for the basic **if** construct are:

$$P_A \land \dot{C_A} \supset P_B$$
$$P_A \land \sim C_A \supset P_B$$

where C_A is the branch condition.

The two verification conditions needed in this case are given below, where the initial values of x and y are respectively α and β

$$VC(A-(t)-B): \textit{true} \land \alpha > \beta \supset ((\alpha \leqslant \beta) \land (\beta = \alpha \land \alpha = \beta)) \lor (\beta = \beta \land \alpha = \alpha)$$

Since $\alpha > \beta$ is true and the second part of the conclusion (i.e. $\alpha = \alpha \land \beta = \beta$) is true, the verification condition for the *true* path is true.

The verification condition for the *false* path is:

$$VC(A-(f)-B): \textit{true} \land \sim(\alpha > \beta) \supset ((\alpha \leqslant \beta) \land (\alpha = \alpha \land \beta = \beta)) \lor (\alpha = \beta \land \beta = \alpha)$$

Since $\sim(\alpha > \beta) \supset (\alpha \leqslant \beta)$ and the conclusion ($\alpha = \alpha \land \beta = \beta$) is true the verification condition for the *false* path is true. It follows that the labelled program segment $(A-B)$ is true. Case statements can be treated similarly.

1.5.6   Verification of program segments with loops

There are problems with trying to verify loop segments directly by symbolic execution because the number of iterations required is usually arbitrary. To overcome this problem, a special kind of assertion called a *loop invariant* must be employed. A loop invariant should be a property (predicate) that captures the progressive computational role of the loop while at the same time remaining true before and after each loop traversal irrespective of how many times the loop is executed. Once the loop invariant is established, there are several steps that must be taken to verify the loop segment. To understand this loop verification procedure, we will use the following single-loop program structure as our model.

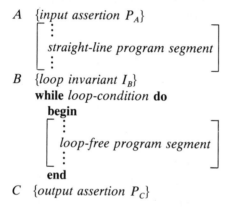

A {*input assertion P_A*}

  ⋮

  straight-line program segment

  ⋮

B {*loop invariant I_B*}

  while *loop-condition* **do**

    begin

      ⋮

      loop-free program segment

      ⋮

    end

C {*output assertion P_C*}

(a)   The first step that must be taken is to show that the loop invariant is true initially, before the loop is entered. This can be done by setting up a verification condition $VC(A-B)$ for the program segment from A to B. That is, the input assertion, together with any changes to variables caused by the segment $A-B$, must imply that the loop invariant is true. We can use symbolic execution to carry out this verification step. That is, we must show $P_A \supset I_B$.

(b)   The second part of verifying a loop involves showing that the loop invariant is still true *after* the segment of program within the loop has been executed. To do this we can set up a verification condition $VC(B-B)$. This involves showing that the loop invariant with initial values of variables set, together with the condition for loop execution C_B, implies the truth of the loop invariant with final values of variables, i.e.

$$I_B \wedge C_B \supset I_B$$

Symbolic execution can also be used to verify this step.

(c)   As a final step in verifying a loop segment, it is necessary to show that the invariant, together with the negation of the loop-entry condition, implies the assertion that applies on exiting from the loop. The verification condition in this case for our basic loop structure will be $VC(B-C)$. The corresponding proposition will be:

$$I_B \wedge \sim C_B \supset P_C$$

A better understanding of the application of the loop verification technique can be gained by studying a specific example. Consider the following program segment which can be used to compute factorial.

```
A   {assert P_A: n>=0}
    i := 0;
    fact := 1;
B   {invariant I_B: fact = i!∧i≤n}
    while i<n do
        begin
            i := i+1;
            fact := i*fact
        end
C   {assert P_C: fact = n!}
```

Assume the input value of n is γ and the current values of i and $fact$ are α and β respectively. Using symbolic execution we can show that the associated verification conditions that must be proved are:

1. $VC(A-B) : P_A \supset I_B$
     : $\gamma \geqslant 0 \supset 1 = 0! \wedge 0 \leqslant \gamma$
     Now $1 = 0!$ is true by definition and $\gamma \geqslant 0 \supset 0 \leqslant \gamma$ is trivially true and so the verification condition $VC(A - B)$ is true.

2. $VC(B-B) : I_B \wedge C_B \supset I_B$
     : $\underbrace{\beta = \alpha! \wedge \alpha \leqslant \gamma}_{I_B} \wedge \underbrace{\alpha < \gamma}_{C_B} \supset (\alpha+1)\beta = (\alpha+1)! \wedge (\alpha+1) \leqslant \gamma$
     Since $\beta = \alpha!$
     we have $(\alpha+1)\beta = (\alpha+1)\alpha! = (\alpha+1)! \equiv (\alpha+1)\alpha!$ by definition
     and so $\beta = \alpha! \supset (\alpha+1)\beta = (\alpha+1)!$ is true.
     Also $\alpha \leqslant \gamma \wedge \alpha < \gamma \supset \alpha < \gamma$
     and so $(\alpha+1) \leqslant \gamma$ for integer α and γ.
     It follows that the verification condition $VC(B-B)$ is true.

3. $VC(B-C) : I_B \wedge \sim C_B \supset P_C$
     : $\beta = \alpha! \wedge \alpha \leqslant \gamma \wedge \sim(\alpha < \gamma) \supset \beta = \gamma!$
     Since $\sim(\alpha < \gamma) \supset \alpha \geqslant \gamma$
     then $\alpha \leqslant \gamma \wedge \alpha \geqslant \gamma \supset \alpha = \gamma$
     and so because $\alpha = \gamma$ it follows that $\beta = \alpha! \supset \beta = \gamma!$ is true
     and so the verification condition $VC(B-C)$ is true.

Since the verification conditions for all three program segments are correct, the complete program segment is said to be *partially correct*.

What the verification method we have described gives us is only a proof of *partial correctness*, with the implication that if the algorithm terminates the result produced will be correct. For programs that contain loops we are therefore left with the separate but necessary task of proving that the program terminates in order to establish *total correctness*.

Before considering in detail a method for proof of termination, we will consider setting up the verification conditions for a program example that employs an array.

1.5.7   Verification of program segments that employ arrays

The idea of symbolic execution developed in the preceding sections can be extended to some of the simpler examples that employ arrays although it now becomes necessary to account for the symbolic values of *all* array elements. As an example of verification of a program segment containing an array we will set up the verification conditions for a program that finds the position of the smallest element in the array.

The program annotated with assertions may take the following form:

A {*assert* P_A: $n \geqslant 1$}
    $i := 1$;
    $p := 1$;
B {*invariant* I_B: $(1 \leqslant i \leqslant n) \wedge (1 \leqslant p \leqslant i) \wedge (a[p] \leqslant a[1], a[2], ..., a[i])$}
    while $i < n$ **do**
        begin
            $i := i+1$;
            if $a[i] < a[p]$ **then** $p := i$
        end
C {*assert* P_C: $(1 \leqslant p \leqslant n) \wedge (a[p] \leqslant a[1], a[2], ..., a[n])$}

where we have used the shorthand convention that:

$$a[p] \leqslant a[1], a[2], ..., a[n] \equiv a[p] \leqslant a[1] \wedge a[p] \leqslant a[2] \wedge \cdots \wedge a[p] \leqslant a[n]$$

Assuming that the initial values of $a[1], a[2], ..., a[n]$ are respectively $\alpha_1, \alpha_2, ..., \alpha_n$, and that the initial value of n is δ, we can use symbolic execution to check the verification conditions:

$$VC(A-B): \delta \geqslant 1 \supset (1 \leqslant 1 \leqslant \delta) \wedge (1 \leqslant 1 \leqslant 1) \wedge \alpha_1 \leqslant \alpha_1$$

With i and p having initial values of β and γ respectively, the verification conditions for the two paths through the loop are:

$VC(B-(t)-B)$: $(1\leqslant\beta\leqslant\delta)\wedge(1\leqslant\gamma\leqslant\beta)\wedge(\alpha_\gamma\leqslant\alpha_1, \alpha_2, ..., \alpha_\beta)\wedge\beta<\delta\wedge\alpha_{\beta+1}<\alpha_\gamma$
$\qquad\supset(1\leqslant\beta+1\leqslant\delta)\wedge(1\leqslant\beta+1\leqslant\beta+1)\wedge\alpha_{\beta+1}\leqslant\alpha_1, \alpha_2, ..., \alpha_{\beta+1}$
$VC(B-(f)-B)$: $(1\leqslant\beta\leqslant\delta)\wedge(1\leqslant\gamma\leqslant\beta)\wedge(\alpha_\gamma\leqslant\alpha_1, \alpha_2, ..., \alpha_\beta)$
$\qquad\wedge\beta<\delta\wedge\sim(\alpha_{\beta+1}<\alpha_\gamma)$
$\qquad\supset(1\leqslant\beta+1\leqslant\delta)\wedge(1\leqslant\gamma\leqslant\beta+1)\wedge (\alpha_\gamma\leqslant\alpha_1, \alpha_2, ..., \alpha_{\beta+1})$
$VC(B-C)$: $(1\leqslant\beta\leqslant\delta)\wedge(1\leqslant\gamma\leqslant\beta)\wedge(\alpha_\gamma\leqslant\alpha_1, \alpha_2, ..., \alpha_\beta)\wedge\sim(\beta<\delta)$
$\qquad\supset(1\leqslant\gamma\leqslant\delta)\wedge(\alpha_\gamma\leqslant\alpha_1, \alpha_2, ..., \alpha_\delta)$

The example above should give some flavor of how programs with arrays may be treated. We will now return to consideration of the problem of proving program termination.

1.5.8 Proof of termination

To prove that a program terminates, it is necessary to show that it accomplishes its stated objective in a finite number of steps. This amounts to showing that *every* loop in the program terminates in a finite number of steps. In many instances, proof of termination follows directly from the properties of the various iterative constructs. Consider, for example, the **for**-loop below:

      for $i := 1$ **to** n **do**
         begin
          $\vdots$
         end

When n is positive and finite this is guaranteed to terminate because, with each iteration, the number of steps to the termination condition being satisfied is reduced by at least one. This reduction can only be carried out a finite number of times and so the loop must terminate.

There are obviously loops for which the proof of termination is much more subtle and elusive. One of two situations usually prevails in such circumstances. When there is no single variable that is monotonically progressing towards the termination condition, we often find that an arithmetic combination of two (or more) variables makes progress towards termination with each iteration.

If the termination characteristic of the program is not of this type, it usually remains to show that there is some property of the data (perhaps a sentinel) that will guarantee termination.

More formally, the problem of proving loop termination can often be approached by associating another expression, in addition to the loop invariant, with each loop. The expression, ϵ, should be chosen to be a function of the variables used in the loop. It should *always* be non-negative and it must be shown to decrease in value with each loop iteration. If these criteria are satisfied, the loop must terminate. Proof of termination can therefore be reduced to establishing the truth of the following *termination conditions*.

(i)   Referring back to our generalized loop structure we must show that the truth of the loop invariant I_B, together with condition for loop execution C_B, implies that the value of the expression ϵ is greater than zero. That is,

$$TC1(B): I_B \wedge C_B \supset \epsilon > 0$$

The condition $\epsilon \geqslant 0$ becomes an invariant of the loop.

In some instances, the invariant used for establishing partial correctness is not sufficient for use in a proof of termination. This problem can be overcome by attaching additional conditions (derived from earlier assertions) to the invariant.

(ii) The second proposition that must be proven is to show that the loop invariant I_B, together with the condition for loop execution, C_B, implies that the value ϵ_0 of the expression *before* execution is strictly greater than its value ϵ after loop execution, i.e. for a loop B

$$TC2(B-B): I_B \wedge C_B \supset (\epsilon_0 > \epsilon) \wedge (\epsilon \geqslant 0)$$

The final value of ϵ can be obtained by symbolic execution of the statements in the loop.

Once these two propositions have been shown to be true, we can immediately conclude that the repetition process is finite since ϵ can only be decreased a finite number of times while remaining positive as required by $TC1(B)$. The considerations of termination for **repeat** .. **until** loops follow a similar line of reasoning.

A proof of termination for the quotient/remainder program given below will now be outlined.

```
        ⋮
        begin
A         {assert P_A: (x≥0)∧(y>0)}
          r := x; q := 0;
B         {invariant I_B: r≥0∧x=y*q+r}
          while y≤r do
              begin
                  r := r−y;
                  q := q+1
              end
C         {assert P_C: (x=y*q+r)∧(0≤r<y)}
```

To prove termination for this program segment we will use:

$$\epsilon = r + y$$

In order to establish the first termination condition, we will need to attach the additional condition $y > 0$ from P_A to the invariant I_B. We then have

$$TC1(B): (r \geqslant 0) \wedge (x = y*q + r) \wedge (y > 0) \wedge (y \leqslant r) \supset (r + y > 0)$$

Now

$$(r \geqslant 0) \wedge (y > 0) \supset (r + y > 0)$$

and so $TC1(B)$ can be shown to be true.

Assuming that x, y, r and q respectively have the symbolic values α, β, γ, and δ on entering the loop, then for $TC2(B-B)$ we have:

$$TC2(B-B): (\gamma \geqslant 0) \wedge (\alpha = \beta*\delta + \gamma) \wedge (\beta > 0) \wedge (\beta \leqslant \gamma) \supset \gamma + \beta > (\gamma - \beta) + \beta$$

where

$$\epsilon_0 = \gamma + \beta \qquad \text{and} \qquad \epsilon = (\gamma - \beta) + \beta$$

which can easily be shown to be true and so the proof of termination is complete.

Once both partial correctness and termination have been established, the proof is complete. To embark on detailed formal proofs of programs requires a considerable degree of mathematical maturity and experience. The length and detail of such proofs is usually considerably greater than the size of the original program text. In the discussions which follow, we will therefore only attempt to annotate programs with relevant assertions.

1.6   THE EFFICIENCY OF ALGORITHMS

Efficiency considerations for algorithms are inherently tied in with the design, implementation, and analysis of algorithms. Every algorithm must use up some of a computer's resources to complete its task. The resources most relevant in relation to efficiency are *central processor time* (CPU time) and *internal memory*. Because of the high cost of computing resources it is always desirable to design algorithms that are economical in the use of CPU time and memory. This is an easy statement to make but one that is often difficult to follow either because of bad design habits, or the inherent complexity of the problem, or both. As with most other aspects of algorithm design, there is no recipe for designing efficient algorithms. Despite there being some generalities each problem has its own characteristics which demand specific responses to solve the problem efficiently. Within the framework of this last statement we will try to make a few suggestions that can sometimes be useful in designing efficient algorithms.

1.6.1   Redundant computations

Most of the inefficiencies that creep into the implementation of algorithms come about because redundant computations are made or unnecessary storage is used. The effects of redundant computations are most serious when they are embedded within a loop that must be executed many times. The most common mistake using loops is to repeatedly recalculate part of an expression that remains constant throughout the entire execution phase of the loop. The example below illustrates this point:

```
x := 0;
for i := 1 to n do
   begin
      x := x+0.01;
      y := (a*a*a+c)*x*x+b*b*x;
      writeln ('x = ' , x,'y = ',y)
   end
```

This loop does *twice* the number of multiplications necessary to complete the computation. The unnecessary multiplications and additions can be removed by precomputing two other constants *a3c* and *b2 before* executing the loop:

```
a3c := a*a*a+c;
b2 := b*b;
x := 0;
for i := 1 to n do
   begin
      x := x+0.01;
      y := a3c*x*x+b2*x;
      writeln ('x = ',x,'y = ',y)
   end
```

The savings in this instance are not all that significant but there are many other situations where they are much more significant. It is always most important to strive to eliminate redundancies in the innermost loops of computations as these inefficiencies can be most costly.

1.6.2 Referencing array elements

If care is not exercised redundant computations can also easily creep into array processing. Consider, for example, the two versions of an algorithm for finding the maximum and its position in an array.

Version (1)

```
p := 1;
for i := 2 to n do
    if a[i]>a[p] then p := i;
max := a[p]
```

Version (2)

```
p := 1;
max := a[1];
for i := 2 to n do
    if a[i]>max then
        begin
            max := a[i];
            p := i
        end
```

The version (2) implementation would normally be preferred because the conditional test (i.e. $a[i]>max$) which is the dominant instruction is more efficient to perform than the corresponding test in version (1). It is more efficient because to use the variable *max* only one memory reference instruction is required, whereas to use the variable $a[p]$ requires two memory references and an addition operation to locate the correct value for use in the test. Also in version (2), introduction of the variable *max* makes it clearer what task is to be accomplished.

1.6.3 Inefficiency due to late termination

Another place inefficiencies can come into an implementation is where considerably more tests are done than are required to solve the problem at hand. This type of inefficiency can be best illustrated by example. Suppose we had to linear search an alphabetically ordered list of names for some particular name. An inefficient implementation in this instance would be one where *all* names were examined even if the point in the list was reached where it was known that the name could not occur later (e.g. suppose we were looking for the name MOORE, then, as soon as we had encountered a name that occurred alphabetically later than MOORE, e.g. MORRIS, there would be no need to proceed further). The inefficient implementation could have the form:

1. **while** name sought $<>$ current name and no end-of-file **do**
    (a) get next name from list.

A more efficient implementation would be:

1. **while** name sought $>$ current name and not end-of-file **do**
    (a) get next name from list.
2. test if current name is equal to name sought.

The same sort of inefficiency can be built into the bubblesort algorithm (algorithm 5.3) if care is not taken with the implementation. This can happen if the inner loop that drives the exchange mechanism always goes the full length of the array. For example,

> **for** $i := 1$ **to** $n-1$
> > **for** $j := 1$ **to** $n-1$
> > > **if** $a[j]>a[j+1]$ **then** "exchange $a[j]$ with $a[j+1]$"

With this sorting mechanism, after the ith iteration, the last i values in the array will be in sorted order. Thus, for any given i the inner loop should not proceed beyond $n-i$. The loop structure will then be:

> **for** $i := 1$ **to** $n-1$
> > **for** $j := 1$ **to** $n-i$
> > > **if** $a[j]>a[j+1]$ **then** "*exchange $a[j]$ with $a[j+1]$*"

The lesson to be learned from this is that we should always try to take advantage of any order or structure in a problem.

1.6.4   Early detection of desired output conditions

The bubblesort also provides us with an example of another related type of inefficiency involving termination. It sometimes happens, due to the nature of the input data, that the algorithm establishes the desired output condition *before* the general conditions for termination have been met. For example, a bubblesort might be used to sort a set of data that is already almost in sorted order. When this happens it is very likely that the algorithm will have the data in sorted order long before the loop termination conditions are met. It is therefore desirable to terminate the sort as soon as it is established that the data is already sorted. To do this all we need to do is check whether there have been any exchanges in the current pass of the inner loop. If there have been no exchanges in the current pass the data must be sorted and so early termination can be applied (a check of algorithm 5.3 reveals how this is implemented for the bubblesort). In general, we must include additional steps and tests to detect the conditions for early termination. However, if they can be kept inexpensive (as in the bubblesort) then it is worth including them. That is, when early termination is possible, we always have to trade tests and maybe even storage to bring about the early termination.

1.6.5 Trading storage for efficiency gains

A trade between storage and efficiency is often used to improve the performance of an algorithm. What usually happens in this type of tradeoff is that we precompute or save some intermediate results and avoid having to do a lot of unnecessary testing and computation later on. (See for example the longest monotone subsequence problem—algorithm 4.7.)

One strategy that it sometimes used to try to speed up an algorithm is to implement it using the least number of loops. While this is usually possible, inevitably it makes programs much harder to read and debug. It is therefore usually better to stick to the rule of having *one loop do one job* just as we have one variable doing one job. When a more efficient solution to a problem is required it is far better to try to improve the algorithm rather than resorting to "programming tricks" that tend to obscure what is being done. A clear implementation of a better algorithm is to be preferred to a "tricky" implementation of an algorithm that is not as good. We are now left with the task of trying to measure the efficiency of algorithms.

1.7 THE ANALYSIS OF ALGORITHMS

There are usually *many* ways to solve any given problem. In computing, as in most efforts of human endeavor, we are generally concerned with "good" solutions to problems. This raises certain questions as to just what do we mean by a "good" solution to a problem? In algorithm design "good" has both qualitative and quantitative aspects. There are often certain esthetic and personal aspects to this but, on a more practical level, we are usually interested in a solution that is *economical in the use of computing and human resources*. Among other things, good algorithms usually possess the following qualitites and capabilities:

1. They are simple but powerful and general solutions.
2. They can be easily understood by others, that is, the implementation is clear and concise without being "tricky".
3. They can be easily modified if necessary.
4. They are correct for clearly defined situations.
5. They are able to be understood on a number of levels.
6. They are economical in the use of computer time, computer storage and peripherals.
7. They are documented well enough to be used by others who do not have a detailed knowledge of their inner workings.
8. They are not dependent on being run on a particular computer.
9. They are able to be used as a subprocedure for other problems.
10. The solution is pleasing and satisfying to its designer—a product that the designer feels proud to have created.

These qualitative aspects of a good algorithm are very important but it is also necessary to try to provide some quantitative measures to complete the evaluation of "goodness" of an algorithm. Quantitative measures are valuable in that they can give us a way of directly predicting the performance of an algorithm and of comparing the relative performance of two or more algorithms that are intended to solve the same problem. This can be important because the use of an algorithm that is more efficient means a saving in computing resources which translates into a saving in time and money.

1.7.1 Computational complexity

To make a quantitative measure of an algorithm's performance it is necessary to set up a computational model that reflects its behavior under specified input conditions. This model must capture the essence of the computation while at the same time it must be divorced from any programming language.

We are therefore required to characterize an algorithm's performance in terms of the size (usually n) of the problem being solved. Obviously, more computing resources are needed to solve larger problems in the same class. The important question that we must settle is, how does the cost of solving the problem vary as n increases? Our first response to this question might be that as n increases then so does the cost in the same manner (e.g. a problem for $n = 200$ takes twice as long as a problem for $n = 100$). While this *linear* dependence on n is true for some simple algorithms in general the behavior with n follows some other completely different pattern. At the lower end of the scale we have algorithms with logarithmic (or better) dependence on n, while at the higher end of the scale we have algorithms with an exponential dependence on n. With increasing n the relative difference in the cost of a computation is enormous for these two extremes. Table 1.5 illustrates the comparative cost for a range of n values.

Table 1.5 Computational cost as a function of problem size for a range of computational complexities

$\log_2 n$	n	$n \log_2 n$	n^2	n^3	2^n
1	2	2	4	8	4
3.322	10	33.22	10^2	10^3	$>10^3$
6.644	10^2	664.4	10^4	10^6	$>>10^{25}$
9.966	10^3	9966.0	10^6	10^9	$>>10^{250}$
13.287	10^4	132,877	10^8	10^{12}	$>>10^{2500}$

What is obvious from this table is that we can solve only *very small* problems with an algorithm that exhibits exponential behavior. Even assuming that a computer can do about one million operations per second, an exponential algorithm with $n = 100$ would take immeasurably longer than the existence of the earth to terminate. At the other extreme, for an algorithm with logarithmic dependence on n, a problem with $n = 10^4$ would require only 13 steps which amounts to about 13 microseconds of computer time. These examples emphasize how important it is to have an understanding of the way in which algorithms behave as a function of the problem size. What can also come out of analyzing algorithms is a theoretical model of the inherent computational complexity of particular problems.

In deciding how to characterize the behavior of an algorithm as a function of the size of the problem n, we must study the mechanism very carefully to decide just what constitutes the dominant mechanism. It may be the number of times a particular arithmetic (or other) expression is evaluated, or the number of comparisons or exchanges that must be made as n grows. For example, comparisons, exchanges, and moves characterize most sorting algorithms. The number of comparisons usually dominates so we use comparisons in our computational model for sorting algorithms.

1.7.2   The order notation

A standard notation has been developed to represent functions which bound the computing time for algorithms. It is an order notation and it is usually referred to as the *O-notation*. An algorithm in which the dominant mechanism is executed cn^2 times for c, a constant, and n the problem size, is said to have an *order n^2* complexity which is written as $O(n^2)$. Formally, a function $g(n)$ is $O(f(n))$ provided there is a constant c for which the relationship

$$g(n) \leq cf(n)$$

holds for all values of n that are finite and positive. With these conventions we have a means of characterizing the asymptotic complexity of an algorithm and hence of determining the size of problems that it can solve using a conventional sequential computer. We can write the above relationship in the form:

$$\lim_{n \to \infty} \frac{g(n)}{f(n)} = c \qquad \text{where } c \text{ is not equal to zero}$$

As an example, suppose we have an algorithm that requires $(3n^2+6n+3)$ comparisons to complete its task. According to the convention just outlined we have:

$$g(n) = 3n^2+6n+3 \qquad \text{and} \qquad \lim_{n \to \infty} \frac{3n^2+6n+3}{n^2} = 3$$

It follows that this particular algorithm has an asymptotic complexity of $O(n^2)$. In using this methodology to decide upon the superiority of one algorithm over another we need to pay careful attention to the constants of proportionality. It can happen that an algorithm with a higher asymptotic complexity has a very small constant of proportionality and hence for some particular range of n it will give better performance than an algorithm with lower complexity and a higher proportionality constant.

1.7.3   Worst and average case behavior

In analyzing any given algorithm there are two measures of performance that are usually considered. These are the *worst* and *average case* behavior of the algorithm. These two measures can be applied to both the time and space complexity of an algorithm. The *worst case complexity* for a given problem size n corresponds to the maximum complexity encountered among *all* problems of size n. Determination of the worst case complexity for many algorithms is relatively straightforward. We choose a set of input conditions that force the algorithm to make the least possible progress towards its final goal at each step.

In many practical applications it is much more important to have a measure of the *expected complexity* of a given algorithm rather than the worst case behavior. The expected complexity gives a measure of the behavior of the algorithm *averaged* over all possible problems of size n. In comparing two algorithms to solve a given problem, we would generally opt in preference for the algorithm that has the lower expected complexity. Unfortunately, setting up a computational model to characterize the average behavior often involves very complex and sophisticated combinatorial analyses.

1.7.4 Probabilistic average case analysis

As a simple example, suppose we wish to characterize the behavior of an algorithm that linearly searches an ordered list of elements for some value x.

1	2	...		n

In the *worst case* it will be necessary for the algorithm to examine *all n* values in the list before terminating.

The *average case* situation is somewhat different. For a probabilistic average case analysis it is generally assumed that all possible points of termination are *equally likely*, i.e. the probability that x will be found at position 1 is $1/n$, and at position 2 is $1/n$, and so on. The average search cost is therefore the sum of all possible search costs each multiplied by their associated probability. For example, if $n = 5$ we would have:

$$\text{average search cost} = 1/5 \ (1+2+3+4+5) = 3$$

Noting that $1+2+3+ \cdots +n = n(n+1)/2$ (i.e. from Gauss' formula) then in the general case we have:

$$\text{average search cost} = \frac{1}{n}\left(\frac{n}{2}\,(n+1)\right) = \frac{n+1}{2}$$

As a second, slightly more complicated example, let us consider the average case analysis for the binary search procedure described in algorithm 5.7. What we wish to establish in this analysis is the *average number of iterations* of the search loop that are required before the algorithm terminates in a *successful* search. This analysis will correspond only to the *first* binary search implementation proposed in algorithm 5.7 which terminates as soon as the search value is found. The associated binary search tree for an array of size 15 is given in Fig. 1.2.

Referring to the tree we see that 1 element can be found with 1 comparison, 2 elements with 2 comparisons, 4 elements with 3 comparisons, and so on, i.e. sum over all possible elements $= 1+2+2+3+3+3+3+4+ \cdots$. In the general case, 2^i elements require $i+1$ comparisons. Now assuming that all items present in the array are equally likely to be retrieved (i.e. their probability of retrieval is $1/n$), then the average search cost is again just the sum over all possible search costs, each multiplied by their associated probability. That is,[†]

$$\text{average search cost} = \frac{1}{n} \sum_{i=0}^{\lfloor \log_2 n \rfloor} (i+1) \times 2^i = \frac{1}{n} \left\{ \sum_{i=0}^{\lfloor \log_2 n \rfloor} i \times 2^i + n \right\}$$

[†] Where $\lfloor \ \rfloor$ is used to indicate that $\lfloor \log_2 n \rfloor$ is the greatest integer less than or equal to $\log_2 n$ (it is referred to as "Floor" $\log_2 n$), and $\sum$ is the mathematical summation symbol.

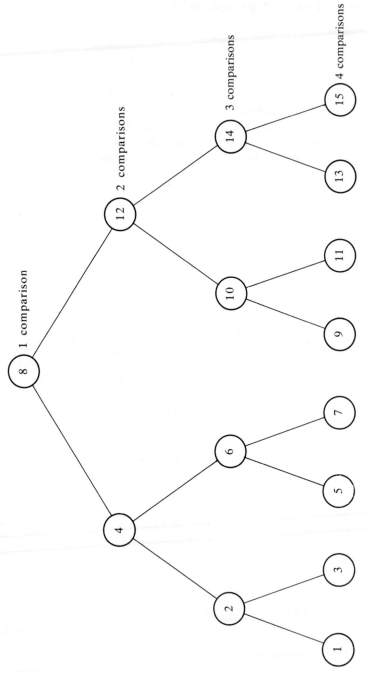

Fig. 1.2   Binary decision tree for a set of 15 elements.

This formula is exact only when n is one less than a power of two. Some calculus is needed to evaluate the sum:

$$s = \sum_{i=0}^{\lfloor \log_2 n \rfloor} i \times 2^i$$

We may recognize that this sum is a geometric progression and we know that in general:

$$1 + x + x^2 + \cdots + x^k = \frac{x^{k+1} - 1}{x - 1}$$

We may also note that:

$$i \times 2^i = \frac{d}{dx} (2x^i)_{x=2}$$

It follows that to compute our sum we can take the derivative of $(x^{k+1} - 1)/(x-1)$ multiplied by 2 and evaluated at $x = 2$ where $k = \lfloor \log_2 n \rfloor$. When this is done we get:

$$s = \sum_{i=0}^{\lfloor \log_2 n \rfloor} i \times 2^i = (n+1)(\lfloor \log_2 n \rfloor - 1) + 2$$

And, after substituting for the sum in our average search cost expression, we find:

$$\text{average search cost} = \frac{(n+1) \lfloor \log_2 n \rfloor + 1}{n} \approx \lfloor \log_2 n \rfloor \text{ for large } n.$$

This example illustrates that even for a relatively simple example, a degree of mathematical sophistication is required to carry out the analysis. We now have some of the tools necessary to embark on a study of algorithm design.

BIBLIOGRAPHY

Problem-solving

The classic book on problem-solving is Polya's *How to Solve It* (1971), which was first published in the 1940s. This book is highly recommended to all embarking on computer problem-solving. Polya's other works on mathematical problem-solving contain a wealth of useful hints and exercises. Gardiner's *Aha! Insight* is also a delightful book. The other references listed also contain important ideas on problem-solving.

1. Gardiner, M., *Aha! Insight*, Freeman, N.Y., 1978.
2. Polya, G., *How to Solve It*, Princeton University Press, Princeton, N.J., 1971.
3. Polya, G., *Mathematical Discovery: On Understanding, Learning and Teaching Problem-Solving*, Vols I and II, Wiley, N.Y., 1962.
4. Polya, G., *Mathematics and Plausible Reasoning*, Vols I and II, Princeton University Press, Princeton, N.J., 1954.
5. Watkins, R. P., *Computer Problem-Solving*, Wiley, Hong Kong, 1974.
6. Wickelgren, W. A., *How to Solve Problems: Elements of a Theory of Problems and Problem-Solving*, Freeman, S.F., 1974.

Top-down design

The references in this section provide a valuable scholarly treatment of structured programming.

1. Alagic, S. and M. A. Arbib, *The Design of Well-Structured and Correct Programs*, Springer-Verlag, N.Y., 1978.
2. Dahl, O.-J., E. W. Dijkstra and C. A. R. Hoare, *Structured Programming*, Academic Press, N.Y., 1972.
3. Dijkstra, E. W., *A Discipline of Programming*, Prentice-Hall, Englewood Cliffs, N.J., 1976.
4. Wirth, N., "Program development by stepwise refinement", *Comm. ACM*, **14**, 221-7, 1971.
5. Wirth, N., *Systematic Programming: An Introduction*, Prentice-Hall, Englewood Cliffs, N.J., 1973.

Program verification

The references in this section represent some of the most important and influential contributions to the discipline of computing science. The article by Kidman (1978) provides a very good tutorial introduction to program verification for beginners. The paper by Wegbreit (1977) also provides important guidelines. The original and most influential contributions to the field of program verification were made by Floyd (1967) and Hoare (1969).

1. Elspas, B., K. N. Levitt, R. J. Waldinger and A. Waksman, "An assessment of techniques for proving program correctness", *Comp. Surv.*, **4**, 97-147, 1972.
2. Floyd, R. W., "Assigning meanings to programs", in *Proc. Symp. in Appl. Math.*, Mathematical Aspects of Computer Science, ed. J. T. Schwartz, Am. Math. Soc., Vol. 19, pp.19-32, 1967.
3. Dijkstra, E. W., *A Discipline of Programming*, Prentice-Hall, Englewood Cliffs, N.J., 1976.
4. Hantler, S. L. and J. C. King, "An introduction to proving the correctness of programs", *Comp. Surv.*, **18**, 331-53, 1976.
5. Hoare, C. A. R., "An axiomatic basis for computer programming", *Comm. ACM*, **12**, 576-80, 1969.
6. Kidman, B. P., "An introduction to program verification", *Proc. 8th Australian Comp. Conf.*, Canberra, Vol. 2, 877-902, 1978.

7.   Linden, T. A., "A summary of progress toward proving program correctness", *Fall Joint Computer Conf.*, Vol. 41, Part 1, 201–11, 1972.
8.   Manna, Z., *Mathematical Theory of Computation*, McGraw-Hill, N.Y., 1974.
9.   Ramamoorthy, C. V. and R. T. Yeh, *Tutorial: Software Methodology*, IEEE Computer Society, Chicago, 1978.
10. Wegbreit, B., "Constructive methods in program verification", *IEEE Trans. Soft. Eng.*, **SE-3**, 193–209, 1977.

Design and analysis of algorithms

The contribution of Knuth (1969, 1972) has been singularly outstanding in this field. The book by Aho *et al.* (1974) is also an important contribution.

1.   Aho, A. V., J. E. Hopcroft and J. D. Ullman, *The Design and Analysis of Computer Algorithms*, Addison-Wesley, Reading, Mass., 1974.
2.   Goodman, S. E. and S. T. Hedetniemi, *Introduction to the Design and Analysis of Algorithms*, McGraw-Hill, N.Y., 1977.
3.   Guttmann, A. J., *Programming and Algorithms*, Heinemann, London, 1977.
4.   Knuth, D. E., *The Art of Computer Programming*, Vol. 1: *Fundamental Algorithms*, Addison-Wesley, Reading, Mass., 1969.
5.   Knuth, D. E., "Mathematical analysis of algorithms", *Proceedings IFIP Congress*, Ljubljana, 135–143, 1972.
6.   Maly, K. and A. R. Hanson, *Fundamentals of Computing Science*, Prentice-Hall, Englewood Cliffs, N.J., 1978.

Chapter 2
FUNDAMENTAL ALGORITHMS

INTRODUCTION

The computer has come close to reaching the status of a universal machine because of its unique ability to perform an almost infinite range of tasks. It combines versatility with lightning speed. What comes as a surprise in this context is that only a very small number of basic instructions are used to perform all computations. At the most fundamental level a computer has instructions for storing information, for performing arithmetic, and comparing information. There are also instructions for controlling the way a computation is performed. These very basic instructions are used to ultimately build the more powerful and complex instructions that we find as primitives in the high level programming languages like Pascal. At the programming language level the same thing happens. Once again, a few computational mechanisms are used to build much larger computational procedures. It is the latter fundamental mechanisms along with considerations of computer information representation that we will examine in this chapter.

One of the most widely used of these fundamental mechanisms is that for interchanging the values associated with two variables. In particular, this operation is widely used in many sorting algorithms. The idea of counting is also an essential part of many more elaborate computational procedures. An extension of the counting idea forms the basis of the often-used mechanism for summing a set of data.

Seemingly, an unlimited number of problems can be expressed in a way that allows them to be solved by repeating a very basic mechanism over and over. For example, a set of n numbers can be summed by simply adding successive numbers from the set to an accumulating sum (see algorithm 2.3). The basic mechanism that is used in the iterative or repetitive process must cause changes in the variables and/or information considered by the mechanism. Only in this way can progress be made towards termination of the iterative process which is always conditionally terminated.

In implementing computer solutions to problems, probably the most important skill that we need to develop is the ability to phrase problems in a way that will allow an iterative solution to be formulated. Unfortunately, for most of us, before our first encounter with computer problem-solving we have had little experience (at the conscious level, at least) of formulating iterative solutions to problems. Time and again in our early programming days we are confronted by simple problems that we can solve very easily (e.g. like picking the maximum number in a set) but for which we have great difficulty in formulating an iterative solution. This happens because we can solve many problems without explicitly formulating or understanding the method used to obtain the solution. When dealing with computers, we are not granted such a luxury. Once we have grasped the idea of "thinking iteratively (and also recursively)", we start to place ourselves in a position where we can formulate computer solutions to otherwise very complex problems.

Another foundation that we must build early in our computing days, is an understanding of the way in which computers represent and manipulate information. In particular, we must appreciate the differences between number and character representations of information and how to manipulate and convert between the various representations.

Only after we have digested the essence of these fundamental concepts are we in a position to tackle the more involved aspects of computer problem-solving.

Algorithm 2.1
EXCHANGING THE VALUES OF TWO VARIABLES

Problem

Given two variables, *a* and *b*, exchange the values assigned to them.

Algorithm development

The problem of interchanging the values associated with two variables involves a very fundamental mechanism that occurs in many sorting and data manipulation algorithms. To define the problem more clearly we will examine a specific example.

Consider that the variables *a* and *b* are assigned values as outlined below. That is,

Starting configuration

This means that memory cell or variable *a* contains the value 721, and memory cell or variable *b* contains the value 463. Our task is to replace the contents of *a* with 463, and the contents of *b* with 721. In other words we want to end up with the configuration below:

Target configuration

To change the value of a variable we can use the assignment operator. Because we want *a* to assume the value currently belonging to *b*, and *b* the value belonging to *a* we could perhaps make the exchange with the following assignments:

$$a := b; \qquad\qquad (1)$$
$$b := a \qquad\qquad (2)$$

where ":=" is the assignment operator. In (1) ":=" causes the value stored in memory cell *b* to be *copied* into memory cell *a*.

Let us work through these two steps to make sure they have the desired effect.

We started out with the configuration

a		*b*
721		463

then after execution of the assignment $a := b$ we have

a		*b*
463		463

The assignment (1) has *changed* the value of *a* but has left the value of *b* untouched. Checking with our target configuration we see that *a* has assumed the value 463 as required. So far so good! We must also check on *b*. When the assignment step (2) i.e. $b := a$ is made *after* executing step (1) we end up with:

a		*b*
463		463

In executing step (2) *a is not changed* while *b* takes on the value that *currently* belongs to *a*. The configuration that we have ended up with does not represent the solution we are seeking. The problem arises because in making the assignment:

$$a := b$$

we have lost the value that *originally* belonged to *a* (i.e. 721 has been lost). It is this value that we want *b* to finally assume. Our problem must therefore be stated more carefully as:

> new value of *a* := old value of *b*;
> new value of *b* := old value of *a*

What we have done with our present proposal is to make the assignment

new value of b := new value of *a*

In other words when we execute step (2) we are *not* using the value *a* that will make things work correctly—because *a* has already *changed*.

To solve this exchange problem we need to find a way of not destroying "*the old value of a*" when we make the assignment

$$a := b$$

A way to do this is to introduce a temporary variable *t* and *copy* the original value of *a* into this variable before executing step (1). The steps to do this are:

$$t := a;$$
$$a := b$$

After these two steps we have

a	*t*	*b*
463	721	463

We are better off than last time because now we still have the old value of *a* stored in *t*. It is this value that we need for assignment to *b*. We can therefore make the assignment

$$b := t$$

After execution of this step we have:

a	*t*	*b*
463	721	721

Rechecking with our target configuration we see that *a* and *b* have now been interchanged as required.

The exchange procedure can now be outlined.

Algorithm description

1. Save the original value of a in t.
2. Assign to a the original value of b.
3. Assign to b the original value of a that is stored in t.

The exchange mechanism as a programming tool is most usefully implemented as a procedure that accepts two variables and returns their exchanged values.

Pascal implementation

```
procedure exchange (var a,b : integer);
var t : integer;
begin {save the original value of a then exchange a and b}
  {assert : a = a0 ∧ b = b0}
  t := a;
  a := b;
  b := t
  {assert : a = b0 ∧ b = a0}
end
```

Notes on design

1. The use of an intermediate temporary variable allows the exchange of two variables to proceed correctly.
2. This example emphasizes that at any stage in a computation a variable always assumes the value dictated by the most recent assignment made to that variable.
3. Working through the mechanism with a particular example can be a useful way of detecting design faults.
4. A more common application of exchange involves two array elements (e.g. $a[i]$ and $a[j]$). The steps for such an exchange are:

```
t := a[i];
a[i] := a[j];
a[j] := t
```

Applications

Sorting algorithms.

Supplementary problems

2.1.1   Given two glasses marked A and B. Glass A is full of raspberry drink and glass B is full of lemonade. Suggest a way of exchanging the contents of glasses A and B.

2.1.2   Design an algorithm that makes the following exchanges:

$$(a \rightarrow b \rightarrow c)$$

The arrows indicate that b is to assume the value of a, c the value of b, and so on.

2.1.3   Design an algorithm that makes the following exchanges:

$$(a \leftarrow b \leftarrow c \leftarrow d)$$

2.1.4   Given two variables of integer type a and b, exhange their values *without* using a third temporary variable.

2.1.5   What happens when the arguments given to the procedure *exhange* are i and $a[i]$?

Algorithm 2.2
COUNTING

Problem

Given a set of n students' examination marks (in the range 0 to 100) make a count of the number of students that passed the examination. A pass is awarded for all marks of 50 and above.

Algorithm development

Counting mechanisms are very frequently used in computer algorithms. Generally a count must be made of the number of items in a set which possess some particular property or which satisfy some particular condition or conditions. This class of problems is typified by the "examination marks" problem.

As a starting point for developing a computer algorithm for this problem we can consider how we might solve a particular example by hand.

Suppose that we are given the set of marks

$$55, 42, 77, 63, 29, 57, 89$$

To make a count of the passes for this set we can start at the left, examine the first mark (i.e. 55), see if it is ≥ 50, and remember that one student has passed so far. The second mark is then examined and no adjustment is made to the count. When we arrive at the third mark we see it is ≥ 50 and so we add one to our previous count. The process continues in a similar manner until *all* marks have been tested.

In more detail we have:

	Marks	Counting details for passes
	55	previous count = 0 current count = 1
Order in	42	previous count = 1 current count = 1
which marks	77	previous count = 1 current count = 2
are	63	previous count = 2 current count = 3
examined	29	previous count = 3 current count = 3
	57	previous count = 3 current count = 4
	89	previous count = 4 current count = 5

$$\therefore \text{ Number of students passed} = 5$$

After each mark has been processed the current count reflects the number of students that have passed in the marks list so far encountered.

We must now ask, how can the counting be achieved? From our example above we see that every time we need to increase the count we build on the previous value. That is,

$$current\_count = previous\_count + 1$$

When, for example, we arrive at mark 57, we have

$$previous\_count = 3$$

Current_count therefore becomes 4. Similarly when we get to the next mark (i.e. 89) the *current_count* of 4 must assume the role of *previous_count*. This means that whenever a new *current_count* is generated it must then assume the role of *previous_count* before the next mark is considered. The two steps in this process can be represented by

$$current\_count := previous\_count + 1 \qquad (1)$$
$$previous\_count := current\_count \qquad (2)$$

These two steps can be repeatedly applied to obtain the count required. In conjunction with the conditional test and input of the next mark we execute step (1), followed by step (2), followed by step (1), followed by step (2) and so on.

Because of the way in which *previous_count* is employed in step (1) we can substitute the expression for *previous_count* in step (2) into step (1) to obtain the simpler expression

$$current\_count := current\_count + 1$$
$$\uparrow \qquad\qquad \uparrow$$
$$\text{(new value)} \qquad \text{(old value)}$$

The *current_count* on the RHS (right-hand side) of the expression assumes the role of *previous_count*. As this statement involves an assignment rather than an equality (which would be impossible) it is a valid computer statement. What it describes is the fact that the *new value* of *current_count* is obtained by adding 1 to the old value of *current_count*.

Viewing the mechanism in this way makes it clear that the existence of the variable *previous_count* in its own right is unnecessary. As a result we have a simpler counting mechanism.

The essential steps in our pass-counting algorithm can therefore be summarized as:

while less then *n* marks have been examined do

(a)   read next mark,
(b)   if current mark satisfies pass requirement then add one to count.

Before any marks have been examined the count must have the value zero. To complete the algorithm the input of the marks and the output of the number of passes must be included. The detailed algorithm is then as described below.

Algorithm description

1.   Prompt then read the number of marks to be processed.
2.   Initialize count to zero.
3   While there are still marks to be processed repeatedly do
    (a)   read next mark,
    (b)   if it is a pass (i.e. ≥ 50) then add one to count.
4.   Write out total number of passes.

Pascal implementation

```
program passcount (input, output);
const passmark = 50;
var count {contains number of passes on termination},
    i {current number of marks processed},
    m {current mark},
    n {total number of marks to be processed}: integer;

begin {count the number of passes (>=50) in a set of marks}
    writeln ('enter a number of marks n on a separate line followed by the
    marks');
    readln (n);
    {assert: n>=0}
    count := 0;
    i := 0;
    {invariant: count = number of marks in the first i read that
    are >= passmark ∧ i =<n}
    while i<n do
```

```
        begin {read next mark, test it for pass and update count if necessary}
          i := i+1;
          read (m);
          if eoln (input) then readln;
          if m>=passmark then count := count+1
        end;
      {assert : count =number of passes in the set of n marks read}
      writeln ('number of passes =', count)
    end.
```

Notes on design

1. Initially, and each time through the loop, the variable *count* represents the number of passes so far encountered. On termination (when $i = n$) *count* represents the total number of passes in the set. Because i is incremented by 1 with each iteration, eventually the condition $i < n$ will be violated and the loop will terminate.
2. It was possible to use substitution to improve on the original solution to the problem. The simplest and most efficient solution to a problem is usually the best all-round solution.
3. An end-of-line test is included to handle multiple lines of data.

Applications

All forms of counting.

Supplementary problems

2.2.1   Modify the algorithm above so that marks are read until an end-of-file is encountered. For this set of marks determine the total number of marks, the number of passes, and the percentage pass rate.

2.2.2   Design an algorithm that reads a list of numbers and makes a count of the number of negatives and the number of non-negative members in the set.

2.2.3   You are given the problem described above. However, assume that your program is to start out with the variable *count* initialized to the total number of students n. On termination, the value of count should again represent the number of students that passed the examination. If there were more passes than fails, why would this implementation be better than the original one?

Algorithm 2.3
SUMMATION OF A SET OF NUMBERS

Problem

Given a set of n numbers design an algorithm that adds these numbers and returns the resultant sum. Assume n is greater than or equal to zero.

Algorithm development

One of the most fundamental things that we are likely to do with a computer is to add a set of n numbers. When confronted with this problem in the absence of a computer we simply write the numbers down one under the other and start adding up the right-hand column. For example, consider the addition of 421, 583 and 714.

$$
\begin{array}{r}
421 \\
583 \\
\underline{714} \\
\cdots\ \underline{8}
\end{array}
$$

In designing a computer algorithm to perform this task we must take a somewhat different approach. The computer has a built-in device which accepts two numbers to be added, performs the addition, and returns the sum of the two numbers (see Fig. 2.1). In designing an algorithm to add a set of numbers a primary concern is the mechanism for the addition process. We will concentrate first on this aspect of the problem before looking at the overall design.

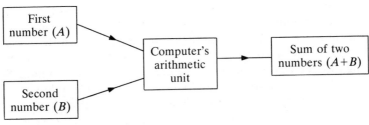

Fig. 2.1   Schematic mechanism for computer's addition process.

The simplest way that we can instruct the computer's arithmetic unit to add a set of numbers is to write down an expression that specifies the addition we wish to be performed. For our three numbers mentioned previously we could write

$$s := 421+583+714 \qquad (1)$$

The assignment operator causes the value resulting from the evaluation of the right-hand side of statement (1) to be placed in the memory cell allocated to the variable s.

Expression (1) will add three *specific* numbers as required. Unfortunately it is capable of doing little else. Suppose we wanted to sum three other numbers. For this task we would need a new program statement.

It would therefore seem reasonable that all constants in expression (1) could be replaced by variables. We would then have

$$s := a+b+c \qquad (2)$$

Expression (2) adds *any* three numbers provided they have been previously assigned as values or contents of a, b, and c respectively. Expression (2) as the basis of a program for adding numbers is more general and more useful than expression (1). It still has a serious deficiency—it can only add sets of three numbers.

A fundamental goal in designing algorithms and implementing programs is to make the programs general enough so that they will successfully handle a wide variety of input conditions. That is, we want a program that will add any n numbers where n can take on a wide range of values.

The approach we need to take to formulate an algorithm to add n numbers in a computer is different from what we would do conventionally to solve the problem. Conventionally we could write the general equation

$$s = (a_1+a_2+a_3+ \cdots +a_n) \qquad (3)$$

or equivalently $\qquad s = \sum_{i=1}^{n} a_i \qquad (4)$ (*Reminder:* $\sum$ is the mathematical summation operator)

We could also write a computer program statement somewhat like equation (3) to add our n numbers but this is not very practical because we want to be able to change n (we may want to use the program to sum a different sized set of numbers). We must therefore look for a better mechanism more in keeping with the way a computer is naturally designed to do things. Several facts about computers are relevant for our current problem. Firstly, computers are well suited to do repetitive things. Secondly, the computer's adding device is designed so that it can only add two numbers at a time. We might therefore ask how we can formulate an algorithm for the addition of n numbers that makes best use of these facts.

One way to do this that takes note of the fact that the computer adds two numbers at a time is to start by adding the first two numbers a_1 and a_2. That is,

$$s := a_1 + a_2 \qquad\qquad (1)$$

We could then proceed by adding a_3 to the s computed in step (1).

$$s := s + a_3 \qquad\qquad (2) \quad \text{(cf. counting statement in algorithm 2.2)}$$

In a similar manner:

$$\left.\begin{array}{l} s := s + a_4 \\ s := s + a_5 \\ \vdots \quad \vdots \quad \vdots \\ s := s + a_n \end{array}\right\} \qquad (3, \ldots, n-1)$$

From step (2) onwards we are actually repeating the same process over and over—the only difference is that values of a and s change with each step. For general i^{th} step we have

$$s := s + a_{i+1} \qquad\qquad (i)$$

This general step can be placed in a loop to iteratively generate the sum of n numbers.

The algorithm we want to develop for summing n numbers should perform correctly for all values of n greater than or equal to 0 (i.e. $n \geqslant 0$). It must therefore work correctly for the sum of zero ($n = 0$) and the sum of 1 ($n = 1$) numbers. This means the step (1) we have used is not appropriate. However, if we replace $i+1$ in the general step (i), by i and substitute $i = 1$ we get:

$$s := s + a_1 \qquad\qquad (1')$$

The step $(1')$ will be correct *provided $s := 0$ before* this step is executed. It follows that *all sums for $n \geqslant 1$ can be generated iteratively*. The instance where $n = 0$ is a special case which cannot be generated iteratively. The sum of zero numbers is zero and so we can generate the first sum directly by the assignment

$$s := 0$$

The core of the algorithm for summing n numbers therefore involves a special step followed by a set of n iterative steps. That is,

1. Compute first sum ($s = 0$) as special case.
2. Build each of the n remaining sums from its predecessor by an iterative process.
3. Write out the sum of n numbers.

The only other considerations involve the input of n, the number of numbers to be summed, and the input of successive numbers with each iterative step. Our complete algorithm can now be outlined.

Algorithm description

1. Prompt and read in the number of numbers to be summed.
2. Initialize sum for zero numbers.
3. While less than n numbers have been summed repeatedly do
    (a)   read in next number,
    (b)   compute current sum by adding the number read to the most recent sum.
4. Write out sum of n numbers.

Pascal implementation†

```
program sum (input, output);‡
var i {summing loop index},
    n {number of numbers to be summed}: integer;
    a {current number to be summed},
    s {sum of n numbers on termination}: real;

begin {computes sum of n real numbers for n>=0}
    writeln ('input n on a separate line, followed by the numbers to be
    summed');
    readln (n);
    {assert: n>=0}
    i := 0;
    s := 0.0;
    {invariant: s =sum of first i numbers read ∧ i=<n}
    while i<n do
        begin {calculate successive partial sums}
            i := i+1;
            read (a);
            if eoln (input) then readln;
            s := s+a
        end;
    {assert: s =sum of n numbers read}
    writeln ('sum of n =', n, ' numbers =', s)
end.
```

---

† See (7) in Notes on design (next section).
‡ A **while**-loop has been used to emphasize iteration and termination. A **for**-loop could equally well have been used.

Notes on design

1. To sum n numbers $(n-1)$ additions must be performed. The present algorithm has used n additions instead to allow a simpler and cleaner implementation.
2. Initially, and each time through the loop, the sum s reflects the sum of the first i numbers read. On termination (when $i = n$) s will represent the sum of n numbers. Because i is incremented by 1 with each iteration eventually the condition $i<n$ will be violated and the loop will terminate.
3. The design employed makes no consideration of the accuracy of the resultant sum or the finite size of numbers that can be accurately represented in the computer. An algorithm that minimizes errors in summation does so by adding, at each stage, the two smallest numbers remaining.
4. Observe that only general algorithms should be implemented as programs. A program parameterized to solve *just one* problem is usually a wasted effort.
5. The obvious or direct solution to the problem is considerably different to the computer solution. The requirement of flexibility imposes this difference on the computer solution.
6. Consideration of the problem at its lowest limit (i.e. $n = 0$) leads to a mechanism that can be extended to larger values of n by simple repetition. This is a very common device in computer algorithm design.
7. A program that reads and sums n numbers is not a very useful programming tool. A much more practical implementation is a function that returns the sum of an array of n numbers. That is,

```
function asum(var a:nelements;n:integer):real;
var sum {the partial sum},
    i:integer;
begin {compute the sum of n real array elements (n⩾0)}
    sum := 0.0;
    for i := 1 to n do
        sum := sum+a[i];
    asum := sum
end
```

Applications

Average calculations, variance and least squares calculations.

Supplementary problems

2.3.1 Design an algorithm to compute the average of n numbers.

2.3.2 Redesign the algorithm so that it only needs to perform $n-1$ additions to sum n numbers.

2.3.3 Design an algorithm to compute the sum of the squares of n numbers. That is,

$$s = \sum_{i=1}^{n} (a_i)^2$$

2.3.4 The harmonic mean defined by

$$H = \frac{n}{\sum_{i=1}^{n} (1/a_i)}$$

is sometimes used as a mean of central tendency. Develop an algorithm to compute the harmonic mean of n data values.

2.3.5 Develop an algorithm to compute the sums for the first n terms $(n \geqslant 0)$ of the following series:

(a) $s = 1+2+3+ \cdots$
(b) $s = 1+3+5+ \cdots$
(c) $s = 2+4+6+ \cdots$
(d) $s = 1+1/2+1/3+ \cdots$

2.3.6 Generate the first n terms of the sequence

$$1 \quad 2 \quad 4 \quad 8 \quad 16 \quad 32 \quad \cdots$$

without using multiplication.

2.3.7 Develop an algorithm that prints out n values of the sequence

$$1 \quad -1 \quad 1 \quad -1 \quad 1 \quad -1 \quad \cdots$$

2.3.8 Develop an algorithm to compute the sum of the first n terms $(n \geqslant 1)$ of the series

$$s = 1-3+5-7+9-\cdots$$

Algorithm 2.4
FACTORIAL COMPUTATION

Problem

Given a number n, compute n factorial (written as $n!$) where $n \geqslant 0$.

Algorithm development

We can start the development of this algorithm by examining the definition of $n!$. We are given that

$$n! = 1 \times 2 \times 3 \times \cdots \times (n-1) \times n \qquad \text{for } n \geqslant 1$$

and by definition

$$0! = 1$$

In formulating our design for this problem we need to keep in mind that the computer's arithmetic unit can only multiply *two* numbers at a time.

Applying the factorial definition we get

$$0! = 1$$
$$1! = 1 \times 1$$
$$2! = 1 \times 2$$
$$3! = 1 \times 2 \times 3$$
$$4! = 1 \times 2 \times 3 \times 4$$
$$\vdots$$

We see that 4! contains *all* the factors of 3!. The only difference is the inclusion of the number 4. We can generalize this by observing that $n!$ can always be obtained from $(n-1)!$ by simply multiplying it by n (for $n \geqslant 1$). That is,

$$n! = n \times (n-1)! \qquad \text{for } n \geqslant 1$$

Using this definition we can write the first few factorials as:

$$1! = 1 \times 0!$$
$$2! = 2 \times 1!$$
$$3! = 3 \times 2!$$
$$4! = 4 \times 3!$$
$$\vdots$$

If we start with $p = 0! = 1$ we can rewrite the first few steps in computing $n!$ as:

$p := 1$	(1)	$= 0!$
$p := p*1$		$= 1!$
$p := p*2$		$= 2!$
$p := p*3$	$(2 \ldots n+1)$	$= 3!$
$p := p*4$		$= 4!$
$\vdots$		$\vdots$

From step (2) onwards we are actually repeating the same process over and over. For the general $(i+1)^{\text{th}}$ step we have

$$p := p*i \qquad (i+1)$$

This general step can be placed in a loop to iteratively generate $n!$. This allows us to take advantage of the fact that the computer's arithmetic unit can only multiply two numbers at a time.

In many ways this problem is very much like the problem of summing a set of n numbers (algorithm 2.3). In the summation problem we performed a set of additions, whereas in this problem we need to generate a set of products. It follows from the general $(i+1)^{th}$ step that all factorials for $n \geqslant 1$ can be generated iteratively. The instance where $n = 0$ is a special case which must be accounted for directly by the assignment

$$p := 1 \qquad \text{(by definition of 0!)}$$

The central part of the algorithm for computing $n!$ therefore involves a special initial step followed by n iterative steps.

1.   Treat 0! as a special case ($p := 1$).
2.   Build each of the n remaining products p from its predecessor by an iterative process.
3.   Write out the value of n factorial.

Algorithm description

1.   Establish n, the factorial required where $n \geqslant 0$.
2.   Set product p for 0! (special case). Also set product count to zero.
3.   While less than n products have been calculated repeatedly do
     (a)   increment product count,
     (b)   compute the ith product p by multiplying i by the most recent product.
4.   Return the result $n!$.

This algorithm is most usefully implemented as a function that accepts as input a number n and returns as output the value of $n!$. In the Pascal implementation p has been replaced by the variable *factor*.

Pascal implementation

```
function nfactorial (n : integer): integer;
var i {loop index representing ith factorial}: integer;
   factor {i!}:integer;

begin {computes and returns n! for n >= 0}
   {assert:n >= 0}
   factor := 1;
   {invariant : factor = i! after the ith iteration ∧ i = <n}
   for i := to n do
     factor := i * factor;
   nfactorial := factor
   {assert: nfactorial = n!}
end
```

Notes on design

1. The algorithm uses n multiplications to compute $n!$. There is in fact a more efficient algorithm that computes $n!$ in essentially $\log_2 n$ steps. (See note 5 below).

2. After the ith time through the loop the value of *factor* is $i!$. This condition holds for all i. On termination (when $i = n$) *factor* will correspond to $n!$. Because i is incremented by 1 with each iteration, eventually the condition $i = n$ will be reached and the loop will terminate. The algorithm performs correctly for all $n \geqslant 0$. However, no consideration is given to the finite size of numbers that can be represented in the computer.

3. Careful definition of the problem and examination of some specific examples is central to the development of the algorithm. The simplest problem leads to a generalization that forms the basis of the algorithm.

4. The idea of accumulating products is very similar to that of accumulating sums (see algorithm 2.3).

5. A more efficient mechanism is based on the fact that it is possible to express $n!$ in terms of $(n/2)!$. In principle, the mechanism is similar to that used in calculating the nth Fibonacci number (ref. A. Shamir, "Factoring numbers in $O(\log n)$ arithmetic steps," *Inf. Proc. Letts.*, **8** 28–31, 1979). See also algorithm 3.8.

Applications

Probability, statistical and mathematical computations.

Supplementary problems

2.4.1 For a given n, design an algorithm to compute $1/n!$.

2.4.2 For a given x and a given n, design an algorithm to compute $x^n/n!$.

2.4.3 Design an algorithm to determine whether or not a number n is a factorial number.

2.4.4 Design an algorithm which, given some integer n, finds the largest factorial number present as a factor in n.

2.4.5 Design an algorithm to simulate multiplication by addition. Your program should accept as input two integers (they may be zero, positive, or negative).

2.4.6 The binomial theorem of basic algebra indicates that the coefficient ^nC_r of the rth power of x in the expansion of $(x+1)^n$ is given by

$$^nC_r = \frac{n!}{r!(n-r)!}$$

Design an algorithm that evaluates all coefficients of x for a given value of n.

Algorithm 2.5
SINE FUNCTION COMPUTATION

Problem

Design an algorithm to evaluate the function $\sin(x)$ as defined by the infinite series expansion

$$\sin(x) = \frac{x}{1!} - \frac{x^3}{3!} + \frac{x^5}{5!} - \frac{x^7}{7!} + \cdots$$

Algorithm development

This problem embodies some of the techniques we have seen in earlier algorithms. Studying the expression for $\sin(x)$ we see that powers and factorials following the sequence

$$1, 3, 5, 7, \ldots$$

are required. We can easily generate this odd sequence by starting with 1 and successively adding 2. Our other problem is to compute the general term $x^i/i!$ which can be expressed as

$$\frac{x^i}{i!} = \frac{x}{1} \times \frac{x}{2} \times \frac{x}{3} \times \cdots \times \frac{x}{i} \qquad \text{for} \quad i \geqslant 1$$

The function we need to compute this will involve the following steps:

```
fp := 1;
j := 0;
while j<i do
   begin
      j := j+1;
      fp := fp*x/j
   end
```

The algorithm can be completed by implementing the additions and subtractions and making the appropriate termination. With this approach *each* term (i.e. $x^i/i!$) is computed by starting at the smallest j value and working upwards. In calculating $n!$ we used the efficient approach of calculating each term from its predecessor. The question this raises is can we do the same with the present problem? To explore this possibility we can examine the overlap for some specific terms of the series. For example,

$$\frac{x^3}{3!} = \frac{x \times x \times x}{3 \times 2 \times 1} \qquad = \frac{x^2}{3 \times 2} \quad \frac{x^1}{1!} \qquad i = 3$$

$$\frac{x^5}{5!} = \frac{x \times x \times x \times x \times x}{5 \times 4 \times 3 \times 2 \times 1} \qquad = \frac{x^2}{5 \times 4} \quad \frac{x^3}{3!} \qquad i = 5$$

$$\frac{x^7}{7!} = \frac{x \times x \times x \times x \times x \times x \times x}{7 \times 6 \times 5 \times 4 \times 3 \times 2 \times 1} = \frac{x^2}{7 \times 6} \quad \frac{x^5}{5!} \qquad i = 7$$

Each of the terms $x^2/(3 \times 2)$, $x^2/(5 \times 4)$, $x^2/(7 \times 6)$, ... can be described by the general term:

$$\frac{x^2}{i(i-1)} \qquad \text{for } i = 3,5,7, \dots$$

Therefore to generate consecutive terms of the sine series we can use

$$\text{current } i^{\text{th}} \text{ term} = \frac{x^2}{i(i-1)} \times (\text{previous term})$$

To get the terms to *alternate* in sign we can use the device employed in problem 2.3.8. Repeatedly executing

$$sign := -\ sign$$

will generate alternating positive and negative terms. This can be incorporated directly into our term expression. The initial conditions are therefore

$$\left. \begin{array}{l} tsin = x; \\ term := x; \\ i := 1 \end{array} \right\}$$

The ith term and summation which can be generated iteratively from their predecessors are:

$$i := i+2;$$
$$term := -term*x*x/(i*(i-1));$$
$$tsin = tsin + term$$

We now have an effective iterative mechanism for generating successive terms of the sine function. The only other consideration is how to terminate the algorithm.

Clearly we can only evaluate sin (x) to a finite number of terms. An important consideration here is the desired accuracy we require for sin (x). Because x is in the range $-1 \leqslant x \leqslant 1$ we can see that the contribution from higher terms quickly becomes very small. For example the 4th term (i.e. $x^7/7!$) makes a contribution of less than 0.0002. In circumstances like this a useful way to bring about termination is to fix an acceptable error level (e.g. 1×10^{-6}) and generate successive terms until the contribution of the current term is *less* than the acceptable error. A detailed error analysis of the problem confirms that this is an acceptable termination condition. Because the terms alternate in sign we will have to use the absolute error term value for the termination test.

The overall strategy for our sine function algorithm can be summarized as follows.

Algorithm description

1. Set up initial conditions for the first term that cannot be computed iteratively.
2. While the absolute value of current term is greater than the acceptable error do
   (a) identify the current i^{th} term,
   (b) generate current term from its predecessor,
   (c) add current term with the appropriate sign to the accumulated sum for the sine function.

Since the sine expression involves the calculation of a single value it is best implemented as a function.

Pascal implementation

```
function sin (x: real): real;
const error = 1.0e-6;
var i {variable to generate sequence 1 3 5 7}: integer;
    x2 {x squared},
    term {current sum of terms – eventually approximates sin}: real;

begin {function returns sin (x) with an accuracy of =<error}
    {assert:-1.0 =<x =<1.0}
    term := x;
    tsin := x;
    i := 1;
    x2 := x * x;
    {invariant: after the jth iteration, i = 2j + 1 ∧term = (-1)↑j * (x↑i) / i!
      ∧tsin is sum of first (j+1) terms}
    while abs (term)>error do
        begin {generate and accumulate successive terms of sine
        expression}
            i := i+2;
            term := -term * x2 / (i * (i-1));
            tsin := tsin +term
        end;
    sin := tsin
    {assert: sin ≈sine (x)∧abs (term)=<error}
end
```

Notes on design

1. The number of loop iterations for this algorithm is a function of the error requirements. For an error of less than 10^{-6} only 5 terms need to be evaluated. This accuracy will suffice for most practical applications. The cost of generating successive terms of the series is *constant*. This is more favorable than the original design where the cost of generating successive terms was proportional to the position of the terms in the series (i.e. later terms required more computation).

2. Before, and throughout the iterative process, at the jth pass (j is not explicitly defined) *term* represents the jth term in the sine series expansion and *tsin* contains the appropriately signed summation of the first j terms in the series expansion. The invariant restrictions on the variables *tsin* and *term* hold for all $j \geqslant 1$. We can be confident that the algorithm will terminate because for the chosen x range (i.e. $-1 \leqslant x \leqslant 1$) the absolute value of *term* is a *strictly decreasing* function. It will therefore eventually become less than the set error level. In this discussion we have not considered contributions from round-off errors.

3. The number of multiplications is reduced by precomputing the $x*x$ term.

4. This algorithm embodies the same basic mechanism that is applied in the factorial and summation algorithms. The only differences involve choice of initial conditions, choice of iterative terms, and choice of termination conditions.

5. Where it is appropriate, generation of each term from its predecessor usually leads to the simplest and most efficient implementation for a problem. It is therefore usually worth putting in the extra effort to see if terms can be generated from their predecessors. Specific examples are good for this purpose.

6. Take particular note of the way the alternating sign effect is achieved and also of the way termination is brought about.

Applications

Mathematical and statistical computations.

Supplementary problems

2.5.1   Design an algorithm to find the sum of the first n terms of the series

$$f_s = 0! + 1! + 2! + 3! + \cdots + n! \qquad (n \geqslant 0)$$

2.5.2   The exponential growth constant e is characterized by the expression

$$e = \frac{1}{0!} + \frac{1}{1!} + \frac{1}{2!} + \frac{1}{3!} + \cdots$$

Devise an algorithm to compute e to n terms.

2.5.3   Design an algorithm to evaluate the function cos (x) as defined by the infinite series expansion

$$\cos{(x)} = 1 - \frac{x^2}{2!} + \frac{x^4}{4!} - \frac{x^6}{6!} + \cdots$$

The acceptable error for the computation is 10^{-6}.

Algorithm 2.6
GENERATION OF THE FIBONACCI SEQUENCE

Problem

Generate and print the first n terms of the Fibonacci sequence where $n \geqslant 1$. The first few terms are:

$$0, 1, 1, 2, 3, 5, 8, 13, \ldots$$

Each term beyond the first two is derived from the sum of its two nearest predecessors.

Algorithm development

From the definition we are given that:

new term = preceding term + term before preceding term

The last sentence of the problem statement suggests we may be able to use the definition to generate consecutive terms (apart from the first two) iteratively.

Let us define:

    a as the *term before the preceding term*
    b as the *preceding term*
    c *new term*

Then to start with we have:

        $a := 0$ first Fibonacci number
        $b := 1$ second Fibonacci number
and $c := a + b$ third Fibonacci number (from definition)

When the new term c has been generated we have the third Fibonacci number. To generate the fourth, or next Fibonacci number, we need to apply the *same* definition again. Before we can make this *next* computation we need to make some adjustments. The fourth Fibonacci number is derived from the sum of the second and third Fibonacci numbers. With regard to the definition the second Fibonacci number has the role of the *term before the preceding term* and the third Fibonacci number has the role of "*the preceding term*". Therefore, before making the *next* (i.e. the fourth) computation we must ensure that:

(a)   new term (i.e. the third) assumes the role of the preceding term,
(b)   and what is currently the preceding term must assume the role of the term before the preceding term.

That is,

$a := 0$	[1]	term before preceding term
$b := 1$	[2]	preceding term
$c := a+b$	[3]	new term
$a := b$	[4]	term before preceding term becomes preceding term
$b := c$	[5]	preceding term becomes new term

After making step [5] we are in a position where we can use the definition to generate the next Fibonacci number. A way to do this is to loop back to step [3]. Further investigation of steps [3]→[5] indicates they can be placed in a loop to iteratively generate Fibonacci numbers (for $n>2$). The essential mechanism we could use is:

```
a := 0;
b := 1;
i := 2;
while i<n do
    begin
        i := i+1;
        c := a+b;
        a := b;
        b := c
    end
```

Before leaving off this discussion we should ask can any improvements be made to our algorithm? With the mechanism we have, as each new term c is computed, the term before the preceding term, a, loses its relevance to the calculation of the *next* Fibonacci number. To restore its relevance we made the assignment

$$a := b$$

We know that at *all* times only two numbers are relevant to the generation of the next Fibonacci number. In our computation, however, we have introduced a third variable, c. What we can therefore attempt to do is keep the two variables a and b always relevant. Because the first Fibonacci number becomes irrelevant as soon as the third Fibonacci is computed we can start with:

$$a := 0; \qquad [1]$$
$$b := 1; \qquad [2]$$
$$a := a+b \qquad [3]$$

(this keeps a relevant to generate the next Fibonacci number)

If we iterate on step [3] to generate successive Fibonacci numbers we run into trouble because we are not changing b. However, after step [3] we know the next (i.e. fourth) Fibonacci number can be generated using

$$next := a+b \qquad [4] \qquad \text{(fourth Fibonacci number)}$$

So we need to ask where is the fault in our reasoning? When we do step [4], the old value of b, as defined by step [2], loses its relevance. To keep b relevant at step [4] we can make the assignment:

$$b := a+b$$

The first four steps then become

$$a := 0; \qquad [1]$$
$$b := 1; \qquad [2]$$
$$a := a+b; \qquad [3]$$
$$b := a+b \qquad [4]$$

After step [4] we find that a and b as defined are correct for generating the fifth Fibonacci number. At this point the old a value becomes irrelevant. Working through several more steps confirms that we can safely iterate on steps [3] and [4] to generate the required sequence. Because the algorithm generates Fibonacci numbers in pairs care must be taken to write out exactly n numbers. The easiest way to do this is to keep the output one step behind the generation phase.

The complete algorithm description can now be given.

Algorithm description

1. Prompt and read n, the number of Fibonacci numbers to be generated.
2. Assign first two Fibonacci numbers a and b.
3. Initialize count of number generated.
4. While less than n Fibonacci numbers have been generated do
   (a) write out next two Fibonacci numbers;

(b)   generate next Fibonacci number keeping *a* relevant;
(c)   generate next Fibonacci number from most recent pair keeping *b* relevant for next computation;
(d)   update count of number of Fibonacci numbers generated, *i*.
5.   If *n* even then write out last two Fibonacci numbers else write out second last Fibonacci number.

Pascal implementation

```
program Fibonacci (input, output);
var a {Fibonacci number variable},
    b {Fibonacci number variable},
    i {number of Fibonacci numbers generated},
    n {number of Fibonacci numbers to be generated}: integer;

begin {generate each Fibonacci number from the sum of its two
predecessors}
    a := 0;
    b := 1;
    i := 2;
    writeln ('enter n the number of Fibonacci numbers to be
      generated');
    readln (n);
    {assert: n>0}
    {invariant: after jth iteration i = 2j + 2∧first i Fib. numbers have
      been generated ∧a = (i–1)th Fib. no. ∧b =ith Fib. no.
      ∧i =<n + 1}
    while i <n do
      begin
        writeln (a, b);
        a := a +b;
        b := a +b;
        i := i +2
      end;
    if i =n then writeln (a, b) else writeln (a)
    {assert: first n Fibonacci numbers generated and written out}
end.
```

Notes on design

1.   To generate *n* Fibonacci numbers essentially *n* steps are required. The algorithm functions correctly for all values of $n \geqslant 1$.
2.   Throughout the computation the variables *a* and *b* always contain the two most recently generated Fibonacci numbers. Therefore, whenever an addition is made to generate the next Fibonacci number, the requirements for that number to be a Fibonacci number are always satisfied. Because *i* is increased with each iteration the condition $i < n$ will eventually be violated and the algorithm will terminate.

3.   The second algorithm is more efficient than the first algorithm because it makes only one assignment per Fibonacci number generated. The first algorithm makes three assignments per Fibonacci number generated.

4.   With the present algorithm Fibonacci numbers are generated in pairs. When n is odd one more number will be generated than is required. It will not, however, be printed. This is a small sacrifice for the other gains.

5.   A more advanced algorithm that can calculate the nth Fibonacci number in $\log_2 n$ steps will be discussed in algorithm (3.8).

Applications

The Fibonacci sequence has practical applications in botany, electrical network theory, sorting and searching.

Supplementary problems

2.6.1   Implement the Fibonacci algorithm as a function that accepts as input two consecutive Fibonacci numbers and returns as output the next Fibonacci number.

2.6.2   The first few numbers of the Lucas sequence which is a variation on the Fibonacci sequence are:

$$1 \quad 3 \quad 4 \quad 7 \quad 11 \quad 18 \quad 29 \quad ...$$

Design an algorithm to generate the Lucas sequence.

2.6.3   Given $a = 0$, $b = 1$, and $c = 1$ are the first three numbers of some sequence. All other numbers in the sequence are generated from the sum of their three most recent predecessors. Design an algorithm to generate this sequence.

2.6.4   Given that two numbers d and e are suspected of being consecutive members of the Fibonacci sequence design an algorithm that will refute or confirm this conjecture.

2.6.5   The ascending sequence of all reduced fractions between 0 and 1 which have denominators $\leqslant n$ is called the Farey series of order n. The Farey series of order 5 is:

$$\frac{0}{1} \quad \frac{1}{5} \quad \frac{1}{4} \quad \frac{1}{3} \quad \frac{2}{5} \quad \frac{1}{2} \quad \frac{3}{5} \quad \frac{2}{3} \quad \frac{3}{4} \quad \frac{4}{5} \quad \frac{1}{1}$$

Denoting this series by

$$\frac{x_0}{y_0} \quad \frac{x_1}{y_1} \quad \frac{x_2}{y_2} \quad ...$$

it can be shown that

$$x_0 = 0 \qquad y_0 = 1 \qquad x_1 = 1 \qquad y_1 = n$$

and in general for $k \geqslant 1$

$$x_{k+2} = \left\lfloor \frac{(y_k + n)}{k_{k+1}} \right\rfloor x_{k+1} - x_k$$

$$y_{k+2} = \left\lfloor \frac{(y_k + n)}{k_{k+1}} \right\rfloor y_{k+1} - y_k$$

where $\lfloor q \rfloor$ is the greatest integer less than or equal to q.

Design an algorithm to generate the Farey series for a given n. (See D. E. Knuth, *The Art of Computer Programming*, Vol. 1, *Fundamental Algorithms*, Addison-Wesley, Reading, Mass., p. 157, 1969.)

2.6.6 Generate the sequence where each member is the sum of adjacent factorials, i.e.

$$f_3 = 1! + 0!$$
$$f_4 = 2! + 1!$$
$$f_5 = 3! + 2!$$

Note that by definition $0! = 1$.

Algorithm 2.7
REVERSING THE DIGITS OF AN INTEGER

Problem

Design an algorithm that accepts a positive integer and reverses the order of its digits.

Algorithm development

Digit reversal is a technique that is sometimes used in computing to remove bias from a set of numbers. It is important in some fast information-retrieval algorithms. A specific example clearly defines the relationship of the input to the desired output. For example,

Input: 27953
Output: 35972

Although we might not know at this stage exactly how we are going to make this reversal one thing is clear—we are going to need to access individual digits of the input number. As a starting point we will concentrate on this aspect of the procedure. The number 27953 is actually

$$2\times10^4+7\times10^3+9\times10^2+5\times10+3$$

To access the individual digits it is probably going to be easiest to start at one end of the number and work through to the other end. The question is at which end should we start? Because other than visually it is not easy to tell how many digits there are in the input number it will be best to try to establish the identity of the least significant digit (i.e. the rightmost digit). To do this we need to effectively "chop off" the least significant digit in the number. In other words we want to end up with 2795 with the 3 removed and identified.

We can get the number 2795 by integer division of the original number by 10

i.e. 27953 **div** 10→2795

This chops off the 3 but does not allow us to save it. However, 3 is the remainder that results from dividing 27953 by 10. To get this remainder we can use the **mod** function. That is,

27953 **mod** 10→3

Therefore if we apply the following two steps

$r := n$ **mod** 10   (1)⇒($r = 3$)
$n := n$ **div** 10   (2)⇒($n = 2795$)

we get the digit 3, and the new number 2795. Applying the same two steps to the new value of n we can obtain the 5 digit. We now have a mechanism for iteratively accessing the individual digits of the input number.

Our next major concern is to carry out the digit reversal. When we apply our digit extraction procedure to the first two digits we acquire first the 3 and then 5. In the final output they appear as:

3 followed by 5   (or 35)

If the original number was 53 then we could obtain its reverse by first extracting the 3, multiplying it by 10, and then adding 5 to give 35. That is,

$3\times10+5$→35

The last three digits of the input number are 953. They appear in the "reversed" number as 359. Therefore at the stage when we have the 35 and then extract the 9 we can obtain the sequence 359 by multiplying 35 by 10 and adding 9. That is,

$$35\times10+9\rightarrow359$$

Similarly

$$359\times10+7\rightarrow3597$$

and

$$3597\times10+2\rightarrow35972$$

The last number obtained from the multiplication and addition process is the "digit-reversed" integer we have been seeking. On closely examining the digit extraction, and the reversal process, it is evident that they both involve a set of steps that can be performed iteratively.

We must now find a mechanism for building up the "reversed" integer digit by digit. Let us assume that the variable *dreverse* is to be used to build the reversed integer. At each stage in building the reversed integer its *previous* value is used in conjunction with the most recently extracted digit.

Rewriting the multiplication and addition process we have just described in terms of the variable *dreverse* we get

	Iteration	Value of dreverse
[1]	*dreverse* := *dreverse*∗10+3	3
[2]	*dreverse* := *dreverse*∗10+5	35
[3]	*dreverse* := *dreverse*∗10+9	359
	⋮	⋮

Therefore to build the reversed integer we can use the construct:

$$dreverse := \text{(previous value of } dreverse)*10$$
$$+\text{(most recently extracted rightmost digit)}$$

The variable *dreverse* can be used on *both* sides of this expression. For the value of *dreverse* to be correct (i.e. *dreverse* = 3) after the first iteration it must initially be zero. This initialization step for *dreverse* is also needed to ensure that the algorithm functions correctly when the input number to be reversed is zero.

What we have not established yet is under what conditions should the iterative process terminate. The termination condition must in some way be related to the number of digits in the input integer. In fact as soon as all digits have been extracted and processed termination should apply. With each iteration the number of digits in the number being reversed is reduced by one, yielding the sequence shown in Table 2.1. Accumulative integer division of the "number being reversed" by 10 produces the sequence 27953, 2795, 279, ... In our example, when the integer division process is applied for a 5th time a zero results since 2 is less than 10. Since at this point in the computation the "reversed" number has been fully constructed we can use the zero result to terminate the iterative process.

Table 2.1 Steps in digit reversal

Number being reversed	Reversed number being constructed	Step
27953	3	[1]
2795	35	[2]
279	359	[3]
27	3597	[4]
2	35972	[5]

The central steps in our digit reversal algorithm are:

1. While there are still digits in the number being reversed do
    (a) extract the righmost digit from the number being reversed and append this digit to the right-hand end of the current reversed number representation;
    (b) remove the rightmost digit from the number being reversed.

When we include input and output considerations and details on initialization and termination we arrive at the following algorithm description.

Algorithm description

1. Establish n, the positive integer to be reversed.
2. Set the initial condition for the reversed integer *dreverse*.
3. While the integer being reversed is greater than zero do

    (a) use the remainder function to extract the rightmost digit of the number being reversed;
    (b) increase the previous reversed integer representation *dreverse* by a factor of 10 and add to it the most recently extracted digit to give the current *dreverse* value;
    (c) use integer division by 10 to remove the rightmost digit from the number being reversed.

This algorithm is most suitably implemented as a function which accepts as input the integer to be reversed and returns as output the integer with its digits reversed.

Pascal implementation

```
function dreverse (n: integer): integer;
var reverse: integer;

begin {reverse the order of the digits of a positive integer}
   {assert: n >= 0 ∧ n contains k digits a(1), a(2), a(3),..., a(k)}
   reverse := 0;
```

{*invariant*: after jth iteration, $n = a(1), a(2), a(3), \ldots a(k-j) \wedge$
    $reverse = a(k), a(k-1), \ldots, a(k-j+1)$}
while $n > 0$ **do**
    begin
        $reverse := reverse * 10 + n$ **mod** $10;$
        $n := n$ **div** 10
    end;
    {*assert*: $reverse = a(k), a(k-1), \ldots, a(1)$}
    $dreverse := reverse$
end

Notes on design

1. The number of steps to reverse the digits in an integer is directly proportional to the number of digits in the integer.

2. After the ith time through the loop (i is not explicitly defined in the algorithm) the variable *dreverse* contains the i leftmost digits in the reversed integer. This condition remains invariant for all i. Also after i iterations the variable n is reduced by i digits. On termination when n has been reduced to zero digits the variable *dreverse* will contain the same number of digits as the input integer. The algorithm will terminate because the variable n is reduced by one more digit with each iteration. The algorithm performs correctly for all values of $n \geqslant 0$.

3. In this design we see once again how a complete solution to a problem is built iteratively from a succession of partial solutions. This is the fundamental design framework for many algorithms.

4. In designing this algorithm we have implicitly been working back from the solution to the starting point. This idea of working backwards is a very powerful and important concept in computing science which we will exploit much more explicitly in the design of more advanced algorithms.

5. A specific example helps to lead us to a method for building the reversed representation.

Applications

Hashing and information retrieval, data base applications.

Supplementary problems

2.7.1   Design an algorithm that counts the number of digits in an integer.

2.7.2   Design an algorithm to sum the digits in an integer.

2.7.3   Design an algorithm that reads in a set of n single digits and converts them into a single decimal integer. For example, the algorithm should convert the set of 5 digits {2,7,4,9,3} to the integer 27493.

Algorithm 2.8
BASE CONVERSION

Problem

Convert a decimal integer to its corresponding octal representation.

Algorithm development

Frequently in computing it is necessary to convert a decimal number to the binary, octal or hexadecimal number systems. To design an algorithm for such conversions we need to understand clearly what the base change entails.

Because initially we probably have no firm ideas on the mechanism for base conversion we will begin with some groundwork. We can start by trying to come to terms with exactly what is a decimal number and an octal number. For this exploration we can look at some specific examples.

The decimal (i.e. base 10) number 275 by its representation, is seen to consist of:

$$
\begin{array}{ll}
5 \text{ units} & 5 \times 1 \\
7 \text{ tens} & 7 \times 10 \\
2 \text{ hundreds} & \underline{2 \times 100} \\
& 275
\end{array}
$$

The decimal system uses the ten digits 0,1,2,3, ..., 9 to represent numbers. The actual *position* of each digit in a number determines its value.

Similar conventions apply for the octal (or base 8) number system. The octal system uses *only* the eight digits 0,1,2,3, ..., 7 to represent numbers. In the octal system the position of each digit determines its value in a similar (but different) way to the decimal system. Taking a few steps ahead for the purposes of illustration it can be shown that the octal representation of the decimal number 275 is 423. The octal number consists of:

$$
\begin{array}{ll}
3 \text{ units} & 3 \times 1 \\
2 \text{ eights} & 2 \times 8 \\
4 \text{ sixty-fours} & \underline{4 \times 64} \\
& 275 \text{ decimal}
\end{array}
$$

As another illustration in contrast to the decimal number 275 (written as 275_{10}) the octal number 275 (written as 275_8) consists of:

5 units	5×1
7 eights	7×8
2 sixty-fours	$\underline{2 \times 64}$
	$\overline{189 \text{ decimal}}$

We can see that 275_8 is much smaller in magnitude than 275_{10}.

With this groundwork complete we can now return to our base conversion problem. We have learned that in changing the base of a number we are not in any way changing the magnitude of the number but rather we are changing the way the number is represented.

As a starting point we will consider the conversion of a particular decimal number to its octal representation. This will hopefully reveal much of the mechanics of the algorithm we are seeking.

Consider that we wish to convert the decimal number 93 to its octal representation. We know that 93 is made up of 3 units and 9 tens. In diagram form we have:

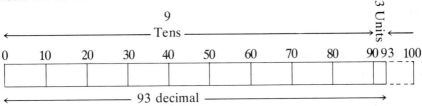

The corresponding octal number will need to be divided up into "blocks" of units, eights, sixty-fours and so on, rather than units, tens, hundreds and so on. Using a diagram for the octal representation we get:

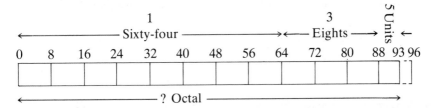

From our diagram we can see that when we divide 93 decimal up into blocks of eight there are 5 units left over at the end. Our octal representation must therefore be of the form ...5. In dividing 93_{10} up into blocks of eight we also discover that there are 11 blocks of eight (i.e. $11 \times 8 = 88$) present in 93_{10}. At this stage we might be tempted to write down 115 as our octal representation of 93_{10}. There is a problem with this, however, because 11 is not a valid octal digit (the only octal digits that we can use are 0,1,2,3, ..., 7). We might therefore ask where do we go from here? With only eight digits the maximum number of eights we can represent is 7. Remembering our previous examples we know that sixty-fours can be used in the representation. In fact 8 eights can (and must) be represented as 1 sixty-four. It follows that 11 eights can be represented as 1 sixty-four and 3 eights. Applying the positional conventions we have encountered earlier we can conclude that the octal representation of 93 decimal is 135.

The octal number 135 consists of

$$
\begin{array}{ll}
5 \text{ units} & 5 \times 1 \\
3 \text{ eights} & 3 \times 8 \\
1 \text{ sixty-four} & \underline{1 \times 64} \\
& \underline{93 \text{ decimal}}
\end{array}
$$

Using a diagram we have arrived at the octal representation for 93_{10}. What we must now do is translate what was done with the diagram into an algorithm. Integer division of 93 by 8 will tell us how many eights are in 93_{10}; that is,

$$93 \ \mathbf{div} \ 8 \rightarrow 11 \text{ eights}$$

The number of sixty-fours in 93_{10} must also be found. This involves breaking the 11 eights into 1 sixty-four and 3 eights. To be systematic about the process we should first find the units, then the eights, then the sixty-fours, and then the five-hundred-and-twelves and so on. We have

93 units→11 eights and 5 units
11 eights→1 sixty-four and 3 eights
1 sixty-four→0 five-hundred-and-twelves and 1 sixty-four

We can now more explicitly identify the base conversion mechanism

$$
\begin{array}{r|r|l}
8 & 93 & \\
8 & 11 & 5 \text{ remainder} \\
8 & 1 & 3 \text{ remainder} \\
& 0 & 1 \text{ remainder}
\end{array}
$$

In changing a decimal number to its octal representation we start by dividing the decimal number by 8. The remainder of this operation is the least significant digit (i.e. 5) of the octal representation. The quotient (i.e. 11) is then taken and divided by 8. The remainder of this operation is the second least significant digit of the octal representation. The process of dividing the quotient and using the remainder as the next least significant digit of the octal representation continues until a zero quotient is encountered. This situation marks the fact that there are no higher order digits in the octal representation (in the example above a zero quotient after 3 divisions by 8 indicates that there are no five-hundred-and-twelves in our original number 93—this is clearly true).

We now have the essentials for implementing our base conversion algorithm. It involves an iterative process where successive octal digits are derived as remainders from a sequence of quotients, each of which is in turn derived from its predecessor by division by 8. More specifically starting with $q := 93$ we have

$$q := q \ \textbf{div} \ 8 {\Rightarrow} q := \ 11 \ \text{with remainder 5} \quad [1]$$
$$q := q \ \textbf{div} \ 8 {\Rightarrow} q := \ \ 1 \ \text{with remainder 3} \quad [2]$$
$$q := q \ \textbf{div} \ 8 {\Rightarrow} q := \ \ 0 \ \text{with remainder 1} \quad [3]$$

To get *both* the quotient q and the remainder r at each step we will need to employ both the integer division and remainder functions. For the general i^{th} step we will need

$$r := q \ \textbf{mod} \ 8 {\Rightarrow} \text{remainder}$$
$$q := q \ \textbf{div} \ 8 {\Rightarrow} \text{reduced quotient}$$

As we have already established, the iterative process needs to be terminated as soon as a zero quotient is encountered. The initial value of the quotient q should be the original decimal value of the number to be converted to octal. The essential steps in the algorithm are:

1. Initialize the quotient q to the decimal number to be converted.
2. Derive the octal digits iteratively using a succession of remainder and quotient computations on consecutive quotient values. Terminate the process when a zero quotient is encountered.

The algorithm should be implemented so that it will also handle conversions other than decimal to octal (e.g. decimal to binary, decimal to ternary). To allow this the inputs to the algorithm should be the new base required and the decimal number to be converted. For convenience of output the digits of the new representation should be stored in an array and written out only after the loop has terminated. Incorporating these refinements we get the following detailed algorithm.

Algorithm description

1. Establish the *newbase* and initialize the quotient q to the decimal number to be converted.
2. Set the new digit count *ndigit* to zero.
3. Repeatedly
    (a) compute the next most significant digit (i.e. octal) from the current quotient q as the remainder r after division by *newbase*,

(b) convert r to appropriate *ascii* value,†
(c) increment new digit count *ndigit* and store r in output array *newrep*,
(d) compute the next quotient q from its predecessor using integer division by *newbase*

until the quotient is zero.

A character array is used is for output to accommodate newbase values of more than 10 (see notes 5 and 6).

Pascal implementation

```
procedure basechange(n,newbase: integer);‡
var i {index for new digit output array},
    ascii {ascii value for current digits},†
    ndigit {current counter of new digits computed},
    q {current quotient},
    r {current digit for newbase representation},
    zero {ascii value of zero character}: integer;
    newrep: array[1..100] of char {output array};

begin {changes base of integer from decimal to any base <= 36}
    {assert: n>0∧2=<newbase=<36}
    zero := ord('0');
    q := n;
    ndigit := 0;
    {invariant: after the ndigitth iteration, q=n div (newbase↑ndigit)
        ∧newrep[1..ndigit] contains the ndigit least significant digits
        of n in newbase in reverse order∧r contains ndigit least
        significant digit}
    repeat
        r := q mod newbase;
        ndigit := ndigit+1;
        ascii := zero+r;
        if ascii>ord ('9') then ascii := ascii+7;
        newrep[ndigit] := chr (ascii);
        q := q div newbase
    until q=0;
    {assert: newrep[1..ndigit] contains the ndigit representation of n in the
        base newbase in reverse order}
    writeln ('Base ', newbase, ' representation of ', n, ' is ');
    for i := ndigit downto 1 do
        write (newrep[i]);
    writeln
end
```

---

† See algorithm 2.9 for explanation of ascii.
‡ The parameters *n* and *newbase* should be checked for range requirements by the calling procedure.

Notes on design

1. The number of steps in this algorithm is a function of the *newbase*, and the magnitude of the integer n. More specifically the number of steps is proportional to x, where x is the smallest integer satisfying the condition $n < (newbase)^x$.

2. Throughout the iterative process after the $ndigit^{th}$ iteration the *ndigit* rightmost digits of the *newbase* representation have been computed. This condition remains invariant throughout the iterative process. On termination the *ndigit* digits have been computed. After each iteration r contains the *ndigit* digit in the new base representation as measured from the right. Since *newbase* is an integer greater than one and the integer division is performed on q with each iteration q will be decreased until $q = 0$. Termination is therefore ensured. The algorithm functions correctly for all storable integers greater than or equal to zero. If the output contains more digits than can be printed on a line then an error will occur.

3. In designing this algorithm a clear understanding of the nature of the data we are working with is essential. Specific examples help to lead us to the required iterative construct and the appropriate termination condition.

4. Once again in this algorithm we see the general framework of establishing an initial condition and then building the solution iteratively from a succession of predecessors.

5. The algorithm will not handle *newbase* values of more than 36 (i.e. ten digits plus 26 alphabetic characters) because of lack of suitable characters for representing digits.

6. The algorithm relies on the fact that the alphabetic characters follow seven characters after the character 9 as in the ascii (American Standard Code for Information Interchange) character set.

7. The algorithm could be made more general by providing for the input numbers to be in any base up to 36.

Applications

Interpretation of stored computer data and instructions.

Supplementary problems

2.8.1 Modify the algorithm to incorporate the generalization suggested in note (7).

2.8.2 Design an algorithm that converts binary numbers to octal.

2.8.3 Design an algorithm to convert binary numbers to decimal.

2.8.4 Design an algorithm that accepts as input a decimal number and converts it to the binary-coded decimal (bcd) representation. In the bcd scheme each digit is represented by a 4-bit binary code.

2.8.5 Design an algorithm that accepts as input a decimal fraction and converts it to the corresponding binary fraction of a fixed accuracy (e.g. $0.625_{10} = 0.101_2 = 1\times2^{-1}+0\times2^{-2}+1\times2^{-3}$).

Algorithm 2.9
CHARACTER TO NUMBER CONVERSION

Problem

Given the character representation of an integer convert it to its conventional decimal format.

Algorithm development

Before we embark on a solution to this conversion problem, we must fully appreciate the difference between the character representation of an integer and its conventional number representation.

The number of different characters needed to represent textual and string information is relatively small. The upper and lower case alphabetic characters, the ten digits, and various punctuation and control characters make up only about one hundred different characters. In contrast to this, the range of different integers (and real numbers) that are needed may extend into the millions, the billions and even further. To obtain *unique* representations for such a large span of numbers requires a considerable amount of "space" to store each individual number. Numbers are represented in the computer in binary positional notation using just the 0 and 1 digits. As an example, let us examine the binary and decimal positional representations for the decimal number 221.

decimal notation $\equiv 2\times10^2+2\times10^1+1\times10^0 \equiv 221$

binary notation $\equiv 1\times2^7+1\times2^6+0\times2^5+1\times2^4+1\times2^3+1\times2^2+0\times2^1+1\times2^0$
$\equiv 11011101$

Comparing the two representations for 221, we see that only 3 decimal digits are needed to represent 221 whereas 8 binary digits are used. To represent one billion, we need 10 decimal digits and about 32 binary digits or bits. The fundamental unit or computer word size for storing numbers is usually one of 16, 32, 36, 60 or 64 bits. Since only 7 or 8 bits (8 bits are called a byte) are all that is needed to distinguish among the hundred or so characters that we are likely to need (i.e. $2^8 \equiv 256$) it is therefore very wasteful of computer memory to store only one character in the basic storage unit for numbers. The solution is therefore to pack several characters into each computer word. For example, on 32-bit computers we find that four 8-bit characters are usually stored in each computer word.

To make this packing possible it has been necessary to assign fixed 8-bit codes to the one hundred or so characters. One of the most widely used of these coding systems is called the American Standard Code for Information Interchange or *ascii* code. Some examples from this system are shown in Table 2.2.

Table 2.2   Ascii character codes and their decimal equivalents

Character	8-bit code	Decimal value
0	00110000	48
1	00110001	49
2	00110010	50
3	00110011	51
⋮	⋮	⋮
A	01000001	65
B	01000010	66
C	01000011	67
⋮	⋮	⋮
a	01100001	97
b	01100010	98
⋮	⋮	⋮

Note that the decimal digits, 0, 1, 2, 3, ..., 9, are also assigned 8-bit character code values. Because of this it is convenient in many applications to represent numbers as sequences of characters. For example, we might represent a date by a string of characters; for example,

23 April 1984

With representations like this there are times when it is necessary to do conventional arithmetic calculations on the numbers represented as sequences of 8-bit characters. In our example above the 23 does not have the value of 2 tens and 3 units but rather there are the decimal values 50 and 51 in successive 8-bit bytes. We cannot do the arithmetic operations directly on the character code representations because the corresponding binary representation does not conform to the standard binary positional notation used to represent numbers in the computer. Our only alternative in such circumstances is to convert the number from its character representation to its conventional number internal representation. This brings us back to our original character-to-number conversion problem.

Our task is therefore to accept as input a character representation of a number containing a known number of characters and make the conversion to the conventional decimal representation. To do this it will be necessary to use our knowledge of the particular character code being employed. In this example, we will choose to work with the ascii code. Fortunately, most programming languages including Pascal provide some additional functions to make tasks like this relatively straightforward to perform.

Suppose as an example we wanted to convert the four-character sequence 1984 to the decimal number 1984. The representation we start out with is

$$\begin{array}{cccc} 1 & 9 & 8 & 4 \\ \downarrow & \downarrow & \downarrow & \downarrow \end{array} \quad \text{characters}$$

$$\boxed{49 \mid 57 \mid 56 \mid 52} \quad \text{ascii values}$$

To make the conversion, the 49 will need to be converted to 1000, the 57 to 900, the 56 to 80 and the 52 to 4 units. To get the appropriate decimal digit in each case we have had to subtract 48 (the ascii value of character 0) from the ascii value of each character. Pascal makes this job easier by providing a function called *ord* which accepts an 8-bit character as its argument and returns as output its corresponding decimal (in our case ascii) value, e.g. the statement

$$x := ord('9')$$

will assign to x the decimal value 57. In our example, to get the decimal digits we will need to subtract $ord('0')$ from the ascii values of each of the characters in the sequence.

Having progressed this far, our next step is to use the digits to construct the corresponding decimal number. The character sequence will need to be processed one character at a time to obtain the decimal digits. What we must now work out is how each digit is to be converted to make its appropriate contribution to the decimal number we are seeking. If we start processing the characters from the left, when we encounter the "1" it is not immediately obvious what power of ten it should be multiplied by after the ascii conversion. However, by the time we have encountered a second character in the sequence we know it should be multiplied by at least 10. And, at the time we have encountered the third character, we know the second digit should have been multiplied by 10 and the first digit multiplied by 100. What this suggests is that we can proceed using essentially the same mechanism as we used in algorithm 2.7 to build up the required integer. That is, for our example of 1984,

$$1 \rightarrow 1 \qquad\qquad \rightarrow \quad 1$$
$$9 \rightarrow 1 \times 10 + 9 \quad \rightarrow \quad 19$$
$$8 \rightarrow 19 \times 10 + 8 \quad \rightarrow \quad 198$$
$$4 \rightarrow 198 \times 10 + 4 \rightarrow 1984$$

All that is left now is to work out the details of the mechanism for implementing this process. The "shifting-to-the-left" mechanism can be obtained at each step by multiplying the previous decimal value by 10 and adding in the current decimal digit. Details of our implementation can now be outlined. It is assumed that the length of the character string has been determined and that a check has been made to confirm that the string represents a positive integer.

Algorithm description

1. Establish the character string for conversion to decimal and its length n.
2. Initialize decimal value to zero.
3. Set *base0* value to the ascii or ordinal value of '0'.
4. While less than n characters have been examined do
   (a) convert next character to corresponding decimal digit,
   (b) shift current decimal value to the left one digit and add in digit for current character,
5. Return decimal integer corresponding to input character representation.

Pascal implementation

```
function chrtodec (string: nelements; n: integer): integer;
var i {index for count of characters converted},
    dec {used to build converted decimal integer},
    base0 {ascii or ordinal value of character 0 }: integer;

begin {converts character string integer representation to decimal}
    {assert: n>=0∧string[1..n] represents a non-negative number}
    dec := 0;
    base0 := ord ('0');
    {invariant: after the ith iteration, dec contains the i leftmost digits
        of the string in integer form ∧i =<n}
    for i := 1 to n do
        dec := dec * 10 + ord (string[i]) − base0;
    {assert: dec contains the integer representation of the n digits in string}
    chrtodec := dec
end
```

Notes on design

1. The number of steps to perform the conversion of the character representation of an integer to decimal is directly proportional to n, the number of characters in the original representation.
2. After the ith time through the loop the first i characters of the string representation will be converted to digits. Also after i iterations, the variable dec will contain the i leftmost digits of the decimal representation with the leftmost digit multiplied by 10^{i-1}, the next digit by 10^{i-2} and the rightmost of the i digits multiplied by 10^0. Termination of the **for**-loop is guaranteed after n iterations. This algorithm does not handle real numbers nor does it protect against the situation where the string being converted will cause integer overflow.

Applications

Business applications, tape processing.

Supplementary problems

2.9.1   Design an algorithm that will handle conversions to decimal where the input character string may contain a decimal point.

2.9.2   Design an algorithm to convert a decimal representation for a number to the corresponding character string representation.

2.9.3   Given that all ascii codes are less than 128, design an algorithm that reads a given set of data and decides whether or not it may contain decimal data.

BIBLIOGRAPHY

Most of the algorithms in this chapter are covered in introductory texts. Bartee (1977) provides a detailed discussion on number systems.

1.   Bartee, T. C., *Digital Computer Fundamentals*, 4th edn, McGraw-Hill, Tokyo, 1977.

Chapter 3
FACTORING METHODS

INTRODUCTION

Throughout the long history of mathematics dating as far back as the early Greeks, the theory of numbers in general, and factoring methods in particular, has been extensively studied. Up until more recent times these studies were for the most part carried out purely for interest's sake.

With the development of computers an understanding of these techniques has begun to be important for very practical reasons as well as their theoretical interest. Many of the algorithms developed long before the advent of computers are now very much a part of important computer applications.

Prime numbers, for example, are used in a number of applications. Recently developed methods for encrypting text to make its contents obscure to any outside observer rely on the fact that the product of two very large primes (more than 100 digits each) is effectively impossible to factorize in an acceptable time with known factoring methods. The best known factoring algorithms rely upon the use of greatest common divisors and related techniques. Prime numbers also play a role in fast methods for information retrieval that employ hashing algorithms (hashing is discussed in Chapter 5). With some hashing schemes it turns out to be appropriate to choose table sizes that are prime numbers. In encryption algorithms, as well as working with large primes, there is a need to raise numbers to large powers by efficient means. In this chapter we will consider a technique for this purpose.

Random numbers are extensively used in many simulation studies. The method for random number generation that we will consider has evolved from theoretical developments in the theory of congruences.

Algorithm 3.1
FINDING THE SQUARE ROOT OF A NUMBER

Problem

Given a number m devise an algorithm to compute its square root.

Algorithm development

When initially confronted with the problem of designing an algorithm to compute square roots, we may be at a loss as to just where to start. In these circumstances we need to be really sure of what is meant by "the square root of a number". Taking some specific examples, we know that the square root of 4 is 2, the square root of 9 is 3, and the square root of 16 is 4 and so on. That is,

$$2 \times 2 = 4$$
$$3 \times 3 = 9$$
$$4 \times 4 = 16$$
$$\vdots \quad \vdots \quad \vdots$$

From these examples we can conclude that in the general case the square root n, of another number m must satisfy the equation

$$n \times n = m \qquad (1)$$

If we are still unsure as to what to do next, we can take a guess at the square root and then use equation (1) to check whether or not we have guessed correctly. Suppose, for example, we do not know the square root of 36. We might guess that 9 could be its square root. Using equation (1) to check our guess we find that $9 \times 9 = 81$ which is greater than 36. Our guess of 9 is too high so we might next try 8. For example, $8 \times 8 = 64$ which is still greater than 36 but closer than our original guess.

The investigation we have made suggests that we could adopt the following systematic approach to solve the problem.

1. Choose a number n less than the number m we want the square root of.
2. Square n and if it is greater than m decrease n by 1 and repeat step 2, else go to step 3.
3. When the square of our guess at the square root is *less* than m we can start increasing n by 0.1 until we again compute a guess greater than m. At this point, we start decreasing our guess by 0.01 and so on until we have computed the square root we require to the desired accuracy.

Diagramatically, we can see in Fig. 3.1 how this algorithm approaches the desired solution.

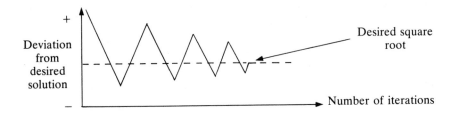

Fig. 3.1   Oscillating convergence to square root.

Studying our algorithm carefully, we observe that the number of iterations it requires depends critically on how good our initial guess is (e.g. if m is 10,000 and our initial guess n is 500 we will need over 400 iterations before we start to converge rapidly on the square root). This observation raises the question, can we derive a quicker way of homing in on the square root that is not so critically dependent on our initial guess?

To try to make progress towards a better algorithm, let us again return to the problem of finding the square root of 36. In choosing 9 as our initial guess, we found that

$$9^2 = 81 \text{ which is } greater \text{ } than \text{ } 36.$$

We know from equation (1) that the 9 should divide into 36 to give a quotient of 9 if it is truly the square root. Instead 9 divides into 36 to give 4. Had we initially chosen 4 as our square root candidate, we would have found

$$4^2 = 16 \text{ which is } less \text{ } than \text{ } 36.$$

From this we can see that when we choose a square root candidate that is too large, we can readily derive from it another candidate that is too small. The larger the guess is that is too large, the correspondingly smaller will be the guess that is too small. In other words, the 9 and the 4 tend to cancel out each other by deviating from the square m in opposite directions. Thus,

Square	Square Root
81 – – – – – – – – – – –	9
36 – – – – – – – – – – –	??
16 – – – – – – – – – – –	4

The square root of 36 must lie somewhere between 9, which is too big, and 4, which is too small. Taking the average of 9 and 4:

$$\frac{(9+4)}{2} = 6.5$$

gives us an estimate "in between" 9 and 4. This new estimate may again be either greater than 36, equal to, or less than 36. We find that $6.5^2 = 42.25$ which is greater than 36. Dividing this new value into 36:

$$\frac{36}{6.5} = 5.53$$

we see that it again has a complementary value (i.e. 5.53) that is less than 36. Thus,

Square		Square Root
81	greater	9
42.25	than 36	6.5
36 – – – – – – – – – – –		??
30.5809	less	5.53
16	than 36	4

We now have two estimates of the square root, one on either side, that are closer than our first two estimates.

We can proceed to get an even better estimate of the square root by averaging these two most recent guesses:

$$(6.5+5.53)/2 = 6.015$$

where $6.015^2 = 36.6025$ which is only slightly greater than the square we are seeking. Although we have not proved it, we may suspect that the strategy of averaging complementary estimates of the square root will converge very rapidly to the desired result even for bad initial estimates. At this stage we should do some mathematical analysis to confirm the validity of this strategy (see Notes on design). However, we will assume that it is a good strategy and proceed with the development of the algorithm.

Our first task now is to clarify the averaging rule that we intend to use to generate successively better approximations to the desired square root. To work this out, let us return to the "square root of 36 problem". As our initial guess *g1* we chose 9. We then proceeded to average this guess with its complementary value $(36/9 = 4)$. In the general case, the complementary value is given by

$$\text{complementary value} := \frac{m}{g1}$$

Our next step was to get an improved estimate of the square root, *g2*, by averaging *g1* and its complementary value (i.e. $(9+36/9)/2 = 6.5$). We can therefore write the expression for *g2* in the general case as

$$g2 := \big(g1 + (m/g1)\big)/2$$

We should now be able to use this expression as the basis of our square root finding algorithm.

In our example for finding the square root of 36, we began with $g1 = 9$ and established that $g2 = 6.5$. We then repeated the averaging process. However, now 6.5 (i.e. $g2$) assumed the role that previously belonged to $g1$ in order to compute an even better estimate. We can achieve this repetitive interchanging of roles by setting up the following loop

$$
\begin{aligned}
g2 &:= (g1 + m/g1))/2; \\
g1 &:= g2
\end{aligned}
$$

This loop will give us progressively better approximations $g2$ to the square root of m.

A question that still remains open is how are we to terminate the iterative process? We seem to have no way of knowing in advance how many iterations will be needed in the general case to calculate an acceptable value for a given square root. We are therefore going to need some other criterion for stopping the iterative process. We know that with successive iterations our algorithm produces closer and closer approximations to the square root. For example, for our square root of 36 problem, we have the sequence

$$9 \rightarrow 6.5 \rightarrow 6.015 \rightarrow \ldots$$

As the iterations increase, we can expect that the differences between the square roots estimated with successive iterations will become progressively smaller. We can therefore terminate the algorithm when the difference between $g1$ and $g2$ becomes less than some fixed error (e.g. 0.0001 might be an acceptable error). We cannot be sure in advance whether or not $g2$ will be progressively larger or smaller than $g1$. To be safe, the *absolute difference* between $g1$ and $g2$ should be used as our termination criterion.

The only other question that remains open is just how should we choose our initial guess? Our considerations so far tell us that in one sense it does not matter much what initial guess we make since the balancing mechanism of our algorithm will ensure that we fairly rapidly converge on an acceptable square root. We might therefore be tempted to choose the number m itself or perhaps $m/2$ as our initial guess and leave it at that (see Notes on design). Our square root algorithm can now be described in detail.

Algorithm description

1. Establish m the number whose square root is required and the termination condition error e.
2. Set the initial guess $g2$ to $m/2$.
3. Repeatedly
   (a) let $g1$ assume the role of $g2$,

(b)   generate a better estimate *g2* of the square root using the averaging formula,
until the absolute difference between *g1* and *g2* is less than *error e*.
4.   Return the estimated square root *g2*.

Pascal implementation

```
function sqroot(m,error: real): real;
var g1 {previous estimate of square root},
    g2 {current estimate of square root}: real;

begin {estimates square root of number m}
   {assert: m>0∧g1=m/2}
   g2 := m/2;
   {invariant: |g2 * g2−m|=<|g1 * g1−m|∧g1>0∧g2>0}
   repeat
     g1 := g2;
     g2 := (g1+m/g1)/2
   until abs(g1−g2)<error;
   {assert: |g2 * g2−m|=<|g1 * g1−m|∧|g1−g2|<error}
   sqroot := g2
end
```


Notes on design

1.   It is not easy to show how many iterations are needed to find the square
root to a given accuracy in the general case. We can, however, show
relatively simply that the method converges rapidly. At the nth step we
have

$$g_n = s - e$$

where s is the desired square root of m and e is the corresponding error
term. Making this substitution in our averaging formula, we get

$$g_{n+1} = \left((s-e) + \frac{m}{(s-e)} \right) \Big/ 2$$

and with $m = s^2$ and for e small we get

$$g_{n+1} = s - e + \frac{e^2}{2s}$$

and so

$$g_{n+1} = g_n + \frac{e^2}{2s}$$

The quadratic term confirms that the method will converge rapidly to the desired result. Also the relative error $e_n = |1-(g_n/\sqrt{m})|$ decreases rapidly since $e_{n+1} = e_n^2/2$.

2. After inspecting the averaging formula, we conclude that in the limit when $g1 = \sqrt{m}$ our formula yields

$$g2 = \left(g1 + \frac{m}{g1}\right)\Big/2 = (g1+g1)/2 = g1$$

The method therefore shows in principle convergence to the desired limit. To establish that the algorithm terminates we must show that the absolute difference between successive iterations is strictly decreasing to the limit. This follows directly from the fact that the algorithm shows quadratic convergence.

3. In this design, we have applied a feedback principle. That is, we keep making corrections to our estimate in a way dependent on how much the previous solution deviated from the desired result. The more drastic the deviation the more drastic the correction. This is a very important principle.

4. A specific example has given us the clues we need to set up a general model.

5. The formula we have developed for computing the square root can be derived alternatively from Newton's formula.

$$x_{n+1} = x_n + \frac{f(x_n)}{f'(x_n)}$$

6. To compute the nth root (i.e. where $x^n = m$) we can use

$$x_{i+1} = \left((n-1)x_i + \frac{m}{x_i(n-1)}\right)\Big/n$$

7. It is possible to set up a polynomial expression that will give optimum starting values for $g1$ (see E. G. Maursund, "Optimal starting values for Newton–Raphson calculation of $\sqrt{x}$", *Communications ACM*, **10**, 430–2 (1967)). The square root function in a computer system may be used thousands of times in a day. In such circumstances it would be worthwhile using some mathematical knowledge to find an improved algorithm. For such an often-used routine, the extra cost or research will probably pay for itself time and time again.

Supplementary problems

3.1.1   Implement the square-root-finding algorithm that was originally proposed.

3.1.2 The geometric mean is used to measure central tendency. It is defined as

$$G.M. = \sqrt[n]{(x_1 \times x_2 \times x_3 \times \cdots \times x_n)}$$

Develop an algorithm to input n numbers and compute their geometric mean.

3.1.3 Design an algorithm that finds the integer whose square is closest to but greater than the integer number input as data.

3.1.4 Design and implement an algorithm to iteratively compute the reciprocal of a number.

Algorithm 3.2
THE SMALLEST DIVISOR OF AN INTEGER

Problem

Given an integer n devise an algorithm that will find its smallest exact divisor other than one.

Algorithm development

Taken at face value, this problem seems to be rather trivial. We can take the set of numbers $2, 3, 4, \ldots, n$ and divide each one in turn into n. As soon as we encounter a number in the set that *exactly* divides into n our algorithm can terminate as we must have found the smallest exact divisor of n. This is all very straightforward. The question that remains, however, is can we design a more efficient algorithm?

As a starting point for this investigation, let us work out and examine the complete set of divisors for some particular number. Choosing the number 36 as our example, we find that its complete set of divisors is

$$\{2, 3, 4, 6, 9, 12, 18\}$$

We know that an *exact divisor* of a number divides into that number leaving no remainder. For the exact divisor 4 of 36, we have:

										36
4	4	4	4	4	4	4	4	4		
1	2	3	4	5	6	7	8	9		

That is, there are exactly 9 fours in 36. It also follows that the bigger number 9 also divides *exactly* into 36. That is,

$$\frac{36}{4} \to 9$$

$$\frac{36}{9} \to 4$$

$$\text{and } \frac{36}{4 \times 9} \to 1$$

Similarly, if we choose the divisor 3, we find that it tells us that there is a bigger number 12 that is also an exact divisor of 36. From this discussion we can draw the conclusion that exact divisors of a number must be paired.

Clearly, in this example we would not have to consider either 9 or 12 as potential candidates for being the smallest divisor because both are linked with another smaller divisor. For our complete set of divisors of 36, we see that:

Smaller factor		Bigger factor	
2	is linked with	18	(i.e. $\frac{36}{2} \to 18$)
3	is linked with	12	
4	is linked with	9	
6	is linked with	6	

From this set, we can see that the smallest divisor (2) is linked with the largest divisor (18), the second smallest divisor (3) is linked with the second biggest divisor (12) and so on. Following this line of reasoning through we can see that our algorithm can safely terminate when we have a pair of factors that correspond to

(a)   the biggest smaller factor s,
(b)   the smallest bigger factor b.

Or, in other words, we want an s and b that satisfy

$$s \times b = n$$

and for which s is less than b. The crossover point and limiting value must occur when $s = b$, i.e. when

$$s \times s = n$$

It follows that it is not necessary to look for smallest divisors of n that are greater than the square root of n.

This consideration is particularly relevant if we are likely to have to deal with large prime numbers (a prime number is an integer that is only exactly divisible by 1 and by itself).

What this square root limit allows us to do is stop the search for a valid exact divisor much earlier than we would otherwise be able to if the number we were considering was a prime number (e.g. for the prime number 127 our algorithm can terminate after only 10 iterations).

Before being completely satisfied with our new design, we should once again ask are there any other improvements we can make? The set of divisors that we would now consider are all integers up to $\sqrt{(n)}$. For the prime number 127, the divisors we would consider are

$$2, 3, 4, 5, 6, 7, 8, 9, 10, 11$$

We know that *all* even numbers are divisible by 2. It follows that if the number we are testing is not divisible by 2 then it certainly will not be divisible by 4, 6, 8, 10, ... And so if the number we are testing is odd, we need only consider odd numbers as potential smallest divisor candidates (i.e. we need only consider 3, 5, 7, 9, ...).

In fact, consideration of odd numbers is more than we need to do. We will not pursue this latter "improvement" here as it is related to the more challenging problem of generating prime numbers, which we will consider later.

The overall strategy for our algorithm can now be summarized:

1. If the number n is even, then the smallest divisor is 2
    else
    (a) compute the square root r of n,
    (b) while no exact divisor less than square root of n do
        (b.1) test next divisor in sequence 3, 5, 7, ...

All that is left to do now is work out the implementation details. The divisors to test can be generated by starting d at 3 and using

$$d := d+2$$

To determine whether or not a number is an exact divisor of another number, we can check if there is any remainder after division. For this we can use the **mod** function. If n **mod** $d = 0$ then d is an exact divisor of n.

The two conditions for termination can be applied directly. It is possible that our algorithm may terminate when either or both of the conditions n **mod** $d = 0$ and $d \geq r$ apply. An additional test is therefore needed after termination to check whether or not n does in fact have an exact divisor. We can now proceed with the detailed description of the algorithm.

Algorithm description

1. Establish n the integer whose smallest divisor is required.

2. If *n* is not odd then return 2 as the smallest divisor
    else
    (a)   compute *r* the square root of *n*,
    (b)   initialize divisor *d* to 3,
    (c)   while not an exact divisor and square root limit not reached do
          (c.1)   generate next member in odd sequence *d*,
    (d)   if current odd value *d* is an exact divisor
          then return it as the exact divisor of *n*
          else return 1 as the smallest divisor of *n*.

Pascal implementation

```
function sdivisor (n: integer): integer;
var d {current divisor and member of odd sequence},
    r {integer less than or equal to square root of n}: integer;

begin {finds the smallest exact divisor of an integer n, returns 1 if n
prime}
    {assert: n > 0}
    if not odd(n) then
        sdivisor := 2
    else
        begin {terminate search for smallest divisor at sqrt (n)}
            r := trunc(sqrt(n));
            d := 3;
            {invariant: d = <r + 1 ∧ no odd integer in [3..d − 2] exactly
            divides n}
            while (n mod d < >0) and (d <r) do d := d + 2;
            {assert: d is smallest exact divisor of n ∧ d = <r ∨ (d = <r + 1) ∧ n
            is prime}
            if n mod d = 0 then
                sdivisor := d
            else
                sdivisor := 1
        end
end
```

Notes on design

1. The algorithm takes at most $\lfloor \sqrt{n} \rfloor /2$ (i.e. strictly the largest integer less than or equal to $(\sqrt{n})/2$) iterations to determine the smallest divisor of a number *n*. If *n* is even, no iterations are performed.

2. After the ith iteration of the **while**-loop, the first *i* members of the odd sequence 3, 5, 7, 9, ... will have been tested for exact division into *n*. Also after the ith iteration it will be established that the ith member of the sequence 3, 5, 7, ... is the smallest exact divisor of *n* or that the

smallest exact divisor of n is not among the first i members of the odd sequence. The algorithm is guaranteed to terminate because with each iteration, d is incremented by 2 and so eventually the condition $d \geqslant r$ will be satisfied.

3. We observe that, as is usually the case, the most obvious solution to a problem is not the best. When designing algorithms we should always keep this thought in mind.

4. Consideration of a specific example tells us a lot about the design although we should always be watchful that we have not picked some special case.

5. We should always be on the lookout for doing unnecessary steps in our algorithms (e.g. it is no good considering even numbers as divisor candidates when the input number n is odd). Even our algorithm as it stands considers unnecessary candidates (e.g. 9, 15, ...). Ideally, we should consider only prime numbers as divisor candidates but this is a difficult problem in itself (see algorithm 3.4).

6. It is possible with extra assignments to terminate the **while**-loop with a single test. This usually results in a more efficient implementation. In the present problem, the gains, if any, will be marginal. Notice that there is no need to assign n **mod** d to a variable. We would not, however, use $(d \geqslant sqrt(n))$ as a termination condition because re-computing $sqrt(n)$ after each iteration is costly and unnecessary.

7. Dijkstra also gives an interesting and efficient method for finding the smallest prime factor of a large number (see E. Dijkstra, *A Discipline of Programming*, Prentice-Hall, Englewood Cliffs, N.J., p. 143, 1976).

Applications

Allocation problems.

Supplementary problems

3.2.1   Modify the algorithm so that the square root of n does not need to be explicitly computed.

3.2.2   Design an algorithm to produce a list of all exact divisors of a given positive integer n.

3.2.3   Design and implement an algorithm that finds the smallest positive integer that has n or more divisors.

3.2.4   For the integers in the range 1 to 100 find the number that has the most divisors.

3.2.5   It is possible to improve the efficiency of our smallest divisor algorithm by generating a sequence of ds that excludes multiples of

3 as well as multiples of 2. Implement an algorithm that includes this refinement.

3.2.6   An algorithm due to Fermat can be used to find the largest factor f (less than or equal to $\sqrt{n}$) of an odd integer. Fermat established that the following relations hold for n.

$$n = f \times g \text{ with } f \leq g$$
$$n = x^2 - y^2 \text{ with } 0 \leq y < x \leq n$$
$$\text{where } x = \lfloor (f+g)/2 \rfloor, \ y = \lfloor (g-f)/2 \rfloor$$

The algorithm can be implemented by introducing two auxiliary variables x' and y' such that

$$x' = 2x + 1$$
$$y' = 2y + 1$$

The odd values that these two variables can assume are:

$$x': 2\lfloor \sqrt{n} \rfloor + 1, \ 2\lfloor \sqrt{n} \rfloor + 3, \ 2\lfloor \sqrt{n} \rfloor + 5, \ ...$$
$$y': 1, 3, 5, 7, ...$$

Noting that successive squares can be generated by summing the odd sequence, the error e (initially set to $[\lfloor \sqrt{n} \rfloor^2 - n]$) when positive is reduced by subtracting successive y' values until it is made zero or negative, and, when negative it is reduced by adding successive x' values. This process terminates when $e = 0$. At this point the factor f can be found from

$$f = \lfloor (x' - y')/2 \rfloor$$

Implement Fermat's algorithm.

Algorithm 3.3
THE GREATEST COMMON DIVISOR OF TWO INTEGERS

Problem

Given two positive non-zero integers n and m design an algorithm for finding their greatest common divisor (usually abbreviated as gcd).

Algorithm development

When initially confronted with this problem, we see that it is somewhat different from other problems we have probably encountered. The difficult aspect of the problem involves the relationship between the divisors of two numbers. Our first step might therefore be to break the problem down and find all the divisors of the two integers n and m independently. Once we have these two lists of divisors we soon realize that what we must do is select the largest element common to both lists. This element must be the greatest *common* divisor for the two integers n and m.

We may expect that this algorithm will be relatively time consuming for large values of n and m because of the tedious step of having to generate all factors of two integers.

It was the Greek philosopher, Euclid, who more than 2000 years ago first published a better way to solve this problem. The algorithm published, which has come to be known as Euclid's algorithm, was probably invented by a predecessor of Euclid's called Eudorus. The ancient Chinese also discovered this algorithm.

To embark on our search for a better algorithm, a good place to start is with a careful look at just what is the greatest common divisor of two integers. The gcd of two integers is the largest integer that will divide *exactly* into the two integers with no remainder. We can build up to the common divisor of two integers by first considering an exact divisor of a *single* integer. An exact divisor of a number is another smaller number that divides the original number up into a set of equal parts. For example, the divisor 5 divides the number 30 up into 6 equal parts. Diagrammatically this can be represented as:

$$0 \quad 5 \quad 10 \quad 15 \quad 20 \quad 25 \quad 30$$

P_1	P_2	P_3	P_4	P_5	P_6

$$P_1 = P_2 = P_3 = P_4 = P_5 = P_6$$

Now let us extend this idea and representation to two integers, 30 and 18, whose gcd x we may be seeking. Studying Fig. 3.2, we see that for the common divisor situation *both* n and m can be thought of as being divided up into segments of size x. When the two blocks for n and m are aligned from the left, the section AB of n must match the full length of m. The number n, however, exceeds m by the length BC. The question is, what can we say about the segment BC? If x is going to be an exact divisor of *both* n and m and if AB is exactly divided by x, then so too must BC be *exactly* divided up into segments of size x.

Having made this observation, our next problem is to try to work out how to find the largest of the common divisors that n and m may share. Considering the simpler problem first, we know that the greatest divisor of a single number is the number itself (e.g. the greatest exact divisor of 30 is 30).

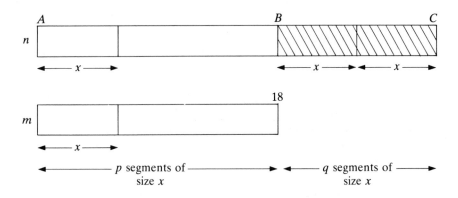

Fig. 3.2 Schematic representation of the gcd problem.

For our example, we have:

(a) the greatest divisor of 30 is 30;
(b) the greatest divisor of 18 is 18.

Our problem is to find the greatest *common* divisor of *two* numbers rather than one number. Clearly no number greater than 18 can be a candidate for the gcd because it will not divide exactly into 18. We can in fact generalize this statement to say that the gcd of two numbers cannot be bigger than the smaller of the two numbers. The next question we might ask is, can the gcd of two numbers be *equal to* the smaller of those two numbers (this is not true in the case of 18 and 30 but if we were considering 12 and 36 we would find that 12 is the gcd)? We can therefore conclude that the smaller of the two numbers n and m must be the upper limit for the gcd.

We must now decide how to continue when the smaller of the two numbers n and m is not their gcd.

To try to answer this question let us return to our specific problem of trying to find the gcd of 18 and 30. We have the situation shown in Fig. 3.3. The other piece of information available to us is that the segment BC will need to be exactly divided by the gcd. And since 18 is not the gcd the number x we are seeking must be less than 18 and it must exactly divide into the segment BC. The biggest number that exactly divides into BC must be 12 since BC is itself 12. If 12 is to be the gcd of 18 and 30 it will have to divide exactly into both 18 and 30. In taking this step, we have actually reduced our original problem to the smaller gcd problem involving 12 and 18, as shown in Fig. 3.4.

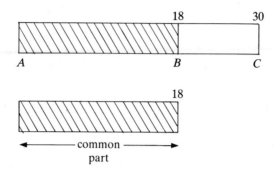

Fig. 3.3 Schematic representation of gcd problem showing common part.

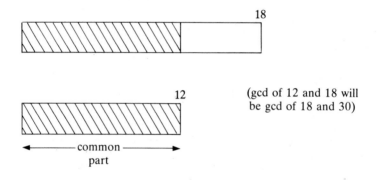

Fig. 3.4 Smaller gcd problem to be solved.

Applying a similar argument to our smaller problem, we discover that since 12 is not a divisor of 18, we are going to end up with a still smaller problem to consider. That is, we have the situation shown in Fig. 3.5. With this latter problem, the smaller of the two numbers 6 and 12 (i.e. 6) is an exact divisor of 12. Once this condition is reached we have established the gcd for the current problem and hence also for our original problem.

We can now summarize our basic strategy for computing the gcd of two numbers:

1. Divide the larger of the two numbers by the smaller number.
2. If the smaller number exactly divides into the larger number
    then the smaller number is the gcd
    else remove from the larger number the part common to the smaller
       number and repeat the whole procedure with the new pair of
       numbers.

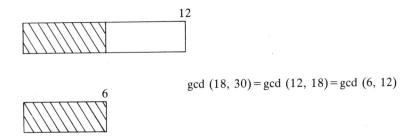

gcd (18, 30) = gcd (12, 18) = gcd (6, 12)

Fig. 3.5   A still smaller gcd problem to be solved.

Our task now is to work out the details for implementing and terminating the gcd mechanism. First let us consider how to establish if the smaller number exactly divides into the larger number. Exact division can be detected by there being no remainder after integer division. The **mod** function allows us to compute the remainder resulting from an integer division. We can use:

$$r := n \textbf{ mod } m$$

provided we had initially ensured that $n \geqslant m$. If r is zero, then m is the gcd. If r is not zero, then as it happens it corresponds to the "non-common" part between n and m. (E.g. 30 **mod** 18 = 12.) It is therefore our good fortune that the **mod** function gives us just the part of n we need for solving the new smaller gcd problem. Furthermore, r by definition must be smaller than m. What we need to do now is set up our iterative construct using the **mod** function. To try to formulate this construct, let us return to our gcd (18, 30) problem.

For our specific example we have:

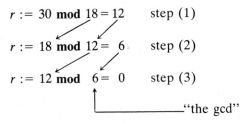

$$r := 30 \textbf{ mod } 18 = 12 \qquad \text{step (1)}$$

$$r := 18 \textbf{ mod } 12 = 6 \qquad \text{step (2)}$$

$$r := 12 \textbf{ mod } 6 = 0 \qquad \text{step (3)}$$

"the gcd"

Our example suggests that with each reduction in the problem size the smaller integer assumes the role of the larger integer and the remainder assumes the role of the smaller integer.

The reduction in problem size and role changing steps are carried out repeatedly. Our example therefore suggests that the gcd mechanism can be captured iteratively with a loop of the form:

while gcd not found do
(a)   get remainder by dividing the larger integer by the smaller integer;
(b)   let the smaller integer assume the role of the larger integer;
(c)   let the remainder assume the role of the smaller integer.

Now we must decide in detail how the loop should terminate. Our earlier discussion established that the current divisor will be the gcd when it divides exactly into the integer that is the larger (or equal) member of the pair. The exact division will correspond to a zero remainder. It follows that we can use this condition to terminate the loop. For example:

while non-zero remainder do
   "continue search for gcd".

Examining the mechanism we have constructed a little more carefully we see that there are two things we have not considered. Firstly, when the termination condition is tested on entering the loop we will not have computed any remainder. One way to overcome this would be to compute the remainder for the original pair of integers before entering the loop. That is,

1.   compute remainder for original pair of integers.
2.   while non-zero remainder do
         "continue search for gcd".

We see that with this mechanism, since the remainder has to be computed at least once, we have a situation where termination could be tested after first passing through the loop once. This suggests that a simpler mechanism in this case would be:

repeatedly
   "search for gcd"
until zero remainder.

The other consideration we must attend to is that when the original pair of integers is passed to the loop we do not know which is the larger. A way around this problem would be to exchange the two integers before entering the loop if their roles are wrongly assigned. This looks clumsy so let's see what goes wrong if we fail to make this change before entering the loop. For our earlier example, if we enter the loop with

$$r := 18 \bmod 30$$

the remainder becomes 18, the larger integer becomes 30, and the smaller integer becomes 18. What has happened is that the roles of the larger and smaller integers have been interchanged, which amounts to the exchange we had originally intended. It follows that we need not concern ourselves with the problem of deciding which of the input pair of integers is the larger. A final point to consider is, which variable will contain the gcd when the mechanism terminates? Referring back to our earlier description of the mechanism we see that in the final iteration before termination, the smaller integer which is the gcd gets assigned the role of the larger integer. Noting this fact we can now describe our algorithm in detail.

Algorithm description

1. Establish the two positive non-zero integers smaller and larger whose gcd is being sought.
2. Repeatedly
    (a) get the remainder from dividing the larger integer by the smaller integer;
    (b) let the smaller integer assume the role of the larger integer;
    (c) let the remainder assume the role of the divisor
    until a zero remainder is obtained.
3. Return the gcd of the original pair of integers.

Pascal implementation

```
function gcd(n,m: integer): integer;
var r {remainder after integer division of n by m}: integer;

begin {computes the greatest common divisor for two positive
non-zero integers}
  {assert: n>0∧m>0}
  repeat
    {compute next gcd candidate and associated remainder}
    r := n mod m;
    n := m;
    m := r
  until r = 0;
  {assert: n = gcd of original pair n, and m}
  gcd := n
end
```

Notes on design

1. The number of iterations required by the gcd algorithm is highly dependent on the input data and whether or not the two integers have a common divisor greater than 1. A "worst-case" type situation occurs when the original pair of integers are adjacent Fibonacci numbers. Then successive remainders follow the Fibonacci sequence down to

zero. The number of iterations is therefore bounded by the number of terms in the Fibonacci sequence up to the point that includes the original pair of integers. If N is the smallest Fibonacci number greater than the larger of n and m, then it can be shown that there will be $\lceil \log_\Phi(\sqrt{(5N)}) \rceil - 2$ iterations where $\Phi = 0.5(1 + \sqrt{5})$.

2. The algorithm we have implemented, although logically tidy, is not easy to prove correct because it does not have a suitable invariant relation that holds throughout the computation. If we make the necessary changes to allow our loop to take the form:

> **repeat**
> $n := m$;
> $m := r$;
> $r := n \bmod m$
> **until** $r := 0$

we will get an algorithm that is easier to prove correct. Starting with $m := a$ and $r := b$ (where a and b are the original pair of numbers whose gcd is sought) we will have the following invariant relation:

$$\gcd(n, m) = \gcd(a, b) \wedge r \geqslant 0$$

On termination, we will have

$$m = \gcd(n, m) = \gcd(a, b) \wedge r = 0$$

We can conclude that the algorithm terminates because $n \bmod m$ is always less than m and so r is strictly decreasing and so eventually the condition $r = 0$ will be met.

3. We observe that the solution to the gcd problem is brought about by taking a problem and breaking it down into a smaller problem that can be solved by the same mechanism. We will see later that this is a very powerful technique that usually suggests the use of recursion.

4. Definitions play an important role in solving this problem.

5. Simple diagrams are often helpful in discovering algorithms as we have observed with this problem.

Applications

Reducing a fraction to its lowest terms.

Supplementary problems

3.3.1 Implement a gcd algorithm that uses a **while**-loop rather than a **repeat**-loop.

3.3.2   Design a gcd algorithm that does not use either division or **mod** functions.

3.3.3   Design an algorithm that will find the gcd of n positive non-zero integers.

3.3.4   If the two integers whose gcd is sought may contain multiples of two, then a better way to proceed is by first reducing each of the integers by their common multiples of two, taking into account their contribution to the gcd. When one integer contains multiples of two it is best to remove these contributions before proceeding with the standard gcd mechanism. Try to incorporate these ideas into a more efficient gcd algorithm.

3.3.5   Design an algorithm to find all common prime divisors of two numbers. (*Hint*: Algorithm 3.5 may be useful).

3.3.6   It is well known that adjacent Fibonacci numbers do not share a common divisor greater than 1 (they are relatively prime). Design an algorithm that tests this observation for the first n integers.

3.3.7   Design an algorithm to compute the smallest common multiple (scm) of two non-zero positive integers n and p. The scm is defined as the smallest integer m such that n and p divide exactly into m.

3.3.8   Design an algorithm to compute the smallest common divisor other than one of two positive non-zero integers.

3.3.9   Given the two fractions a/b and c/d, design an algorithm that computes their sum in terms of the smallest common denominator.

Algorithm 3.4
GENERATING PRIME NUMBERS

Problem

Design an algorithm to establish all the primes in the first n positive integers.

Algorithm development

The efficient generation of prime numbers is an open problem. We will consider here the more restricted problem of generating all primes in the first n integers. *A prime number is a positive integer that is exactly divisible only by 1 and itself.* The first few primes are:

$$2 \quad 3 \quad 5 \quad 7 \quad 11 \quad 13 \quad 17 \quad 19 \quad 23 \quad 29 \quad 31 \quad 37 \quad \ldots$$

All primes apart from 2 are odd.

As a starting point in developing our prime number generator let us explore how we can establish whether or not a particular number is a prime number. To do this we can pick a particular example (i.e. the number 13). The definition of a prime number gives us the start we need. We know that if the number we are testing is prime it will have no exact divisors other than 1 and itself. This suggests that to determine whether or not 13 is prime we need to divide it in turn by the set of numbers 2, 3, 4, 5, ... , 12. If any of these numbers divide into 13 without remainder we will know it cannot be prime. Therefore to test 13 for primality, eleven calls to the *mod* function are required. It is easy to see that as *n* grows, the cost of making these divisions and tests is going to get very expensive. We must therefore look for ways of improving the efficiency of our algorithm. A little thought reveals that there are several avenues open to us. Firstly, we can try to keep to a minimum the number of numbers that we have to test for primality and secondly we can try to improve the efficiency of testing a number for primality.

Following up the first suggestion, we know that apart from 2 we do not need to examine *any* of the even numbers. Starting *x* at 1 and using the increment

$$x := x+2$$

gives us the sequence of numbers

$$3, 5, 7, 9, 11, 13, 15, 17, ...$$

For large *n* this still leaves us with a large set of numbers to consider. So far we have eliminated numbers divisible by 2. Can we extend this to eliminating numbers divisible by 3, 5, and so on? To explore this idea let us first write down the odd sequence with the multiples of 3 removed. We have:

Beyond 5 we have the alternating sequence of differences 2, 4. This alternating difference sequence should be able to be generated. We will not dwell on it here but it is easy to see that the construct below with *dx* initially 4

$$dx := abs(dx-6)$$

has the desired behavior. This device will allow us to eliminate two-thirds of the numbers from consideration as potential prime numbers candidates.

We might now ask can we eliminate multiples of 5 in a similar manner?

The answer is yes but it would be slightly more involved. This line of attack does not seem as though it is going to be very fruitful. What we do see from this however is that one way to generate prime numbers is to simply write down the list of all integers then cross out multiples of 2, 3, 5, 7, 11, and so on.

(a)   2   3   4̸   5   6̸   7   8̸   9   1̸0̸   11   1̸2̸   13   1̸4̸   15   1̸6̸   17   1̸8̸   19

multiples of 2 crossed out

(b)   2   3   5   7   9̸   11   13   1̸5̸   17   19

multiples of 3 crossed out

(c)   2   3   5   7   11   13   17   19

At stage (c) in this instance we are left with all prime numbers less than 20. If we start out with a much larger list and successively cross out multiples of 2, 3, 5, 7, 11, ... the numbers that are not crossed out will be prime numbers. This idea for generating primes dates back to the early Greek mathematician, Eratosthenes and is usually referred to as the "sieve of Eratosthenes".

There is a problem in implementing this method directly if it is necessary to generate a large number of primes. Storage proportional to the span of integers up to n may be required.

Further investigation of the "crossing out" mechanism indicates that for large n most elements are crossed out a number of times (e.g. 15 is crossed out twice because it is a multiple of 3 and also a multiple of 5).

These observations suggest that it is worth while trying to see if there is any way in which we can cut down on the amount of storage and testing needed to find a set of primes.

We have previously seen that to determine that 13 is a prime it would need to be divided by the set of numbers 2, 3, 4, ... , 11, 12. Studying this mechanism carefully and noting how the search for the smallest divisor of a number was terminated (algorithm 3.2) we can see that it is not necessary to test divisors beyond $\lfloor \sqrt{13} \rfloor$. If a number x has an exact divisor then there will have to be a factor less than or equal to $\sqrt{x}$. (See the reasoning in algorithm 3.2 for an explanation of this.) For large x termination of the divisor testing at $\sqrt{x}$ will be a relatively efficient operation (e.g. when x is approximately 1000, division by only the primes up to 31 is all that is needed to test x for primality—this involves only 10 divisions). Division by composite numbers is never needed because if a composite number is an exact divisor, this implies that a smaller prime factor of the composite has already been an exact divisor.

At this stage we can propose a basic structure for our algorithm:

while $x<n$ **do**
    begin
        (a)   generate next x using the construct $dx := abs(dx-6)$,
        (b)   test whether x is prime using all primes $\leqslant\sqrt{x}$,
        (c)   if a prime is found that is less than $\sqrt{n}$ then store it for
               later testing against larger x values.
    end

To test all integers up to n for primality we will need to retain all primes up to $\sqrt{n}$.

Every time a new x is brought up for testing we will need to ensure that we have the appropriate set of primes to divide into x.

Working through some examples we find:

x range	prime divisors required
$2\leqslant x<9$	2
$9\leqslant x<25$	2, 3
$25\leqslant x<49$	2, 3, 5
$49\leqslant x<121$	2, 3, 5, 7
$\vdots \qquad \vdots$	$\vdots \qquad \vdots$

Our method for generating x values excludes all multiples of 2 and 3. Therefore our method for generating x values will produce only primes for values of x less than 25. As soon as x reaches 25 the divisor 5 will need to be used in the prime test. We can then proceed until x reaches 49 at which stage 7 must be included as a divisor and so on.

Starting out with

$$p[1] := 2; \; p[2] := 3; \; p[3] := 5;$$
and $plimsq := 25; \; limit := 3$

we can include the following conditional statement *before* testing each x value for primality

if $x >= plimsq$ **then**
    begin
    $limit := limit+1;$
    $plimsq := sqr(p[limit])$
    end

It is only necessary to increase *limit* by 1 with this test because the difference between the squares of adjacent primes is always greater than 4, the largest increment that is made in x.

There would appear to be a risk here that we may run out of primes to test against x as it gets very large. To avoid this risk we could ensure that the program terminates if we run out of divisors to test for primality. To make things easier we will use a result from number theory that tells us that:

$$p[i] < p[i-1]^2$$

This condition is sufficient to ensure that we will never run out of divisors.

Once we have established the proper set of prime divisors we need to test a given x, the next step is to actually test x for primality. For this purpose we can use a loop that successively tests all the prime divisors with indices less than *limit* against x.

Some thought reveals there are two conditions under which this loop should terminate:

1. an exact divisor of x has been found—so it cannot be prime;
2. we have reached the divisor with index one less than limit.

Using the **mod** function to test for exact division and using the remainder *rem* to set the Boolean condition *prime* we get:

```
j := 3; prime := true;
while prime and (j<limit) do
   begin
      rem := x mod p[j];
      prime := rem <> 0;
      j := j+1
   end
```

We may anticipate that this loop will be heavily used for large values of n and so in a practical implementation it would be better to reduce the two loop tests to a single test by removing the test $j<limit$. This can be done by *temporarily* replacing the element in $p[limit]$ with a sentinel equal to x and making a test on j *outside* the loop. This is left as an exercise for the reader.

All that is now needed is a test to see if the prime-testing loop established that x is prime. If it is, then, providing x is less than $\sqrt{n}$ it is saved, otherwise it can be written out directly.

The central part of our more detailed algorithm then has the form below assuming *limit*, dx, and *plimsq* have been appropriately initialized.

```
while x<n do
   begin
      dx := abs(dx-6);
      x := x+dx;
      if limit≤i then
         if x≥plimsq then
            begin {include next prime as divisor}
```

```
            limit := limit+1;
            if limit≤i then
                plimsq := sqr(p[limit])
         end;
       j := 3;
       prime := true;
       while prime and (j<limit) do
          begin {test next number x for primality}
              rem := x mod p[j];
              prime := rem <> 0;
              j := j+1
          end
          if prime then "write out x and save if necessary"
   end
```

We now have the basis of a workable algorithm for finding primes. For large n a lot of time will be spent in the inner loop doing costly divisions (in the **mod** function). We might therefore ask is there any way we can alleviate this division testing? What we get from any division test is either a zero or a non-zero integer. A non-zero remainder tells us that the particular prime being used is not an exact divisor of x. Its value also tells us the next value in the x range where the current divisor $p[k]$ will be an exact divisor. For example:

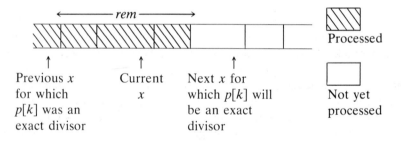

We can use this information to "*cross out*" in advance the next value of x divisible by $p[k]$. To do this another array $out[1..\sqrt{n}]$ will be needed to store values crossed out in advance. The crossing out is done by

$$nxtout := p[k]- rem;$$
$$out[nxtout] := false$$

The idea will then be to check the array *out before* testing a given number for primality. If it is already "crossed out" no prime testing need be done. An investigation and testing of this idea shows that it will allow us to cut down by a factor of 4 or 5 the number of numbers that have to be tested for primality.

This sounds like a useful refinement. Unfortunately whenever a prime x is encountered *all* prime divisors less than $\sqrt{x}$ must be tested against it. For large n establishing the primes by this method is going to be computationally costly.

It may therefore be better to go back to the sieve of Eratosthenes and see if there is anything we can do about its large storage cost. The advantage that the sieve method has is that it does not involve any costly divisions to establish the primes. To generate all the primes up to n we need to cross out all multiples less than n of all the primes less than or equal to $\sqrt{n}$. We want to do this using considerably less than a storage cost of n. The question is how can we achieve a useful reduction in storage? Our sieve algorithm as originally proposed needs to generate multiples of the primes 5, 7, 11, ..., $\sqrt{n}$ in storage of size n. For example, for 5 we have the multiples

$$5, 10, 15, 20, 25, 30, 35, ...$$

With this set we notice that every second multiple is even and so it cannot be a prime candidate. Each new member of the "multiple-of-5" sequence is generated by adding the original prime on to the previous accumulated multiples of 5. The same condition applies for all multiple sequences. Using n storage locations for $n < 49$ we only need to cross out multiples of 3 and 5. For this example we have:

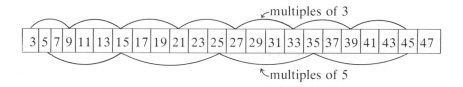

multiples of 3

| 3 | 5 | 7 | 9 | 11 | 13 | 15 | 17 | 19 | 21 | 23 | 25 | 27 | 29 | 31 | 33 | 35 | 37 | 39 | 41 | 43 | 45 | 47 |

multiples of 5

The numbers that have not been crossed out are prime. What we do with the sieve method is cross out all the multiples in advance and then make a single pass through the array and pick out the numbers not crossed out.

It is apparent that once we have "crossed out" the 9 the space that 3, 5, 7, 9 occupy is no longer needed because at that time we will know all primes less than 9. A similar argument applies when we discover the 15 has been crossed out. This suggests if we can in some way do our crossing out in a localized fashion we may not have to pay such a high storage cost. We know that for $n < 49$ we only need to consider multiples of 3 and 5 (assuming multiples of 2 are automatically neglected). We would only need space for *two* variables in this instance if we could generate all the multiples of 3 and 5 in consecutive order; e.g., 3×3, 3×5, 3×7, 5×5, 3×9, ... A way in which we can do this is to have a variable x (as in the previous method) which assumes all possible odd values. Whenever x is incremented what we must do is increment the multiples of 3 and/or 5 while they are *less* than x. The next step is then to check if the current multiples of 3 and 5 are equal to x. If neither multiple is equal to x then x must be prime. In the general case this check will need to be made with the multiples of all primes less than or equal to $\lfloor \sqrt{x} \rfloor$.

If *limit* marks the index of the largest prime less than or equal to $\lfloor \sqrt{x} \rfloor$ then our prime test for the current value of x will be

```
while prime and (j<limit) do
   begin
      while multiple[j]<x do multiple[j] := multiple[j]+p[j]*2;
      prime := x <> multiple [j];
      j := j+1
   end
```

Where the array *multiple* contains at each stage the multiples of all primes $\leqslant \lfloor \sqrt{x} \rfloor$. $2*p[k]$ is used rather than $p[k]$ to avoid generating even-numbered multiple candidates. This less expensive method of prime testing can replace the prime testing by division used in our previous algorithm. Because of the way the array *multiple* is used a new prime is not added to the multiple list until its square has been reached. The new prime multiple can be included by the test

```
if limit≤i then
   if x≥plimsq then
      begin
         multiple[limit] := plimsq;
         limit := limit+1;
         if limit≤i then
            plimsq := sqr(p[limit])
      end
```

With these changes to the previous algorithm we now have a method for generating primes that *avoids the division test* but achieves the same result. The cost has been additional storage to store the multiples of the primes less than $\sqrt{n}$. Our detailed algorithm is now given below.

Algorithm description

1. Initialize and write out the first 3 primes. Also initialize the square of the 3rd prime.
2. Initialize x to 5.
3. While x less than n do
    (a) get next x value excluding multiples of 2 and 3;
    (b) if not past end of multiples list then

(b.1)   if $x \geqslant$ square of largest prime then
      (1.a)   include next prime multiple as its square,
      (1.b)   update square by squaring next prime $> \sqrt{x}$;
(c)   while have not established x is non-prime with valid prime multiples do
      (c.1)   while current prime multiple is less than x, increment by current prime value doubled,
      (c.2)   do prime test by comparing x with current multiple;
(d)   if current x prime then
      (d.1)   write out x and if it is less than $\sqrt{n}$ store it.

Pascal implementation

```
procedure primes (n: integer);
const np = 100;
var multiple: array[1..np] of integer; {multiples of primes}
    p: array[1..np] of integer; {primes up to sqrt (n)}
    i {index for primes saved},
    j {index of primes and multiple array},
    limit {upper index for primes less than sqrt(x)},
    plimsq {square of largest prime included so far},
    rootn {truncated sqrt(n)},
    dx {increment either 2 or 4 to avoid multiples of 3},
    x {current candidate for prime test}: integer;
    prime: boolean;

begin
    {assert: n > 1}
    p[1] := 2; p[2] := 3; p[3] := 5; i := 3;
    if n < 5 then for j := 1 to (n + 1) div 2 do writeln (p[j])
    else
      begin
        for j := 1 to 3 do writeln (p[j]);
        x := 5; plimsq := 25; limit := 3; dx := 2;
        rootn := trunc(sqrt(n));
        {invariant: after current iteration all primes in [2..x] have been
        written out ∧ x = <n + 2}
        while x < n do
          begin {test x for primality}
            x := x + dx;
            dx := abs(dx − 6);
            if limit <= i then
              if x >= plimsq then
                begin
                  multiple[limit] := plimsq;
                  limit := limit + 1;
                  if limit <= i then
                    plimsq := sqr(p[limit])
                end;
```

```
prime := true;
j := 3;
{invariant: after jth iteration x not divisible by primes
p[1..j − 1]∧j =<limit∧x <p[limit] * p[limit]}
while prime and (j <limit) do
   begin {test x by comparing with all multiples of primes}
      while multiple[j]<x do
      multiple[j] := multiple[j]+p[j] * 2;
      prime := x <>multiple[j];
      j := j +1
   end;
{assert: (j =limit∧x is prime) ∨ (j =<limit∧x not prime)}
if prime then
   begin
      writeln (x);
      if x <=rootn then
         begin
            i := i +1;
            p[i] := x
         end
   end
   end
   end
{assert: all primes in range [2..n +2] have been written out}
end
```

Notes on design

1. There are approximately $n/\log_e n$ primes in the first n positive integers. The analysis of the final algorithm is rather complex and so we will not pursue it here. Essentially $(n^{3/2}/\log_e^3 n)$ additions are required to establish the primes in the first n integers.

2. After the current pass through the outermost **while**-loop the value x has been tested for primality and all elements of the array in positions less than j (excluding positions 1 and 2) are greater than or equal to x. Also after the current pass, x is less than *plimsq*. The variable *prime* will be true after the current pass if x is prime, otherwise it will be false. In the inner **while**-loop for prime-testing after the jth step the first $(j-1)$ elements of *multiple* will be $\geq x$ and the variable *prime* will be true if none of the first $j-1$ primes are multiples or exact divisors of x. The innermost **while**-loop maintains the invariant relation that *multiple*[j]$\geq x$ after the $(j-1)^{th}$ pass through the prime-test loop.

    The outermost loop will terminate because the difference between x and n decreases by at least 2 with each pass through the outermost loop.

    The prime-test loop will terminate because the difference between j and *limit* decreases by 1 with each pass through this loop. The innermost **while**-loop involving multiples will terminate because *multiple*[*j*] is incremented by $2 * p[j]$ a positive integer with each iteration and so eventually its termination condition will be met. Since all loops terminate the whole process will terminate. The mechanism will function correctly for values of $n > 1$. The fact that n may exceed the word size or that the array limits may be exceeded has not been allowed for.

3. In this problem we have seen how a gain in computational efficiency is made by using additional storage. Divisions are generally costly and so in computation-bound applications an attempt should be made to limit them.

4. Most of the computation time for this problem is spent in the prime-testing loop. Every effort should therefore be made to keep this loop as simple and efficient as possible. In practice it would be better to use a single conditional test on the prime-testing loop (see discussion).

Supplementary problems

3.4.1   At the cost of some additional storage the prime-testing loop can be simplified and speeded up. This involves moving the step for updating the *multiple* array outside this loop. Try to modify the algorithm to incorporate this refinement.

3.4.2   It is possible to implement a sieving algorithm which crosses out each composite (non-prime) number exactly once rather than a number of times. The algorithm is based on the idea that any non-prime x can be written as $x = p^k q$ where $k \geqslant 1$ and q is a prime $\geqslant p$. Try to implement this algorithm (ref. D. Gries and J. Misra, "A linear sieve algorithm for finding prime numbers", *Comm. ACM*, **21**, 999–1003 (1978)).

3.4.3   Another interesting sequence of numbers is produced by starting out with the list of all integers 1, 2, 3, ..., n. From this list every *second* number is removed to produce a new list. From the new list every *third* number is removed to give yet another list. Every *fourth* number is removed from this list and so the process continues. The numbers that remain after this process are called the *lucky numbers*. The first seven lucky numbers are 1, 3, 7, 9, 13, 15, 21, ... Design an algorithm to list the lucky numbers in the first n integers.

3.4.4   The largest known primes are called the Mersenne primes. They are of the form $2^p - 1$ where p is prime. A test called Lucas' test can be used to check whether a number of this form is prime. The test can be stated as follows. If $p > 2$ then $2^p - 1$ is prime only if $l_{p-2} = 0$ where the sequence l can be generated using

$$l_0 = 4, \quad l_{i+1} = (l_i^2 - 2) \mod (2^p - 1).$$

Design an algorithm to generate the Mersenne primes in the first n integers.

Algorithm 3.5
COMPUTING THE PRIME FACTORS OF AN INTEGER

Problem

Every integer can be expressed as a product of prime numbers. Design an algorithm to compute all the prime factors of an integer n.

Algorithm development

Examination of our problem statement suggests that

$$n = f_1 \times f_2 \times f_3 \cdots \times f_k \text{ where } n > 1 \text{ and } f_1 \leqslant f_2 \leqslant \cdots \leqslant f_k$$

The elements $f_1, f_2, \ldots, f_k$ are all prime numbers. Applying this definition to some specific examples we get:

$$8 = 2 \times 2 \times 2$$
$$12 = 2 \times 2 \times 3$$
$$18 = 2 \times 3 \times 3$$
$$20 = 2 \times 2 \times 5$$
$$60 = 2 \times 2 \times 3 \times 5$$

An approach to solving this factorization problem that immediately comes to mind is to start with the divisor 2 and repeatedly reduce n by a factor of 2 until 2 is no longer an exact divisor. We then try 3 as a divisor and again repeat the reduction process and so on until n has been reduced to 1. Consider the case when $n = 60$.

Marking with an asterisk the unsuccessful attempts to divide, we have

2	2	2	3	3	4	5	
60	30	15*	15	5*	5*	5	1

We can make several observations from this example. Firstly, 2 is the only even number that we need to try. In fact if we pay careful attention to our original definition we will see that only *prime numbers should be considered as candidate divisors*. Our present approach is going to test a lot of unnecessary divisors. From this we can begin to see that generation of a set of prime numbers should be an integral part of our algorithm. From our earlier work on primes and smallest divisors (algorithms 3.2 and 3.4) we know that all prime factors of n must be less than or equal to $\sqrt{n}$. This suggests that we should perhaps produce a list of primes up to $\sqrt{n}$ *before* going through the process of trying to establish the prime factors of n. Further thought reveals that there is a flaw in this strategy which comes about because prime factors may occur in multiples in the factorization we are seeking. A consequence of this is that in precomputing all the primes up to $\sqrt{n}$ we may end up computing a lot more primes than are needed as divisors for the current problem. (As an extreme example if n were 1024 we would calculate primes up to 32 whereas in fact the largest prime factor of 1024 is only 2.)

A better and more economical strategy is therefore to only compute prime divisors as they are needed. For this purpose we can include a modified version of the sieve of Eratosthenes that we developed earlier. As in our earlier algorithm as soon as we have discovered n is prime we can terminate. At this stage let us review the progress we have made. The top-level description of the central part of our algorithm is:

> **while** "it has not been established that n is prime" **do**
>   **begin**
>   (a)   if *nxtprime* is divisor of n then save *nxtprime* as a factor and
>   reduce n by *nxtprime*
>   else get next prime,
>   (b)   try *nxtprime* as a divisor of n.
>   **end**

We now must work out how the "not prime" test for our outer loop should be implemented. The technique we employed earlier was to use integer division and test for zero remainder. Once again this idea is applicable. We also know that as soon the prime divisor we are using in our test becomes greater than $\sqrt{n}$ the process can terminate.

Initially when the prime divisors we are using are much less than $\sqrt{n}$ we know that the testing must continue. In carrying out this process we want to avoid having to calculate the square root of n repeatedly. Each time we make the division:

$$n \textbf{ div } nxtprime \qquad (\text{e.g. } 60 \textbf{ div } 2)$$

we know the process must continue until the quotient q resulting from this division is less than *nxtprime*.

At this point we will have:

$$(nxtprime)^2 > n$$

which will indicate that n is prime. The conditions for it not yet being established that n is prime are therefore:

(a)   exact division   (i.e. $r := n \textbf{ div } nxtprime = 0$),
(b)   quotient greater than divisor   (i.e. $q := n \textbf{ mod } nxtprime > nxtprime$).

The truth of either condition is sufficient to require that the test be repeated again.

Now we need to explore how the algorithm will terminate. If we follow the factorization process through for a number of examples we discover that there are two ways in which the algorithm can terminate. One way for termination is where n is eventually reduced to 1. This can happen when the largest prime factor is present more than once (e.g. as in the case of 18 where the factors are $2 \times 3 \times 3$). The other possible situation is where we terminate with a prime factor that only occurs once (e.g. the factors of 70 are $2 \times 5 \times 7$). In this instance we have a termination condition where n is >1. Therefore, after our loop terminates we must check which termination condition applies and adjust the prime factors accordingly.

The only other considerations are the initialization conditions and the dynamic generation of primes as required. Since we have already considered the prime number generation problem before we will assume there is a function available which when given a particular prime as an argument returns the next prime. The sieve of Eratosthenes can be readily adapted for this purpose and in the present example we will assume that the procedure *eratosthenes* which returns *nxtprime* is available. The prime factorization algorithm can now be given in detail.

Algorithm description

1. Establish n the number whose prime factors are sought.
2. Compute the remainder r and quotient q for the first prime *nxtprime* = 2.
3. While it is not established that n is prime do
   (a)   if *nxtprime* is an exact divisor of n then
         (a.1)   save *nxtprime* as a factor f,
         (a.2)   reduce n by *nxtprime*,
      else
            (a'.1)   get next biggest prime from sieve of Eratosthenes,
   (b)   compute next quotient q and remainder r for current value of n and current prime divisor *nxtprime*.
4. If n is greater than 1 then
      add n to list as a prime factor f.
5. Return the prime factors f of the original number n.

Pascal implementation

```
procedure primefactors (var f: nelements; var i: integer; n: integer);
var
   q {quotient of n div nxtprime},
   r {remainder of n div nxtprime},
   nxtprime {next prime divisor to be tested}: integer;
   d: array[1..100] of integer; {multiples array for sieve}
```

```
begin {computes the prime factors f of n by division by successive
primes}
   {assert: n > 1}
   nxtprime := 2;
   q := n'div nxtprime;
   r := n mod nxtprime;
   i := 0;
   {invariant: after current iteration f [1..i] will contain all prime factors
   (including repeats) < nxtprime
   ∧ one or more contributions of nxtprime if it is a factor}
   while (r = 0) or (q > nxtprime) do
      begin {record factor if exact divisor or get next prime}
         if r = 0 then
            begin {exact divisor so save prime factor and reduce n}
               i := i + 1;
               f[i] := nxtprime;
               n := q
            end
         else eratosthenses (d,nxtprime); {get next prime}
            q := n div nxtprime;
            r := n mod nxtprime
      end;
   if n > 1 then
      begin {n is a prime factor}
         i := i + 1;
         f[i] := n
      end
   {assert: f[1..i] will contain all prime factors (including repeats) of
   original n}
end
```

Notes on design

1. The computational cost for this algorithm can be divided into two
    parts. The part for generating the prime divisors (which we have
    considered before) and the part for computing the prime factors. In the
    worst case (when n is prime) of the order of $\sqrt{n}$ steps will be needed to
    compute the prime factors of n. Average behavior is not easy to
    characterize.

2. The condition that remains invariant for the prime factoring loop is
    after an iteration with the divisor *nxtprime* all prime factors *less* than
    nxtprime will have been established. At the same time n will have been
    reduced at least by the product of all its prime factors (including
    multiples) less than *nxtprime*. On termination the condition that (n **div**
    nxtprime ≤ *nxtprime*) must hold. The algorithm must eventually termi-
    nate because with each iteration either n is decreased or *nxtprime* is
    increased. Both these changes have the effect of reducing the ratio of n
    to *nxtprime* until eventually the condition $q > nxtprime$ no longer holds.

3. The algorithm we have developed here, although correct, is only suitable for numbers with 6 or less digits. Beyond this it starts to become computationally expensive and so more sophisticated factoring algorithms are needed. As a final comment a practical method (i.e. one that is economical in both space and time) for factoring very large numbers has yet to be developed. Modern encryption algorithms rely on this fact.

4. If this algorithm were to be used on a routine basis, a better strategy would be to precompute a table of primes *once* rather than generating the primes as required.

5. Knuth gives a practical method for factoring large numbers (*The Art of Computer Programming*, Vol. 2, pp. 347–9).

Applications

Factoring numbers with up to six digits.

Supplementary problems

3.5.1 Implement a version of the prime factorization algorithm that incorporates a sieve of Eratosthenes procedure.

3.5.2 Implement a prime factorization algorithm that eliminates only multiples of 2, 3 and 5 as divisors and compare it with 3.5.1 in terms of the number of divisions made.

3.5.3 Amicable numbers are pairs of numbers each of whose divisors add to the other number. (*Note*: 1 is included as a divisor but the numbers are not included as their own divisors.) Design and implement an algorithm that tests whether a given pair of numbers are amicable numbers.

3.5.4 A perfect number is one whose divisors add up to the number. Design and implement an algorithm that prints all perfect numbers between 1 and 500.

Algorithm 3.6
GENERATION OF PSEUDO-RANDOM NUMBERS

Problem

Use the linear congruential method to generate a uniform set of pseudo-random numbers.

Algorithm development

Random number generators are frequently used in computing science for among other things, testing and analysing the behavior of algorithms. A sequence of random numbers should exhibit the following behavior.

1. The sequence should appear as though each number had occurred by chance.
2. Each number should have a specified probability of falling within a given range.

The approach generally taken in computing science for random number generation is to simulate random processes by deterministically producing a sequence of numbers that appear to exhibit random behavior. These sequences are predictable in advance and for this reason they are usually referred to as *pseudo-random* sequences. There are many methods for generating pseudo-random numbers. Perhaps the most widely used of these algorithms is the *linear congruential method*. When this method is appropriately parameterized it will generate pseudo-random sequences that, for practical purposes, satisfy statistical criteria required of uniformly distributed random variables. In a uniform distribution each possible number is equally probable.

The implementation of the linear congruential method is very straightforward. Successive members of the linear congruential sequence $\{x\}$ are generated using the expression:

$$x_{n+1} = (ax_n + b) \bmod m \qquad \text{for} \quad n \geq 0$$

where the parameters a, b, m, and x_0 must be carefully chosen in advance according to certain criteria. The parameters a, b, and m are referred to as the multiplier, increment, and modulus respectively. Knuth (*The Art of Computer Programming*, Vol. 2, pp.9–157) gives an excellent theoretical basis for the choice of these parameters. These results can be summarized as follows:

All parameters should be integers greater than or equal to zero and m should be greater than x_0, a, and b.

Parameter x_0
The parameter x_0 can be chosen arbitrarily within the range $0 \leq x_0 < m$.

Parameter m
The value of m should be greater than or equal to the length of the random sequence required. In addition it must be possible to do the computation $(a*x+b) \bmod m$ without roundoff.

Parameter a

The choice of a depends on the choice of m. If m is a power of 2 then a should satisfy the condition:

$$a \bmod 8 = 5$$

If m is a power of 10, then a should be chosen such that:

$$a \bmod 200 = 21$$

Further requirements on a are that it should be larger than $\sqrt{m}$ and less than $m - \sqrt{m}$, $(a-1)$ should be a multiple of every prime dividing into m, and if m is a multiple of 4 then $(a-1)$ should also be a multiple of 4. These conditions, together with the requirement that b should be relatively prime to m are needed to guarantee that the sequence has a period of m.

Parameter b

The constant b should be odd and not a multiple of 5.

When a, b, and m are chosen according to the conditions outlined above a sequence of m pseudo-random numbers in the range 0 to $(m-1)$ can be generated before the sequence begins to repeat. A Pascal implementation of the linear congruential method is given below for an m value of 4096.

Pascal implementation

```
procedure random (var x: integer);
var
  a {multiplier},
  b {increment},
  m {modulus}: integer;

begin {generates pseudo-random numbers x by the linear
congruential method}
  m := 4096;
  {assert: 0 =< x =< m - 1}
  b := 853;
  a := 109;
  x := (a * x + b) mod m
  {assert: 0 =< x =< m - 1}
end
```

Notes on design

1. The linear congruential method is a simple, efficient and practical method for generating pseudo-random numbers.
2. A uniform distribution of pseudo-random numbers can be used as a basis for generating other distributions such as the normal and exponential distributions.

3. The theoretical basis for the choice of parameters involves a highly sophisticated analysis.

Applications

Analysis of algorithms, simulation problems and games.

Supplementary problems

3.6.1　Confirm that the algorithm repeats after generating m random numbers. Compute the mean value and variance for the set of m pseudo-random numbers.

3.6.2　Check the uniformity of the distribution produced by the linear congruential method for $m = 4096$ by accumulating random numbers in blocks of 64 in the range $0 \rightarrow 4095$ (e.g. the first block is $0 \rightarrow 63$). Make a plot of the resulting histogram.

3.6.3　Uniformly distributed random numbers $\{r\}$ can be used to generate a random set that are exponentially distributed $\{x\}$ using the formula

$$x_i = -\frac{1}{\lambda} \log_e (1-r_i)$$

where λ is a parameter of the exponential distribution. Implement the algorithm.

3.6.4　The polar method can be used to generate normally distributed random numbers in the range 0 to 1. It involves first generating two uniform random numbers r_1 and r_2. Then if the expression for d below is $\geqslant 1$ two normally distributed random numbers can be computed as n_1 and n_2. That is,

$$d = (2r_1-1)^2 + (2r_2-1)^2$$

$$n_1 = (2r_1-1)\left(\frac{-2 \log_e(d)}{d}\right)^{\frac{1}{2}}$$

$$n_2 = (2r_2-1)\left(\frac{-2 \log_e(d)}{d}\right)^{\frac{1}{2}}$$

Use these expressions to generate normally distributed random numbers.

3.6.5　For some applications, a "better" random generator than the simple linear congruential method is needed. To do this, two *independent* sets of random numbers $\{r_i\}$ and $\{s_i\}$ must be generated using two sets of a and b values and the *same* m value. An auxiliary storage area of 100 elements $\{t_i\}$ is then filled with the first 100 random values of the sequence $\{r_i\}$. Having carried out this initialization step we can then generate successively pairs of random numbers r_i and s_i. To output the ith "better" random number, we use s_i and the modulus m to compute an index j to the table $t[1...100]$, i.e.

$$j = \lfloor 100 \ s_i/m \rfloor$$

The ith "better" random number is then found at position $t[j]$. After $t[j]$ has been referenced it is *replaced* by the current r_i value. Implement this "better" random number generator. (Ref. M. O. MacLaren and G. Marsaglia, "Uniform random number generators", *J. ACM*, **12**, 83–9, (1965)).

Algorithm 3.7
RAISING A NUMBER TO A LARGE POWER

Problem

Given some integer x, compute the value of x^n where n is a positive integer considerably greater than 1.

Algorithm development

Evaluating the expression

$$p = x^n$$

where x and n are given is a straightforward task. A simple method of evaluation is to repeatedly multiply an accumulating product p by x for n iterations, for example,

```
p := 1
for i := 1 to n do p := p*x
```

In most cases, evaluating x^n in this way is satisfactory. There are, however, occasions (e.g. as in a recently published encryption algorithm) where it is necessary to strive for higher efficiencies in evaluating the power of some integer. Let us therefore concern ourselves with trying to discover a more efficient algorithm for power evaluation.

It is not obvious where to start in designing a more efficient algorithm for evaluating x^n. In these circumstances it is probably best to study how a specific example is evaluated using the first algorithm to see if this will help us to get started.

Consider the evaluation of x^{10}. In our stepwise approach we have:

$$p_1 = x^1 = x$$
$$p_2 = x^2 = x \times x$$
$$p_3 = x^3 = x^2 \times x$$
$$p_4 = x^4 = x^3 \times x$$
$$\vdots$$
$$p_{10} = x^{10} = x^9 \times x$$

Studying these steps carefully, we see that x is increasing by one power at each step. In trying to evaluate x^{10} more efficiently, what are we really trying to do? To evaluate x^{10} more efficiently implies that we will need to take *fewer* steps to complete the task. The question is just how can we do this? Looking back at our example, we see that we could have generated x^4 by simply multiplying x^2 by itself, for example,

$$x^4 = x^2 \times x^2$$

This requires *just one* multiplication rather than the two multiplications used in our example above. In terms of power addition we have $2+2=4$ compared with $2+1+1=4$. This new way of evaluating x^4 may provide the lead we need so we should investigate further along these lines. In one sense, what this most recent example tells us is that we will have solved our problem in the most efficient way when we discover the set of numbers that add to 10 in the least number of steps. (Remember, multiplication in this instance translates into the *addition* of powers).

Some sets of numbers that add up to 10 are:

$$8+2 = 10$$
$$7+3 = 10$$
$$6+4 = 10$$
$$5+5 = 10$$
$$4+4+2 = 10$$
$$\vdots$$

What we observe is that whichever one of these possibilities we choose we are going to be faced with a smaller power evaluation problem that needs to be solved efficiently. Also since adding three numbers is not going to be as efficient as adding two numbers, our "best" solution to the problem is not likely to come from adding sets like $4+4+2$. This leads us to the question as to what is the pair of numbers that we can choose to add to 10 that leaves us with the *smallest* smaller power evaluation problem?

Suppose we choose 8 and 2 as our pair of powers to generate x^{10} (i.e. $x^8 \times x^2 = x^{10}$). If we made this choice we would need to generate x^8 which is already close to x^{10} before we could complete the task. *Putting it another way, we need to ask what is the "smallest" pair of numbers that we can choose that add up to* 10? The answer to this question has to be two 5s. For example,

$$5+5 = 10$$

All other combinations, e.g. 6+4, etc., leave us with a larger smaller power evaluation problem to solve (in this case x^6). That is, for our current power evaluation problem, once we have generated x^5 we can go *directly* to x^{10} by simply multiplying x^5 by itself.

Our next concern is to try to work out how to compute x^5 efficiently. Again we can try the power-halving approach. Unfortunately, half of 5 is 2.5 which is not an integral power. Our only useful alternative in this case is to generate x^5 by squaring x^2 to give x^4 and then multiplying that result by x. For example,

$$x^5 = x^2 \times x^2 \times x$$

The steps to compute x^{10} are therefore:

$$x^2 = x \times x$$
$$x^4 = x^2 \times x^2$$
$$x^5 = x^4 \times x$$
$$x^{10} = x^5 \times x^5$$

With this scheme we have used *only four* rather than nine multiplications to evaluate x^{10}. On this basis, it would be reasonable to expect that for larger powers the savings would be much greater.

We are still quite a long way from coming to terms with the implementation of this algorithm, so let us consider another example to see what generalizations we can make. Consider the case of evaluating x^{23}. In working out the steps required to compute x^{10} we actually started with the final power and worked *backwards*. We can try the same idea with this second example.

$$x^{23} = x^{22} \times x$$
$$x^{22} = x^{11} \times x^{11}$$
$$x^{11} = x^{10} \times x$$
$$x^{10} = x^5 \times x^5$$
$$x^5 = x^4 \times x$$
$$x^4 = x^2 \times x^2$$
$$x^2 = x \times x$$

Here we can see that only 7 multiplications have been required to raise a number to the power 23. We can also see after studying these last two examples that a definite pattern has evolved.

At each stage in the power generation process, one of two conditions apply:

(a) Where we have an *odd* power it must have been generated from the power that is one less (e.g. $x^{23} = x^{22} \times x$).
(b) Where we have an *even* power, it can be computed from a power that is *half* its size (e.g. $x^{22} = x^{11} \times x^{11}$).

These last two statements capture the essence of the algorithm. This means that our algorithm will need to be in two parts:

1. a part that determines the multiplication strategy, and
2. a second part that actually does the power evaluation.

To map out the multiplication procedure, we can start with the power required and determine whether it is even or odd. The next step is to integer-divide the current power by 2 and repeat the even/odd determination procedure. From our two examples we can see that this whole process must be continued until 2 is reached. The even/odd information can be recorded in an array by storing a 1 for odd and a 0 for even powers.

For our second example we would have:

$$
\begin{array}{ll}
x^{23} & d[1] = 1 \\
x^{11} & d[2] = 1 \\
x^{5} & d[3] = 1 \\
x^{2} & d[4] = 0 \\
x^{1} & d[5] = 1
\end{array}
$$

To carry out the second part of the algorithm (i.e. the power evaluation), we need to work *forwards* rather than backwards. This implies that we must start with the highest element in the d array (in our example $d[4]$) and work back down to $d[1]$.

Starting out with our product p equal to 1 we can proceed with the power evaluation using the following rule:

if the current d array element is zero then
   (a)   we simply square the current power product p,
else
   (a')   we square the current product p and multiply by x to generate an odd power.

For the evaluation of x^{23} the steps are:

$$
\begin{array}{llll}
d[5] = 1 \Rightarrow p := p \times p \times x & (1 \times 1 \times x) & = x \\
d[4] = 0 \Rightarrow p := p \times p & (x \times x) & = x^2 \\
d[3] = 1 \Rightarrow p := p \times p \times x & (x^2 \times x^2 \times x) & = x^5 \\
d[2] = 1 \Rightarrow p := p \times p \times x & (x^5 \times x^5 \times x) & = x^{11} \\
d[1] = 1 \Rightarrow p := p \times p \times x & (x^{11} \times x^{11} \times x) & = x^{23}
\end{array}
$$

From our earlier work on base conversion (Chapter 2) we may recognize that repeated division of the power n by 2 has the effect of computing its binary representation. Since efficient power evaluation is based on the binary representation of the power we may ask can it be done directly rather than after deriving the binary representation? If we could proceed in this way there would be no need to save the multiplication strategy for later use.

To try to discover if a direct approach is viable we can return to our earlier example and its binary representation:

$$23_{10} = 10111$$

Our original scheme builds up the power by left-shifting the most significant digits, i.e. we have:

$$
\begin{array}{ll}
1 & x \\
10 & x^2 \\
101 & x^5 \\
1011 & x^{11} \\
10111 & x^{23}
\end{array}
$$

With this scheme the contributions of the most significant digits are incorporated *first*. In contrast, derivation of the binary representation of the power gives us the binary digits in the order from the *least* significant to the most significant. The question we may therefore ask is, can the power evaluation also take place in this order? Referring to the binary representation for x^{23} we see that it can be written as

$$x^{23} = x^1 x^2 x^4 x^{16}$$

where

$$1 \times 2^0 + 1 \times 2^1 + 1 \times 2^2 + 0 \times 2^3 + 1 \times 2^4 = 23$$

which suggests that power evaluation can be coupled *directly* with the derivation of the binary representation of the power n.

For our example we will need to be able to consecutively generate the powers

$$x^1, \ x^2, \ x^4, \text{ and } x^{16}$$

as successive binary digits are established.

Each of these powers can be generated by multiplying its predecessor by itself: for example,

$$x^4 = x^2 \times x^2$$

Notice that x^8 is missing from the list but it still must be computed when the 0 binary digit is established if x^{16} is to be obtained at the next step. Studying our example once again more thoroughly we see that power evaluation involves the following steps.

1. Successive generation of numbers of the power sequence $x, x^2, x^4, x^8, x^{16}, \ldots$

2. Inclusion of the current power member into the accumulated product when the corresponding binary digit is one.

Table 3.1 summarizes the power evaluation for x^{23} by our new proposal.

Table 3.1 Power evaluation by doubling strategy for x^{23}

Binary digit	Power sequence	Accumulated product
1	x	x
1	x^2	$x^2 \times x = x^3$
1	x^4	$x^4 \times x^3 = x^7$
0	x^8	—
1	x^{16}	$x^{16} \times x^7 = x^{23}$

The test $n \bmod 2 = 1$ can be used to check if the next most significant binary digit is one. If the accumulated product is labelled *product* and successive members of the power sequence are labelled *psequence* then to include the current power sequence member into the accumulated product we can use the following standard form:

$$product := product \times psequence$$

The variable *product* will need to be initially set to 1 to allow for the case where the power n is zero. The power sequence variable *psequence* will need to be initialized to x, the number that is to be raised to the power n. The initialization steps are therefore:

$$product := 1;$$
$$psequence := x$$

With successive iterations the power value of *psequence* will need to be *doubled*. This step can be accomplished using:

$$psequence := psequence \times psequence$$

The other step that must take place with each iteration is that n must be divided by 2. For example,

$$n := n \textbf{ div } 2$$

The algorithm will need to terminate when n is reduced to zero.

We now have all the details needed to describe the power evaluation algorithm in full.

Algorithm description

1. Establish n, the integer power, and x the integer to be raised to the power n.

2. Initialize the power sequence and product variable for the zero power case.
3. While the power n is greater than zero do
   - (a) if next most significant binary digit of power n is one then
     - (a.1) multiply accumulated product by current power sequence value;
   - (b) reduce power n by a factor of two using integer division;
   - (c) get next power sequence member by multiplying current value by itself.
4. Return x raised to the power n.

Pascal implementation

```
function power(x, n: integer): integer;
var product {current accumulated product, eventually contains result},
    psequence {current power sequence value}: integer;

begin {computes x raised to the power n using doubling strategy}
  {assert: x>0∧n>=0∧n0=n}
  product := 1;
  psequence := x;
  {invariant: product * (psequence) ↑n =x↑n0 ∧n >=0}
  while n>0 do
    begin {incorporate power for next most significant binary digit if
    not zero}
      if (n mod 2)=1 then
        product := product * psequence;
      n := n div 2;
      psequence := psequence * psequence
    end;
  {assert: product =x↑n0}
  power := product
end
```

Notes on design

1. Multiplications of the order of $\lceil \log_2 n \rceil$ are needed to raise x to the power n. This method of power evaluation, although not optimum for all values of n, is an efficient method for large values of n.
2. The **while**-loop generates the binary representation of the integer n for all values of $n>0$. After the ith iteration the i rightmost bits of the binary representation of n have been generated and x has been raised to a power equal to the value of these i rightmost bits. At the same time n

has been reduced by 2^i. The algorithm terminates because with each iteration n is reduced and so eventually the condition $n>0$ will be false.

The algorithm will function correctly for all values of $n \geq 0$. For large values of n the value of x^n will quickly exceed the limits of most computers' integer wordsize representations. No attempt has been made in the current algorithm to protect against this possibility. Obviously an extended representation using arrays or modular arithmetic is needed in such circumstances. Functionally, however, the above method of power evaluation can be used.

3. Our original doubling method is not as attractive as the final algorithm because it requires separate array storage.

4. A specific example has been very helpful in isolating the mechanism for power evaluation.

5. In this algorithm, we see that a divide-and-conquer strategy is applied. The original problem is solved by repeatedly solving a problem half its size. This idea is applied recursively. This divide-and-conquer strategy as is often the case leads to a balanced and efficient algorithm.

Applications

Encryption (secret coding of information), and testing for non-primality of numbers.

Supplementary problems

3.7.1   Design an algorithm for power evaluation that is built upon a base 3 strategy rather than the current base 2 method. Compare the results for this new method with the current algorithm.

3.7.2   Design a complete precision power evaluation algorithm for values of x^n that may exceed the computer's integer representation limit.

3.7.3   It is sometimes important to establish that a number is not a prime. To do this we can use a result that follows from the work of Fermat. It is possible to show that for all prime numbers except 2, the following condition holds:

$$2^{p-1} \bmod p = 1$$

This test can be performed in the order of $\log_2(p)$ steps. Design an algorithm to test a number for non-primality. For simplicity, choose a prime such that 2^{p-1} does not exceed your computer's integer word size representation limit.

Algorithm 3.8
COMPUTING THE nth FIBONACCI NUMBER

Problem

Given a number n generate the nth member of the Fibonacci sequence.

Algorithm development

Remembering back to algorithm (2.6) we are given that the nth member of
the Fibonacci sequence f_n is defined recursively as follows:

$$f_1 = 0$$
$$f_2 = 1$$
$$f_n = f_{n-1} + f_{n-2} \qquad \text{for } n > 2$$

We have previously seen how this definition can be used in conjunction with
an iterative construct to generate Fibonacci numbers. What we are concerned with here is whether or not there is a more efficient way of generating
the nth Fibonacci number rather than the complete sequence of n Fibonacci
numbers. It sometimes happens when one member of a set is required the
job can be done more efficiently than generating the $(n-1)$ predecessors. For
example, in algorithm (3.7) we saw how this principle was very effectively
applied. That is, we were able to raise a number to the nth power, not by
generating its $(n-1)$ predecessors but instead by generating only of the order
of $\log_2 n$ of its predecessors. What we are interested in here is whether or not
we can apply this divide-and-conquer strategy to our current problem. In the
power generation problem, our task was straightforward because the relationship between powers of i and the powers of $2i$ was simple and easily
defined (e.g. $x^6 = x^3 \times x^3$).

In our present problem we are not sure whether such a "doubling
relationship" exists. To explore this possibility let us write down the first few
members of the Fibonacci sequence.

Fibonacci number	0	1	1	2	3	5	8	13	21	34
index	1	2	3	4	5	6	7	8	9	10

To pick an example let us see if the 8th Fibonacci number can be related to
the 4th Fibonacci number. We have:

$$f_4 = 2$$
$$f_8 = 13$$

The relationship is:

$$f_8 = 6 \times f_4 + 1$$

Trying this relationship out with f_{10} and f_5 we discover that it does not generalize. We may suspect that no doubling relationship exists between just two Fibonacci numbers. The next thing we can try is some combination of two Fibonacci numbers to generate the "doubled" Fibonacci number. This might have more chance of success since in the original scheme for generating Fibonacci numbers, two numbers are used to generate the next. Let us therefore try to write f_8 in terms of only f_4 and f_5. To do this we will need to use the original definition for the sequence. That is,

$$f_4 = 2$$
$$f_5 = 3$$
$$f_6 = f_5 + f_4$$
$$f_7 = f_6 + f_5 = (f_5 + f_4) + f_5 \quad \text{(substituting for } f_6)$$
$$f_8 = f_7 + f_6 = [(f_5 + f_4) + f_5] + f_5 + f_4$$

collecting terms we get:

$$f_8 = 3f_5 + 2f_4 = 3 \times 3 + 2 \times 2 = 13$$

Since $f_5 = 3$ and $f_4 = 2$ the last expression suggests:

$$f_8 = f_5^2 + f_4^2$$

Checking with f_{10}, f_5 and f_6 to see if the formula generalizes, we get

$$f_{10} = f_6^2 + f_5^2 = 5^2 + 3^2 = 34$$

Without going into a detailed proof, we might be satisfied that in general:

$$f_{2n} = f_{n+1}^2 + f_n^2$$

Further checks with the sequence confirm this expression.

We are almost there, or are we? Looking back at our algorithm for computing powers, we found that on occasions, to get the optimum final solution, we sometimes had to multiply by just x to take into account odd powers. We might expect that the same idea will have to carry through to our current problem. That is, we will need to have on hand the Fibonacci number f_{2n+1} as well as the Fibonacci number f_{2n} to extend the process. To generate the f_{2n+1} Fibonacci number we need f_{2n} and f_{2n-1}:

$$f_{2n+1} = f_{2n} + f_{2n-1}$$

The problem is we do not have f_{2n-1} and so we are not much better off. We are therefore going to need to try to generate f_9 from f_5 and f_4. Applying the same substitution method as we used to establish:

$$f_{2n} = f_{n+1}^2 + f_n^2 \quad \text{(for } n > 1)$$

we finally get, after some substitution and checking:

$$f_{2n+1} = 2f_n f_{n+1} + f_{n+1}^2 \qquad \text{(for } n \geqslant 1)$$

To double the next time, f_{2n} and f_{2n+1} assume the role originally assigned to f_n and f_{n+1} respectively. We now have the basis of a method for generating the nth Fibonacci number in a similar manner to raising x to the power n as in algorithm (3.7).

In this case our algoirthm will need to be in two parts:

1. a part that determines the doubling strategy by generating the binary representation of n, and
2. a second part that actually computes the nth Fibonacci number according to the doubling strategy.

We now need to work through some examples to see just how these doubling formulas can be applied. To start with, we can generate the binary representation of n using the method in algorithm 3.7. Let us consider $n = 10$ (Table 3.2).

Table 3.2

Pair of Fibonacci numbers needed	Fibonacci number	Binary representation
(f_{10}, f_{11})	f_{10}	$d[1] = 0$
(f_5, f_6)	f_5	$d[2] = 1$
(f_2, f_3)	f_2	$d[3] = 0$
(f_1, f_2)	f_1	$d[4] = 1$

Notice that "doubling" (f_2, f_3) only gives us (f_4, f_5). However, to generate the next "doubled" pair (f_{10}, f_{11}) we need the pair (f_5, f_6). Fortunately we can simply use the standard formula to generate f_6 (i.e. $f_6 = f_5 + f_4$).

Consider another example where $n = 13$ (Table 3.3).

Table 3.3

Pair of Fibonacci numbers needed	Fibonacci number	Binary representation
(f_{13}, f_{14})	f_{13}	$d[1] = 1$
(f_6, f_7)	f_6	$d[2] = 0$
(f_3, f_4)	f_3	$d[3] = 1$
(f_1, f_2)	f_1	$d[4] = 1$

After studying these two examples carefully, it becomes clear how the binary representation can be used to generate the Fibonacci number we require.

We always start out with the pair (f_1, f_2) and to generate the required Fibonacci number we will always need to make one less doubling step $(i-1)$

than there are binary digits i in the representation of n (e.g. the binary representation of $n = 13$ is 1011 and hence $4-1 = 3$ doubling steps are required). The binary digit that is always accounted for by the initial conditions is always the most significant digit (e.g. for $n = 13$ it is $d[4]$) when n has been reduced to 1. We can eliminate this digit by stopping generating binary digits one step earlier.

Considering our example for $n = 13$, we must start by applying the doubling rule to the pair (f_1, f_2). This yields the pair (f_2, f_3). Before we can proceed, we need the pair (f_3, f_4) which we can derive directly from the pair (f_2, f_3) by applying the standard formula $f_{k+1} = f_k + f_{k-1}$. In general, whenever the corresponding binary digit (in this case $d[3]$) is odd, we need to carry out the doubling process and then extend the sequence by one before doubling again.

If we use fn and $fnp1$ for the Fibonacci numbers f_n and f_{n+1} respectively and $f2n$ and $f2np1$ for f_{2n} and f_{2n+1} we will have the initial doubling steps:

$fn := fn*fn + fnp1*fnp1;$
$f2np1 := 2*fn*fnp1 + fnp1*fnp1$

and then the following reassignments in preparation for the next doubling step:

$fn := f2np1;$
$fnp1 := f2np1 + f2n$ (extension by 1)

At this point the variables fn and $fnp1$ are correctly assigned to allow the next doubling step to be taken.

Returning to our example, once we have the pair (f_3, f_4) we get the next pair (f_6, f_7) just by doubling. The zero for $d[2]$ tells us that we can use the pair (f_6, f_7) *directly* for the next doubling step without having to extend the sequence by 1.

Using the variables $fn, fnp1, f2n, f2np1$ again, we have in this case first the initially doubling steps as before: that is,

$f2n := fn*fn + fnp1*fnp1;$
$f2np1 := 2*fn*fnp1 + fnp1*fnp1$

and then the following reassignments in preparation for the next doubling step:

$fn := f2n;$
$fnp1 := f2np1$

At this point the variables fn and $fnp1$ are correctly assigned to allow the next doubling step to be taken. In the actual implementation, since the square of $fnp1$ occurs twice, it is more efficient to precompute it.

The doubling step is common to both the case when $d[k] = 0$ and

$d[k] = 1$. It can therefore be put *before* the two possible reassignment cases. The reassignments in preparation for the next doubling can then be made conditional on the value of the current binary digit. Noting these facts the detailed description of our algorithm can now be given. The method used for establishing the binary representation for n is exactly the same as that used in algorithm 3.7.

Algorithm description

1. Establish n, indicating the nth Fibonacci number is required.
2. Derive the binary representation of n by repeated division by 2 and store representation in array $d[1..i-1]$.
3. Initialize the first two members of the doubling sequence.
4. Stepping down from the $(i-1)^{th}$ most significant digit in the binary representation of n to 1 do
    (a) use current pair of Fibonacci numbers f_n and f_{n+1} to generate the pair f_{2n} and f_{2n+1},
    (b) if current binary digit $d[k]$ is zero
         then make the reassignments to f_n and f_{n+1}
         else extend sequence by 1 number and then make the reassignments to f_n and f_{n+1}.
5. Return the nth Fibonacci number f_n.

Pascal implementation

```
function nfib (n: integer): integer;
var d: array [1..100] of integer; {array containing binary digits}
    fn {the nth fibonacci number – on termination contains final result},
    f2n {the 2nth fibonacci number},
    fnpl {the (n + 1)th fibonacci number},
    f2npl {the (2n + 1)th fibonacci number},
    i {binary digit count less 1 of n and index for binary array},
    k {index for array of binary digits},
    sqfnpl {square of the (n + 1)th fibonacci number}: integer;

begin {generate the nth fibonacci number by repeated doubling}
    {assert: n > 0 ∧ n has = < 100 digits in its binary representation}
    i := 0;
    {invariant: after the ith iteration the i least significant bits of binary
    representation of original n stored in d[i..1]}
    while n > 1 do
        begin {generate binary digits for n without the most significant
        digit}
            i := i + 1;
            if odd(n) then d[i] := 1 else d[i] := 0;
            n := n div 2
        end;
```

```
fn := 0;
fnpl := 1;
{invariant: after current iteration fn = fibonacci number
corresponding to i − k + 1 leftmost bits of binary representation
of n}
for k := i downto 1 do
    begin {generate the 2n and (2n + 1)th fibonacci numbers from
    the nth and (n + 1)th}
        sqfnpl := fnpl * fnpl;
        f2n := fn * fn + sqfnpl;
        f2npl := 2 * fn * fnpl + sqfnpl;
        if d[k] = 0 then
            begin {reassign nth and (n + 1)th ready for next doubling
            phase}
                fn := f2n;
                fnpl := f2npl
            end
        else
            begin {extend sequence by one and reassign nth and
            (n + 1)th}
                fn := f2npl;
                fnpl := f2npl + f2n
            end
    end;
    {assert: fn = the nth fibonacci number}
    nfib := fn
end
```

Notes on design

1. For a given value of n the algorithm requires of the order of $\log_2 n$ steps to compute the nth Fibonacci number.

2. The **while**-loop generates the binary representation of n for values of n greater than 1. After the ith iteration, the i rightmost bits of the binary representation of n have been generated. On termination, when $n = 1$ all but the leftmost significant digit of the binary representation of n has been generated.

   After the jth iteration of the **for**-loop (j is not explicitly defined) a Fibonacci number fn has been generated which corresponds to the $(j+1)$ leftmost binary digits of n. On termination when $j = i$ and $k = 1$ the variable fn corresponds to the nth Fibonacci number.

   The **while**-loop terminates because n follows a strictly decreasing sequence to 1 due to the repeated division by 2. By definition, the **for**-loop will also terminate.

   The algorithm will function correctly for all values of $n \geq 1$. For large values of n the value of fn will quickly exceed the limits of most computers' integer word size representations. No attempt has been made in the current algorithm to protect against this possibility.

3. In this problem we have been able to carry over a design that we learned about in the previous algorithm.
4. The algorithm in itself is not all that useful. The technique that it illustrates however is very important.
5. In this problem we were able to make progress by having a goal (i.e. a way in which we wanted to try to compute the nth Fibonacci number) and then using a specific example to invent the formula we needed to achieve the goal.
6. Notice that to save on multiplications it is preferable to precompute f_{n+1}.

Supplementary problems

3.8.1   Develop a recursive implementation that incorporates the ideas above for calculating the nth Fibonacci number. Compare the performance of the recursive method with the iterative solution.

3.8.2   What sequence of pairs of Fibonacci numbers would be needed to compute the 23rd Fibonacci number using the present algorithm?

3.8.3   It is possible to multiply two numbers x and y by repeatedly halving y (i.e. integer division) when it is even and reducing it by 1 when it is odd. When y is odd the current value of x is accumulated. When y is even, x is doubled. Implement this multiplication algorithm. (*Note:* Doubling and halving operations correspond to "shift" operations which are very efficient on most computers.)

3.8.4   It is possible to compute $n!$ in $O(\log_2 n)$ steps. Try to develop such an algorithm for computing $n!$ (Ref. A. Shamir, "Factoring numbers in $O(\log n)$ arithmetic steps", *Inf. Proc. Letts.*, **8**, 28–31 (1979)).

BIBLIOGRAPHY

Most of the algorithms in this chapter are covered in introductory computing texts. Knuth (1969) provides a detailed discussion on factoring methods.

1. Knuth, D. E., *The Art of Computer Programming*, Vol. 2: *Seminumerical Algorithms*, Addison–Wesley, Reading, Mass., 1969.

Chapter 4
ARRAY TECHNIQUES

INTRODUCTION

The array is a powerful tool that is widely used in computing. Arrays provide for a very special way of storing or organizing data in a computer's memory. The power of the array is largely derived from the fact that it provides us with a very simple and efficient way of referring to and performing computations on collections of data that share some common attribute. For someone just starting to work with computers it often takes a considerable time, and a number of examples, to fully appreciate the different ways in which arrays can be used in computations. An analogy that often helps to reinforce the concept involves thinking that an array is much like a street with a row of houses. The attribute that all the houses share is the *name* of the street. Each house in the street has a *unique address* which distinguishes it from all other houses in the street. The address is made up of two parts, the *street name* and the *number* of the lot. The street name corresponds to the array name and the street number corresponds to the *suffix*.

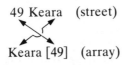

The house at each address corresponds to the memory storage unit or computer word (or byte) at each address in the array. People and furniture etc. are "stored" in houses while we store numbers or characters in fixed-length binary representation in array locations. It is a copy of the number or characters stored in an array location that we retrieve when we reference a particular array location by specifying its array name and suffix. The processing of arrays is simplified by using variables to specify suffixes. In processing a particular array it does not matter what name we give the array suffix—it is only the suffix value which determines which array location is referenced (i.e. if the variables i and j both have the value 49 then the references $a[i]$ and $a[j]$ *both* reference the *same* array location which is $a[49]$).

The concept of a one-dimensional array which we have been considering extends in a natural way to multidimensional arrays.

Arrays play an integral part in many computer algorithms. They simplify the implementation of algorithms that must perform the same computations on collections of data. Furthermore, employment of arrays often leads to implementations that are more efficient than they would otherwise be.

The contents of array locations can be changed and used in conditional expressions etc. in the same way as single variables. Also the suffix can be the result of a computation as well as a single variable (e.g., $a[2*i+1]$ and $a[j-1]$ are valid references to array locations provided the resulting suffix is within the array bounds).

The most important basic ways in which we change the contents of an array location are by direct computation and assignment, by exchange of the contents of two array locations, and by counting. In the algorithms which follow we will examine a variety of basic array techniques and applications. We will also see in later chapters how arrays are used to simulate stacks and queues and other important data structures. Non-linear data structures such as trees and graphs can also be maintained using one-dimensional and two-dimensional arrays.

In more advanced computer applications arrays can be used to build and simulate finite state automata.

Algorithm 4.1
ARRAY ORDER REVERSAL

Problem

Rearrange the elements in an array so that they appear in reverse order.

Algorithm development

The problem of reversing the order of an array of numbers appears to be completely straightforward. Whilst this is essentially true, some care and thought must go into implementing the algorithm.

We can start the design of this algorithm by careful examination of the elements of an array before and after it has been reversed; for example,

| 1 | 2 | 3 | 4 | 5 | 6 | 7 | before reversal

| 7 | 6 | 5 | 4 | 3 | 2 | 1 | after reversal

What we observe from our diagram is that the *first* element ends up in the *last* position. The *second* element ends up in the *second last* position and so on. Carrying this process through we get the following set of exchanges:

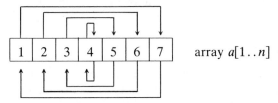

array $a[1..n]$

In terms of suffixes the exchanges are:

step [1] $a[1]<=>a[7]$
step [2] $a[2]<=>a[6]$
step [3] $a[3]<=>a[5]$
step [4] $a[4]<=>a[4]$ there is no exchange here

Examining the effects of these exchanges we discover that after step [3] the array is completely reversed. We see that with each step the suffixes on the left are increasing by one while at the same time the suffixes on the right are decreasing by one. In setting up our algorithm we need a pair of suffixes that model this *increasing–decreasing* behavior. Our increasing suffix can be the variable i which is simply incremented by one with each step.

For our decreasing suffix we might try $[n-i]$ since this decreases by 1 with each increase in i by 1. The problem with this suggestion is that when $i=1$ we find that $[n-i]$ is equal to $n-1$ rather than n as we require for our exchange. We can correct this by adding 1. The suffix $[n-i+1]$ can then be used as our decreasing suffix. With these suffixes we have

i	$n-i+1$
1	$7-1+1=7$
2	$7-2+1=6$
3	$7-3+1=5$
4	$7-4+1=4$

Each exchange (cf. algorithm 2.1) can be achieved by a mechanism of the form

$$t := a[1];$$
$$a[i] := a[n-i+1];$$
$$a[n-i+1] := t$$

The only other aspect of the algorithm that we need to consider is the range that i can assume for a given n. Studying our original array it is clear that only 3 exchanges are needed to reverse arrays with either 6 or 7 elements. Consideration of further examples leads us to the generalization that the number of exchanges r to reverse the order of an array is always the nearest integer that is less than or equal half the magnitude of n. Our algorithm now follows directly from the above results and discussion.

Algorithm description

1. Establish the array $a[1..n]$ of n elements to be reversed.
2. Compute r the number of exchanges needed to reverse the array.
3. While there are still pairs of array elements to be exchanged
   (a) exchange the ith element with the $[n-i+1]^{th}$ element.
4. Return the reversed array.

The algorithm can be suitably implemented as a procedure that accepts as input the array to be reversed and returns as output the reversed array.

Pascal implementation

```
procedure reverse (var a: nelements; n: integer);
var i {increasing index for array},
    r {number of exchanges required}: integer;
    t {temporary variable needed for exchange}: real;

begin {reverses an array of n elements}
   {assert: n>0∧a[1]=a1, a[2]=a2,...,a[n]=a(n)}
   r := n div 2;
   {invariant: 1=<i=<⌊n/2⌋∧a[1]=a(n), a[2]=a(n-1),...,
   a[i]=a(n-i+1),
   a[i+1]=a(i+1), a[n-i]=a(n-i), a[n-i+1]=a(i), ..., a[n]=a1}
   for i := 1 to r do
      begin {exchange next pair}
         t := a[i];
         a[i] := a[n-i+1];
         a[n-i+1] := t
      end
      {assert: a[1]=a(n), a[2]=a(n-1),...,a[n-1]=a2, a[n]=a1}
end
```

Notes on design

1. To reverse an array of n elements $\lfloor n/2 \rfloor$ exchanges are required.
2. There are $r = \lfloor n/2 \rfloor$ pairs of elements in an array of n elements. To reverse an array of n elements r pairs of elements must be exchanged. After the ith iteration (for i in the range $1 \leq i \leq r$) the first i pairs of elements have been interchanged. This relation remains invariant. The ith pair consists of the ith element and the $(n-i+1)$th element. The algorithm will terminate because with each iteration i is advanced by 1 so eventually r pairs will have been exchanged.
3. In practice where array elements need to be accessed in reverse order it is usually not necessary to actually reverse the order of the array elements. Instead simply using a standard decreasing subscript device like $(n-i+1)$ will do the job. Alternatively, with appropriate initialization, $j := j-1$ can be used.
4. An example makes it easier to establish how many pairs of exchanges are required in general for both even and odd array sizes.
5. To exchange a pair of array elements the same technique is employed as is used for exchanging a pair of single variables.
6. There is a simpler algorithm for array reversal that starts out with two indices, $i = 0$ and $j = n+1$. With each iteration i is increased and j is decreased for $i < j$.

Applications

Vector and matrix processing.

Supplementary problems

4.1.1   What happens if the exchange process continues for n steps rather than $\lfloor n/2 \rfloor$ steps?

4.1.2   Implement the array reversal algorithm suggested in note 6.

4.1.3   Design an algorithm that places the kth element of an array in position 1, the $(k+1)$th element in position 2, etc. The original 1st element is placed at $(n-k+1)$ and so on.

4.1.4   Design an algorithm that rearranges the elements of an array so that all those originally stored at odd suffixes are placed before those at even suffixes. For example, the set

1	2	3	4	5	6	7	8

would be transformed to

1	3	5	7	2	4	6	8

Algorithm 4.2
ARRAY COUNTING OR HISTOGRAMMING

Problem

Given a set of *n* students' examination marks (in the range 0 to 100) make a count of the number of students that obtained each possible mark.

Algorithm development

This problem embodies the same principle as algorithm 2.2 where we had to make a count of the number of students that passed an examination. What we are required to do in this case is obtain the distribution of a set of marks. This problem is typical of frequency counting problems. One approach we could take is to set up 101 variables $C0$ $C1$, $C2$, ..., $C100$ each corresponding to a particular mark. The counting strategy we could then employ might be as follows:

while less than *n* marks have been examined do
(a)   get next mark *m*,
(b0)   if $m = 0$ then $C0 := C0+1$;
(b1)   if $m = 1$ then $C1 := C1+1$;
(b2)   if $m = 2$ then $C2 := C2+1$;
(b3)   if $m = 3$ then $C3 := C3+1$;
$\vdots$

(b100) if $m = 100$ then $C100 := C100+1$.

The difficulty with this approach is that we need to make 101 tests (only one of which is successful) just to update the count for one particular mark. Furthermore our program is very long. It therefore seems that there should be an easier way to solve the problem.

To begin the search for a better solution let us consider first how we might solve the problem without a computer. An approach we could take is illustrated by the following diagram:

It involves taking a piece of graph paper or dividing plain paper up into slots each of which can be identified with a particular mark value. The next step is to examine each mark, and, depending on its value, we place a star in the corresponding mark's slot. If we applied this step to all marks when the task was completed the number of stars associated with each slot would represent the mark's count for that particular mark.

The method we have outlined is certainly a workable hand solution. The question we must now ask is can we use these ideas in developing a useful computer solution to the problem? In the method we have proposed it is not necessary to compare each mark with all possible marks' values. *Instead, the value of a particular mark leads us directly to the particular slot that must be updated.* This one-step procedure for each mark would certainly be very attractive if it could be carried across to the computer algorithm.

It is at this point that we need to recognize that an array can be usefully employed in the solution to our problem. We can very easily set up an array with 101 locations, each location corresponding to a particular mark value. For example,

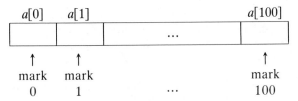

If we store in each array location the *count* of the number of students that obtained that mark we will have the required solution to the problem (e.g. if 15 students obtained the mark 57, then we will have the number 15 in location 57 when all marks have been examined).

What we must now consider is just how the count for each array location is achieved. In setting up our mechanism we want to try to incorporate the one-step procedure that was possible in the hand solution. Initially we can consider what happens when a particular mark is encountered. Suppose the current mark to be counted is 57. In using the array for counting we must at this stage add one to the count stored in location 57. For this step we can use the actual mark's value (i.e. 57) to reference the array location that we wish to update. That is, the mark's value can be employed as an array suffix. Because it is necessary to add one to the previous count in location 57, we will need a statement of the form:

new count in location 57 := previous count in location 57+1

Since location $a[57]$ must play both the "previous count" and "new count" roles, we can write

$$a[57] := a[57]+1$$

or for the general mark m we can write

$$a[m] := a[m]+1$$

This last statement can form the basis of our marks-counting algorithm. By using the mark value to address the appropriate array location, we have modelled the direct update method of the hand solution.

To complete the algorithm, all that is necessary is to include details for the input of the marks and the output of the marks frequency distribution. Prior to beginning the counting process the array must have all its elements set to zero. The details of the algorithm are then as given below.

Algorithm description

1. Prompt and read in n the number of marks to be processed.
2. Initialize all elements of the counting array $a[0..100]$ to zero.
3. While there are still marks to be processed, repeatedly do
    (a) read next mark m,
    (b) add one to the count in location m in the counting array.
4. Write out the marks frequency count distribution.

Pascal implementation

```
program histogram (input, output);
var i {current number of marks processed},
    m {current mark},
    n {number of marks to be processed}: integer;
    a: array [0..100] of integer;

begin {compute marks frequency distribution}
    writeln ('enter number of marks n on a separate line followed by
    marks');
    readln (n);
    for i := 1 to 100 do a[i] := 0;
    {assert: n >= 0 ∧ all a[0..100] are set to 0}
    {invariant: when i marks read, for j in range 0 =< j =< 100, all a[j]
    will represent the number of marks j in the first i read ∧ i =< n}
    for i := 1 to n do
        begin {read next mark and update appropriate array elements}
            read (m);
            if eoln (input) then readln;
            {assert: m in range 0 =< m =< 100}
            a[m] := a[m] + 1
        end;
    {assert: when n marks read, for j in range 0 =< j =< 100, all a[j]
    will represent the number of marks j in the set}
        for i := 0 to 100 do
            begin
                write (a[i]);
                if i mod 8 = 0 then writeln
            end
end.
```

Notes on design

1. Essentially n steps are required to generate the frequency histogram for a set of n marks.
2. After i iterations the jth element in the a array will contain an integer representing the number of marks j encountered in the first i marks. This relation holds for all j in the range $0 \leq j \leq 100$ and for all i in the range $1 \leq i \leq n$. On termination, when $i = n$, all array elements will reflect the appropriate marks' counts for the complete set. It follows from the definition of the **for**-loop that both loops terminate.
3. The idea of *indexing by value* is important in many algorithms because of its efficiency.

Applications

Statistical analyses.

Supplementary problems

4.2.1   Modify the algorithm above so that a histogram is obtained only for each ten percentile range (e.g. $0 \rightarrow 10\%$, $11 \rightarrow 20\%$, ...) rather than for each individual mark.

4.2.2   It is required to generate a histogram distribution for a set of daily average temperatures recorded in Antarctica. The temperatures are integer values in the range $-40°C$ to $+5°C$. Design an algorithm to input n such temperatures and produce the appropriate distribution.

4.2.3   Modify the marks algorithm so that the mean and the median mark for the set are obtained. The median mark is that mark for which essentially half the candidates received that mark or some smaller mark.

Algorithm 4.3
FINDING THE MAXIMUM NUMBER IN A SET

Problem

Find the maximum number in a set of n numbers.

Algorithm development

Before we begin to work on the algorithm for finding the maximum we need to have a clear idea of the definition of a maximum. After consideration we can conclude that the maximum is that number which is greater than or equal to all other numbers in the set. This definition accommodates the fact that the maximum may not be unique. It also implies that the maximum is only defined for sets of one or more elements.

To start on the algorithm development for this problem let us examine a particular set of numbers. For example,

8	6	5	15	7	19	21	6	13

After studying this example we can conclude that *all* numbers need to be examined to establish the maximum. A second conclusion is that comparison of the relative magnitude of numbers must be made.

Before proceeding with our algorithm let us consider how we solve the problem in the absence of a computer. When we are given a short list of numbers and asked to find the maximum we simply scan the list and supply the answer. For the list above we will quickly be able to respond that 21 is the maximum. The mechanism we "seem" to apply is to scan the numbers and select one which we "feel" is bigger than the rest. We then rescan the numbers to check the validity of our assumption. If we encounter a larger number we rescan the set comparing the numbers with our new candidate. The process is repeated until we are satisfied with our choice. For short lists this whole process is so fast that we are not usually aware of the details of the mechanism we use.

For longer lists (perhaps of a thousand or more numbers) it is not nearly so easy to apply the strategy we have outlined. Instead we need to simplify and systematize our approach to prevent the problem from becoming beyond our capabilities.

The simplest and most systematic way to examine every item in a list is to start at the beginning of the list and work through, number by number, until the end of the list is reached. It is not going to be enough just to examine each item. At each step a comparison is needed.

Imagine for a moment that we are given the task of finding the maximum among one thousand numbers by having them flashed up on a screen one at a time. This task is close to the problem that must be solved to implement the computer algorithm. When the *first* number appears on the screen we have no way of knowing whether or not it is the maximum. In this situation the best that we can do is write it down as our temporary candidate for the maximum. Having made the decision to write down the first number we must now decide what to do when the second number appears on the screen. Three situations are possible:

1. the second number can be *less* than our temporary candidate for the maximum;

2. the second number can be *equal* to our temporary candidate for the maximum;
3. the second number can be *greater* than our temporary candidate for the maximum.

If situations (1) or (2) apply our temporary candidate for the maximum is still valid and so there is no need to change it. In these circumstances we can simply go ahead and compare the third number with our temporary maximum which we will call *max*.

However, if the second number is *greater* than our temporary maximum, we must cross out our original temporary maximum and write down the second number as the new temporary maximum. We then move on and compare the third number with the new temporary maximum. The whole process will need to continue until all elements in the set have been examined. As larger values are encountered they assume the role of the temporary maximum. At the time when all numbers have been examined the temporary maximum that is written down is the maximum for the complete set. This strategy can form the basis of our computer algorithm.

As with most algorithms we must take care in getting the starting conditions correct. We can use an iterative procedure to examine all the elements in the set (we will assume they are actually in an array). Our initial proposal might therefore be:

1. While all array elements not examined do
    (a) if the current array element > temporary maximum then update the temporary maximum.

When we start out we realize there is a problem with this proposal. There is no temporary maximum at the time when the first element is considered so no valid comparison with the first element can be made. We must therefore look for a way around this problem. Remembering back to our numbers-on-a-screen example we see that when the first number appeared we immediately, without comparison, considered it as the temporary maximum. We can apply the same idea to our algorithm by initially setting the temporary maximum variable *max* to the first array element. This corresponds to solving the *smallest* problem. All other elements can be examined iteratively and comparisons can be made with a valid temporary maximum. With these modifications to our initial approach we have the essentials for our maximum-finding algorithm.

Algorithm description

1. Establish an array $a[1..n]$ of n elements where $n \geqslant 1$.
2. Set temporary maximum *max* to first array element.

3. While less than n array elements have been considered do
   (a) if next element greater than current maximum *max* then
       assign it to *max*.
4. Return maximum *max* for the array of n elements.

This algorithm can be implemented as a function that accepts as input an array of length n and returns as output *max*, the maximum value in the array of n numbers.

Pascal implementation

```
function amax (a: nelements; n: integer): real;
var i {array index}: integer;
    max {current maximum}: real;

begin {find the maximum in an array of n numbers}
  {assert: n>0}
  i := 1;
  max := a[i];
  {invariant: max is maximum in a[1..i]∧i=<n}
  for i := 2 to n do
    if a[i]>max then max := a[i];
  {assert: max is maximum in a[1..n]}
  amax := max
end
```

Notes on design

1. The number of comparisons needed to find the maximum in an array of n elements is $n-1$.
2. For all i in the range $1 \leqslant i \leqslant n$ when i elements have been examined the variable *max* is greater than or equal to all elements in the range 1 to i. This relation remains invariant throughout the computation. On termination when $i = n$ the variable *max* contains the maximum value for the complete set. The algorithm will terminate because with each iteration the variable i is incremented by 1 and so eventually the condition when $i = n$ is reached. The algorithm will function correctly for values of $n \geqslant 1$.
3. A way of establishing the initializing step is to consider the smallest possible problem that can be solved by the algorithm. In this case the smallest problem is that of finding the maximum in an array of one number (i.e. $n = 1$). This problem can only be solved by direct assign-

ment of the *max* variable. With the initial step established larger problems (i.e. $n > 1$) can be solved by iteration.

4. Sometimes algorithms to find the maximum are initialized by setting $max = 0$. Setting *max* initially to any fixed constant is bad programming practice (e.g. the program would fail if all values were negative and *max* was initialized to zero).

5. The generalization of this problem involves finding the kth smallest element in an array. We will consider this problem later.

Applications

Plotting, scaling, sorting.

Supplementary problems

4.3.1   Design an algorithm to find the minimum in an array.

4.3.2   Design an algorithm to find the number of times the maximum occurs in an array of n elements. Only one pass through the array should be made.

4.3.3   Design an algorithm to find the maximum in a set and the position
        (a)   where it first occurs;
        (b)   where it last occurs.

4.3.4   Design an algorithm to find the maximum absolute difference between adjacent pairs of elements in an array of n elements.

4.3.5   Design an algorithm to find the second largest value in an array of n elements.

4.3.6   Find the position of a number x (if it occurs) in an array of n elements.

4.3.7   Design an algorithm for finding the maximum in a set by comparing *each* number with *all* other numbers. Your algorithm should terminate when it finds a number that is greater than or equal to all other numbers. What happens when you look for the most efficient implementation of this method?

4.3.8   Design an algorithm to find the minimum, the maximum, and how many times they both occur in an array of n elements.

4.3.9   The minimum and maximum in an array of size n can be found using $(3/2)n$ comparisons instead of $2n$ comparisons by considering the elements in pairs and comparing the larger element of the pair against the current maximum and the smaller element of the pair against the current minimum. Implement this algorithm.

Algorithm 4.4
REMOVAL OF DUPLICATES FROM AN ORDERED ARRAY

Problem

Remove all duplicates from an ordered array and contract the array accordingly.

Algorithm development

As a starting point for this design let us focus on a specific example so that we have a clear idea of exactly what is required.

```
 1  2  3   4   5   6   7   8   9  10  11  12  13
┌──┬──┬──┬──┬──┬──┬──┬──┬──┬──┬──┬──┬──┐
│ 2│ 2│ 8│15│23│23│23│23│26│29│30│32│32│   Before duplicate removal
└──┴──┴──┴──┴──┴──┴──┴──┴──┴──┴──┴──┴──┘
 . . . . .      . . . . . . . . . . . .          . . . .
```

After a brief examination of the array we will be able to produce the contracted array below:

```
 1  2   3   4   5   6   7   8
┌──┬──┬──┬──┬──┬──┬──┬──┐
│ 2│ 8│15│23│26│29│30│32│   After duplicate removal
└──┴──┴──┴──┴──┴──┴──┴──┘
```

Having seen what our goal is we must now discover a suitable mechanism for the process. Comparing the two arrays we see that all elements, apart from the first, have shifted their positions in the array. In other words, each *unique* element in the original array has been moved as far to the left as possible.

Whatever mechanism we finally decide upon is going to need to be built around the detection of duplicates in the original data. A duplicate pair is identified when two adjacent elements are equal in value. With each comparison, only two situations are possible:

1.   a pair of duplicates has been encountered;
2.   the two elements are different.

It is fairly obvious that these two situations will always need to be treated differently. To try to understand this, consider what happens when the four 23s are encountered.

We have:

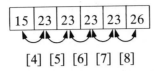

[4] [5] [6] [7] [8]

When the 15 is compared with 23 (step [4]) the 23 is the most recent *unique* element encountered and so it should be moved as far to the left as possible. At the next step, two 23s are compared. Since the 23 has already been accounted for in the previous step, the only action we must take is to move to the next pair. Once again, two 23s are compared and so again all we can do is move to the next step. At step [8] 26 is compared with 23. Here the 26 is the most recently encountered unique element. It must therefore be appropriately relocated in the array.

Study of our example reveals that the position in the array where each most recently encountered unique element must be located is determined at each instance by the number of unique elements met so far. In the case of the 26, it is the fifth unique element and so it must accordingly be placed in position 5. This suggests the use of a counter, the value of which at each instance reflects the number of unique elements encountered to date. If i is the position where the most recently encountered unique element is found and j is the count of the number of unique elements to date, then an assignment of the form:

$$a[j] := a[i]$$

will model the contraction mechanism.

For example, when the 26 is encountered and recorded as the next unique element, we have the configuration below:

			5					9	
2	8	15	23	23	23	23	23	26	...

$$\uparrow_j \qquad\qquad \uparrow_i$$

Summarizing the basic steps so far in our mechanism we have:

while all adjacent pairs of elements have not been compared do
(a)   if they are not equal, shift the rightmost element in the next pair to the array position determined by the current unique element count.

Having established the basic mechanism, we need to work out details of the initialization process. After studying our example, we can conclude that the first array element will always remain untouched. To accommodate the fact that the first two elements may be identical, the comparison process will need to start by comparing the first two elements. To do this we have two initialization choices:

1. $i := 1$
    $a[i] = a[i+1]$?   (comparison)
2. $i := 2$
    $a[i-1] = a[i]$?   (comparison)

When we consider how the algorithm must terminate, we discover that the second alternative is better because it allows the algorithm to terminate directly when i is equal to n, the number of elements in the original array.

We may have noticed in exploring the problem that if there are no duplicates in the array, then the repeated assignment

$$a[j] := a[i]$$

is unnecessary because all elements are already in their correct place. Even if duplicates are present in an array it is only necessary to start shifting elements *after* the first duplicate is encountered. How can these situations best be accommodated? One way is to compare pairs of elements until a duplicate is encountered. For this we can use a loop of the form

while $a[i-1] <> a[i]$ **do** $i := i+1$

When a duplicate is encountered, the unique element count will be $i-1$. The variable j should be set to this value.

There is a problem of termination with this loop if there are no duplicates in the array. The easiest way around this problem is to force the loop to terminate by including the test $i < n$.

We can now describe our algorithm in more detail.

Algorithm description

1. Establish the array $a[1..n]$ of n elements.
2. Set loop index i to 2 to allow correct termination.
3. Compare successive pairs of elements until a duplicate is encountered then set unique element count j.
4. While all pairs have not been examined do
    (a) if next pair not duplicates then
         (a.1) add one to unique element count j,
         (a.2) move later element of pair to array position determined by the unique element count j.

Pascal implementation

```
procedure duplicates (var a: nelements; var n: integer);
var i {at all times i −1 is equal to the number of pairs examined},
    j {current count of the number of unique elements encountered}:
    integer;

begin {deletes duplicates from an ordered array}
    {assert: n >1 ∧elements a[1..n]in non-descending order}
    i := 2;
    while (a[i −1]<>a[i]) and (i <n) do i := i +1;
    if a[i −1]<>a[i] then i := i +1;
    {assert: i >=2∧a[1..i −1]unique ∧in ascending order}
    j := i −1;
    {invariant: after the ith iteration j <=i −1∧i =<n +1∧there are no
    equal adjacent pairs in the set a[1..j]}
    while i <n do
        begin {examine next pair}
            i := i +1;
            if a[i −1]<>a[i] then
                begin {shift latest unique element to unique count position}
                    j := j +1;
                    a[j] := a[i]
                end
        end;
        {assert: there are no equal adjacent pairs in a[1..j]}
    n := j
end
```

Notes on design

1. To delete duplicates from an array of n elements $(n-1)$ comparisons are required. The number of data movements (i.e. $a[j] := a[i]$ instructions) required is at best 0 and at worst $(n-2)$. In general it will be somewhere between these two extremes.

2. At the end of each iteration, the variable j represents the number of unique elements encountered in examining the first $(i-1)$ pairs of elements. The j unique elements encountered are located in the first j locations of the array. On termination when $i = n$ or $n+1$ the value of j will represent the number of unique elements in the original input data. The algorithm will terminate because the variable i advances by one towards n with each iteration. The algorithm will function correctly for values of $n>1$. In the case when all elements are unique the second **while**-loop is not entered.

3. It may be conceptually convenient in this algorithm to think of the original data set as a *source* array and the final data set with duplicates removed as the *target* data set.

4. A specific example is useful in developing the algorithm.
5. Inclusion of the first **while**-loop prevents unnecessary data movement operations.

Applications

Data compression and text processing problems.

Supplementary problems

4.4.1   Remove from an ordered array *all* numbers that occur more than once.

4.4.2   Delete from an ordered array all elements that occur more than k times.

4.4.3   Give an example of an array configuration that will lead to $(n-2)$, data movement operations.

4.4.4   Design an algorithm for storing an ordered array that has many duplicates. It can be assumed there are no negative array elements.

4.4.5   Given a large ordered array that may contain many elements that are multiply occurring (it may be assumed that on average when an element is multiply occurring it will occur many times). Devise an *adaptive* duplicate deletion algorithm that is more efficient than the above algorithm for this particular type of data.

Algorithm 4.5
PARTITIONING AN ARRAY

Problem

Given a randomly ordered array of n elements, partition the elements into two subsets such that elements $\leq x$ are in one subset and elements $>x$ are in the other subset.

Algorithm development

This problem is relevant to some sorting and median finding algorithms. To try to focus on what must be done, we can consider a particular example. Given the random data set below, we are asked to partition it into two subsets, one containing elements ≤ 17 and the other containing elements >17.

a[1]   *a*[10]

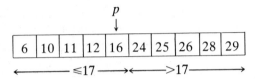

Top end of array

Clearly we need to be able to separate the two subsets. To do this, we could put those elements >17 at the top end (the high suffix end) of the array and those ≤17 at the bottom of the array.

One straightforward way of making this transfer is to sort the array into ascending order. When we do this we get the configuration below.

p

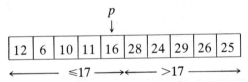

After sorting we can easily find the location that partitions the elements into the two subsets we require.

With this solution to the problem, we have actually *ordered* the two subsets in addition to separating them. In our original statement of the problem it was *not* required that the elements be ordered. For our example the configuration below:

p

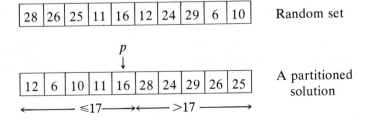

would equally well have satisfied the requirements of the problem. Notice in this data set that while the data is still partitioned into two subsets the elements are no longer ordered. Sorting of data is usually a costly operation. We might therefore suspect that there may be a simpler, less costly solution to the problem than our original proposal.

If sorting does not seem necessary, we might therefore ask what other alternatives do we have? To try to come to terms with this, let us re-examine and compare the original random set and the "unordered" solution to the problem.

| 28 | 26 | 25 | 11 | 16 | 12 | 24 | 29 | 6 | 10 |

Random set

p

| 12 | 6 | 10 | 11 | 16 | 28 | 24 | 29 | 26 | 25 |

←——— ≤17——→←—— >17 ——→

A partitioned solution

Comparing these two data sets, we see that elements at the left-hand end >17 must be moved to the right-hand end of the partitioning point p.

Elements ≤17 that are to the left of p need not be moved because they are already in their proper partition. This saving will result in fewer exchanges being required than in the sort method. When we are initially presented with the random set we do not know how many elements are ≤17. One way to overcome this would be to make a pass through the array counting all values ≤17. Once we know the value of p we can then make another pass through the array. This time when we encounter a value >17 on the left side of p we must move it to the right of p. For example, the 28 could be placed where the 12 is and the 12 could be placed in the 28's original position. This idea can be extended and so we end up with the steps illustrated below.

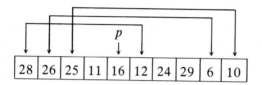

Whenever we encounter a value on the left that must be moved to the right partition, we simply search for the *next* value on the right that has to be moved to the left partition and exchange them. When we reach p by moving from the left all the exchanges needed will have been made.

This proposal is much more efficient than the method involving sorting as now only *two* passes need to be made through the array.

Before settling on this partitioning method we should explore whether or not the partitioning might be possible with just *one* rather than two passes through the data set. In the first pass through the data set, in our most recent proposal, no partitioning or exchanging takes place because we do not know where the two partitions will eventually split.

Studying the random set again more closely we observe that the 28 could *safely* be exchanged with the 10 *without* knowing where the final partition will be. That is,

| 28 | 26 | 25 | 11 | 16 | 12 | 24 | 29 | 6 | 10 |

Similarly the 26 could be exchanged with the 6. What this exploration is starting to suggest is that we can *move in from both ends*. When we do this we are actually "growing" both the left and right partitions towards the middle. That is

Left partition (growing to the right) →		Right partition (growing to the left) ←

If we continue this "pincer" process, the two partitions will eventually meet and when they do we will have the desired partition for our complete data set. Working completely through our example above, we get:

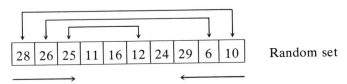

Random set

With these exchanges we end up with the partitioned set below:

$$p \atop \downarrow$$

10	6	12	11	16	25	24	29	26	28

It can be seen that this approach enables us to partition the data by making *just one* pass rather than two passes through the array. We might therefore propose the following basic partitioning mechanism:

while the two partitions have not met do
(a)   extend the left and right partitions inwards exchanging any wrongly placed pairs in the process.

Having worked out the basic mechanism, we must now turn our attention to the details of the algorithm.

The first consideration is to model the "moving inwards" process. Movement inwards from the left can proceed until we encounter an element larger than the partitioning value x (in the above example $x = 17$). This can be accomplished by a loop of the form:

while $a[i] \leqslant x$ **do** $i := i+1$

Movement inwards from the right can proceed until we encounter an element smaller than or equal to x; for this we can use a decreasing loop:

while $a[j] > x$ **do** $j := j-1$

The starting value for i must be 1 and the starting value for j must be n, the number of elements in the array. As soon as both loops have terminated we have detected an element at position i, that must be moved to the right partition, and an element at j, that must be moved to the left partition.

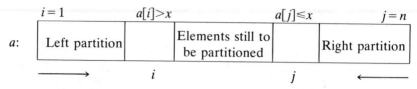

At this point the ith and j^{th} elements can be exchanged. For the exchange we can use the standard technique:

$$t := a[i];$$
$$a[i] := a[j];$$
$$a[j] := t$$

After the exchange we can start the "moving inwards" process again at positions $(i+1)$ and $(j-1)$.

The only other implementation considerations we need to make involve termination of the loops. Only when the two partitions meet do we need to terminate the "pincer" process. That is, the main loop should progress only while the i index is less than the j index. That is,

while $i<j$ do
(a)   move i and j towards each other exchanging any wrongly placed pairs in the process.

Incorporating the ideas for moving inwards and exchanging wrongly placed pairs we get:

```
while i<j do
  begin
    while a[i]≤x do i := i+1;
    while a[j]>x do j := j−1;
    t := a[i];
    a[i] := a[j];
    a[j] := t;
    i := i+1;
    j := j−1
  end
```

With this loop structure we see that because of the way i and j are changed after each exchange, they can cross over when the two partitions meet. It follows that we can end up with the configuration shown below:

1		j	i		n
$a[1..j]\leq x$ ...				... $a[i..n]>x$	

The index j will therefore indicate the upper limit for the left partition. At this point we may feel that the development is complete. However, because there are two loops that can change i and j within our main loop we need to investigate further how any special cases may influence the conditions for termination of all three loops. There are several possible configurations that can apply when the two partitions are about to meet.

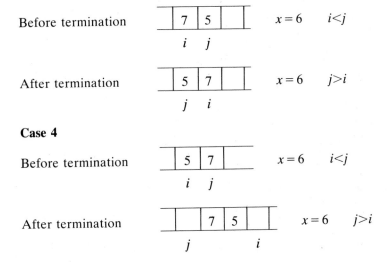

Case 1

Before termination   7 6 5 $x = 6$ $i < j$
                       i j

After termination   5 6 7 $x = 6$ $i = j$
                        i,j

Case 2

Before termination   5 6 7 $x = 6$ $i < j$
                       i j

After termination   5 7 6 $x = 6$ $j < i$
                       j i

There is a problem here because i, and j cross over *before* the last exchange is made. This will lead to incorrect partitioning of the array. We will come back to this problem again when we have looked at the other cases.

Case 3

Before termination   7 5 $x = 6$ $i < j$
                       i j

After termination   5 7 $x = 6$ $j > i$
                       j i

Case 4

Before termination   5 7 $x = 6$ $i < j$
                       i j

After termination   7 5 $x = 6$ $j > i$
                       j i

As in case 2, there are problems in case 4 as i and j can cross over before the last exchange is made.

At this point let us attempt to solve the problem that is raised by cases 2 and 4. Clearly, from our examples, it is only safe to make an exchange when $i \leq j$. One way to prevent the wrong partitioning would therefore be to include the test

> **if** $i \leq j$ **then**
>> "exchange $a[i]$ and $a[j]$"

The problem with this extra test is that it is included to cope with just two special cases. Is there any other way around the problem? Our problem arises in cases 2 and 4 because the elements are already correctly placed *before* the last exchange is made. We already have the condition

$$\textbf{while } i < j \textbf{ do}$$

in our main outer loop but it does not prevent the exchange from taking place. We might therefore ask can it be used to prevent the exchange in cases 2 and 4?

Re-examining the basic mechanism of the main loop we see that the following basic steps are repeated over and over:

1. move towards middle from the left and right;
2. exchange wrongly partitioned pair;
1. move towards middle from left and right;
2. exchange wrongly partitioned pair;
1. ...
2. ...
⋮

If the loop condition were to prevent the exchange it would need to come directly before the exchange. That is,

```
while i<j do
  begin
    t := a[i];
    a[i] := a[j];
    a[j] := t;
    i := i+1;
    j := j-1;
    while a[i]≤x do i := i+1;
    while a[j]>x do j := j-1
  end
```

There is a problem with this because the first time through the main loop we do not know whether $a[i]$ and $a[j]$ should be automatically exchanged since there has been no initial move inwards from the left and right to establish that an exchange is necessary. Again looking at the basic mechanism we see that the easiest and cleanest way around this problem is to take the very first "move towards the middle from the left and right" *outside* the loop as an initializing step and precondition for entering the loop. We then get:

```
while a[i]≤x do i := i+1;
while a[j]>x do j := j−1;
while i<j do
  begin
    t := a[i];
    a[i] := a[j];
    a[j] := t;
    i := i+1;
    j := j−1;
    while a[i]≤x do i := i+1;
    while a[j]>x do j := j−1
  end
```

Re-examining our four test cases again we see that there are no longer any difficulties with crossover. There is still a problem with this implementation because we have not allowed for the fact that x could be either greater than or less than *all* the elements. In both these cases one of the initializing-step loops can cause a reference to an out-of-bounds array location. Our only alternative is to include bounds checks on the i and j indices in the first two loops. They will then become:

```
while (a[i]≤x) and (i<j) do i := i+1;
while (a[j]>x) and (i<j) do j := j−1
```

When x is greater than or equal to all the array values these two loops will terminate with $i=j=n$ and all $a[1..j]≤x$. In the other case where x is less than all the array elements, these two loops will terminate with $i=j=1$. In this case, to be strictly correct j should have the value 0. To cover this case we need to include the following statement:

```
if a[j]>x then j := j−1
```

Our development of the algorithm is now complete.

Algorithm description

1. Establish the array $a[1..n]$ and the partitioning value x.
2. Move the two partitions towards each other until a wrongly placed pair of elements is encountered. Allow for special cases of x being outside the range of array values.

3. While the two partitions have not met or crossed over do
   (a) exchange the wrongly partitioned pair and extend both partitions inwards by one element;
   (b) extend left partition while elements less than or equal to x;
   (c) extend the right partition while elements are greater than x.
4. Return the partitioning index p and the partitioned array.

Pascal implementation

```
procedure xpartition (var a: nelements; n: integer; var p: integer; x:
real);
var i {current upper boundary for values in partition =<x},
    j {current lower boundary for values in partition >x}: integer;
    t {temporary variable for exchange}: real;

begin {partition array into two subsets (1) elements =<x
(2) elements>x}
  {assert: n>0}
  i := 1; j := n; .
  while (i<j) and (a[i]<=x) do i := i+1;
  while (i<j) and (a[j]>x) do j := j−1;
  if a[j]>x then j := j−1;
  {invariant: after the ith iteration a[1..i−1]=<x∧a[j+1..n]>x
  ∧i=<n+1∧j>=0∧i=<j+1}
  while i<j do
    begin {exchange current pair that are in wrong positions}
      t := a[i];
      a[i] := a[j];
      a[j] := t;
      {move inwards past the two exchanged values}
      i := i+1;
      j := j−1;
      {extend lower partition}
      while a[i]<=x do i := i+1;
      {extend upper partition}
      while a[j]>x do j := j−1
    end;
  {assert: a [1..i−1]=<x∧a[j+1..n]>x∧i>j}
  p := j
end
```

Notes on design

1. To partition an array into two subsets at most $(n+2)$ comparisons of the form $a[i] \leqslant x$ and $a[j] > x$ must be made. The number of exchanges required can vary between 0 and $\lfloor n/2 \rfloor$ depending on the distribution of the array elements. If a sorting method had been used for partitioning,

of the order of $n\log_2 n$ (written $O(n\log_2 n)$) comparisons would have been required.

2. After each iteration the first $(i-1)$ elements in the array are $\leq x$ and the last $(n-j)$ elements are $> x$. The variables i and j are increased and decreased respectively in such a way that these two relations hold. The outer **while**-loop will terminate because with each iteration the distance between i and j is decreased by at least 2 because the statements $i := i+1$ and $j := 1$ are executed at least once.

3. In designing an algorithm, do not do more than is required. Sorted partitions are not needed to solve the problem.

4. In the final design the problem is solved by only moving data when it is absolutely necessary. This is a sound algorithm design principle.

5. The final design is superior to the second design because it achieves the partitioning more efficiently without knowledge of the partition location. The lesson from this is do not bother to compute unnecessary information.

6. The idea of working inwards from both ends of the array gives the algorithm balance.

7. If there are a lot of duplicates, some unnecessary exchanges are made.

Applications

Sorting, statistical classification.

Supplementary problems

4.5.1   Another simple but less efficient way to partition the data is to apply the following rules with each iteration:

(a)   if $a[i] \leq x$ then increase i;
(b)   otherwise if $a[j] > x$ then decrease j;
(c)   if neither of the above conditions apply then exchange $a[i]$ and $a[j]$ and increase i and decrease j.

Implement this algorithm. (Ref. J. Reynolds, *The Craft of Programming*, Prentice-Hall, London, 1981, p.126.)

4.5.2   Design an algorithm to extract the subset of values in a randomly ordered array that are within a specific range. What we want is:

values $\leq$	range	values $\geq$

Modify the selection sort (algorithm 5.2) so that it sorts all values less than x. Varying x randomly, compare this algorithm with the partitioning algorithm.

4.5.3   The problem of the Dutch national flag involves starting out with a row of n buckets, i.e. *bucket*$[1..n]$, each bucket containing a single pebble that is either red, white or blue.

The task is to arrange the pebbles so that all reds occur before all whites which in turn occur before all blue pebbles. Design and implement an algorithm to solve the Dutch national flag problem. (See E. W. Dijkstra, *A Discipline of Programming*, Prentice-Hall, Englewood Cliffs, N.J., 1976, p.111.)

Algorithm 4.6
FINDING THE kth SMALLEST ELEMENT

Problem

Given a randomly ordered array of n elements determine the kth smallest element in the set.

Algorithm development

We have already seen an algorithm for finding the largest value in a set. The current problem is a generalization of this problem. As we saw in the partitioning problem (algorithm 4.5), one way to find the kth smallest element would be to simply sort the elements and then pick the kth value. We may, however, suspect that this problem could be treated in a similar fashion to the partitioning problem. In the partitioning problem, we knew in advance the value x about which the array was to be partitioned but we did not know how many values were to be partitioned on either side of x. The current problem represents the complementary situation where we are given how the array is to be partitioned but we do not know in advance the value of x (i.e. the kth smallest value).

The partitioning algorithm can only partition data into two subsets when it has in advance the value about which the two subsets are to be partitioned. The question is, then, how can we apply the partitioning algorithm to the current problem *without* knowing in advance the kth smallest value?

Since we have no idea in advance what the kth smallest value is, we might therefore be tempted to choose a value x at random from the array and partition the array about x. The variables l and u are initially assigned to the bounds of the array. For example,

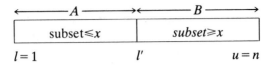

Unless we are very lucky we will not pick the kth smallest value with our random guess. However, the value x will cause the original data set to be divided into two *smaller* subsets. The kth smallest value will have to be in one or the other of these two subsets A and B. If, for example, the kth smallest value is in subset B (i.e. in the subset with elements $\geq x$) then we can completely disregard subset A and start trying to find the kth smallest value in subset B. The easiest way to do this is to replace l by l' and start searching for the kth smallest value again in the smaller subset B. If we repeatedly apply this partitioning process to smaller and smaller subsets that contain the kth smallest value we will eventually obtain the desired result.

The two cases where further processing is required are:

1. k^{th} smallest in subset $\geq x$:

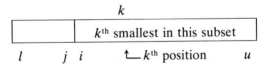

Here we set $l := i$ and repeat the partitioning process for the new limits of l and u.

2. k^{th} smallest in subset $\leq x$:

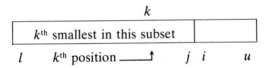

Here we set $u := j$ and repeat the partitioning process for the new limits of u and l. By examining the values of i and j on termination of the partitioning loop we know which subset contains the kth smallest value and hence which limit must be updated. The two tests we can use are

> **if** $j<k$ **then** $l := i$;
> **if** $i>k$ **then** $u := j$

The partitioning process need only continue while $l<u$. The variables i and j will need to be reset to the adjusted limits l and u before beginning each new partitioning phase.

The basic mechanism may therefore take the form:

while $l<u$ do
(a)   choose some value x about which to partition the array,
(b)   partition the array into two partitions marked by i and j,
(c)   update limits using the tests
     if $j<k$ then $l := i$
     if $i>k$ then $u := j$

What we must now decide is how x should be selected. Since the algorithm is designed for random data it should not matter which array element is assigned to x. It is therefore tempting to select as our guess at the kth smallest value the element stored in the kth position simply because it allows the special case of sorted data to be handled most efficiently. What are the implications of this choice? If the partitions do not meet at k (i.e. further partitioning is necessary) then a different value will need to be moved there for selection in the next partitioning pass. Before considering this detail let us consider the partitioning process. The strategy developed in algorithm 4.5 should be applicable (perhaps in some modified form) to the present problem. The difference we may anticipate at this stage is that x will be selected using

$$x := a[k]$$

rather than having x with a given value as in the earlier problem. Unlike in the partitioning problem, because x is selected from the array, we should be able to avoid the complications caused by the fact that it could be outside the bounds of the array. In the "moving-inwards" process the loop

while $a[j]>x$ **do** $j := j-1$

is guaranteed to stop because it must eventually run into x. There is, however, a problem with

while $a[i] = <x$ **do** $i := i+1$

because it will not stop on encountering the array value equal to x. Can we prevent this? The answer is yes, if we change the $\leq$ to a $<$ sign, for example,

while $a[i]<x$ **do** $i := i+1$

What are the implications of this? A careful examination of some examples reveals that it has no serious effect on the partitioning process other than causing array values equal to x to be swapped (perhaps unnecessarily), i.e. we may have values equal to x in either or both partitions after a partitioning pass. This does not present any difficulties with regard to our overall strategy. Furthermore, a side-effect of changing $a[i]\leq x$ to $a[i]<x$ is to guarantee that the value at position k is *moved* with each partitioning pass

that does not result in termination of the algorithm. This fits in nicely with our earlier requirement on the occupancy of $a[k]$. In detail, if the i-loop *passes* the kth position, then a *smaller* value than the current guess (i.e. $x = a[k]$) from the righthand side will be placed in the kth position. The fact that the i-loop has reached the kth position first can only mean that the current k^{th} smallest choice is too large and so it needs to be replaced by a smaller guess. The complementary argument applies if the j-loop reaches the kth position first.

A further examination of the details for updating l and u suggests that changes are needed to handle the case where i and j both reach k in the same pass. The easiest way out of this problem is to allow the loop to make an extra iteration. Filling in the details, and making the modifications we have outlined, the central part of our partitioning algorithm can take the form:

```
while l<u do
  begin {make next partitioning pass}
    i := l; j := u;
    x := a[k];
    while a[i]<x do i := i+1;
    while a[j]>x do j := j−1;
    while i≤j do
      begin {exchange and extend partitions}
        t := a[i];
        a[i] := a[j];
        a[j] := t;
        i := i+1;
        j := j−1;
        while a[i]<x do i := i+1;
        while a[j]>x do j := j+1
      end;
    if j<k then l := i;
    if i>k then u := j
  end
```

At this point we have a useful mechanism for finding the kth smallest element. How well this algorithm performs depends on how lucky we are with our choices of x at each partitioning stage. For example, if x is much too small, we may end up with the two partitions meeting at the far left, a long way from the kth position. For example,

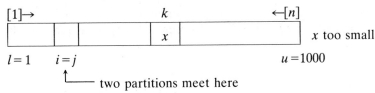

— two partitions meet here

With $n = 1000$, $k = 500$ and if i and j meet at position 20, then with our current choice of x we have only reduced the problem size from $l := 1$, $u = 1000$ to $l = 21$, $u = 1000$. So in effect we have had to pay the price of a large number of comparisons with very little gain or reduction in the problem size. We might therefore ask, is there a way in which we can do anything about having made a bad guess x at the kth value? What we need is a way of being able to detect as soon as possible that we have made a bad guess at the kth smallest value. If we can do this we should be able to cut down on comparisons that are not very fruitful. Studying our diagram above we see that as soon as the j index passes k on its way to meeting up with i we know that our choice of x must have been too small. Similarly, the complementary argument indicates that as soon as i passes k on its way to meeting with j we know that our choice of x must have been too big.

Therefore, in the first case (when i meets j at a position *less* than k) we can *stop* the "pincer" process when $j<k$ rather than when $i>j$. The saving in making this early termination is illustrated in Fig. 4.1. A similar argument can be made for the other case when i meets j at a position *greater* than k. Using this approach we are able to stop making comparisons and exchanges as soon as we have detected that our current choice of x is not the kth smallest value.

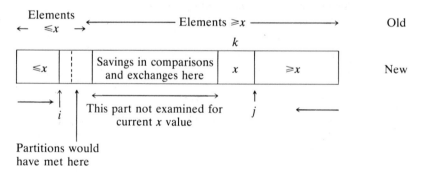

Fig. 4.1   Partitioning with early termination.

To implement this alternative method of termination, we need two tests, one checking whether i has passed k and a second to check whether j has passed k. We can use:

while $(i{\leq}k)$ **and** $(j{\geq}k)$ **do** ...

Once again we must consider what happens in terms of exchanges when one of the partitions reaches the kth position. Using the configuration:

	i	k	j		
...	250	292	300	...	$x = 292$

We are better off this time than with the earlier algorithm because it is no longer possible for the two **while**-loops to cause i and j to cross over *before* the last exchange in the current iteration of the outer partition loop. This is because x is always kept *between* the i and j positions. The conditional test controlling exchanges:

$$\textbf{if } i \leqslant j \textbf{ then } \text{"exchange"}$$

becomes unnecessary. We now, therefore, have a simpler and more efficient algorithm. The detailed description of our final algorithm is given below.

Algorithm description

1. Establish $a[1..n]$ and the requirement that the kth smallest element is sought.
2. While the left and right partitions do not overlap do
    (a) choose $a[k]$ as the current partitioning value x;
    (b) set i to the upper limit l of the left partition;
    (c) set j to the lower limit u of the right partition;
    (d) while i has not advanced beyond k and j is greater than or equal to k do
        (d.1) extend the left partition while $a[i]<x$;
        (d.2) extend the right partition while $x<a[j]$;
        (d.3) exchange $a[i]$ with $a[j]$;
        (d.4) extend i by 1 and reduce j by 1;
    (e) if k^{th} smallest in left partition, update upper limit u of left partition;
    (f) if k^{th} smallest in right partition, update lower limit l of right partition.
3. Return the partitioned array with elements $\leqslant a[k]$ in the first k positions in the array. -

Pascal implementation

```
procedure kselect (var a: nelements; k, n: integer);
var i {temporary extension of left partition for current guess at kth
   smallest element x},
   j {temporary extension of right partition for current guess at kth
   smallest element x},
   l {upper limit for left partition},
   u {lower limit for right partition} integer;
   x {current guess at kth element in array},
   t {temporary variable used to exchange a[i] with a[j] }: real;

begin {finds kth smallest element in array a. on termination kth
   smallest is in position k}
```

```
{assert: n>0∧1=<k=<n}
l := 1;
u := n;
{invariant: all a[1..l−1]=<all a[u+1..n]∧l=<k+1∧k−1=<u}
while l<u do
   begin {using new estimate of kth smallest x try to extend left
   and right partitions}
      i := l;
      j := u;
      x := a[k];
      {invariant: all a[l..i−1]=<all a[j+1..u]∧i=<k+1∧j>=k−1
      ∧1=<k=<n}
      while (i<=k) and (j>=k) do
         begin {extend left and right partitions as far as possible, then
         exchange}
            while a[i]<xdo i := i+1;
            while x<a[j] do j := j−1;
            t := a[i];
            a[i] := a[j];
            a[j] := t;
            i := i+1;
            j := j−1
         end;
      {update limits of left and right positions as required}
      if j<k then l := i;
      if i>k then u := j
   end
   {assert: all a[1..k]=<all a[k..n]}
end
```

Notes on design

1. The algorithm must make at least $(n+1)$ comparisons to find the kth smallest among n elements. This occurs when the kth smallest element has been chosen as the initial partitioning value. In the worst case where a search is made for the median m (i.e. $m=[n+1]\ div\ 2$) and the problem space is reduced by 1 with each pass then $(n/2+1)$ $(n/2+2)/2=(n+2)(n+4)/8$ comparisons are required. This result follows from the summation formula where the sum S_q of $1+2+\cdots+q$ is $S_q = q(q+1)/2$. In the average case (which is rather difficult to analyze) about $3n$ comparisons are required to find the median. For k *very* small relative to n the number of comparisons is on average less than $2n$. In the limit when $k=1$ on average close to $n+1+\log_e n$ comparisons are required. We will not consider the exchanges required here but it should be noted that the final algorithm makes considerably fewer exchanges than the earlier version of the algorithm.

2. The detailed proof of correctness of this algorithm is rather lengthy. We will only summarize the most important details. To do this we need to characterize the behavior of the four variables, l, u, i, and j. After each pass through the outermost **while**-loop, all elements in positions $a[1]$, $a[2]$,... , $a[i-1]$ are less than or equal to x and all elements in positions $a[u+1]$, $a[u+1]$, ... , $a[n]$ are greater than or equal to x. On termination, the elements $a[1]$, $a[2]$, ... , $a[k-1]$ are less than or equal to $x = a[k]$ and elements $a[k+1]$, $a[k+2]$, ... , $a[n]$ are greater than or equal to $x = a[k]$. After each pass through the loop "**while** ($i \le k$) **and** ($j \ge k$) **do**" all elements in positions $a[1]$, $a[2]$, ... , $a[i-1]$ are less than or equal to x and all elements in positions $a[j+1]$, $a[j+2]$, ... , $a[n]$ are greater than or equal to the current $x = a[k]$ value. On termination of the outer loop, $j = k-1$ and $i = k+1$ and the above condition remains invariant. The exchange does not alter the invariant relations for i and j. The innermost **while**-loops terminate because x is in $a[1..n]$ and between $a[i]$ and $a[j]$. The loop "**while** $i \le k$..." terminates because with each iteration i increases towards k by at least 1 and j decreases towards k by at least 1. The outermost **while**-loop terminates because with each iteration either i is incremented by at least 1 and j is decremented by at least 1.

3. We have seen two useful algorithms developed for finding in general the kth smallest element in a random set (and in particular the median of a random set). The final algorithm is better for several reasons. It only persists with a given guess x at the kth smallest element as long as is essential. As soon as it is known x is incorrect, a new x is considered. This idea saves on both exchanges and comparisons (in particular when k is small relative to n). The mechanism is simpler because it is not necessary to guard against making exchanges as in the earlier algorithm.

4. In this problem the strategy of setting out with a large problem and quickly reducing it to smaller and smaller problems is effectively applied.

Applications

Finding the median and finding percentiles.

Supplementary problems

4.6.1   Implement and compare the two algorithms given for varying k values relative to n. For the comparison measure the number of exchanges in each case. Use a random number generator to produce suitable data sets.

4.6.2   For very small values of k relative to n (i.e. for $k<10$ and large n) it is possible to design a more efficient algorithm using the following idea. At *each* stage in the algorithm the *largest element in the first k values* is exchanged with progressively smaller values in the set $a[k+1], a[k+2], \ldots, a[n]$. Design and implement this algorithm and compare it with the algorithm above for very small k relative to n.

4.6.3   If the first k elements in the array are maintained as a heap or a tree data structure, we get a more efficient version of algorithm 4.6.2. Implementation of this algorithm involves some rather sophisticated concepts.

4.6.4   The algorithm we have described can be improved by using a sampling method. The idea is to use say a 1% sample and find the kth smallest as the estimate of x (ref. R. W. Floyd and R. L. Rivest, "Expected time bounds for selection," *Comm. ACM*, **18**, 165–172, 1975). Implement and test this approach.

Algorithm 4.7
LONGEST MONOTONE SUBSEQUENCE

Problem

Given a set of n distinct numbers, find the length of the longest monotone increasing subsequence.

Algorithm development

A monotone increasing subsequence is a subset of numbers which are *strictly increasing* from left to right. This definition does not require that the numbers be adjacent in the original set or that the longest sequence is unique. For example in the set below:

x	x		x	x		x			
1	2	9	4	7	3	11	8	14	6

the sequence 1, 2, 4, 7, 11, 14, is a monotone increasing subsequence. The task at hand is to find the longest such subsequence for a given sequence of integers.

Although it is not too difficult by eye to pick out monotone increasing subsequences, implementation of a systematic procedure seems somewhat more challenging.

To try to make a start on developing an algorithm, let us examine more carefully the subsequence we have selected and its relation to the complete sequence. Our subsequence is again:

$$1 \quad 2 \quad 4 \quad 7 \quad 11 \quad 14$$

In deriving this subsequence we notice that there are many other monotone increasing subsequences present in the data:

$$1 \quad 2 \quad 9$$
$$1 \quad 2$$
$$2 \quad 9$$
$$1 \quad 2 \quad 3 \quad 6$$

Our task in solving this problem involves being able to "recognize" monotone increasing subsequences and, having done so, being able to decide which is the longest. From the subsequences we have examined, we notice that they have no unique starting point and no unique ending point and, also more than one subsequence may start and end at the same point. (For example, we have discovered that two monotone subsequences 1, 2, 9 and 2, 9 end with a 9.) The longest subsequence that can end with 9 is of length 3. Our problem is that we do not know where the longest subsequence ends.

These observations suggest that we will need to have a systematic way of generating and examining subsequences in order to make progress in finding the longest monotone increasing subsequence. We know that the longest subsequence must end with one particular number in the original sequence. At the same time we might suspect that the task of finding the longest subsequence that ends at a particular point might be easier to solve than our original problem. If we can first solve this smaller problem for all possible points of termination (i.e. for the longest subsequences terminating at *each* position in the array), we should be able to select from this set the solution to our original problem.

In order to try to develop an algorithm for finding the longest subsequence terminating at a particular point, we can return to our specific example. Let us suppose that we wish to determine the longest monotone increasing subsequence ending at position 6.

To start with we will write down the lengths of the first five longest subsequences by inspection and then we will try to work out a suitable mechanism.

1	2	3	4	5	6	index
1	2	9	4	7	3	sequence
1	2	3	3	4		sequence lengths

In carrying out these steps we notice that each sequence must be of length *at least* one. Also we see that the subsequence terminating at position 4 (i.e. 1, 2, 4) can only be of length 3. To work this out we had to disregard the 9. From this we can see that there is no point in considering values larger than the terminating value (in this case 4) in determining the length of the longest sequence ending with a 4. Applying this observation to the longest sequence ending at position 6, we determine that this sequence must be:

$$1 \quad 2 \quad 3$$

which is of length 3. This sequence is made up of the subsequence terminating at position 2 and the element in position 6. What this suggests is that to determine the longest subsequence terminating at position 6, we need to examine all the other subsequences terminating before 6 and see if the 3 can be added to the end of these subsequences. For example, we have:

Sequence	Valid/not valid	Old sequence length
1 3	√	1
1 2 3	√	2
1 2 9 3	×	3
1 2 4 3	×	3
1 2 4 7 3	×	4

The subsequences that do not maintain the monotone increasing criterion are marked with crosses.

To implement this process of extending the earlier subsequences we need to have access to the lengths of all preceding subsequences. *The longest new extended subsequence terminating at position 6 must be derived from the longest earlier subsequence to which the element in position 6 can be appended.* The same process can be used to determine the longest subsequence ending in position 7 and so on.

We now have the basis of a method for finding the longest monotone increasing subsequence, that is,

1. For each subsequence termination position do
   (a) append the current element onto the longest of the preceding subsequences that allows the monotone increasing criterion to be maintained.

We will need two loops to implement this process, one to examine each new termination position, and a second to examine all preceding subsequences. A basic structure we can use for an array $a[1..n]$ is:

```
for i := 2 to n do
   begin
   (a)  for j := 1 to i−1 do
```

begin

(a.1)   "find the longest monotone increasing subsequence in the set $a[1..i-1]$ terminated by a value $<a[i]$"

       end

(b)   "append the ith element to the appropriate preceding monotone increasing subsequence and update the maximum subsequence to date as necessary"

     end

The outer loop must start at $i=2$ so that there can always be a valid predecessor. The inner loop must examine all elements that precede the current i^{th} element (i.e. $a[1..i-1]$).

To find the longest monotone increasing subsequence within the inner loop, we need to exclude elements larger than the latest element being considered, $a[i]$. If *last* is set to $a[i]$ this can be achieved by the test:

     if $a[j]<last$ **then**

       "see if length of jth sequence is longest encountered to date"

Another simple conditional test is needed to detect and retain the length of the longest sequence encountered. The append operation simply involves storing the length of the longest monotone increasing subsequence terminating at the ith position. A separate array $b[1..n]$ can be used for this purpose.

We have now worked out essentially all the details of our algorithm. Before proceeding, we should ask is there any way in which we can improve the efficiency of our algorithm? A lot of time is spent in the inner loop going over and over the same set of data. What we need to do is see if there is any way in which we can cut down on the number of steps made in the inner loop. It would seem desirable to examine the preceding subsequences in the order from longest to shortest. The problem with this is that it would probably require sorting the predecessors by length which in itself is a costly operation (see Notes on design).

What other alternatives do we have? Our algorithm, as it stands, does keep track of the longest monotone increasing subsequence encountered to date. Provided we have the position where this longest subsequence terminates, we can test directly to see if the latest element can be appended onto the longest subsequence. If it can, there is no need to go through the inner loop at all. Placing this test before the inner loop will considerably improve the efficiency of our algorithm particularly if the longest monotone increasing subsequence is quite long in relation to the total length of the sequence. In the instance where the sequence to be examined is in ascending order, the algorithm will take of the order of n operations rather than of the order of n^2 operations. In many applications, the longest subsequence will be considerable in size, so this refinement to our algorithm will be very useful. Our algorithm can now be described in detail.

Algorithm description:

1. Establish the data set $a[1..n]$ of n elements.
2. Set initial conditions for subsequence terminating in the first position.
3. For the remaining $(n-1)$ positions in the array do
    (a) if current element less than maximum in the longest previous set then
        (a.1) locate position and value of maximum among the predecessors;
        (a.2) update position and length of maximum if required;
        else update length, position of maximum and the maximum length so far.
4. Return length of longest monotone increasing subsequence.

Pascal implementation

```
procedure monotone (a: nelements; n: integer; var maxlength:
integer);
var
  length: array [1..100] of integer;
  i {index for current terminating subsequence},
  j {index for predecessors of current terminating subsequence},
  maxj {length of current longest predecessor subsequence},
  pmax {position of current longest monotone increasing
  subsequence}: integer;
  current {current element to be appended to appropriate preceding
  subsequence}: real;

begin {find longest monotone increasing subsequence}
  {assert: n>0}
  length [1] := 1;
  pmax := 1;
  maxlength := 1;
  {invariant: after ith iteration length[1..i] are lengths of lmss ending
  at a[1..i]∧1 =<i =<n ∧maxlength =length of lmss in first i
  positions ∧pmax is where it terminates}
  for i := 2 to n do
    begin {append current element to its longest valid predecessor
    subsequence}
      current := a[i];
      if current<a[pmax] then
        begin {search for longest predecessor subsequence}
          maxj := 1;
          {invariant: after jth iteration maxj =length of lmss in a[1..j]
          terminating in a value less than a[i]∧j =<i −1}
          for j := 2 to i −1 do
            begin {reject subsequence with too large a terminator}
              if a[j]<current then
```

```
        begin
          if maxj<length[j] then maxj := length[j]
        end
      end;
      length[i] := maxj + 1;
      if length[i]>maxlength then
        begin {save length and position of longest subsequence
        to date}
          maxlength := maxlength + 1;
          pmax := i
        end
    end
  else
    begin {append directly to longest predecessor}
      maxlength := maxlength + 1;
      length [i] := maxlength;
      pmax := i
    end
end,
{assert: maxlength = length of lmss in a[1..n]∧pmax is where it
terminates}
end
```

Notes on design

1. In the worst case (for a sequence in descending order) the algorithm
    will examine data elements $\frac{1}{2}n(n-1)+n = \frac{1}{2}n(n+1)$ times. In the best
    case when the data is in ascending order, essentially n tests will be made
    on the data. On average the number of tests will fall somewhere
    between these two extremes. The longer the longest monotone increas-
    ing subsequence, the more comparisons the test guarding the inner
    loop will save. In contrast to the final implementation, our first pro-
    posal would always involve examination of $\frac{1}{2}n(n-1)$ data elements.

2. After the ith step in the outer loop the longest subsequences terminat-
    ing with the first i elements will have been determined. Also, after the
    i^{th} step the termination position and length of the longest monotone
    increasing sequence among the first i elements will be established. In
    the inner loop after the jth step, the longest subsequence terminating
    with a value less than $a[i]$ will be established.

3. In the development of this algorithm small specific examples play an
    important role.

4. The idea of breaking a large problem down into a set of smaller simpler
    problems is a valuable strategy in designing algorithms.

5. In this design we have seen how it is always important to try to make
    the best use of a given piece of information (i.e. we have used know-
    ledge of the longest subsequence to date to improve the efficiency of

our algorithm).

6. Because it is more efficient to reference a single variable than an indexed variable, the current term $a[i]$ (which is referenced frequently) has been assigned to a single variable *current*.

7. With an additional n storage elements, it is possible to implement a more efficient algorithm for this problem by linking together all elements with sequences of the same length. We can then easily examine sequences in order from the largest to the smallest.

Applications

Studying random sequences, file comparison.

Supplementary problems

4.7.1 Implement the first design that was proposed for finding the longest monotone increasing subsequence.

4.7.2 Compare the performance of the algorithm in 4.7.1 with the algorithm above for
(a) random data,
(b) data with a long monotone increasing subsequence (say $0.5n$).

4.7.3 Design and implement an algorithm that prints out the longest monotone increasing subsequence for a given set of data.

4.7.4 Design and implement an algorithm that determines the length of the longest monotone (it may be either increasing or decreasing) subsequence.

4.7.5 Design and implement an algorithm that uses the suggestion in note 7.

BIBLIOGRAPHY

Most of the algorithms in this chapter can be found in introductory computing texts.

1. Hoare, C. A. R., "Proof of a program: FIND", *Comm. ACM*, **14**, 39–45, (1971).

Chapter 5
MERGING, SORTING AND SEARCHING

INTRODUCTION

The related activities of sorting, searching and merging are central to many computer applications. Sorting alone has been said to account for more than 30% of all computer time spent.

Sorting and merging provide us with a means of organizing information to facilitate the retrieval of specific data. Searching methods are designed to take advantage of the organization of information and thereby reduce the amount of effort to either locate a particular item or to establish that it is not present in a data set.

Sorting algorithms arrange items in a set according to a predefined ordering relation. The two most common types of data are string information and numerical information. The ordering relation for numeric data simply involves arranging items in sequence from smallest to largest (or vice versa) such that each item is *less than or equal to* its immediate successor. This ordering is referred to as *non-descending order*. The items in the set below have been arranged in non-descending numeric order.

$$\{7, 11, 13, 16, 16, 19, 23\}$$

Sorted string information is generally arranged in standard lexicographical or dictionary order. The following list has been arranged in dictionary order

$$\{a, abacus, above, be, become, beyond\}$$

Because of its economic importance, the problem of sorting has been extensively studied both from theoretical and practical standpoints. As a result, there are numerous algorithms available for sorting information. Sorting algorithms usually fall into one of two classes:

1. The simpler and less sophisticated algorithms are characterized by the fact that they require of the order of n^2 comparisons (i.e. $O(n^2)$) to sort n items.

2. The advanced sorting algorithms take of the order of $n \log_2 n$ (i.e. $O(n \log_2 n)$) comparisons to sort n items of data. Algorithms within this set come close to the optimum possible performance for sorting random data.

It is instructive to compare n^2 and $n \log_2 n$ as a function of n. Table 5.1 makes this comparison for various values of n.

Table 5.1   A comparison of sorting algorithm complexities as a function of n

n	n^2	$n \log_2 n$	$n^2/n \log_2 n$
10	100	33.2	3.01
100	10,000	664.4	15.05
1,000	1,000,000	9,966	100.34
10,000	100,000,000	132,877	752.58

Clearly, as n becomes larger the advanced methods establish their superiority over the simpler methods. The $n^2/n\log_2 n$ ratio emphasizes this difference with increasing n.

The advanced methods gain their superiority because of their ability to exchange values over large distances in the early stages of the sort. It can be shown that, on average, for random data, items need to be moved a distance of about $n/3$. The simpler and less efficient methods tend to only move items over small distances and consequently they end up having to make many more moves before the final ordering is achieved.

No one sorting method is best for all applications. Performances of the various methods depend on parameters like the size of the data set, the degree of relative order already present in the data, the distribution of values of the items, and the amount of information associated with each item. For example, if the data is almost in sorted order, the bubblesort (which is normally the least efficient for random data) can give better performance than one of the advanced methods.

In this chapter we will examine a variety of the simple and more advanced sorting algorithms. We will do this in an attempt to get a better overall picture of the wide variety of techniques that can be used to manipulate data in a computer.

Algorithm 5.1
THE TWO-WAY MERGE

Problem

Merge two arrays of integers, both with their elements in ascending order, into a single ordered array.

Algorithm development

Merging two or more sets of data is a task that is frequently performed in computing. It is simpler than sorting because it is possible to take advantage of the partial order in the data.

Examination of two ordered arrays should help us to discover the essentials of a suitable merging procedure.

Consider the two arrays:

a: | 15 | 18 | 42 | 51 | m elements

b: | 8 | 11 | 16 | 17 | 44 | 58 | 71 | 74 | n elements

A little thought reveals that the merged result should be as indicated below. The origins (array a or b) are written above each element in the c array.

b	b	a	b	b	a	a	b	a	b	b	b
8	11	15	16	17	18	42	44	51	58	71	74

c: $(n+m)$ elements

What can we learn from this example? The most obvious thing we see is that c is longer than either a or b. In fact c must contain a number of elements corresponding to the sum of the elements in a and b (i.e. $n+m$). Another thing that comes from this example is that to construct c it is necessary to examine *all* elements in a and b. The example also indicates that to achieve the merge a mechanism is needed for appropriately selecting elements from a and b. To maintain order in placing elements into c it will be necessary to make comparisons in some way between the elements in a and the elements in b.

To see how this might be done let us consider the smallest merging problem (that of merging two elements).

To merge the two one-element arrays all we need to do is select the smaller of the a and b elements and place it in c. The larger element is then placed into c. Consider the example below:

a: | 15 |

b: | 8 |

The 8 is less than 15 and so it must go into $c[1]$ first. The 15 is then placed in $c[2]$ to give:

c: | 8 | 15 |

We should be able to make a similar start to our larger problem of merging m and n elements. The comparison between $a[1]$ and $b[1]$ allows us to set $c[1]$.

We then have:

| a: | 15 | 18 | 42 | ... |

| b: | 8 | 11 | 16 | ... |

| c: | 8 | ... |

After the 8 has been placed in $c[1]$ we need a way of deciding which element must be placed *next* in the c array. In our two-element merge the 15 was placed next in c. However, with our larger example placing 15 in $c[2]$ will leave the 11 out of order. It follows that to place the next element in c we must compare the *next* element in b (i.e. 11) with the 15 and then place the smaller of these into c.

We can now start to see what is happening. In the general case the next element to be placed into c is always going to be the *smaller* of the first elements in the "*unmerged*" *parts* of arrays a and b.

After the second comparison (i.e. $a[1]<b[2]$?) we have Fig. 5.1(a), and by repeating the process (i.e. comparing $a[1]$ and $b[3]$) we obtain Fig. 5.1(b). To keep track of the start of the "yet-to-be-merged" parts of both the a and b arrays two index pointers i and j will be needed. At the outset they must both have the value 1. As an element is selected from either a or b the appropriate pointer must be incremented by 1. This ensures that i and j are always kept pointing at the respective first elements of the yet-to-be-merged parts of both arrays. The only other pointer needed is one that keeps track of the number of elements placed in the merged array to date. This pointer, denoted k, is simply incremented by 1 with each new element added to the c array.

If we follow the step-by-step merging process that we began above we eventually get to the situation shown in Fig. 5.1(c).

When we run out of elements to be merged in one of the arrays we can no longer make comparisons between elements in the two arrays. We must therefore have a way of detecting when one of the arrays runs out. Which array runs out first depends on the particular data set.

One approach we can take with this problem is to include tests to detect when either array runs out. As soon as this phase of the merge is completed another mechanism takes over which copies the yet-to-be-merged elements into the c array. An overall structure we could use is:

1. while ($i \leqslant m$) and ($j \leqslant n$) do
    (a) compare $a[i]$ and $b[j]$ then merge the smaller member of the pair into c array,
    (b) update appropriate pointers,

2. if $i < m$ then
    (a)   copy rest of a array into c,
    else
    (a') copy rest of b array into c.

A careful study of this proposal reveals that it results in a rather clumsy implementation. It is therefore worthwhile looking to see if there are any simpler alternatives.

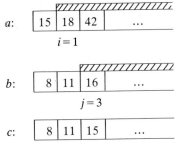

(a)   Merge of first two elements.

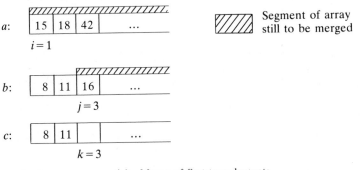

(b)   Merge of first three elements.

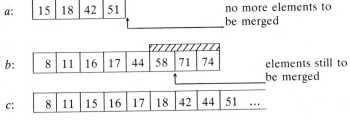

(c)   State of merge after a array exhausted.

Fig. 5.1

A place to start on this new line of attack is with the segment that had to be copied in our example. Studying this we see that the *largest* value from the *a* and *b* arrays ends up as the *last* value to be merged into the *c* array. What does this observation suggest? If for a moment we imagined that the largest value on the end of the *a* array were a 74 then the merge would progress in such a way that completion of *c* would occur when the ends of *both a* and *b* were reached. That is,

a: | 15 | 18 | 42 | 51 | 74 | the largest value in the two arrays

b: | 8 | 11 | 16 | 17 | 44 | 58 | 71 | 74 |

This observation gives us the clue we need to set up a simpler merging mechanism. If we ensure that the largest element in the two arrays is present on the ends of *both* arrays then the last two elements to be merged must be the last element in the *a* array and the last element in the *b* array. With this situation guaranteed we no longer have to worry about which array runs out first. We simply continue the merging process until $(n+m)$ elements have been inserted in the *c* array.

The central part of this implementation could be:

```
if a[m]<b[n] then a[m+1] := b[n] else b[n+1] := a[m];
i := 1;
j := 1;
nm := n+m;
for k := 1 to nm do
  begin {merge next element}
    if a[i]<b[j] then
      begin
        c[k] := a[i];
        i := i+1
      end
    else
      begin
        c[k] := b[j];
        j := j+1
      end
  end
```

This latest proposal although a clean simple implementation can in certain circumstances do considerably more comparisons than are necessary.

In the algorithms above, have we made best use of the information available? Since we have access to the last elements of both arrays it is easy to determine in advance which array will be completed first *in* the merge and which array will need to be copied *after* the merge. With these facts established we should be able to reduce the tests in the **while**-loop from two to one and at the same time cut down on the number of comparisons. A comparison between $a[m]$ and $b[n]$ will establish which array finishes merging first.

We would then have:

> if $a[m] \leq b[n]$ then
> (a)   "merge all of *a* with *b*"
> (b)   "copy rest of *b*"
> else
> (a′)   "merge all of *b* with *a*"
> (b′)   "copy rest of *a*"

A single procedure *mergecopy* can be used to implement these merging and copying steps. The merge and the copying operations can also be implemented as separate procedures. In the merging process it is possible that the two arrays do not overlap. When this happens the *a* and *b* data sets should be copied one after the other. After determining which array finishes merging first it is then a simple matter to determine if there is overlap between the two arrays. A comparison of the *last* element of the array that finishes merging first with the *first* element of the other array will establish whether or not there is overlap. For example if *a* ends first we can use:

> if $a[m] \leq b[1]$ then
> (a)   copy array *a*
> (b)   copy array *b*
> else
> (a′)   merge all of *a* with *b*
> (b′)   copy the rest of *b*

The details of the actual merge are very similar to our second proposal except that now the process only continues until all the *m* values of the *a* array have been merged (when *a* terminates first in the merge). The copying mechanism involves the direct copying from one array to another.

Algorithm description

(1) procedure *merge*

1. Establish the arrays $a[1..m]$ and $b[1..n]$.
2. If last *a* element less than or equal to last *b* element then
   (a)   merge all of *a* with *b*,

(b)   copy rest of *b*,
else
(a')   merge all of *b* with *a*,
(b')   copy rest of *a*.
3.   Return the merged result $c[1..n+m]$.

(2)   procedure *mergecopy*

1.   Establish the arrays $a[1..m]$ and $b[1..n]$ with $a[m] \leq b[n]$.
2.   If last element of *a* less than or equal to first element of *b* then
(a)   copy all of *a* into first *m* elements of *c*,
(b)   copy all of *b* into *c* starting at $m+1$,
else
(a')   merge all of *a* with *b* into *c*,
(b')   copy rest of *b* into *c* starting at position just past where merge finished.

(3)   procedure *shortmerge*

1.   Establish the arrays $a[1..m]$ and $b[1..n]$ with $a[m] \leq b[n]$.
2.   While all of *a* array still not merged do
(a)   if current *a* element less than or equal to current *b* element then
(a.1)   copy current *a* into the current *c* position,
(a.2)   advance pointer to next position in *a* array,
else
(a'.1)   copy current *b* into the current *c* position,
(a'.2)   advance pointer to next position in *b* array;
(b)   advance pointer for *c* array by one.

(4)   procedure *copy*

1.   Establish the arrays $b[1..n]$ and $c[1..n+m]$
and also establish where copying is to begin in *b* (i.e. at *j*)
and where copying is to begin in *c* (i.e. at *k*).
2.   While the end of the *b* array is still not reached do
(a)   copy element from current position in *b* to current position in *c*;
(b)   advance pointer *j* to next position in *b*;
(c)   advance pointer *k* to next position in *c*.

Pascal implementation

```
procedure copy(var b: nelements; var c: npmelements; j,n: integer;
var k: integer);
var i {index for section of b array to be copied}: integer;

begin {copy sequence b[j..n] into merged output}
   {assert: k = k0}
```

{*invariant*: $c[k0]=b[j] \wedge c[k0+1]=b[j+1] \wedge .... c[k-1]=b[i] \wedge 1=<k0$
$\wedge 1=<i=<n \wedge 1=<j=<n \wedge k0=<k=<m+n+1$}
for $i := j$ **to** n **do**
begin
  $c[k] := b[i]$;
  $k := k+1$
end
  {*assert*: $c[k0]=b[j] \wedge c[k0+1]=b[j+1]... \wedge c[k-1]=b[n]$}
end;

procedure *shortmerge*(**var** *a,b*: *nelements*; **var** *c*: *npmelements*; m:
integer; **var** *j,k*: **integer**);
var *i* {*index for the a array that is being merged*}: **integer**;

begin {*merges all of a array with b array elements* <a[m]}
  {*assert*: $m>0 \wedge n>0 \wedge a[1..m]$ *ordered* $\wedge b[1..n]$ *ordered*}
  $i := 1$;
  {*invariant*: *after ith iteration* $a[1..i-1]$ *merged with* $b[1..j-1]$ *and
  stored in* $c[1..k-1]$ *ordered* $\wedge i=<m+1 \wedge j=<n+1 \wedge$
  $k=<m+n+1$}
  while $i<=m$ **do**
    begin
      if $a[i]<=b[j]$ **then**
        begin
          $c[k] := a[i]$;
          $i := i+1$
        end
      else
      begin
        $c[k] := b[j]$;
        $j := j+1$
      end;
      $k := k+1$
    end
    {*assert*: $c[1..k-1]$ *ordered* $\wedge$ *it is made up of only* $a[1..m]$ *and*
    $b[1..j-1]$ *elements* $\wedge k=<m+n+1 \wedge j=<n+1$}
end

procedure *mergecopy*(**var** *a,b*: *nelements*; **var** *c*: *npmelements*; m,n:
integer);
var *i* {*first position in a array*},
  j {*current position in b array*},
  k {*current position in merged array* − *initially* 1}: **integer**;

begin {*merges* $a[1..m]$ *with* $b[1..n]$}
  {*assert*: $m>0 \wedge n>0 \wedge a[1..m]$ *ordered* $\wedge b[1..n]$ *ordered*}
  $i := 1; j := 1; k := 1$;
  if $a[m]<=b[i]$ **then**
    begin {*two sequences do not overlap so copy instead of merge*}
      copy(*a,c,i,m,k*);
      copy(*b,c,j,n,k*)
    end

```
    else
       begin {merge all of a with b then copy rest of b}
          shortmerge(a,b,c,m,j,k);
          copy(b,c,j,n,k)
       end
       {assert: c[1..m +n] ordered ∧it is made up of only a[1..m] and
       b[1..n] elements}
    end


    procedure merge(var a,b: nelements; var c: npmelements; m,n:
    integer);

    begin {merges the arrays a[1..m] and b[1..n] to give c[1..m +n]
    taking advantage of which array is used up first in merge}
       if a[m]<=b[n] then
          mergecopy(a,b,c,m,n)
       else
          mergecopy(b,a,c,n,m)
    end
```

Notes on design

1. For two input arrays of sizes m and n the number of comparisons vary from 2 to $(n+m+1)$ to complete the task. When there is no overlap of the ranges of the two arrays the minimum situation applies.

2. In considering the behavior of this algorithm we will focus on the procedure *shortmerge*. On completion of the ith step of the **while**-loop the first $(i-1)$ elements will have been merged with the first $(j-1)$ elements of the b array. The number of merged elements after the ith step will be $i+j-2$. The first $k-1$ elements after the ith step will be in non-descending order. The loop terminates because with each iteration either i or j is incremented and since it is guaranteed that there exists a j such that $a[m]\leqslant b[j]$ *before shortmerge* is called a condition will eventually be established that i will be incremented beyond m.

3. The final design we have come up with has resulted in a seemingly more complicated implementation than for the two earlier proposals. Although this may be true the actual mechanism for the final algorithm is simpler and cleaner. Furthermore, it uses all the information at hand to the best advantage. Unnecessary comparisons are avoided when the two arrays do not overlap.

4. Consideration of the smallest merging problem gives us a reference point for isolating the basic merging mechanism.

5. The present algorithm is not suitable for merging data sets whose lengths are not known in advance as is often the case when files have to be merged. In that case a modification of the first algorithm must be used.

6. When the sizes of the two data sets are known in advance it is possible
    to use only *two* arrays to complete the merge.

Applications

Sorting, tape sorting, data processing.

Supplementary problems

5.1.1   Implement the first merging algorithm that was developed.

5.1.2   Design and implement a merging algorithm that reads the data sets
        from two files of unknown length. Use end-of-file tests to detect the
        ends of the data sets.

5.1.3   Design and implement a merging algorithm that uses only two
        arrays. It can be assumed that the sizes of the two data sets are
        known in advance. An interesting way to do this is to place the array
        with the biggest element so that it fills up the output (merged) array.
        The following diagram illustrates the idea (the *b* array has the
        largest element).

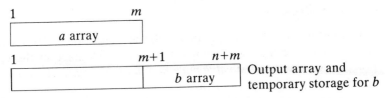

        This simplifies the merge because when the merging of *a* is com-
        pleted the remaining elements of *b* will be in place.

5.1.4   Design an algorithm for merging three arrays.

5.1.5   In the special case where it is necessary to "merge" two files of *m*
        and *n* elements (where $m = 1$ and *n* is large) the problem is best
        solved by binary search. It is also possible to show that conditions
        for merging are "best" when $m = n$. Noting these facts it is possible
        to implement a merging algorithm that couples a binary search with
        a normal merging operation in a way that allows the best features of
        both to be retained. This can be done by imagining that the larger of
        the two data sets is divided up into blocks equal to the size of the
        smaller data set. For example,

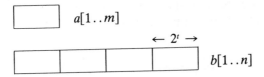

where the blocksize is 2^t and $t = \lfloor \log_2 (n/m) \rfloor$. The merge then starts by moving backwards in steps of size 2^t through $b[1..n]$ until the last element in m is established to be within a given block of size 2^t. The last element of $a[1..m]$ can then be merged with the block in t comparisons using a binary search. The process then repeats for $a[m-1]$. Implement this algorithm. (See F. W. Hwang and S. Lin, "A simple algorithm for merging two disjoint linearly ordered data sets", *SIAM J. Computing*, **1**, 31–39 (1972).)

Algorithm 5.2
SORTING BY SELECTION

Problem

Given a randomly ordered set of n integers, sort them into non-descending order using the selection sort.

Algorithm development

An important idea in sorting of data is to use a selection method to achieve the desired ordering. In its simplest form at each stage in the ordering process, *the next smallest value must be found and placed in order.*
  Consider the unsorted array:

$a[1]\,a[2]\,a[3]$ ... $a[8]$

| 20 | 35 | 18 | 8 | 14 | 41 | 3 | 39 | unsorted array

What we are attempting to do is to develop a mechanism that converts the unsorted array to the ordered configuration below:

$a[1]\,a[2]$ ... $a[8]$

| 3 | 8 | 14 | 18 | 20 | 35 | 39 | 41 | sorted array

Comparing the sorted and unsorted arrays we see that one way to start off the sorting process would be to perform the following two steps:

1. Find the smallest element in the unsorted array;
2. Place the smallest element in position $a[1]$.

| 20 | 35 | 18 | 8 | 14 | 41 | 3 | 39 |

The following construct can be used to find the smallest element:

$min := a[1]$;
for $j := 2$ **to** n **do**
    if $a[j] < min$ **then** $min := a[j]$

Then the assignment below can be used to put the minimum in position $a[1]$.

$$a[1] := min$$

Performing these two steps on the unsorted array we get:

3	35	18	8	14	41	3	39

By applying these two steps we have certainly managed to get the 3 into position $a[1]$ but in doing so we have *lost* the 20 that was there originally. Also we now have two 3s in the array whereas we started out initially with just one. To avoid these problems we will obviously have to proceed somewhat differently. Before placing the 3 in position $a[1]$ we will need to *save* the value (i.e. the 20) that is already there. A simple way to save it would be to store it in a temporary variable (e.g. $t := a[1]$ would save it).

The next question is what can we do with the 20 once the 3 has been stored in position $a[1]$? We need to put it back in the array but the question is, where? If we put it in position 2 we are not much better off because then we need to find a place for the 35. A careful examination of the situation, shown in Fig. 5.2, reveals that we can in fact put it back in the position where we found the smallest value. The 3 still in that position has already been relocated so no information is lost.

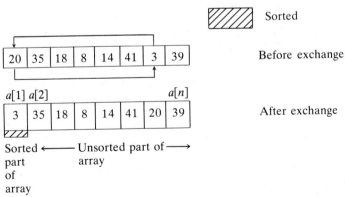

Fig. 5.2 Basic selection and exchange mechanism.

To achieve these two changes we need a mechanism that not only finds the minimum but also remembers the array location where the minimum is currently stored. That is every time the minimum is updated we must save its position. This step can be added to our previous code:

```
min := a[1];
p := 1;
for j := 2 to n do
   if a[j]<min then
      begin
         min := a[j];
         p := j
      end
```

The 20 and the 3 can then be swapped using the following statements (note the 3 is saved in the temporary variable *min*) which will need to be placed *outside* the loop for finding the minimum.

```
a[p] := a[1];      {puts 20 in array position p}
a[1] := min
```

We now have a mechanism that "sorts" one element but what we need is a mechanism that will allow us to sort n elements. The same strategy can be applied to find and place the second smallest element in its proper order. To find the second smallest element we will need to start looking in the array at position 2 because if we start at position 1 we would again find the 3 which would be of no help. The steps we need are therefore:

```
min := a[2];
p := 2;
for j := 3 to n do
   if a[j]<min then ...
```

We can extend this process for finding the 3rd smallest, the 4th smallest, and so on. A conceptually simple way to think about the process is to consider that at each stage the array is divided into an unsorted part and a sorted part. The selection mechanism then involves repeatedly extending the sorted part by one element by finding the next smallest element in the unsorted part of the array and placing it on the end of the sorted array. That is,

while all elements in the array are not yet sorted do

(a)   find the position p, and value $a[p]$, of the smallest element left in the unsorted array;

(b)   exchange the element in $a[p]$ with the element in the *first* position in the unsorted part of the array.

Before actually considering the details of the implementation see Fig. 5.3, where the complete sort for our example is shown.

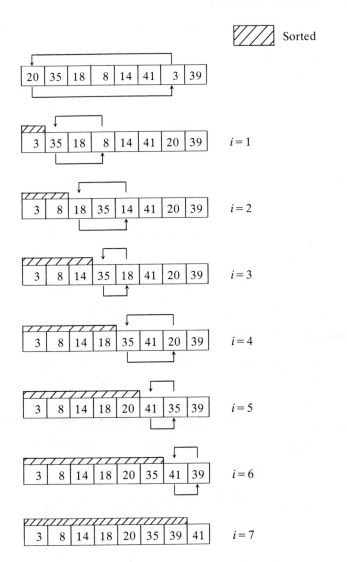

Fig. 5.3 Sorting by the selection method.

Notice that we only need to go through the unsorted part of the array $n-1$ (i.e. in this case 7) times because as soon as $n-1$ elements have been put in order the nth element must by definition be the largest and so by default it must be in order.

To progressively place elements in the sorted array a loop is needed to repeatedly find the smallest element in the remaining unsorted array.

The mechanism we can use for this purpose is:

```
for i = 1 to n−1 do
    begin
        "find and (by exchange) place the iᵗʰ smallest element in order"
    end
```

Our development is now complete.

Algorithm description

1. Establish the array $a[1..n]$ of n elements.
2. While there are still elements in the unsorted part of the array do
   (a) find the minimum *min* and its location p in the unsorted part of the array $a[i..n]$;
   (b) exchange the minimum *min* in the unsorted part of the array with the first element $a[i]$ in the unsorted array.

Pascal implementation

```
procedure selectionsort(var a: nelements; n: integer);
var i {first element in unsorted part of array},
    j {index for unsorted part of array},
    p {position of minimum in unsorted part of array},
    min {current minimum in unsorted part of array}: integer;

begin {sorts array a[1..n] into non-descending order using selection
method}
    {assert: n>0∧i=0}
    {invariant: a[1..i] sorted ∧all a[1..i]=<all a[i+1..n]}
    for i := 1 to n−1 do
        begin {find minimum in unsorted part of array and exchange it
        with a[i]}
            {assert: 1=<i=<n−1∧j=i}
            min := a[i];
            p := i;
            {invariant: min =<all a[i..j]∧i=<n−1∧i=<j=<n
            ∧i=<p=<j ∧min=a[p]}
            for j := i+1 to n do
                if a[j]<min then
                    begin {update current minimum in unsorted part of array}
                        min := a[j];
                        p := j
                    end;
            {assert: min =<all a[i..n]∧min =a[p]}
```

```
        a[p] := a[i];
        a[i] := min
    end
    {assert: a[1..n] sorted in non-descending order ∧ a permutation
    of original data set}
end
```

Notes on design

1. In analyzing the selection sort algorithm there are three parameters that are important: the number of comparisons made, the number of exchanges made, and the number of times the minimum is updated. The first time through the inner loop $n-1$ comparisons are made, the second time $n-2$, the third time $n-3$, and finally 1 comparison is made. The number of comparisons is therefore always:

$$n_c = (n-1)+(n-2)+(n-3)+ \ ... \ +1 = n(n-1)/2$$

(by Gauss' formula)

   The number of exchanges is always $(n-1)$ because it is equal to the number of times the outer loop is executed. Calculation of the number of times the minimum is updated involves a more detailed analysis since it is dependent on the data distribution. On average it can be shown that there are $(n \log_e n + cn)$ updates required for random data.

2. After the ith step of the outer loop the first i values $a[1..i]$ have been placed in non-descending order (i.e. $a[1] \leqslant a[2] \leqslant \ \cdots \ \leqslant a[i]$). Also after the ith step all elements with subscripts $>i$ (i.e. $a[i+1..n]$) are greater than or equal to the first i elements. After the jth step of the inner loop the position p and value min of the smallest element among $a[i..j]$ has been determined. On termination of this loop the position and value of the smallest element among $a[i..n]$ is determined. By definition both for-loops terminate and so the algorithm terminates.

3. Of the simple sorting algorithms the selection sort is one of the best because it keeps to a minimum the number of exchanges made. This can be important if there is a significant amount of data associated with each element.

4. In this design we saw how a complete algorithm is built by first designing an algorithm to solve the simplest problem. Once this is done it can be generalized to provide the complete solution.

5. The number of comparisons required by the selection sort can be reduced by considering elements in pairs and finding the minimum and maximum at the same time. Some care must be taken in implementing this algorithm.

6.   There are more sophisticated and efficient ways of carrying out the selection process. We will examine some of these later.

Applications

Sorting only small amounts of data—much more efficient methods are used for large data sets.

Supplementary problems

5.2.1   Sort an array into descending order.
5.2.2   Implement a selection sort that removes duplicates during the sorting process.
5.2.3   Implement an algorithm that incorporates the idea in note 5, and work out the relative number of comparisons it makes.
5.2.4   Count the number of minimum updates the selection sort requires for sorted, reverse order, and random data.
5.2.5   The selection sort can be modified so that it will terminate as soon as it is established that the data set is sorted. This is done by counting the number of times the minimum is updated in each selection pass. It also involves some other changes. Implement this algorithm.
5.2.6   Implement a function that examines an array and returns the Boolean value *sorted* which is *true* if the array is in non-descending order and *false* otherwise.

Algorithm 5.3
SORTING BY EXCHANGE

Problem

Given a randomly ordered set of n numbers sort them into non-descending order using an exchange method.

Algorithm development

Almost all sorting methods rely on exchanging data to achieve the desired ordering. The method we will now consider relies heavily on an exchange mechanism. Suppose we start out with the following random data set:

$a[1]\,a[2]\;\ldots$ $a[n]$

| 30 | 12 | 18 | 8 | 14 | 41 | 3 | 39 |

With the data as it stands there is very little order present. What we are always looking for in sorting is a way of increasing the order in the array. We notice that the first two elements are "out of order" in the sense that no matter what the final sorted configuration 30 will need to appear *later* than 12. If the 30 and 12 are interchanged we will have in a sense "increased the order" in the data. This leads to the configuration below:

$a[1]\,a[2]\,a[3]$

| 12 | 30 | 18 | 8 | 14 | 41 | 3 | 39 |

After examining the new configuration we see that the order in the data can be increased further by now comparing and swapping the second and third elements. With this new change we get the configuration

| 12 | 18 | 30 | 8 | 14 | 41 | 3 | 39 |

The investigation we have made suggests that the order in the array can be increased using the following steps:

1. For all adjacent pairs in the array do
   (a) if the current pair of elements is not in non-descending order then exchange the two elements.

After applying this idea to all adjacent pairs in our current data set we get the configuration below:

| 12 | 18 | 8 | 14 | 30 | 3 | 39 | 41 |

On studying the mechanism carefully we see that it *guarantees* that the biggest element 41 will be forced into the last position in the array. In effect the last element is at this stage "sorted". The array is still far from being sorted.

If we start at the beginning and apply the same mechanism again we will be able to guarantee that the second biggest value (i.e. 39) will be in the second last position in the array. In the second pass through the array there is no need to involve the last element in comparison of adjacent pairs because it is already in its correct place. By the same reasoning, when a third pass is made through the data the last two elements are in their correct place and so they need not be involved in the comparison–exchange phase.

The repeated exchange method we have been developing guarantees that with each pass through the data one additional element is sorted. Since there are n elements in the data this implies that $(n-1)$ passes (of decreasing length) must be made through the array to complete the sort. It is evident that $(n-1)$ passes rather than n passes are required because by definition once $(n-1)$ values have been sorted the nth value must be in its correct place (in this instance it would be the first element). Combining these observations with our earlier mechanism for comparing and exchanging adjacent pairs the overall structure of our algorithm becomes:

> **for** $i := 1$ **to** $n-1$ **do**
>   **begin**
>   (a)   for all unsorted adjacent pairs do
>   (a.1) if current pair not in non-descending order then
>   exchange the two elements
>   **end**

This mechanism is applied to our original data set in Fig. 5.4.

Our final consideration is to fill in details of inner loop to ensure that it only operates on the "unsorted" part of the array. Adjacent pairs can be compared using a test of the form

$$\textbf{if } a[j] > a[j+1] \textbf{ then } \text{"exchange pair"}$$

Our major concern here is that the index does not intrude into the sorted array. Since the upper limit of the $(j+1)$ index for each pass is directly a function of the number of passes, and hence the i value, the upper limit for the inner loop will need to be $n-i$. A check for the first pass (when $i=1$) confirms this. In this case for the last adjacent pair when $j = n-1$ the index $j+1$ will be equal to n as required. For the complete example we have worked through we see that the array is already sorted by the time i has reached 6.

It is not hard to imagine, because of the nature of this sorting algorithm, that for many data sets the array will be completely ordered well before i reaches $n-1$. Can we take advantage of this? To do this we need some criterion for deciding when the array is completely sorted. To try to work this out let us consider what happens when our algorithm is given an array that is completely sorted. In that case we see that *no exchanges* are made. A relatively easy way to solve our problem is therefore to check whether or not any exchanges have been made in the current pass. If there have been no exchanges, then it follows that all elements in the unsorted part of the array must already be in ascending (or more strictly, non-descending) order. An indicator *sorted* that is set to *true* before the current pass and which is then set to *false* if an exchange is made will do the job. An additional test will then be needed after each pass to see if *sorted* is still *true*. This alters our outermost loop test.

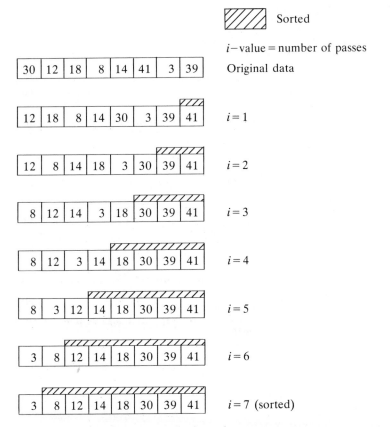

Fig. 5.4   Sorting by exchange.

There are still other refinements that we can make to this algorithm but we will leave these as supplementary problems.

Algorithm description

1. Establish the array $a[1..n]$ of n elements.
2. While the array is still not *sorted* do
   (a) set the order indicator *sorted* to *true*;
   (b) for all adjacent pairs of elements in the unsorted part of the array do
      (b.1) if current adjacent pair not in non-descending order then
         (1.a) exchange the elements of the pair,
         (1.b) set *sorted* to *false*.
3. Return the sorted array.

Pascal implementation

```
procedure bubblesort(var a: nelements; n: integer);
var i {index for number of passes through the array},
    j {index for unsorted part of array},
    t {temporary variable used in exchange}: integer;
    sorted {if true after current pass then array sorted}: boolean;

begin {sorts array a[1..n] into non-descending order by exchange
method}
   {assert: n > 0}
   sorted := false;
   i := 0;
   {invariant: after ith iteration i =< n ∧ a[n − i + 1..n] ordered ∧ all
   a[1..n − i] =< all  a[n − i + 1..n] ∨ (i < n ∧ a[1..n − i] ordered ∧
   a[n − i + 1..n] ordered ∧ all a[1..n − i] =< all a[n − i + 1..n])}
   while (i < n) and (not sorted) do
      begin {make next pass through unsorted part of array}
         sorted := true;
         i := i + 1;
         {invariant: after jth iteration j =< n − i ∧ all a[1..j] =< a[j + 1]}
         for j := 1 to n − i do
            if a[j] > a[j + 1] then
               begin {exchange pair and indicate another pass required}
                  t := a[j];
                  a[j] := a[j + 1];
                  a[j + 1] := t;
                  sorted := false
               end
         {assert: all a[1..n − i] =< a[n − i + 1]}
      end
   {assert: a[1..n] sorted in non-descending order ∧ a permutation
   of original data set}
end
```

Notes on design

1. The relevant parameters for analyzing this algorithm are the number of comparisons and number of exchanges made. The minimum number of comparisons is $(n-1)$ when the data is already sorted. The maximum number of comparisons occur when $(n-1)$ passes are made. In this case $n(n-1)/2$ comparisons are made.

    If the array is already sorted zero exchanges are made. In the worst case there are as many exchanges as there are comparisons, i.e. $n(n-1)/2$ exchanges are required. In the average case $n(n-1)/4$ exchanges are made.

2. After the ith iteration, all $a[n-i+1..n]$ are sorted and all $a[1..n-i]$ are less than or equal to $a[n-i+1]$. In addition, the inner loop may establish that $a[1..n-i]$ are sorted with $i<n$. For the inner loop, after the jth iteration the $a[j+1]$ element will be greater than or equal to all elements in $a[1..j]$. Termination of the **while**-loop is guaranteed because i increases by 1 with each iteration and the **for**-loop must, by definition, always terminate.

3. A weakness of this algorithm is that it relies more heavily on exchanges than most other sorting methods. Since exchanges are relatively time-consuming, this characteristic makes the method very costly for sorting large random data sets. There is, however, one instance where a bubblesort (as it is usually called) can be efficient. If a data set has only a small percentage of elements out of order a bubblesort may require only a small number of exchanges and comparisons.

4. Examination of the intermediate configurations for the sample data set suggests that the algorithm lacks balance and symmetry. While large data elements make rapid progress to the right end of the array small values make only slow progress to the left end of the array (e.g., note the progress of the 3 in the example above). This problem can be alleviated by *alternating* the directions in which passes are made through the data.

Applications

Only for sorting data in which a small percentage of elements are out of order.

Supplementary problems

5.3.1   Use a count of the number of comparisons and exchanges made to compare the selection sort and bubblesort for random data.

5.3.2   Implement a version of the bubblesort that builds up the sorted array from smallest to largest rather than as in the present algorithm.

5.3.3   Design and implement an algorithm that incorporates the suggestion in note 4 above.

5.3.4   Design and implement a modified bubblesort that incorporates exchanges in the reverse direction of fixed length.

5.3.5   Try to design a *less* efficient bubblesort than the present algorithm.

Algorithm 5.4
SORTING BY INSERTION

Problem

Given a randomly ordered set of n numbers sort them into non-descending order using an insertion method.

Algorithm development

Sorting by insertion is one of the more obvious and natural ways to sort information. It approximates quite closely the ordering procedure that card players often use. Central to this algorithm is the idea of building up the complete solution by inserting an element from the unordered part into the current partially ordered solution, extending it by one element. This mechanism is suggestive of a selection sort where we selected the smallest element in the unordered part and placed it on the end of the sorted part. We have:

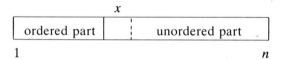

A simple, systematic, and alternative way we could choose the next item to be inserted is to always pick the *first* element in the unordered part (i.e. x in our example). We then need to appropriately insert x into the ordered part and, in the process, extend the ordered section by one element. Diagrammatically what we want to do is illustrated in Fig. 5.5.

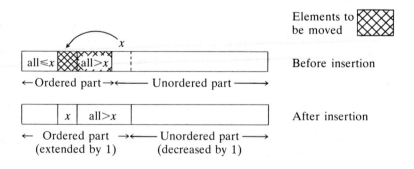

Fig. 5.5   Mechanism for insertion.

Initially the whole array is in an unordered state. For this starting condition x will need to be the second element and $a[1]$ the "ordered part". The ordered part is extended by first inserting the second element, then the third element, and so on. At this stage the outline for our insertion sort algorithm is:

> **for** $i := 2$ **to** n **do**
>   **begin**
>   (a)   choose next element for insertion ($x := a[i]$)
>   (b)   insert x into the ordered part of the array
>   **end**

To make room for x to be inserted all elements greater than x need to be moved up by one place (shaded area in Fig. 5.5). Starting with $j := i$ the following steps will allow us to move backwards through the array and accomplish the task.

> **while** $x < a[j-1]$ **do**
>   **begin**
> $a[j] := a[j-1]$;
> $j := j-1$
>   **end**

As soon as we have established that x is greater than or equal $a[j-1]$ the loop will terminate and we will know that x must be placed in position $a[j]$ to satisfy the non-descending order requirements. There is a problem of termination with this loop when x happens to be less than *all* the elements $a[1..i-1]$. In this instance our loop will cause the suffix $a[0]$ to be referenced. We must therefore protect against this problem. One way around the problem would be to include a check on the j suffix using

> **while** $x < a[j-1]$ **and** $j > 2$ **do**

This is going to mean a more costly test that will have to be executed very frequently. Another approach we can take to terminate the loop correctly is to temporarily place x as a sentinel at either $a[0]$ or $a[1]$ which will force the loop to terminate. This is rather untidy programming. We may therefore ask, is there any other cleaner alternative? Our concern is always that we may want to insert an element that is *smaller* than the element that at each stage occupies position $a[1]$. If the minimum element were in position $a[1]$ we would have no concern about the insertion mechanism terminating. This suggests that the easiest way to overcome our problem is to find the minimum and put it in place *before* starting the insertion process. Once the minimum is put in place the first two elements must be ordered and so we can start by inserting the *third* element. To test our design, Fig. 5.6 shows this mechanism applied to a specific example.

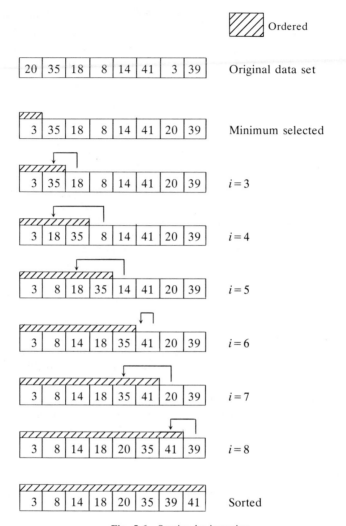

Fig. 5.6 Sorting by insertion.

Our complete algorithm can now be described. There are several ways of improving this basic insertion sort algorithm. These suggestions will be given in the supplementary problems.

Algorithm description

1. Establish the array $a[1..n]$ of n elements.
2. Find the minimum and put it in place to act as sentinel.

3. While there are still elements to be inserted in the ordered part do
    (a) select next element x to be inserted;
    (b) while x is less than preceding element do
         (b.1) move preceding element up one position,
         (b.2) extend search back one element further;
    (c) insert x at current position.

Pascal implementation

```
procedure insertionsort(var a: nelements; n: integer);
var i {increasing index of number of elements ordered at each stage},
    j {decreasing index used in search for insertion position},
    first {smallest element in array},
    p {original position of smallest element},
    x {current element to be inserted}: integer;

begin {sorts array a[1..n] into non-descending order using insertion
method}
   {assert: n>0∧i=1}
   {find minimum to act as sentinal}
   first := a[1]; p := 1;
   for i := 2 to n do
     if a[i]<first then
       begin
         first := a[i];
         p := i
       end;
     a[p] := a[1];
     a[1] := first;
   {invariant: 1=<i=<n∧a[1..i] ordered}
   for i := 3 to n do
     begin {insert ith element — note a[1] is a sentinal}
       x := a[i];
       j := i;
       {invariant: 1=<j=<i∧x=<a[j..i]}
       while x<a[j−1] do
         begin {search for insertion position and move up elements}
           a[j] := a[j−1];
           j := j−1
         end;
       {assert: 1=<j∧x=<a[j+1..i]}
       {insert x in order}
       a[j] := x
     end
   {assert: a[1..n] sorted in non-descending order and a
   permutation of original data}
end
```

Notes on design

1. In analyzing the insertion sort two parameters are important. They are the number of comparisons (i.e. $x<a[j-1]$) made and secondly the number of array elements that need to be moved or shifted. The inner **while**-loop must be executed at least once for each i value. It follows that at least $(2n-3)$ comparisons must be made. At the other extreme at most $(i-1)$ comparisons must be made for each i value. Using the standard summation formula we can show that in the worst case

$$\left(\frac{n^2+n-4}{2}\right)$$

comparisons will be required. Usually the average case behavior is of more interest. Assuming that on average $(i+1)/2$ comparisons are needed before x can be inserted each time it can be shown that

$$\left(\frac{n^2+6n-12}{4}\right)$$

comparisons are required. The performance of the algorithm is therefore $O(n^2)$. Similar arguments can be used to compute the number of move operations.

2. The condition remaining invariant in the outer loop is that after the ith iteration the first i values in the array have been placed in non-descending order (i.e. $a[1] \leqslant a[2] \leqslant \cdots \leqslant a[i]$). After the nth iteration the array is completely sorted. On completion of the iteration with index j of the inner **while**-loop it is established that the subset of elements $a[j..i]$ are all $\geqslant x$ where $1 \leqslant j \leqslant i$. The algorithm functions correctly for all values of $n \geqslant 1$. By definition the **for**-loop will terminate. Termination of the inner loop is guaranteed because the loop index is strictly decreasing and the minimum in $a[1]$ guarantees that the condition $x<a[j-1]$ will eventually be false.

3. The insertion sort is usually regarded as the best of the n^2 algorithms for sorting small random data sets.

4. The design for this algorithm has been arrived at by first working out the mechanism for insertion in an array of size $n=2$. Generalization to larger-sized problems is then straightforward.

5. There is a cleaner way to do an insertion sort that involves a slight increase in loop overhead. This involves searching for the position of insertion from the *beginning* of the array each time. The central part of the insertion sort will then have the form:

$$\vdots$$

```
for i := 2 to n do
    begin {search for x's position then insert it}
        j := 1; x := a[i];
```

```
        while x>a[j] do j := j+1;
        for k := i down to j+1 do a[k] := a[k−1];
        a[j] := x
    end
```

Applications

Where there are relatively small data sets. It is sometimes used for this purpose in the more advanced quicksort algorithm (algorithm 5.6).

Supplementary problems

5.4.1   Compare the selection sort and insertion sort for random data. Use the number of moves and the number of comparisons to make the comparative study.

5.4.2   A small saving can be made with the insertion sort by using a method that does other than selection of the *next* element for insertion. Try to incorporate this suggestion.

5.4.3   A saving on both comparisons and moves can be made by inserting *more than one* element into the ordered part with successive passes. Design such an algorithm that functions by inserting two elements with each pass through the outermost loop.

5.4.4   The algorithm we have produced takes no advantage of the fact the elements in positions $a[1..i]$ are ordered. Use a binary search to speed up the location of the insertion position (see algorithm 5.7).

5.4.5   Modify the insertion sort so that it is more balanced. To do this allow insertions at *both* ends of the array. You may also wish to include an exchange mechanism to speed up the algorithm even further.

5.4.6   The position of the last insertion can be "remembered" and employed when inserting the *next* element. Implement a version of the insertion sort that incorporates this idea.

Algorithm 5.5
SORTING BY DIMINISHING INCREMENT

Problem

Given a randomly ordered set of n numbers sort them into non-descending order using Shell's diminishing increment insertion method.

Algorithm development

A comparison of random and sorted data sets indicates that for an array of size n, elements need to travel on average a distance of about $n/3$ places. This observation suggests that progress towards the final sorted order will be quicker if elements are compared and moved initially over longer rather than shorter distances. This strategy has the effect (on average) of placing each element *closer* to its final position *earlier* in sort. The worst case for this strategy will be when elements are compared and moved over only a distance of one (as in the bubblesort).

We now come to the question of how to implement this idea. A method is needed that initially moves elements over long distances then, as the sort progresses, the distance over which elements are compared and moved is decreased. One strategy for an array of size n is to start by comparing elements over a distance of $n/2$ and then successively over the distances $n/4$, $n/8$, $n/16$, ..., 1.

Consider what happens when the $n/2$ idea is applied to the data set below.

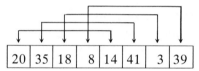

| 20 | 35 | 18 | 8 | 14 | 41 | 3 | 39 | Original data

After comparisons and exchanges over the distance $n/2$ we have $n/2$ chains of length two that are "sorted".

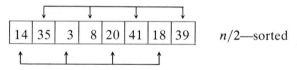

| 14 | 35 | 3 | 8 | 20 | 41 | 18 | 39 | $n/2$—sorted

The next step is to compare elements over a distance $n/4$ and thus produce two sorted chains of length 4.

| 3 | 8 | 14 | 35 | 18 | 39 | 20 | 41 | $n/4$—sorted

Notice that after the $n/4$ sort the "amount of disorder" in the array is relatively small.

The final step is to form a *single* sorted chain of length 8 by comparing and sorting elements distance 1 apart.

| 3 | 8 | 14 | 18 | 20 | 35 | 39 | 41 | $n/8$—sorted

Since the relative disorder in the array is small towards the end of the sort (i.e. when we are $n/8$—sorting in this case) we should choose as our method

for sorting the chains an algorithm that is efficient for sorting partially
ordered data. We have already seen that the insertion sort and bubblesort
are effective for sorting partially ordered data. The insertion sort should be
better because it does not rely so heavily on exchanges. The next question to
ask is will the insertion sort be appropriate in the earlier stages of the sort
where we are concerned with sorting many shorter chains? Since initially the
chains are short we might also expect the insertion sort to work well in these
circumstances.

Our next and most important consideration is to work out how to apply
an insertion sort to the various chains. The overall structure of our algorithm
must allow us to apply insertion sorts over the following distances: $n/2, n/4,$
$n/8, ..., 1$. We can implement this as follows:

> $inc := n;$
> **while** $inc>1$ **do**
> > **begin**
> > (a) $inc := inc$ **div** 2;
> > (b)   "Insertion sort all chains with increment of size inc"
> > **end**

The next steps in the development are to establish first how many chains
are to be sorted for each increment gap and then to work out how to access
the individual chains for insertion sorting. A careful study of our example
reveals that the number of chains to be sorted for each increment size is
always equal to the increment itself (i.e. equal to inc). We can therefore
expand our algorithm to:

> $inc := n;$
> **while** $inc>1$ **do**
> > **begin**
> > (a) $inc := inc$ **div** 2;
> > (b)   **for** $j := 1$ **to** inc **do**
> > > **begin**
> > > "Insertion sort current chain with increment of size
> > > inc"
> > > **end**
> > **end**

Now comes the crucial stage of dovetailing the insertion sort into the
algorithm. (See algorithm 5.4 for a full description of the insertion sort.)

In the standard implementation the first element that we try to insert is
the second element in the array. In the present context for each chain to be
sorted it will need to be the second element in the chain. The position of the
second element k of each of the chains is given by:

$$k := j+inc$$

Successive members of each chain beginning with j can be found using:

$$k := k+inc$$

until k exceeds n, the number of elements in the array.

With these refinements we get:

```
inc := n;
while inc>1
  begin
    inc := inc div 2;
    for j := 1 to inc do
      begin
        k := j+inc;
        while k≤n do
          begin
            x := a[k];
            "Find insertion position current for x"
            a[current] := x;
            k := k+inc
          end
      end
  end
```

A sentinel was used in our earlier implementation of the insertion sort. In the present case we do not have a *single* location (i.e. $a[1]$) where all chains to be sorted terminate. This complicates the issue of trying to use a sentinel to terminate the insertion mechanism. In doing the insertion we must place x (equal to $a[k]$) at its "sorted" position in the chain. Starting with:

$$current := k$$

the first element to be compared with x is at position *previous*, where:

$$previous := current-inc$$

Successively earlier members of the chain can be found using:

$$previous := previous-inc$$

In our earlier algorithm we used the following loop construct to do the insertion:

while $x<a[previous]$ **do**

Because of the problem with sentinels we need another way of terminating this loop. If *previous* is repeatedly decremented by *inc* it will eventually fall below j which marks the *start* of the current chain being insertion-sorted.

Therefore we should only try to do an insertion while:

> $previous \geqslant j$

We may be tempted to write the required condition as:

> **while** $(previous \geqslant j)$ **and** $(x < a[previous])$ **do**

While this seems perfectly reasonable there are problems with such a Pascal implementation because the loop-condition evaluation does not stop as soon as it is discovered the first condition $(previous \geqslant j)$ is not true. As a result it is possible for the test $x < a[previous]$ to be made when *previous* is out of bounds. A way to get around this problem is to place the test in the loop and use a flag (i.e. *inserted*) to indicate whether or not the test $x < a[previous]$ is true or false.

The loop condition then becomes:

> **while** $(previous \geqslant j)$ **and not** $(inserted)$ **do**

Making the actual insertion is then done as in our earlier implementation. At each stage in the iterative process we need to keep track of the *current* and *previous* members of the present sort chain. Each time before *previous* is decreased by *inc* the variable *current* will need to assume its role. This compares with the use of $a[j]$ and $a[j-1]$ in the original insertion sort algorithm. We are now ready to summarize the complete implementation details. The algorithm we have developed is usually referred to as a shellsort after its inventor D. Shell.

Algorithm description

1. Establish the array $a[1..n]$ of n elements.
2. Set the increment size *inc* to n.
3. While the increment size is greater than one do
   - (a) decrease *inc* by a factor of 2;
   - (b) for all the *inc* chains to be sorted at gaps of *inc* do
      - (b.1) determine position k of second member of *current* chain,
      - (b.2) while end of *current* chain not reached do
         - (2.a) use insertion mechanism to put $x = a[k]$ in place,
         - (2.b) move up *current* chain one by increasing k by *inc*.

Pascal implementation

```
procedure shellsort(var a: nelements; n: integer);
var inc {stepsize at which elements are to be sorted},
    current {position in chain where x is finally inserted},
```

```
previous {index of element currently being compared with x},
j {index for lowest element in current chain being sorted},
k {index of current element being inserted},
x {current value to be inserted}: integer;
inserted {is true when insertion can be made}: boolean;

begin {uses a diminishing increment modification to insertion sort}
  {assert: n>0}
  inc := n;
  {invariant: n>=inc>=1 ∧after each iteration all inc chains with
  displacement inc are ordered}
  while inc>1 do
    begin {do insertion sorts with diminishing increments}
      inc := inc div 2;
      {invariant: 1=<j=<inc ∧after jth iteration first j chains with
      displacement inc are ordered}
      for j := 1 to inc do
        begin {sort all chains for current interval inc}
          k := j+inc;
          {invariant: 1=<j=<inc ∧1=<inc=<n ∧k=<n
          ∧a[j]=<a[j+inc]=<a[j+2*inc]=<....=<a[k-inc]}
          while k<=n do
            begin {step through all members of current chain}
              inserted := false;
              x := a[k];
              current := k;
              previous := current-inc;
              {invariant: j<current=<k ∧x<a[current]
              =<a[current+inc] =<...=<a[k]}
              while (previous>=j) and (not inserted) do
                begin {locate position and perform insertion of x}
                  if x<a[previous] then
                    begin {move chain member up one position}
                      a[current] := a[previous];
                      current := previous;
                      previous := previous - inc
                    end
                  else
                    inserted := true
                end;
              {assert: x=<a[current+inc] =<a[current+2*inc]
              =<...=<a[k]}
              a[current] := x;
              k := k+inc
            end
        end
    end
  {assert: a[1..n] sorted in non-descending order ∧ a permutation
  of original data set}
end
```

Notes on design

1. The analysis of shellsort has proven to be a very difficult problem. It can be shown that there are better choices of the decrement sequence than $n/2, n/4, n/8, \ldots, 1$. For the sequence of decrements, $2^p - 1, \ldots,$ 31, 15, 7, 3, 1 the number of comparisons and moves is proportional to $n^{1.2}$. This is obviously clearly superior to the earlier sorting methods we have considered. At the same time it is not as good as the advanced sorting methods that require of the order of $n \log_2 n$ comparisons.

2. The condition remaining invariant for the outermost **while**-loop of shellsort is that after each iteration all chains (there are *inc* of them at each stage) whose elements are separated by *inc* places have been insertion sorted. After the jth step of the next inner **for**-loop the first j chains (with increments of *inc*) have been insertion sorted. For the next inner **while**-loop (i.e. **while** $k \le n$) after the iteration involving k the element at position k has been ordered appropriately in its chain. With the innermost **while**-loop after the iteration involving the index *previous* it is either established that the current element can be inserted in position *current* or that all elements in the *current* chain including $a[previous]$ are greater than x. All these elements have been moved one position in preparation for the eventual insertion of x in the chain.

   The outer loop eventually terminates because *inc* is reduced by a factor of 2 with each pass. By definition the **for**-loop terminates. The **while**-loop for stepping through the *current* chain terminates because k is increased by *inc* with each pass. Finally, the innermost **while**-loop will terminate because *previous* is reduced by *inc* with each pass.

3. In this design an attempt has been made to move elements further earlier on in the sort in order to end up with a faster overall algorithm.

4. The development of this algorithm is slightly more complex than other sorts we have seen. As an example it brings home the importance of good clean top-down design.

Applications

Works well on sorting large data sets but there are more advanced methods with even better performance.

Supplementary problems

5.5.1 Use a measure of comparisons and moves to compare the shellsort with a standard insertion sort. Use random data for the test.

5.5.2   Compare the performance of shellsort implementations that use respectively the sequence of decrements $n/2$, $n/4$, $n/8$, ..., 1 and 2^p-1, ..., 31, 15, 7, 3, 1. Use random data sets and use the number of comparisons and moves as a measure.

5.5.3   Implement a version of shellsort that incorporates a bubblesort in place of the insertion sort. Compare the performance of this implementation with that of the algorithm that incorporates an insertion sort.

5.5.4   Design an algorithm that compares a random and sorted array and establishes the average distance that elements must travel in moving from random to sorted order.

5.5.5   Modify the shellsort so that the test "*previous*≥*j*" is not needed in the innermost **while**-loop.

5.5.6   A cleaner version of shellsort can be obtained by altering the end from which the insertion is made at each step. This involves a slight modification of the idea suggested in note 5 of algorithm 5.4. Incorporate this idea into shellsort.

Algorithm 5.6
SORTING BY PARTITIONING

Problem

Given a randomly ordered set of n numbers, sort them into non-descending order using Hoare's partitioning method.

Algorithm development

The shellsort algorithm introduced us to the idea that data must be moved over large distances in the early stages of a sort if it is to be an efficient algorithm. There is a simpler and more effective way of doing this than the strategy employed in shellsort (algorithm 5.5). Discovering a simpler and more powerful mechanism is probably something that would elude many of us even knowing that it existed. Let us, however, attempt the creative step by considering the sort of questions that we could ask that may lead us in the right direction.

Our initial response to the idea of moving data over long distances might be to ask what is the *maximum* distance over which we can move data? The answer to this question is that we could exchange the first and the last elements if they were out of order. Similarly, we could then exchange the second, and second last elements if they were out of order, and so on.

Applying this mechanism to the unsorted array listed below:

| 20 | 35 | 18 | 8 | 14 | 41 | 3 | 39 |

Unsorted array

we end up with the new configuration:

| 20 | 3 | 18 | 8 | 14 | 41 | 35 | 39 |

Having made this first pass through the array we must now ask, how next to proceed? The first pass has provided us with a set of ordered pairs. One way to proceed might be to try to extend these pairs into larger ordered segments. Exploring this idea we find that it comes down to a merging operation and so loses the characteristic of exchanging data over large distances. Moving in from both ends at first sight seems like a good idea but simply exchanging pairs when they are out of order is not much help. What appears to be wrong with this strategy is that we have not reduced the size of the problem to be solved in any easily recognizable way. We therefore have two alternatives, we can either change the way in which we process the elements, or we can change the criterion used to exchange pairs of elements. If we decided to pursue the latter course we will need to find an alternative criterion for swapping pairs of elements. What other criteria are there? This seems to be a hard problem to decide abstractly so let us refer back to our original data set to see if we can find any clues there.

Examining the data set carefully, we see that when the first and last elements are compared (i.e. the 20 and the 39) no exchange takes place. However, the 20 is the third largest element and so it should really be moved to the righthand end of the array as quickly as possible. There would be no point in exchanging the 20 with the 39 but it would make a lot of sense to exchange the 20 with the small value 3 in the seventh position in the array. What does this approach suggest? It has led us to the idea that it is probably a good strategy to move the big elements to the righthand end as quickly as possible and at the same time to move the smaller elements to the lefthand end of the array. Our problem is then to decide which elements are *big* and which elements are *small* in the general case. Reflecting for a moment we realize that this problem does not have a general solution—we seem to be stuck! The only possibility left is to take a *guess* at the element that might allow us to distinguish between the big and the small elements. Ideally, after the first pass through the data, we would like to have *all* big elements in the right half of the array and all small elements in the left half of the array. This amounts to *partitioning* the array into two subsets. For example,

Partition of all "small" elements	Partition of all "large" elements

We must now decide how to achieve this partitioning process. Following our earlier discussion, the only possibility is to use an element from the array. This raises the question, is partitioning the array compatible with exchanging data over large distances in the early stages of the sort? To try to answer this question, as a test case we can choose 18 as the partitioning value, since it is the fourth largest of the eight values. Carrying out this step the first thing we discover is that 20 should be in the partition for larger elements rather than in the partition for smaller elements. That is,

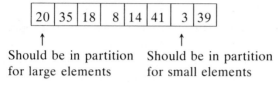

If 20 is in the wrong partition it implies that there must be a small element that is wrongly placed in the other partition. To make progress in partitioning the array, we need to place 20 in the partition for larger elements. The only satisfactory way to do this is to "make room" for it in the partition of larger elements by finding a "small" element in that partition and exchanging the pair. The 3 in position 7 is a candidate for this transfer of data. If we move into the array from the right looking for small elements, and in from the left looking for large elements (where large and small are relative to 18), we will have a way of partitioning the array, and, at the same time, exchanging data over large distances as we had originally set out to do. At this point we may recognize that the first partitioning method considered in the discussion of algorithm 4.6 can be easily adapted to the present situation. Recapitulating, the basic steps in the partitioning algorithm were:

1. Extend the two partitions inwards until a wrongly partitioned pair is encountered.
2. While the two partitions have not crossed
    (a)   exchange the wrongly partitioned pair;
    (b)   extend the two partitions inwards again until another wrongly partitioned pair is encountered.

Applying this idea to the sample data set given above we get:

| 3 | 14 | 8 | 18 | 35 | 41 | 20 | 39 |

↑   ↑   ↑

Partition for   Partition for
smaller elements   larger elements
all ≤18   all ≥18

The partitioning method discussed in algorithm 4.6 can take as many as $n+2$ comparisons to partition n elements. This can be improved by replacing the loop test $i \leq j$ by the test $i < j-1$. For this new implementation, when termination occurs with $i = j-1$ it is then necessary to perform an extra exchange outside the loop.

Unlike our earlier proposal, the smaller elements are now completely separated from the larger elements. How can this result be exploited? We now have *two* partitions whose values can be treated independently. That is, if we sort the first three values and then later sort the last five values, the whole array will be completely ordered. In sorting these two partitions, we want to again try to adhere to the idea of exchanging data over large distances. Since the two partitions are independent, we can treat them as two smaller problems that can be solved in a manner similar to the original problem. Although for small data sets (like the one we have been considering) this looks clumsy, we can imagine that for much larger sets it will provide an efficient way of transferring data over large distances.

What we must now establish is how this partitioning idea and transferring of data over large distances fits in with our goal for sorting the data. To investigate this relationship, we can again apply the partitioning process to the two partitions derived from the original data set. To make it easier to understand the mechanism we can consider a choice of partitioning elements that allows us to divide the two partitions in half. (That is, we can choose 8 for the left partition and 35 for the right partition.) When the partitioning mechanism is applied to these partitions with 8 and 35 as the partitioning elements we get:

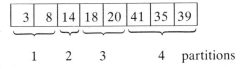

Notice that from this example that an exchange should be made when we encounter elements greater than or equal to our partitioning value. We will come back to this later.

Examining the results of these latest partitioning steps, we see that there are now four partitions. We notice that these partitions are *partially ordered* (i.e. the elements in the first partition are smaller than the elements in the second partition which are in turn smaller than the elements in the third partition and so on. If the partitions of size 2 and 3 are again trivially partitioned it will result in the array being sorted. What we have learned from this consideration is that repeated partitioning gives us a way of moving data over long distances and, at the same time, when the process is taken to the limit, it leads to the complete data set being sorted. We have therefore discovered that repeated partitioning can be used for sorting. Our task now is to work out how to implement this mechanism. Before doing this we can summarize our progress with the algorithm. The basic mechanism we have evolved is:

while all partitions not reduced to size one do
(a)   choose next partition to be processed;
(b)   select a new partitioning value from the current partition;
(c)   partition the current partition into two smaller partially ordered sets.

There are two major issues that must now be resolved. Firstly, we must find a suitable method for selecting the partitioning values. Our earlier discussion led us to the conclusion that the best we would be able to do was "guess" a suitable partitioning value. On average, if the data is random, we may expect that this approach will give reasonable results. The simplest strategy for selecting the partitioning value is to always use the first value in the partition. A little thought reveals that this choice will be a poor one when the data is already sorted and when it is in reverse order. The best way to accommodate these cases is to use the value in the *middle* of the partition. This strategy will not alter the performance for random data but it will result in much better performance for the more common special cases we have mentioned. If *lower* and *upper* specify the array limits for a given partition then the index *middle* for the middle element can be computed by averaging the two limits (see algorithm 5.7):

$$middle := (lower + upper) \textbf{ div } 2$$

In our earlier example we saw how the original data was divided initially into *two* partitions that needed to be processed further. Because only one partition at a time can be considered for further partitioning, it will be necessary to *save* information on the bounds of the other partition so that it can be partitioned later. For example,

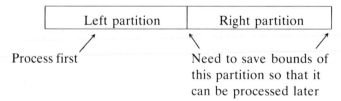

Further consideration of the repeated partitioning mechanism suggests that we will have to save the bounds for a large number (rather than just one) of the partitions as the process extends to smaller and smaller partitions. The easiest way to do this is to store these in an array (it really functions as a stack—see Chapter 7). This raises the question of how much extra storage needs to be allocated for this array. To answer this we will need to look at the worst possible partitioning situation. In the worst case, we could end up with *only one* element in the smaller partition each time. This situation would result in the need to store the bounds for $n-1$ partitions if we were sorting n elements. The associated cost would be $2(n-1)$ array locations. To ensure that our algorithm will handle all cases correctly, it seems that we will need to include the $2(n-1)$ extra locations. This is a costly increase in storage and so we should see if there is any way of reducing it. To do this we will need to take a closer look at the worst case situation where we have assumed that the bounds for partitions of size 1 must be stored away each time. That is,

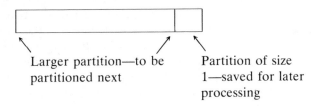

Larger partition—to be   Partition of size
partitioned next   1—saved for later
                                processing

The problem arises here because we always (unknowingly) keep selecting the larger partition to be processed next. If instead for this case we could *control* the situation so that the *smaller* partition was processed next, then only two locations would be needed to save the larger partition bounds for later processing. This improvement comes about because "partitioning" the partition of size 1 leads to no extra partitions being generated *before* the larger partition is again processed. With this strategy, the situation above is no longer the worst case. The worst case will now apply when the "biggest" smaller partition is processed next at each stage. The biggest smaller partition is *half* the size of the current partition. If we start out with an array of size n to be sorted, it can be halved $\log_2 n$ times before a partition of size 1 is reached. Therefore, if we adopt the strategy of always processing the smaller partition next we will only need additional storage proportional to $\log_2 n$. This is much more acceptable even for very large n. (That is, we will only need about twenty locations of partition storage to process an array of 2000.) A simple test that determines where the partitions meet relative to the middle can decide which is the larger partition. That is,

if partitions meet to the left of the middle then
    "process left partition and save right's limits"
else
    "process right partition and save left's limits"

We can now again summarize the steps in our algorithm and incorporate the details of the refinements we have just made.

while all partitions have not been reduced to size 1 do
(a)   choose the smaller partition to be processed next;
(b)   select the element in the middle of the partition as the partitioning
      value;
(c)   partition the current partition into two partially ordered sets;
(d)   save the larger of the partitions from step (c) for later processing.

At this point in our development, the thing that is not very clear is how the
algorithm is going to terminate. In our earlier discussion we established that
when the partitioning process is repeatedly applied, we eventually end up
with a single element to be "partitioned". In concert with this process of
reducing the partition size to 1, the larger of the two partitions is being
"stacked" away for *later* processing. Figure 5.7 illustrates the partitioning
mechanism and the "stacking away" of the larger partition in each case.

     When a partition of size 1 has been reached we have no alternative
other than to start the partitioning process on the partition that has most
recently been stored away. To do this we must *remove* its limits from the top
of the stack.

     For our example it will require that segment $h..c$ is partitioned next.
Our task is to ensure that *all* partitions have been reduced to size 1. When all
partitions have been reduced to size 1 there will be no limits left on the stack
for further processing. We can use this condition to terminate the repeated
partitioning mechanism. The mechanism can start with the limits for the
complete array on the stack. We then proceed with repeated partitioning
until the stack is empty. This can be signalled by maintaining a pointer to the
"top-of-the-stack". When this array index is zero it will indicate that all
partitions have been reduced to size 1. We will see later (algorithm 8.2) in
the recursive implementation of quicksort how Pascal implicitly and automatically implements the stack mechanism.

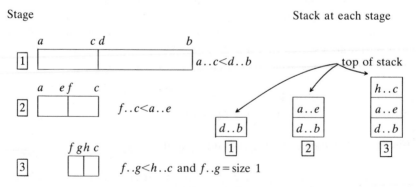

Fig. 5.7   Stack mechanism to save partition limits for later processing.

We have now explored the problem sufficiently to be able to provide a detailed description of the algorithm. Details of the partitioning mechanism follow from algorithm 4.6.

Algorithm description

1. Establish array $a[1..n]$ to be sorted.
2. Place upper and lower limits for array on the stack and initialize pointer to top of stack.
3. While stack is not empty do
   (a) remove upper and lower limits of array segment from top of stack;
   (b) while current segment not reduced to size 1 do
       (b.1) select middle element of array segment from stack;
       (b.2) partition the current segment into two with respect to the current middle value;[†]
       (b.3) save the limits of the larger partition on the stack of later processing and do setup to process the smaller partition next if it contains more than one element.

Pascal implementation

```
procedure quicksort(var a: nelements; n,stacksize: integer);
var left {upper limit of left partition a[1..left]},
    right {lower limit of right partition a[right..n]},
    newleft {upper limit of extended left partition},
    newright {lower limit of extended right partition},
    middle {middle index of current partition},
    mguess {current guess at median},
    temp {temporary variable used for exchange},
    stacktop {current top of stack}: integer;
    stack: array[1..100] of integer;

begin {sort by repeated partitioning of smallest available partition}
    {assert: n>0}
    stacktop := 2;
    stack[1] := 1;
    stack[2] := n;
    {invariant: 1 =<i,p ∧l,s =<n ∧for all unsorted partitions defined on
    stack for which j<k we have all a[1..j]=<all a[k..l]∧for all ordered
    partitions currently in array for which p <r we have all a[p..q]
    =<a[r..s]∧stacktop >=0}
```

---

† A detailed treatment of the partitioning mechanism has been given previously in the text and in the discussion for algorithm 4.6. For reasons of efficiency the partitioning procedure has been included directly into the quicksort algorithm rather than via a procedure call.

```
while stacktop > 0 do
   begin {partition until all partitions reduced to size one}
      right := stack[stacktop];
      left := stack[stacktop - 1];
      stacktop := stacktop - 2;
      {invariant: all a[stack[stacktop - 1]..left - 1 = < all a[left..right]
      = < all a[right + 1..stack[stacktop]] ∧ left = < right ∧ limits for first
      and third positions all stacked}

   while left < right do
      begin {partition the current segment according to mguess}
         newleft := left;
         newright := right;
         middle := (left + right) div 2;
         mguess := a[middle];
         while a[newleft] < mguess do newleft := newleft + 1;
         while mguess < a[newright] do newright := newright - 1;
         {invariant: all a[left..newleft - 1] = < all a[newright + 1..right]}
         while newleft < newright - 1 do
            begin {exchange wrongly partitioned pair and then extend
            both segments}
               temp := a[newleft];
               a[newleft] := a[newright];
               a[newright] := temp;
               newleft := newleft + 1;
            newright := newright - 1;
               while a[newleft] < mguess do newleft := newleft + 1;
               while mguess < a[newright] do newright := newright
            end;
         if newleft <= newright then
         begin {allow for case where two partitions do not
         cross-over}
            if newleft < newright then
               begin {exchange}
                  temp := a[newleft];
                  a[newleft] := a[newright];
                  a[newright] := temp
               end;
            newleft := newleft + 1;
            newright := newright - 1
         end;
         if newright < middle then
            begin {set up to process smaller left partition next}
               stack[stacktop + 1] := newleft;
               stacktop := stacktop + 2;
               stack[stacktop] := right;
               right := newright
            end
         else
            begin {set up to process smaller right partition next}
```

```
                    stack[stacktop + 1] := left;
                    stacktop := stacktop + 2;
                    stack[stacktop] := newright;
                    left := newleft
                  end
            end
         end
         {assert: a[1..n] sorted in non-descending order ∧ a permutation of
         the original data set}
      end
```

Notes on design

1. The quicksort algorithm is recognized as probably the most efficient of
    the internal sorting algorithms. It gains its efficiency by keeping the
    number of data movement operations small. Detailed analysis of the
    algorithm shows that the comparison step dominates. In the average
    case, of the order of $n \log_2 n$ comparisons are made for an array of n
    elements. The worst case, where the largest (or smallest) element is
    always selected as the partitioning value, results in of the order of n^2
    comparisons.

2. For the partitioning part of the implementation, after each iteration
    we have that $a[left..newleft-1] \leqslant mguess$ and $a[newright+1..$
    $right] \geqslant mguess$. With each pass through the "**while** $left < right-1$ **do**"
    loop all elements in the range $a[1..left-1]$ are less than or equal to all
    elements in range $a[left..n]$. Similarly, all elements in the range
    $a[right+1..n]$ are greater than or equal to all elements in the range
    $a[1..right]$ and $left \leqslant right+1$ and $right \geqslant left-1$. After each iteration of
    the stack loop "**while** $stacktop > 0$ **do**", the top of the stack will contain
    the limits for the smallest array segment to date that is yet to be
    partitioned if the stack is not empty. With each iteration of the parti-
    tioning loop either *newleft* or *newright* is changed by at least one and so
    this loop will terminate. It follows that the "**while** $left < right$ **do**" will
    also terminate because *left* and *right* are determined by *newleft* and
    newright. Termination of the outermost loop which depends on the
    stack being empty is harder to understand. Informally, we can use the
    following argument to explain how termination comes about. Re-
    peated partitioning results in smaller and smaller partition limits being
    placed on the stack until eventually we end up with a partition of size
    one. At this point, partitioning ceases and the smallest available parti-
    tion left on the stack is removed and processed. Since all partitions
    considered are eventually reduced to size one and there are only at
    most n such partitions we may expect that the removal-from-the-stack
    operation will guarantee that the algorithm will eventually terminate.

3. The quicksort algorithm has a number of attractive attributes. It has the advantage over most other $O(n \log_2 n)$ algorithms in that it only moves elements when it is absolutely necessary. (That is, it can be said that it achieves its goal by applying the principle of least effort—a powerful and elegant strategy.) This can be important where large amounts of data have to be moved around. (In some cases this can be avoided by swapping pointers rather than the actual data.)

4. The algorithm possesses the highly desirable characteristic of exchanging data over large distances early in the sorting process.

5. The quicksort algorithm is not superior to some of the other $O(n^2)$ algorithms when it comes to sorting small data sets (≈ 12). The algorithm can therefore be speeded up by incorporating an insertion sort into the mechanism. Whenever the algorithm reduces a partition to less than say 12 elements it can be insertion-sorted instead of being partitioned further.

6. Quicksort is by nature a recursive algorithm. As we will see in Chapter 8 it has a very simple recursive implementation.

7. Notice that when all elements to be "sorted" are equal, quicksort does a lot of unnecessary exchanges.

Applications

Internal sorting of large data sets.

Supplementary problems

5.6.1   The number of comparisons required by quicksort can be reduced by a few percent by using the median of three elements whenever a new guess at the median is required. A simple way to do this is to always select the median of the first, middle, and end values in the array segment being partitioned. Implement this refinement and compare it with the original version using the number of comparisons as a measure.

5.6.2   It was mentioned earlier (in note 5) that quicksort can be speeded up by using an insertion sort whenever a segment less than about twelve elements needs to be sorted. Incorporate this suggestion.

5.6.3   The suggestion in the previous problem can result in a considerable overhead for the procedure calls to the insertion sort. An alternative and more effective approach is to postpone the insertion sorting until after *all* partitions have been reduced to a size of less than 12. Implement this version and devise suitable tests to compare it with the 5.6.2 implementation.

5.6.4   A significant saving in comparisons can be made by initially placing the partitioning value selected into the first location of the range to be partitioned and proceeding with the partitioning from the second position. Implement this modification.

Algorithm 5.7
BINARY SEARCH

Problem

Given an element x and a set of data that is in strictly ascending numerical order find whether or not x is present in the set.

Algorithm development

The problem of searching an ordered list such as a dictionary or telephone directory occurs frequently in computing.

Before pursuing the computer solution to such problems it is useful to draw upon our non-computing experience of searching ordered data. For this purpose consider how we use the telephone directory to look up someone's number (perhaps Mr J. K. Smith's number). One way to find his number would be to start at page 1 of the telephone book and progress through page-by-page until we are successful. Personal experience tells us that this method is far too slow and that instead we use a completely different approach to solve the problem. The fact is that we have no trouble in quickly locating a particular person's telephone number in a directory of over a million names. The question is how do we manage this?

In looking for Mr Smith's number we certainly do not start looking near the front of the directory. Instead we would probably open the directory at a page somewhere more than two-thirds of the way through. We would then glance at the name at the top of the page we had opened and decide from this whether or not we had gone too far. From our current position, depending on the name we had encountered, we would apply the same strategy again although most probably on a smaller scale. In this way moving backwards and forwards we would very quickly home in on the page containing the name we were seeking. What we are doing in this search process is discarding from further consideration as quickly as possible large portions of the directory. In fact we are applying what is commonly known as an interpolation search method. It is possible to formulate such a strategy as a computer algorithm but for the present we will concentrate on a somewhat different approach which is more general in that it will yield a very good performance independently of the distribution of the ordered data.

The above strategy at first sight seems somewhat difficult to formalize into a computer algorithm. What we need is a method that allows us to quickly eliminate large portions of the data and systematically home in on the relevant area.

It is easy to see that in all cases the value in the set that we are seeking is either in the first half of the list or the second half of the list (it may also be the middle value in the set). For example,

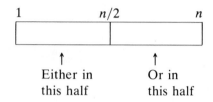

We can establish the relevant half by comparing the value sought with the value in the middle of the set. This single test will eliminate *half* of the values in the set from further consideration. Now we have a problem only *half* the size of the original problem. Suppose it is established that the value we are seeking is in the second half of the list (e.g. somewhere between the $(n/2)^{\text{th}}$ value and the nth value).

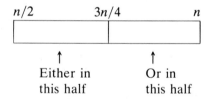

Once again, it is either in the first half or the second half of this reduced set. By examining first the $n/2$ value and then the $3n/4$ value we have been able to eliminate from further consideration essentially three quarters of the values in the original data set in just two comparisons. We can continue to apply this idea of reducing our problem by half at each comparison until we encounter the value we are seeking or until we establish that it is not present in the set. With the telephone directory problem, the latter task is just as easily accomplished. We can expect the same situation to apply to our computer algorithm.

The halving strategy that we have been considering is one of the most widely used methods in computing science. It is commonly known as the *divide-and-conquer* strategy. The corresponding searching method we are starting to develop is known as the *binary search* algorithm.

At this stage we have the general strategy:

repeatedly
 "examine middle value of remaining data and on the basis of this comparison eliminate half of the remaining data set"
until (the value is found or it is established that it is not present)

Let us now consider a specific example in order to try to find the details of the
algorithm needed for implementation.

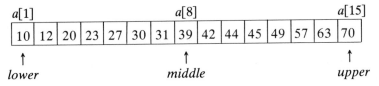

Suppose we are required to search an array of 15 ordered elements to
establish if $x = 44$ is present and, if so, the position that it occupies in the
array. We start by examining the middle value in the array. If the array
contains an even number of values it will not strictly have a middle value. To
get the middle value of an array of size n we can try:

   $middle := n$ **div** 2

for $n = 15$ this yields $middle = 7$ which is not strictly the middle. If we add 1
before carrying out the division we get

   $middle := (n+1)$ **div** $2 \equiv 8$ (the middle)

This gives $a[middle] = a[8] = 39$. Since the value we are seeking (i.e. 44) is
greater than 39 it must be somewhere in the range $a[9] ... a[15]$. That is, $a[9]$
becomes the lower limit of where 44 could be. That is, $lower := middle+1$.
We then have:

	a[9]		a[12]			a[15]	
	42	44	45	49	57	63	70
	↑		↑			↑	
	lower		middle			upper	

To calculate the middle index this time we can subtract 8 from 15 (i.e., the
amount discarded) to give 7 the number of values remaining. We can then
divide it by 2 to give 3 which can be added to 9 to give 12. This approach is
somewhat involved. Studying the *upper* and *lower* index values we see that if
we add them and divide by 2 we end up with 12. Tests on several other values
confirm that this method of calculating the middle works in the general case,
e.g.

   $middle := (lower+upper)$ **div** 2

When $a[12]$ is examined it is established that 44 is *less* than $a[12]$. It follows that 44 (if it is present) must be in the range $a[9]$ ... $a[11]$. Accordingly the upper limit becomes one less than the middle value, i.e.

$upper := middle-1$

We then have:

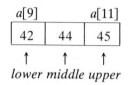

From this we see that with each comparison either the lower limit is increased or the upper limit is decreased.

With the next comparison we find the value we are seeking and its position in the array. That is, in just 3 comparisons we have located the value we wanted. It can be seen that an additional comparison would have been required if the value we had been seeking were either 42 or 45.

Our algorithm must handle the situation where the value we are seeking is *not present* in the array. When the value we are seeking is present the algorithm terminates when the current middle value is equal to the value sought. *Clearly this test can never be true when the value sought is not present.* Some other condition must therefore be included to guarantee that the algorithm will terminate.

To investigate termination when the value is not present consider what happens when we are searching for 43 rather than 44. The procedure progresses as before until we get the configuration below:

$a[9]$ $a[11]$

42	44	45

↑   ↑   ↑
lower middle upper

At this stage we find that 43 is *less* than the middle value and we have:

$upper := middle-1$

This leads to the situation where $lower = upper = middle$ (i.e. they are all 9).

$a[9]$ $a[11]$

42	44	45

↑
lower   (i.e. $lower = 9$
middle $middle = 9$
upper $upper = 9$)

The next comparison of 43 with $a[middle] = a[9]$ tells us the value we are seeking is above the middle value. We therefore get

$$lower := middle + 1 = 10$$

We then have $lower = 10$ and $upper = 9$. That is, $lower$ and $upper$ have crossed over. Another investigation in searching for 45 indicates that $lower$ once again becomes greater than $upper$. When the value we are seeking is present $lower$ may become greater than $upper$ but only when the value sought is found. Since all unsuccessful searches eventually pass through the stage when $upper = lower = middle$ (because of the way in which $middle$ is calculated) we can use the condition

$$lower > upper$$

in conjunction with the equality test of the array value with the value sought to terminate our algorithm. Before leaving off this discussion, we should be sure that the algorithm terminates when the value we are seeking is less than the first value $a[1]$ or greater than the last value $a[n]$.

A further check for the special case when there is only one element in the array confirms that the algorithm functions correctly and also terminates as required. At this stage we have the following algorithm.

1. Establish ordered array size n and the value sought x.
2. Establish the ordered data set $a[1..n]$.
3. Set $upper$ and $lower$ limits.
4. Repeatedly
   (a) calculate middle position of remaining array;
   (b) if value sought is greater than $middle$ value
       then adjust $lower$ limit to one greater than $middle$,
       else adjust $upper$ limit to one less than $middle$
   until value sought is $found$ or $lower$ becomes greater than $upper$.
5. Set $found$ accordingly.

The Pascal implementation is

```
procedure binsch (var a:nelements; n,x:integer; var middle:integer;
    var found:boolean);
var lower, {lower limit}
    upper {upper limit}:integer;
begin
    lower := 1;
    upper := n;
    repeat
        middle := (lower + upper) div 2;
        if x > a[middle] then
            lower := middle + 1
```

```
      else
          upper := middle − 1
      until (a[middle] = x) or (lower > upper);
      found := (a[middle] = x)
  end
```

The termination condition for the algorithm above is somewhat clumsy. Furthermore, it is difficult to prove the algorithm is correct. It is, therefore, useful to investigate whether or not there is a more straightforward implementation. In any particular search the test whether the current middle value (i.e. $a[middle]$) is equal to the value sought usually applies only within one step of where the algorithm would otherwise terminate (see the binary decision tree for an explanation). This means that if the algorithm can be formulated to terminate with a single condition it will lead to a more elegant and also a more efficient solution.

Careful examination of our original algorithm indicates that we cannot simply remove the test $a[middle] = x$ as this leads to instances where the algorithm will not terminate correctly. The problem arises because it is possible to move past a successful match.

To obtain a better solution to the problem we must therefore maintain conditions that prevent this bypass. A way to do this is to ensure that $upper$ and $lower$ home in on the target termination position in such a way that they do not cross over or move past the match condition.

In other words, if x is *present* in the array, we want the following condition to hold after each iteration:

$$a[lower] \leqslant x \leqslant a[upper]$$

It follows that $lower$ and $upper$ will need to be changed in such a way as to guarantee this condition *if x is present*. If we can do this, we should be able to find a suitable termination condition involving just $lower$ and $upper$. Our starting configuration will be:

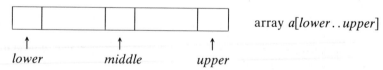

array $a[lower..upper]$

$lower$ $middle$ $upper$

Beginning with:

$$middle := (lower + upper) \text{ div } 2$$

we can make the following conditional test in an effort to bring $upper$ and $lower$ closer together:

$$x > a[middle]$$

If this condition is true then x must be in the range $a[middle+1..upper]$ if it is present in the array. It follows that with this condition true, we can make the assignment:

$$lower := middle+1$$

On the other hand if this condition is not true (i.e. therefore $x \leq a[middle]$) x must be in the range $a[lower..middle]$ if it is present in the array. The variable $upper$ can therefore be reassigned as:

$$upper := middle$$

(Note that the assignment $upper := middle-1$ is not made because the test $x > a[middle]$ is not strong enough to discount the possibility that $a[middle] = x$.)

We are now left with the question of deciding how this mechanism can be terminated. The mechanism by which $lower$ and $upper$ are changed is such that if the element x is present either one of them could reach an array element equal to x first. If $upper$ descends to an array value equal to x first, then $lower$ must increase until this element is reached from below. The complementary situation will apply if $lower$ reaches an array element equal to x first. These two situations suggest that the termination condition:

$$lower = upper$$

is probably the most appropriate if x is present.

The fact that $lower$ is set to $(middle+1)$ rather than just $middle$ guarantees that $lower$ will be increased after each pass through the loop where $lower$ is reassigned.

The guarantee that $upper$ is decreased each time through the loop that it is reassigned is more subtle since it is always assigned to the current $middle$ value. The truncation caused by the integer division, i.e.

$$middle := (lower+upper) \textbf{ div } 2$$

ensures that the $middle$ value is always less than the current $upper$ value (except when $upper = lower$). For example,

$$middle = (2+4) \ div \ 2 = 3 < 4$$
$$middle = (2+3) \ div \ 2 = 2 < 3$$

Because $middle$ is decreased in this way, it follows that $upper$ will also be decreased whenever it is reassigned.

At this point we should also check the special cases when x is not present to ensure that the algorithm always terminates correctly. The most important special cases are:

1. there is only one element in the array;
2. x is less than the first element in the array;

3.   *x* is greater than the last element in the array;
4.   *x* is in the range *a*[1..*n*] but is absent from the array.

A check of these cases reveals that the algorithm terminates correctly when the element *x* is not present in the array. We can now, therefore, give a detailed description of our algorithm.

Algorithm description

1.   Establish the array *a*[1..*n*], and the value sought *x*.
2.   Assign the *upper* and *lower* variables to the array limits.
3.   While *lower<upper* do
     (a)   compute the middle position of remaining array segment to be searched,
     (b)   if the value sought is greater than current middle value then
           (b.1)   adjust lower limit accordingly
           else
           (b'.1)   adjust upper limit accordingly.
4.   If the array element at *lower* position is equal to the value sought then
     (a)   return found
     else
     (a')   return not found.

Pascal implementation

```
procedure binarysearch(var a: nelements; n,x: integer; var found:
boolean);
var lower {lower limit of array segment still to be searched},
    upper {upper limit of array segment still to be searched},
    middle {middle of array segment still to be searched}: integer;

begin {binary searches array a[1..n] for element x}
  {assert: n>0∧a[1..n] sorted in ascending order∧exists k such that
  1=<k=<n∧x=a[k] if x is present}
  lower := 1;
  upper := n;
  {invariant: lower>=1∧upper=<n∧x in a[lower..upper] if present}
  while lower<upper do
    begin {increase lower and decrease upper keeping x in range if
    present}
      middle := (lower+upper) div 2;
      if x>a[middle] then
        lower := middle+1
      else
        upper := middle
    end;
```

{**assert**: *lower = upper = k ∧ x = a[k] if x in a[1..n]*}
found := (*a[lower] = x*)
end

Notes on design

1. The binary search algorithm in general offers a much more efficient alternative than the linear search algorithm. Its performance can best be understood in terms of a binary search tree. For an array of 15 items, the tree has the form shown in Fig. 5.8.

    From this tree it can be seen that at most 4 comparisons are needed. In general no more than $\lfloor \log_2 n \rfloor + 1$ comparisons are required. This means that even for an array of one million entries only about twenty comparisons would be required. By comparison, a linear search requires on average $n/2$ comparisons.

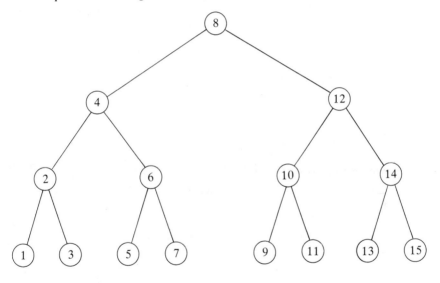

Fig. 5.8 Binary decision tree for binary search algorithm.

2. With each iteration, if *x* is *present* in the array, *lower* will be increased and *upper* will be decreased in such a way that the condition:

    $$a[lower] \leq x \leq a[upper] \text{ and } lower \leq upper$$

    remains true. Termination will occur when *lower = upper* and hence *if x is present* we will have

    $$a[lower] = x = a[upper]$$

3. There have been many implementations of the binary search algorithm
    (see, for example, B. Kidman, "Understanding the binary search",
    Aust. Comp. J., **13**, 7–12 (1981); N. Wirth, *Algorithms + Data Struc-
    tures = Programs*, Prentice-Hall, 1976).

    Most of them are either more complicated, or they possess what
    might be regarded as unusual initialization and termination conditions
    that tend to make them harder to understand.

Supplementary problems

5.7.1   Design and implement versions of the binary search that have the
        following loop structures:

   (a)   **while** *lower<upper+1* **do**
   (b)   **while** *lower<upper−1* **do**

5.7.2   Implement versions of the binary search that make the following
        paired changes to *lower* and *upper*:

   (a)   *lower := middle+1* $\Big\}$
         upper := middle−1

   (b)   *lower := middle* $\Big\}$
         upper := middle

5.7.3   Implement a binary search algorithm that calculates the middle
        using $\lceil (lower+upper)/2 \rceil$.

5.7.4   A variation on the basic binary algorithm involves not centering the
        algorithm around the *lower* and *upper* limits. Instead, two alternate
        parameters are maintained, one that points to the *middle* of the
        array segment still to be searched, and a second marking the half
        width of that segment. A binary search algorithm that uses this
        approach is referred to as a uniform binary search. Design and
        implement a uniform binary search.

5.7.5   Develop an algorithm that uses a random number generator which
        always generates random numbers in the range *lower...upper*. In
        each instance the random number generated should take on the role
        of *middle* in the above algorithms. Compare the performance of this
        algorithm with the binary search algorithm in terms of the number
        of comparisons made.

5.7.6   A searching method that uses linear interpolation can give fast
        retrieval when the ordered data set is relatively evenly distributed
        over its range of possible values. With this method, the magnitude of
        the value *x* we are seeking is used to determine which element of the
        array we should next compare with *x*. When *lower* and *upper* are the
        current limits of the array segment left to be searched we can

examine next the element that is approximately a distance

$$\left(\frac{x-a[lower]}{a[upper]-a[lower]}\right)\times(upper-lower-1)$$

above the current value of *lower*. Implement an interpolation search and compare its performance with the $\log_2 n$ performance of the binary search. Use a uniform random number generator to produce the array *a*. Note that this array will need to be sorted.

Algorithm 5.8
HASH SEARCHING

Problem

Design and implement a hash searching algorithm.

Algorithm development

It usually comes as a surprise to most people when they learn for the first time that there exists a searching method that is on average considerably faster than a binary search and which often only has to examine one or two items before terminating successfully. Having been told that such a method exists, let us consider how we might go about trying to discover this seemingly mysterious super-fast searching algorithm.

To make a start on our task let us take a specific data set and see what we can do with it. To simplify the problem let us first focus on the task of finding the *position* of a number in an array.

$a[1]$							$a[8]$							$a[15]$
10	12	20	23	27	30	31	39	42	44	45	49	53	57	60

Suppose we were to focus on finding the 44 (in the more usual context it would be some information *associated* with the 44 that we would be seeking). Our earlier experience with the binary search illustrated how we could take advantage of the order in an array of size n to locate an item in about $\log_2 n$ steps. Exploitation of order just does not seem to be a strong enough criterion to locate items much faster than this. The almost unbelievable aspect of the faster method is the statement that "it usually only has to look at one, two or three items before terminating successfully". To try to make progress let us focus on the extreme case where it only examines *one* item before terminating. When first confronted with this idea it seems to be impossible—how could we possibly find one item in a thousand first time?

To find the 44 in our example we would have to somehow go "magically" to location 10 first. There does not seem to be any characteristic that 44 possesses that would indicate that it was stored in location 10. All we know about 44 is its *magnitude*. We seem to have come to a dead end! How could 44's magnitude be of any help in locating its position in the array in just one step? Reflecting on this for a while, we come to the conclusion that only if the *number* 44 were stored in array *location* 44 would be able to find it in *one* step. Although the idea of storing each number in the array location dictated by its magnitude would allow us to locate it or detect its absence in one step, it does not seem practical for general use. For example, suppose we wanted to store and rapidly search a set of 15 telephone numbers each of seven digits, e.g. 4971667. With the present scheme, this number would have to be stored at array location 4971667. Any array with such an enormous number of locations just to store and search for 15 numbers does not seem worth it. Before abandoning the idea of looking for a better method let us take one last look at the "progress" we have made. To make things easier let us return to our earlier example. We have a set of 15 numbers between 10 and 60. We could store and search for these elements in an array of size 60 and achieve a one-step retrieval. The problem with this is that in the general case this would mean that too much space would have to be used. This leads to the question, can we apply the same retrieval principles using a *smaller* storage space?

One response to this last question would be that we might proceed by "normalizing" the data. This would amount to applying a transformation to each number before we search for it (i.e. 60 could be transformed so that it becomes 15, 20 becomes 5 and so on, by doing an integer division by 4 and rounding to the nearest integer). When we apply this normalizing transformation to our sample data set and round to the nearest integer we discover that some values *share* the same index in the range 1 to 15 while other indices in this range are not used. Therefore, we see that by reducing the array size from the *magnitude* range (60) to the *occupancy* range (15) we have introduced the possibility of multiple occupancy. Clearly the less we reduce the range the less will be the risk of multiple occupancy or *collisions* as they are usually called.

This proposal that we have made seems to only half-solve our problem. The normalized set of values would be:

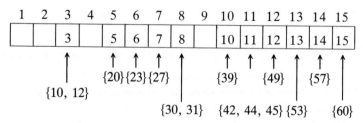

It is easy to imagine situations where this normalizing scheme will introduce even more severe collision situations (i.e. suppose the largest value was *much bigger* than all other values in the set). These observations suggest that our normalizing approach is probably not the best one to take.

Our most recent observations leave us with the question, is there any alternative presearch transformation that we can apply to our original data? What we desire of such a transformation is that for our particular example it produces values in the range $1 \rightarrow 15$ and that it is not badly affected by irregularities in the distribution of the original data. One such alternative transformation would be to compute the values of the original set *modulo* 15 and add 1 (we will assume that the numbers to be stored are all positive). Applying this transformation (which is usually referred to as hashing) to our original data set we get:

1	2	3	4	5	6	7	8	9	10	11	12	13	14	15
30	31			49	20			23	39	10		12		44

↑ under 1: {45, 60}   ↑ under 9: {53}   ↑ under 13: {27, 42, 57}

This result is a little disappointing as there are still nearly as many collisions. We are, however, better off with this method because it can accommodate irregularities in the distribution better.

We made an observation earlier that the more we try to "compress" a data set the more likely it is that there will be collisions. To test out this observation let us see if we can reduce the number of collisions by choosing to use an array with say 19 locations rather than 15 (i.e. we will calculate our numbers modulo 19 rather than 15 and drop the plus one). In most circumstances we would be prepared to concede the use of 20% extra storage if it would give us very fast retrieval with very few collisions.

0	1	2	3	4	5	6	7	8	9	10	11	12	13	14	15	16	17	18
57	20		60	23		44	45	27		10	30	12			53			

↑ under 0: {39}   ↑ under 3: {42}   ↑ under 10: {49} ↑ under 11: {31}

Once again there are a number of collisions but this time there are no multiple collisions. Studying this table we see that 11 of the 15 values have been stored such that they can be retrieved in a *single* step. We are therefore left with the question of what to do about the collisions? If we can find a method of storing the values that collided so that they too can be retrieved quickly then we should end up with an algorithm that has a high average retrieval efficiency. To study this problem let us return to our example.

The situation as it stands is that there are a number of "free" locations in the array which could be used to store the four elements that made collisions. We may therefore ask the question for each individual element—where is the best place to store this element? For example, we can ask where is the best place to store the 31 which collided with the element in location 12. Studying this particular case we see that if 31 is placed in location 13 then we would be able to locate it in *two* steps. The way we could do this would be to compute:

$$31 \textbf{ mod } 19 \rightarrow \text{location } 12$$

We would then examine the element in location 12 and discover that it is not 31. Having made this discovery we could move to the *next* position in the array (i.e. position 13) and discover the 31. We must now ask can we *generalize* this idea? As another example we can ask where should the 49 be placed? If position 13 is occupied by 31 then we have the choice of placing it either in position 14 or position 9 as these are the two *closest* locations. While position 9 might seem the more attractive location to place 49, we see that there are problems because in the general case we will not know in what direction to search. Position 14 therefore seems the best place to store the 49. We can then always use the rule of *searching forward* (modulo the table size) when we do not find the element we are seeking at the hashed location. From this discussion we can conclude that collisions can be resolved by storing the "collided" element in the *next available forward location*. Applying this idea to our particular set we get

0	1	2	3	4	5	6	7	8	9	10	11	12	13	14	15	16	17	18
57	20	39	60	23	42	44	45	27		10	30	12	31	49	53			

The elements that made collisions are underlined. The tail of each arrow indicates where an element that collided should have been stored. Before proceeding further let us try to assess the *average* number of steps to retrieve an element from this table assuming all elements are likely to be retrieved with equal probability.

We have:

(a)   11 elements located in 1 step
(b)   3 elements located in 2 steps
(c)   1 element located in 4 steps

    15   21

Therefore, for this configuration an element will be located in $\simeq 1.4$ steps on average. This seems very promising, particularly if such performance extends to the general case. Rather than pursue this verification here, we will assume it to be true and continue with the development of a hash searching algorithm that will match our proposed storage scheme.

To make things simpler, we will assume that the goal is to construct a hash searching function that simply returns the position of the search key (a number) in the hash table. (As we remarked earlier, in practice we would not be interested just in the position of a key but rather in the information associated with the key—i.e. we might need to locate a person's address by doing a hash search using his/her name.)

Our discussion thus far suggests that the steps in locating an item in the table should be relatively straightforward. Our method for resolving collisions requires that we perform the following basic steps:

1. Derive a hash value modulo the table size from the search key.
2. If the key not at hash value index in array then
    (a)   perform a forward linear search from current position in the array modulo the array size.

For a search item *key* and a table size *n* we can accomplish step (1) using:

$$position := key \bmod n$$

We can then use a test of the form:

$$\textbf{if } table[position] <> key \textbf{ then } ...$$

to decide whether *key* is located at the index *position* in the array *table*.

To complete the development of the algorithm all that remains is to work out the details of the search. In constructing the forward search all we need do is examine successive positions in the table taking note that the index will need to "wrap-around" when it gets to the end of the array (see Fig. 5.9).

We can use the *mod* function to accomplish the wrap-around, that is,

$$position := (position+1) \bmod n$$

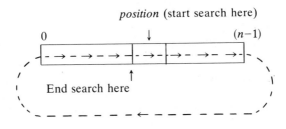

Wrap-around of *position* index

Fig. 5.9 Collision resolution mechanism for hashing scheme.

The final consideration is to work out the details for terminating the search. Several things are relevant in this respect.

To make the search as efficient as possible we must stop it either as soon as we have located the key or as soon as we know that the key is not in the table. A test of the form:

$$\textbf{if } table[position] = key \textbf{ then } \ldots$$

will allow us to identify the presence of *key* in the table. It will not, however, enable us to detect its absence. To establish a good "absence-test" let us return to our earlier example. Suppose that we were to conduct a search in the table for "25" which is not present. The first step would be:

$$position := 25 \textbf{ mod } 19 = 6.$$

We discover that it is not in position 6 and then start searching positions 7, 8, ... In performing this search we find that at position 9 a "blank" is encountered rather than another number. What does this imply?

A blank suggests an *available* position at which to store a number. Furthermore, because of the way keys are inserted in the table it tells us 25 could not be inserted anywhere past position 9—remember the collision resolution rule we proposed, "insert the key in the *first* available location". The first encounter with an *unoccupied* location can therefore be used to signal the end-condition for an unsuccessful search. If we are storing numbers it will not be convenient to mark unoccupied locations with a blank. In practice the value we use to *safely* signal an unoccupied location will depend on the nature of the keys and the way the table is employed. We will therefore avoid the issue by choosing to use a variable *empty* that is passed as a parameter to the procedure. The test we can then use will have the form:

$$\textbf{if } table[position] = empty \textbf{ then } \ldots$$

We might now propose the following search:

while key not found and current position not empty do
(a)   move to next location modulo table size.

This seems to satisfy our requirements. However, when we study the termination conditions carefully we find that we have overlooked the possibility that the table could be *full* and the key may not be present. In that case we have a potentially infinite loop. How can we avoid this? Referring back to Fig. 5.9, we discover that as soon as we arrive back at the position at which we started we will know that the key is not present. An extra test seems to be needed. We now have established *three* ways in which the search can terminate:

1.   successfully on finding the key;

2. unsuccessfully at an *empty* location;
3. unsuccessfully with a *full* table.

The need to test these three conditions as each new position is examined seems rather clumsy. We might, therefore, ask is there a way to reduce the number of tests? Our earlier use of *sentinels* for terminating a search may be relevant. Following this line of reasoning we see that the first and third tests can be combined. We can *force* the search to be successful after examining all elements in the table. The way we can do this is by temporarily storing the key in the table at the original hashed position *after* discovering that the value there does not match the search key. The original value can then be restored after the search is complete. A Boolean variable *active* which is set to false on either finding the key or on finding an empty location can be used to terminate the search loop. A separate Boolean variable *found* can be used to distinguish between the termination conditions. This variable should not be set when the key is found only after a complete search of the table.

Our development of the algorithm is now complete.

Algorithm description

1. Establish the hash table to be searched, the key sought, the empty condition value, and the table size.
2. Compute hash index for key modulo the table size.
3. Set Boolean variables to terminate search.
4. If key located at index position then
   (a) set conditions for termination
   else
   (a) set sentinel to handle full table condition.
5. While no termination condition satisfied do
   (a) compute next index modulo table size;
   (b) if key found at current position then
       (b.1) set termination conditions and indicate found if valid
       else
       (b'.1) if table position empty then signal termination.
6. Remove sentinel and restore table.
7. Return result of search.

Pascal implementation

```
procedure hashsearch(var table: nelements; var position: integer;
var found: boolean; tablesize,empty,key:integer);
var temp {temporary storage for value at position start},
    start {hash value index to table}: integer;
    active {if true continue search of table}: boolean;
```

```
begin {uses hashing technique to search table for key}
  {assert: tablesize > 0}
  active := true; found := false;
  start := key mod tablesize;
  position := start;
  if table[start] = key then
    begin {key found at hash position}
      active := false;
      found := true;
      temp := table[start]
    end
  else
    begin {set up sentinel to terminate on full table}
      temp := table[start];
      table[start] := key
    end;
  {invariant: key not equal to values table[start..(position − 1) mod
  tablesize]∧number of values checked =<tablesize + 1}
  while active do
    begin {linear search table from position start for key}
      position := (position + 1) mod tablesize;
      if table[position] = key then
        begin {found key − make sure not just termination}
          active := false;
          if position <>start then found := true
        end
      else
        if table[position] = empty then active := false
    end;
  table[start] := temp
  {assert: (table[position] = key ∧position <>start ∧found = true ∨
  (complete table searched ∧ found = false)}
end
```

Notes on design

1. The performance of the hash searching algorithm can be characterized
    by the number of items in the table that need to be examined *before*
    termination. This performance is a function of the fraction of occupied
    locations (called the *load factor* α). It can be shown, after making
    certain statistical assumptions, that on average $[1+(1/(1-\alpha))]/2$ loca-
    tions will need to be examined in a successful search (e.g. for a table
    that is 80% full this will be *fewer than three locations* irrespective of
    table size). The cost of making an unsuccessful search is more expen-
    sive. On average $[1+(1/(1-\alpha)^2)]/2$ locations must be examined before
    encountering an empty location (e.g. for a table that is 80% full, this
    will amount to 13 locations).

2. To characterize the behavior of the hash search, we need to focus on the search loop. After each iteration, it will be established that *key* is not in the locations from *start* to *position* or that key occurs at the table location *position*, or if the current position is empty that *key* is not in the table. The algorithm will terminate because with each iteration of the search loop, *position* will be increased by one modulo the table size. Therefore, eventually the sentinel will be encountered. This will bring about termination if it has not happened earlier due to a match or an empty location.

3. In solving this problem, it was useful to focus on an ideal but impractical solution. We were then able to move from this situation to a more practical implementation that retained much of the flavor and desirable properties of the original approach.

4. It would be desirable if the cost of unsuccessful searches was less expensive on average. One way to achieve this is to insert the keys into the table in increasing numerical (or alphabetical) order. For example, consider the five keys 16, 18, 25, 26, 29 inserted in numerical order into the table below of size 5.

0	1	2	3	4
25	16	26	18	29

If we were to search for 17 which hashes to position 2, we can stop the search immediately because there is a key there that occurs *numerically later* than 17. This stopping rule applies in general for tables constructed using an ordering method. The average number of locations that must be examined for an unsuccessful search is then *identical* to that for a successful search.

5. In most (but not all) practical applications, hash tables are not allowed to fill beyond about 80% because of the sharp deterioration in performance beyond this level.

6. The hashing method we have described suffers from the fact that there is a tendency for the keys that are inserted latest to *cluster* around the keys that were inserted without collision. A way to minimize this is to apply what is known as the linear quotient method. The idea is to use the *remainder* of division by the table size (which must be prime) as the first probe of the table. The *quotient* is then used as the *stepsize* to make subsequent probes of the table (if linear probing). With this method, *all* table values are examined before repetition if the table size is prime.

Applications

Fast retrieval from both small and large tables.

Supplementary problems

5.8.1   Extend the hashing algorithm given so that it will work with words rather than numbers. One way to "hash" a word is to take the sum of the collating sequence values for the characters in the word (e.g. $a = 1$, $b = 2$, $c = 3$, ... —the word *ace* will have the hash value $1+3+5 = 9$).

5.8.2   Modify the hashing algorithm given so that it searches a table in which the words have been inserted in alphabetical order (see note 4 above).

5.8.3   It is not always convenient or possible to insert items into a hash table in order as required in the previous problem. An alternative approach that achieves the same effect is to proceed as follows when inserting a new element x. If x hashes to location k and the value there occurs alphabetically later than x, then interchange the roles of x and *table*$[k]$ and repeat the process until an empty location is found. This has the effect of letting x take precedence in ordering over keys that were inserted earlier but occur alphabetically later.

5.8.4   Implement the linear quotient hashing method described in note 6 and compare its performance with the algorithm above for a load factor of 80%. Use a random number generator to provide the key set. Make tests for sets of both successful and unsuccessful searches.

5.8.5   Make a plot of load factor versus search cost (successful *and* unsuccessful) for load factors in the range 50% to 95% at 5% intervals

(a)   using the formulas given in note 1, and
(b)   by doing a simulation with random numbers.

5.8.6   Use random numbers to fill a table to 80% and do a profile of the number of values that were at their hash position, at their hash position+1, at their hash position+2 and so on.

5.8.7   If items are retrieved from a hash table with unequal frequencies a gradual speed-up in retrieval can be obtained by shifting each item as it is retrieved one position closer to its original hash position by performing an exchange. Implement this hash search method.

BIBLIOGRAPHY

Wirth (1976) gives an important treatment of sorting methods. Knuth (1973) gives the most comprehensive treatment of sorting and searching algorithms. The survey of Martin (1971) is also very readable and informative.

1. Aho, A. V., J. E. Hopcroft and J. D. Ullman, *The Design and Analysis of Algorithms*, Addison–Wesley, Reading, Mass., 1974.
2. Knuth, D. E., *The Art of Computer Programming*, Vol. 3: *Sorting and Searching*, Addison–Wesley, Reading, Mass., 1973.
3. Knuth, D. E., "Algorithms", *Sci. Am.*, **237** (4), 63–80 (1977).
4. Lorin, H., *Sorting and Sort Systems*, Addison–Wesley, Reading, Mass., 1975.
5. Martin, W. A., "Sorting", *Comp. Surv.*, **3,** 147–74 (1971).
6. Price, C. E., "Table look-up techniques", *Comp. Surv.* **3,** 49–65 (1971).
7. Wirth, N., *Algorithms + Data Structures = Programs*, Prentice-Hall, Englewood Cliffs, N.J., 1976.

Chapter 6
TEXT PROCESSING AND PATTERN SEARCHING

INTRODUCTION

It has long been recognized that computers are well equipped to perform other than numeric computations. A consequence of this has been the ever-increasing application of computers to the processing of textual information. The nature of textual data as opposed to numerical data forces us to adopt a whole range of new computational strategies and algorithms that are appreciably different from those we have needed for dealing with numeric problems. The basic unit is now a character rather than a number.

Our major concerns in processing text are centered around either manipulation and movement of characters or searching for patterns or words. The first two algorithms we will consider in this chapter convey something of the flavor of text manipulation as it is applied to computer document preparation. The mechanisms for manipulation of text are usually straightforward, although considerable attention must be paid to details and the structure of the text.

Perhaps the single most important part of text processing is centered around the search for particular patterns within the text. The large volumes of text that might have to be processed, and the frequency with which text searches must be conducted, underlines the need for efficient search algorithms. The last half of this chapter is devoted to a study of text and pattern searching algorithms. These algorithms demonstrate the importance of paying attention to the text structure and the information at hand when considering designs.

248

Algorithm 6.1
TEXT LINE LENGTH ADJUSTMENT

Problem

Given a set of lines of text of arbitrary length, reformat the text so that no lines of more than n characters (e.g. 40) are printed. In each output line the maximum number of words that occupy less than or n characters, should be printed and no word should extend across two lines. Paragraphs should also remain indented.

Algorithm development

Let us start thinking about the design for this problem by trying to isolate the basic mechanisms. We could begin by reading text until we have read n characters. The words *completed* at this point can then be printed. We must remember that the input lines may contain *less than n, n* itself, or *more than n* characters.

Consider diagramatically what is involved when the process is beginning. In this case assume that the required n is 40 characters.

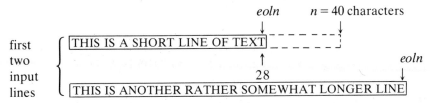

Let us start by reading 40 characters from the input and placing them in an array.

What this suggests is that when we reach the end of the first line and our character count has not yet reached $n = 40$ we are going to need to start reading from the *next* line. After we have placed 28 characters in our array we have reached the end of the first input line. We can then start reading from the second line to make our quota up to 40 characters. If we place the first character of the second input line in position 29 we will end up with:

... OF TEXTTHIS ...

This suggests that when we encounter an end-of-line in the input we need to insert a space to guarantee word separation. The next thing we observe is that at the 40-character position we find that we are right in the middle of the word ANOTHER. Since words are not to be broken in the output no characters of the word ANOTHER should be printed. Instead our first output line will only be 36 characters long.

```
                                              36   40
                                               ↓    ↓
 _____ _ _ _
| THIS IS A SHORT LINE OF TEXT THIS IS!_ _ _!
```

To get this output we need to know where the last full word (in this case IS) ended. There are two ways to establish this. We can either count back from position 41 until we encounter a blank. For example, we could use:

> *back* := 41;
> **while** *a*[*back*] <> ' ' **do** *back* := *back*−1

We need to read *one more* character than we wish to output to allow for the fact that a word may end at position 40. Alternatively, as each new blank is encountered we can update a variable with the current position. When we reach our 41 character limit the current value of the variable will tell us where the last full word ended. This latter approach is more costly.

With the information as to where the last full word ends the current line can be printed. We are then left with ANO.

```
                                              36   40
                                               ↓    ↓
 _____
| THIS IS A SHORT LINE OF TEXT THIS IS ANO |
 ←——————————————— printed ———————————————→
```

What are our options at this point? One simple approach would be to move ANO to the start of the array and then begin to fill up the array again. At the same time we could count the characters in the new output line. Since words are on average only a few characters long this data movement cost is small. It could be achieved in the following way:

> *c* := 0;
> **for** *j* := *back*+1 **to** 41 **do**
>   **begin**
>   *c* := *c*+1;
>   *a*[*c*] := *a*[*j*]
>   **end**

In the copying procedure we need to start at *back*+1 to ensure that the first word in the line does not begin with a blank.

Always in problems of this nature we must make sure that the algorithm will terminate correctly. What are the possibilities here? The most likely thing that will happen is that we will end up with a *partly filled* line at the stage when we encounter the end-of-file. The algorithm as we have developed it so far only prints out full lines. We must, therefore, include steps that will print out any partially filled line after the end-of-file has been encountered.

The algorithm we have developed may be considered as a *line-centered* approach to the problem. The overall strategy can now be summarized.

1. While not at end-of-file do
    (a) fill up output line;
    (b) write out output line up to the last full word;
    (c) move any partial word at end of output line to the beginning of line.
2. Write out any partially filled line.

In our algorithm when a word does not completely fit on a line it must be printed on the *next* line. Thus, whenever there is a word to be printed there is always the question "can it be printed on the current line or rather must it go to the next line?" These observations suggest that it may be fruitful to consider a *word-oriented* approach to the problem. One way to pursue this approach is to read words one at a time. When a given word has been read, one of two situations may prevail:

1. The word can be printed on the *current* line because the character count does not exceed the line length limit.
2. The line length limit is exceeded and so the word must be printed on the *next* line.

The preceding discussion suggests the following very straightforward strategy:

1. While not at end-of-file do
    (a) read next word from input;
    (b) if the line length limit is not exceeded then
        (b.1) print word on the current line
        else
        (b'.1) move to next line and print current word.

Comparing this new mechanism with our original proposal it is easy to see that we now have a clearer, cleaner and simpler algorithm. We can therefore proceed with the refinement of our new algorithm as there does not seem to be any other workable alternative. In the process we should make sure that our method will handle punctuation and leave any paragraphs present in the original text indented (tabs will not be considered).

After examining a variety of text we come to the conclusion that, conventionally, words are either separated by one or more spaces and/or a new line character(s). Any punctuation which generally follows on directly at the end of words need not be distinguished from the words. These observations make our task easier.

The input phase can proceed character-by-character. If the current character is neither a space nor an end-of-line it can simply be added to the current word array. As each word is built, a character count will need to be made. Remember back to our earlier discussion, if it is an end-of-line character it will need to be replaced by a space.

With these refinements our input mechanism becomes:

1. While not end-of-file do
    (a)   read and store next character;
    (b)   if character is a space then
            output current word on appropriate line.

To determine which line the current word is to be printed on, we need to add the current word (plus its trailing blank) length *wordcnt* to the current line length *linecnt*. If the line length *limit* is not exceeded the current word can be written out directly and then we can prepare to accept the next word as input. On the other hand, if the current word causes the line length limit to be exceeded, we will need to move to the next line before writing out the current word. After the current word has been written out on the new line, the character count for the new line will have to be the length of the word just written out.

The only difference between the two word-output situations is that in the instance when the line limit is exceeded the output must be preceded by a move-to-the-next line and a reset of the character count on the new line. The steps needed for output of the current word are therefore:

(a)   if line length limit exceeded then
      (a.1)   move to the next line;
      (a.2)   reset character count on new line *linecnt*;
(b)   write out current word plus its trailing space;
(c)   zero character count for word ready for input of next word.

Recalling our original specifications we require that the algorithm will leave paragraphs present in the original text still indented in the reformatted output. We know that a new paragraph is indicated by one or more blanks at the start of a line. The question is how can we distinguish between multiple blanks embedded in the text and a *new* paragraph? A little thought reveals that the new paragraph *must* follow on directly after encountering an end-of-line. We should therefore be able to use the condition of an *end-of-line*, *eol*, *followed by a space* to detect the start of a new paragraph. (We will assume that the original text has been preprocessed such that only new paragraphs have leading spaces.) Our paragraph test and following action will then be:

if end-of-line true followed by single space then
(a)   move to next line,
(b)   reset character count for new line.

For this test to be workable we will need to "turn-on" an end-of-line flag *eol* at the time when we encounter the end-of-line condition. Since the condition for a new paragraph involves the combination of a new line *followed by* a space it will be necessary to set the flag *after* the paragraph check to avoid getting a new paragraph when a space precedes the end-of-line character. In adopting this strategy we will need to make use of the fact that the character returned in Pascal when we try to read a new line is a space. We will also need to remember to "turn-off" the new line flag as soon as we have begun printing words on the new line. The complete algorithm can now be described.

Algorithm description [†]

1. Establish the line length limit *limit* and add one to it to allow for a space.
2. Initialize word and line character counts to zero and end-of-line flag to *false*.
3. While not end-of-file do
    (a)   read and store next character;
    (b)   if character is a space then
          (b.1)   if a new paragraph then
                  (1.a)   move to next line and reset character count for new line,

---

[†]   The unlikely situation where a word is longer than the line length will cause such words to be written out, exceeding the line length limit. It has also been assumed that there are no end-of-line hyphens. They would produce an unwanted space in each case.

(b.2)   add current word length to current line length,

(b.3)   if current word causes line length limit to be exceeded then

    (3.a)   move to next line and set line length to current word length,

(b.4)   write out current word and its trailing space and reinitialize character count,

(b.5)   turn off end-of-input-line flag,

(b.6)   if at end-of-input-line then

    (6.a)   set end-of-input-line flag and move to next input line.

Pascal implementation

```
procedure textformat(limit: integer);
var i {index for word array},
   linecnt {count of characters on current line},
   wordcnt {count of characters in current word}: integer;
   chr {current character},
   space {the space character}: char;
   eol {flag to mark end of line condition}: boolean;
   word: array[1..30] of char; {storage for current word}

begin {reformats text so no line more than limit long and no broken
words}
   {assert: all words less than 31 characters ∧ limit>=maximum
   wordlength in text}
   wordcnt := 0; linecnt := 0; eol := false; space := ' ';
   limit := limit+1;
   {invariant: after current character read, all lines with maximum
   number of whole words =<linecnt will have been printed ∧ all
   complete words read and identified will have been printed}
   while not eof(input) do
      begin {process character by character using space to signal
      end-of-word}
         read(chr);
         wordcnt := wordcnt+1;
         word[wordcnt] := chr;
         if chr=space then
            begin {possible end of current word}
               if eol and (wordcnt=1) then
                  begin {a new paragraph detected in original text}
                     writeln;
                     linecnt := 0
                  end;
               linecnt := linecnt+wordcnt;
               if linecnt>limit then
                  begin {line length limit exceeded so move to next
                  output line}
```

```
                writeln;
                linecnt := wordcnt
              end;
            {write out current word}
            for i := 1 to wordcnt do
              write(word[i]);
            wordcnt := 0;
            eol := false;
            if eoln(input) then
                begin {set end-of-input-line flag to detect new
                paragraph}
                  eol := true;
                  readln
                end
          end
        end;
        {assert: complete text reformatted and printed such that no line
        contains more than limit characters and each line has the
        maximum number of complete words packed on the line}
      writeln
    end
```

Notes on design

1. The cost of reformatting text is linearly dependent on the number of characters in the original text.

2. At the point when the jth character in the original text has been read all completed words in the first j characters will have been output according to the reformatting requirements established by the variable *limit*. Also all paragraphs within the first j characters will have been indented as in the original text. All lines that have been printed when the jth character is reached will be of length less than or equal to *limit* characters. On each line of output the maximum number of words consistent with the line length *limit* will be printed. With each iteration another character is read from the file and so eventually the end-of-file condition will be met and the loop will terminate.

3. Focusing on the output of words rather than the output of lines of text leads to a clearer and simpler algorithm. We should always be on the lookout for the most fundamental mechanism that will accomplish the task we wish to perform.

4. Notice that the present algorithm handles punctuation and multiple spaces in the text in a straightforward manner. We may imagine that there are *length zero* words between multiple spaces.

5. Comparing the final design with the earlier method we can see that we have managed to set up simpler initialization and termination conditions.

6. A diagram, although helpful in solving this problem, has tended to

influence us to focus on a line-oriented rather than a word-oriented solution to the problem.

Applications

Text processing, report writing and file management.

Supplementary problems

6.1.1   Modify the algorithm so that it removes multiple blanks other than those at the start of new paragraphs.

6.1.2   The algorithm we have developed may not reproduce the original text if the output was used as input. This would happen because if there was a space at the end of an input line it would be turned into *two* spaces in the reformatted output. Modify the algorithm so that it overcomes this problem.

6.1.3   Design an algorithm that reads and left justifies lines of text (as required in our algorithm). The beginning of each new paragraph should not be left justified. Note each new paragraph can be assumed to start with an upper case letter and be preceded by multiple blanks.

6.1.4   Design an algorithm that reads lines of text, reformats it and writes it out in pages of two columns (each forty characters wide) separated by a 10-space gap. The first column of the output should correspond to the first half of the input text page and the second column to the second half of the input text page. Each output page should contain 40 lines of text.

6.1.5   Implement the first text-formatting design proposed. Try to avoid the need for shifting word fragments after the current line is printed.

Algorithm 6.2
LEFT AND RIGHT JUSTIFICATION OF TEXT

Problem

Design and implement a procedure that will left and right justify text in a way that avoids splitting words and leaves paragraphs indented. An attempt should also be made to distribute the additional blanks as evenly as possible in the justified line.

Algorithm development

Books and computer-prepared documents are almost always left and right justified. What this means is that *all* lines have a *fixed* length with the *first* word on the line always starting in a fixed position (except when there is a new paragraph) and the *last* word also finishing in another fixed position. As an example, suppose the problem statement above was to be left and right justified. We might have:

Design and implement a procedure
that will left and right justify text in
a way that avoids splitting words and
leaves paragraphs indented. An attempt

↑   ↑
fixed starting   fixed finishing
position   position

The fixed line length is achieved by inserting *additional* spaces between words. One point which this example raises that we had not considered before is the need to allow the fixed line length to be considerably shorter or longer than the average line length of the unformatted text. This suggests that in some cases before left and right justification can begin, considerable rearrangement of the text will be necessary. Studying our example above more carefully, we come to the conclusion that a line can only be left and right justified when the unformatted line is less than or equal to the fixed length required. It seems, therefore, that the formatting procedure will need to take place in two steps:

(a) rearrange the text so that line lengths do not exceed the fixed output line length;

(b) left and right justify the reformatted text lines.

Essentially the requirements of the first step are fulfilled by the procedure developed in algorithm 6.1. So our task reduces to that of taking the output of the procedure in algorithm 6.1 and running it through the left-and-right-justification procedure. In fact the process can be made even simpler. As procedure *textformat* produces a line of text it can directly call our new procedure to complete the justification. This will require only several small changes to the original procedure *textformat*. These changes are left as an exercise for the reader.

In what follows we will concentrate on the left and right justification procedure under the assumption that the input to this procedure is a line of text that is smaller or equal to the length of the required left and right justified output. Our problem is now one of "*evenly*" distributing the extra spaces among the words in the input line. To make the task easier we will assume that the input line has only one space separating words and there are no added spaces at the end of the line. It is straightforward to alter the formatting procedure so that it guarantees that this condition holds in the output. We will also assume that any punctuation in the text either directly precedes or directly follows words with no intervening spaces.

To make a start on the insertion of spaces we can consider several examples in order to try to understand what is involved. On reflecting about the problem we come to the conclusion that for any particular line one of four possible situations may prevail.

1. The line is already of the correct length and so no processing is required (zero spaces to be added).
2. The number of extra spaces needed to expand the current line to the required length is *equal* to the number of spaces already present in the line. In this case it is simply a matter of adding one space to each existing space.
3. The number of spaces to be added is *greater* than the existing number of spaces in the line.
4. The number of spaces to be added is *less* than the existing number of spaces.

Since the first two cases are straightforward we can concentrate on examples where situations (3) and (4) apply. As an example of case (3) suppose we need to add 10 extra spaces to a line which originally possesses only 7 spaces.

Input line

Our task is to *evenly distribute* the 10 extra spaces among the 7 placement positions. Dividing 10 by 7 we discover that ideally $1^3/_7$ spaces should be added to each existing space. Obviously this is not a great help since we can only add an integral number of spaces to each existing space. Because there are more spaces to be added than there are existing positions, a first step would be to add one space to each position. This will certainly satisfy our criterion for evenness and leave us with only three additional spaces $(10-7)$ to be accounted for. As soon as there are less spaces to be added than there are available positions, situation (4) prevails. Now our problem is to add *less than one* space to each existing position.

At this point we could add one more space to each of the first three positions. If we adopt this strategy then the overall appearance of the output text will tend to become lopsided. We must, therefore, find a way of more evenly distributing these extra spaces among the 7 positions. The sort of thing we would like is if there was one space to be added then it would be added to the middle space. If there were two spaces to be added then the first would be positioned one-third of the way across and the second, two-thirds of the way across. When this approach is coupled with the varying word sizes and input line lengths, the additional spaces will tend to blend into the background. Returning to our example, where we need to distribute 3 spaces over 7 positions, we have:

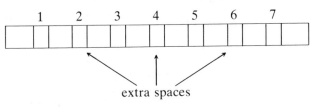

extra spaces

In this particular case the "best" result would probably correspond to the extra spaces being added after words 2, 4 and 6.

Before trying to work out a mechanism we had better look at another example (e.g. distributing 4 additional spaces among 7 positions).

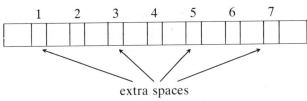

extra spaces

By "eye", it would seem "best" to distribute the extra spaces in this case after words 1, 3, 5 and 7. What we now need to do is develop a mechanism that can distribute spaces in this way. Notice in both cases there is a gap of two between consecutive extra spaces. In the first case where we need to add 3 spaces to 7 positions we can calculate that ideally we should add one space to every $2\frac{1}{3}$ (i.e. $\frac{7}{3}$) positions. This is *closer* to 2 than anything else so adding the extra spaces after every second word (i.e. 2, 4, 6) would appear to be a reasonable strategy. In the second case, where 4 extra spaces need to be added to the line, we find that ideally we should add one space every $1\frac{3}{4}$ positions. Once again, every second position would seem to be the closest we can get. Applying this we get the sequence 2, 4, 6, 8. There is a problem here because the last extra space does not fit within our set of 7 even though 2 seems to be the most suitable increment. In the "hand" solution we used the sequence 1, 3, 5, 7 which again uses an increment of 2 but has its starting position shifted back one position. The last two templates are the same except for their starting positions. The most recent observations raise at least two points. Firstly, the chosen starting position can influence whether or not the required set of spaces can be added. Secondly, there is no guarantee that for a given increment it will be possible to add the required number of spaces. Our algorithm will need to accommodate both these points.

Assuming that we are convinced that a "template" method is a good way to distribute extra spaces evenly let us now try to establish a suitable starting position for the general case where we already know the template increment *delta*. In our example with *delta* = 2 we see that the template could be positioned starting at space 1 or space 2. In the general case, a start anywhere between 1 and *delta* would be possible. The question to ask now is which starting position would give us the most *balanced* distribution of extra spaces?

A starting position *next* of:

$$next := delta \textbf{ div } 2$$

will give us good balance since it is the "average" of the possible range. However, *next* will be zero when *delta* is one because of the integer division. We can allow for this situation by using:

$$next := (delta+1) \textbf{ div } 2$$

There remains the second problem of what to do if our chosen template and starting position does not allow us to expand the line to the desired width. (For example, our template/starting-position combination may have allowed us to add 5 spaces whereas in fact 7 spaces need to be added to produce the desired output line length. Once the 5 spaces have been added there still remains the problem of evenly distributing the remaining 2 spaces.) If this situation prevails after adding the spaces according to the template we will have a smaller problem to solve. This smaller problem should be solvable by exactly the same mechanism. This possibility of repetition in distributing the extra spaces suggests that two loops may be needed—one to distribute the extra spaces according to the current template and a second to repeat the process for other templates as necessary. The central part of our mechanism could be:

while still extra spaces to distribute do
(a)   compute current template increment and starting position according to current extra space count,
(b)   distribute extra spaces guided by template and reduce the extra space count accordingly in the process.

Now that we have evolved a mechanism that will handle the case where there are fewer extra spaces than available positions for placing them, we need to ask how this can be fitted in with the rest of the mechanism. Comparing cases (3) and (4) it is clear that we are effectively using a template mechanism in case (3) also. We may not, therefore, need to treat case (3) as a special case. By choosing an increment of one and a starting position of one, our mechanism will allow us to add a space to every existing space. It may happen, however, that we need to add *more than one* space to each existing space (e.g. we may want to distribute 9 spaces over 4 positions). To accommodate this case a variable *spaceblock* can be used to indicate the number of spaces to be added to each position with the current template pass. Where there are *extraspaces* extra spaces to be added to *nspaces* positions we have:

$$spaceblock := extraspaces \textbf{ div } nspaces$$

Following our earlier argument, the template increment *delta* will be calculated using:

$$delta := \textbf{round}(nspaces/extraspaces)$$

There is a problem with using this in the case where *nspaces* is less than *extraspaces* as it would be possible for *delta* to be set to zero. An additional test:

$$\textbf{if } delta = 0 \textbf{ then } delta := 1$$

is therefore needed to catch this situation.

Having established the mechanics of the procedure for distributing the extra spaces to achieve left and right justification our next task is to build the rest of the mechanism around these steps.

Before we can start to add the extra spaces, we must determine the number of positions in the line where spaces can be added. Under the assumption that there is *only one* space separating each word this amounts to counting the number of spaces in the line. In adopting this procedure we have forgotten that there will be a number of leading spaces at the start of a new paragraph. Therefore, *before* counting the spaces on a given line we need to step past any leading spaces. As a precaution, we should also check for spaces on the end of the line.

The steps will be:

1. Remove spaces from beginning and end of line.
2. Zero space count.
3. While still more characters in line do
   - (a) if current character a space then
     - (a.1) add one to space count.

There now remains the problem of actually adding the extra spaces if it is possible to do so. The mechanism we have developed may need to make one or more passes through the data. When we consider the idea of stepping through the line and adding spaces according to the current template we see that problems start to arise. The problems begin as soon as there is a chance

that more than one pass through the line might be needed to obtain the
distribution we want. It is the introduction of the multiple spaces that is going
to cause the problem. What other alternatives do we have? One approach
would be to completely determine where *all* the extra spaces need to be
added *before* trying to add them to the line. An array equal in length to the
number of positions in the line where spaces could be added would serve the
purpose. We could then use this array to store the number of extra spaces
that would need to be added to each existing space. A still better idea is to
put single spaces in this array at the time when we are doing the space count.
This will then solve the initialization problem when consecutive lines are to
be processed. In the case where 10 extra spaces were to be added to 7
existing positions we would end up with the following values in our space
count array.

1	2	3	4	5	6	7
2	3	2	3	2	3	2

Where only 3 extra spaces were to be added to 7 positions we would have:

1	2	3	4	5	6	7
1	2	1	2	1	2	1

Additions to the table can be made iteratively for each template using the
values *next* and *delta* as determined earlier, i.e.

1. While not past end-of-line do
    (a)   add space block at current template position;
    (b)   move to next template position.

This loop may cause more spaces to be added than are needed. An extra
condition that ensures we do not add more spaces than necessary should
therefore be included. Decrementing and testing the extra space count will
do the job.

   Our only remaining task is to use the space count table or array to
produce the left and right justified output. Following our earlier discussion,
we will need to step through the line character-by-character. Whenever we
encounter a space in the line we will need to refer to the space count table to
decide how many extra spaces (if any) must be added at the current location.
If we are to actually write out the left and right justified line as it is processed
one of two things can happen as each character is considered. If the character
is not a space then it can be written out directly otherwise the table will need
to be used to decide how many spaces are to be written before moving to the
next word. The index to the array will need to be incremented by one as each

new space is encountered. In this procedure we have not catered for the leading spaces at the start of new paragraphs. This can be handled at the time when the initial space count for the line is being made. If *start* is where the first alphabetic character on the line begins we can use:

For from start to end of line do
(a)   if next character a space then
     (a.1)   move to next position in space count table
     (a.2)   write out the number of spaces as determined by the space count table
    else
    (a'.1)   write out current text character.

The complete description of our left and right justification algorithm is described below.

Algorithm description

1.   Establish line to be justified, its current (old) length and the justification (new) length.
2.   Include test to see if it can be justified.
3.   Initialize space count and alphabetic start of line.
4.   While current character a space do
    (a)   shift to next character;
    (b)   increment alphabetic start to line;
    (c)   write out a space.
5.   For from alphabetic start to end of line do
    (a)   if current character a space then
       (a.1)   increment space count,
       (a.2)   set current position in space count table to 1.
6.   Remove any spaces from end of line.
7.   Determine the extra spaces to be added from new and old line lengths.
8.   While still extra spaces to add and possible to do so do
    (a)   compute current template increment from space count and extra spaces count (use rounded values);
    (b)   if increment zero then set to 1 since more extras than spaces;
    (c)   if extra spaces greater than space count then
       (c.1)   determine space block using extra spaces and space count
    else
       (c'.1)   set space block size to 1;
    (d)   determine starting position for template;
    (e)   while not end-of-line and still spaces to add do
       (e.1)   add space block to current template position,

       (e.2)   move to next position in template,

       (e.3)   decrement extra space count by space block size.

9. For from start to end-of-line do

    (a)   if next character a space then

       (a.1)   move to next position in space count table,

       (a.2)   write out number of spaces as per space count table

       else

       (a'.1)   write out current character.

10.   Finish off with an end-of-line.

Pascal implementation

```
procedure leftrightjustify(line: nchars; oldlength,newlength: integer);
const tsize = 40;
var delta {increment for current template},
    extraspaces {number of extra spaces to complete justification},
    j {index for writing out spaces},
    ispace {index for space count template},
    nspaces {number of spaces in input line},
    next {current position in template array},
    position {current position in line},
    start {position of first non-space in line},
    spaceblock {number of spaces to be added to current template}:
    integer;
    space {the space character}: char;
    template: array[1..tsize] of integer;

begin {right and left justifies a line of text to newlength by blank fill}
    if oldlength >newlength then
        writeln('line too long – cannot left and right justify')
    else
        begin {line can be left and right justified}
            space := ' '; start := 1;
            while (line[start] = space) and (start <= oldlength) do
                begin {allow for new paragraph with leading blanks}
                    start := start + 1;
                    write(space)
                end;
            nspaces := 0;
            if start <= oldlength then
                while line[oldlength] = space do oldlength := oldlength – 1;
                {assert: all leading ∧ all trailing spaces removed from line ∧
                nspaces = 0}
                {invariant: start =<position =<oldlength ∧ after current
                iteration ∧ nspaces equals count of all spaces in range
                line[1..position]}
            for position := start to oldlength do
                if line[position] = space then
```

```
        begin {count spaces and initialize space count template}
            nspaces := nspaces + 1;
            template[nspaces] := 1
        end;
    extraspaces := newlength - oldlength;
    {invariant: extraspaces = number of spaces still to be added to
    line}

    while (extraspaces > 0) and (nspaces > 0) do
        begin {set up template according to current space count}
            delta := round(nspaces / extraspaces);
            if delta = 0 then delta := 1;
            if extraspaces > nspaces then
                spaceblock := extraspaces div nspaces
            else
                spaceblock := 1;
            next := (delta + 1) div 2;
            {invariant: after current iteration extraspaces = number of
            spaces still to be added to line ∧ spaceblock spaces to be
            added after (next - delta) word ∧ 1 =< next =< nspaces +
            delta ∧ delta >= 1}

            while (next <= nspaces) and (extraspaces > 0) do
                begin {designate space position for current template
                size}
                    template[next] := template[next] + spaceblock;
                    next := next + delta;
                    extraspaces := extraspaces - spaceblock
                end
        end;
    ispace := 0;

    for position := start to oldlength do
        if line[position] = space then
            begin {write extra spaces if any at current location}
                ispace := ispace + 1;
                for j := 1 to template[ispace] do
                    write(space)
            end
        else
            write(line[position]);
        writeln
    end
    {assert: current line left and right justified to length newlength}
end
```

Notes on design

1. The three iterative phases in this algorithm, the space count, the
   template construction and the output of the justified line of text all
   show linear behavior. The output phase which may dominate when the

output length is much greater than the input length is linear with respect to the output length.

2. There are several loops whose behavior we need to consider. The first is the loop that reads past leading spaces at the start of a new paragraph. After the current iteration of this loop, the first ($start-1$) spaces on the line will have been written. For the space-counting loop after the current iteration the first $position$ spaces in the line will have been checked for space identity. Also after the current iteration the space count in the first $position$ characters will be $nspaces$ (excluding leading spaces). The first $nspaces$ positions in the $template$ array will contain ones.

After each iteration of the outer space template construction loop, the number of extra spaces remaining to be inserted will be $extraspaces$. The template with increment size $delta$ will have been constructed at the end of the current iteration. It will have been positioned starting at the ($delta+1$)**div** 2 space. For the inner template construction loop after the current iteration blocks of spaces of size $spaceblock$ will have been added to the first ($next-delta$) space positions of the template according to the current increment $delta$ starting at ($delta+1$)**div** 2. The number of spaces remaining to be inserted after the current iteration will be $extraspaces$.

With regard to the outer **for**-loop for writing out the justified line after the current iteration the first $position$ characters in the old line will have been written out together with all inserted and original spaces needed to follow the first $ispace$ words on the current line. After the current iteration of the inner **for**-loop the first j spaces will have been written after the $ispace$ word on the current line.

With regard to termination, the first **while**-loop terminates because with each iteration another character on the line will have been considered. The **for**-loop for counting spaces will by definition terminate. The inner **while**-loop needed to construct the template will terminate because with each iteration $next$ is increased by at least one since $delta$ is always ≥ 1. With each iteration of the outer template construction loop, the inner template construction loop (which terminates) will be entered and it will *always* reduce the extra spaces to be added. It follows that the outer loop terminates. The other loops all terminate by definition of the **for**-loop and so the complete algorithm terminates since all its loops terminate.

3. In this problem we have seen how what were initially thought to be special cases of the mechanism could with some careful planning be incorporated into the general mechanism.

4. By using an extra table that stored space positions it would be possible to significantly improve the efficiency of the expansion loop.

5. The algorithm handles correctly the case where there is only one word on a line.
6. The algorithm is made simpler by not adding the extra spaces until their complete distribution is known.
7. It is possible to design more sophisticated left and right justification algorithms that produce a more aesthetically pleasing output.

Applications

Document preparation—limited application.

Supplementary problems

6.2.1 Modify the current algorithm so that while it adheres to the basic template distribution idea, it does not add multiple extra spaces to a location before there has been one extra space added to each location.
6.2.2 Incorporate the suggestion in note 4.
6.2.3 Implement a version of the algorithm that passes the left and right justified line back to the calling procedure.
6.2.4 Include tests in the current algorithm to ensure that the line is *not* expanded if more than twice the number of existing spaces must be added to the line.
6.2.5 Design and implement a simpler justification algorithm that does not require the use of a space table.
6.2.6 Design and implement an algorithm that reverses the justification process by removing multiple blanks. Paragraph indentations should be preserved.
6.2.7 Design and implement a left and right justification algorithm that inserts extra spaces after the longest word first, then after the second longest word and so on. In your implementation, by making certain assumptions, try to avoid having to do a sort. This approach usually produces an aesthetically more pleasing output.

Algorithm 6.3
KEYWORD SEARCHING IN TEXT

Problem

Count the number of times a particular word occurs in a given text.

Algorithm development

The text searching problem and related variations of it are commonly encountered in computing. To give an example, we may wish to determine whether or not the word SENTENCE occurs in the text:

THIS IS A SENTENCE OF TEXT

Solving this problem visually is something we do very easily without being conscious in any way of the mechanism we apply. To design a computer algorithm we are going to need to be considerably more explicit. As a starting point we will need to compare in some way the characters in the word with the characters in the text.

To examine text in a computer we are essentially limited to examining it one character at a time. We therefore need a way of deciding when a match has been made.

Perhaps before starting on this line of attack, we should have a clear idea of exactly what we mean by a word and a text. Observation of any piece of text shows us that a word is a *consecutive* sequence of alphabetic characters. A word in a text may be preceded and followed by one or more non-alphabetic characters (e.g. space(s), punctuation marks, end-of-line characters, end-of-file characters). Closer examination shows that the first word is a special case in that it may or may not be preceded by one or more non-alphabetic characters. It follows from the definition of a word that a text is a sequence of words separated by non-alphabetic characters.

We are now in a better position to define what we mean by a match of two words. Two words can be said to match when they agree character-for-character from the first to the last character. It follows that if the number of character-for-character matches is equal to the length of both the word sought and the text word then we have a match. For example,

$$\ldots \text{SENTENCE} \ldots \qquad \text{(text word—length} = 8)$$
$$\updownarrow \text{ match} \ldots \updownarrow \text{ match}$$
$$\text{SENTENCE} \qquad \text{(word sought—length} = 8)$$

number of character-for-character matches (i.e. $\updownarrow$) is 8.

A *mismatch* between two words must therefore mean that the two words are not the same character-for-character or in other words the number of character-for-character matches is less than the length of the two words. We need to be a little careful here because for example the word SENT matches the word SENTENCE but we cannot say that there is a word-match. We will come back to this question a little later. Having worked out the important definitions that are relevant to this problem we must now try to consider how we can implement the text searching algorithm.

Since we must at all times have access to the word we are seeking in the text we will need to store it in an array. In searching for the word SENTENCE we can store it in the first eight locations of an array called *word*. Our task will then be to examine *all* the words in the text and see if each one in turn matches the word SENTENCE. We can do this by examining first the first word in the text, and then the second word in the text, and so on until we come to the end of the text.

Let us consider first the case where there is a match between the first character of the text and the first character of the word. The next step can be to compare the second character of the text with the second character of the word (we must take care that our algorithm will handle one-letter words). To do this we can read the next character and shift a pointer *i* for the *word* array to the second position in the array. For example, we have

We must then compare the *chr* just read with *word*[2]. If the character *chr* is an "E" the matching process can continue by incrementing *i* reading the next *chr* and so on. If *i* gets to 9 (for our example above) we will know that a match of the word pattern has been made.

Every time it is established that the pattern sought has been *completely* matched, we will need to take additional steps to decide whether or not the pattern is a word rather than a substring of a word. Remembering our definitions we can do this by checking whether the pattern is both preceded and followed by a non-alphabetic character.

The central part of our overall strategy is now:

1.   Set *i* to first position in *word*.
2.   While not end-of-file do
     (a)   read next text character;
     (b)   if current text character matches *i*th character in word then
           (b.1)   extend partial match *i* by one;
           (b.2)   if a pattern match then
                        see if word match also and take appropriate action
           else
                deal with mismatch situation.

In reading the text we *must* take into account end-of-lines.

We are left with the problems of checking the word-match condition and dealing with mismatches. From our earlier discussion, we know that, in general, words are preceded by and followed by non-alphabetic characters.

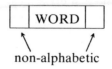

It is easy enough after the pattern-match condition has been met to establish whether or not the next character is alphabetic by simply making the set test

chr in alphabet

provided *alphabet* has been established as the set of alphabetical characters.

The task of checking the character that *precedes* the current pattern is not so easy. Somehow we must find a way to remember the character that precedes the pattern. Characters are eligible to precede a word only when they do not match the current character in the word—that is, when a mismatch condition applies. This suggests that whenever we get a mismatch we should *save* the current text character in case it is needed later to decide whether or not there has been a word-match. The "saved" character will not be changed during a pattern match since it is only changed when a mismatch occurs.

The other step that must be taken when a mismatch occurs is to reset the pointer for the *word* array so that it again points at the first character. The steps to be taken when a mismatch occurs are therefore:

$$\vdots$$

else {mismatch}
(a)   save current text character as *pre*,
(b)   reset *word* array pointer to first position.

To handle the case where the very first word is not preceded by a non-alphabetic character we must initialize the variable *pre* for the character preceding the pattern to a non-alphabetic character. Also the *word* array pointer should be initialized to one.

In our discussion we have not followed through on what must be done when a word-match is established. It turns out that this situation is very similar to the mismatch case. However, now the character that follows the matched word must assume the role of the character that precedes the next word. The pointer for the *word* array will also need to be reset to one. And, finally, the match count will need to be updated. We then have:

if word-match then
(a)   increment match count by one,

(b)   set *pre* to most recent character read,

(c)   reset pointer *i* to first of *word* array.

The complete algorithm for word searching can now be given.

Algorithm description

1.   Establish the word and wordlength *wlength* of the search-word.

2.   Initialize the match-count *nmatches*, set preceding character and set pointer for *word* array *i* to 1.

3.   While not at end-of-file do

    (a)   while not end-of-line do

        (a.1)   read next character;

        (a.2)   if current text character *chr* matches i^{th} character in word then

            (2.a)   extend partial match *i* by 1,

            (2.b)   if a word-pattern match then

                (b.1)   read next character *post*,

                (b.2)   if preceding and following character not alphabetic then

                    (2.a)   update match count *nmatches*,

                (b.3)   reinitialize pointer to *word* array *i*,

                (b.4)   save following character *post* as preceding character

        else

        (2'.a)   save current text character as preceding character for match,

        (2'.b)   reset *word* array pointer *i* to first position;

    (b)   read past end-of-line.

4.   Return word-match count *nmatches*.

The implementation has been designed to handle only lower-case alphabetic characters.

Pascal implementation

```
procedure wordsearch(word: nchars; wlength: integer; var
nmatches: integer);
type letters = 'a'..'z';
var i {position in search word array}: integer;
    chr {current text character},
    pre {candidate for character preceding current word},
    post {candidate for character following current word}: char;
    alphabet: set of letters;
```

```
begin {counts the number of times a word occurs in a given text}
  {assert: wlength > 0}
  alphabet := ['a'..'z'];
  pre := ' '; i := 1;
  while not eof(input) do
    begin {read and process next character}
      {invariant: (i =< wlength ∧ last(i − 1) characters read in text
      match word [1..i − 1]) ∨ (a wordmatch ∧ i = 1) ∧
      nmatches = number of word matches in first (i − 1) characters
      read}
      while not eoln(input) do
        begin
          read(chr);
          if chr = word[i] then
            begin {see if partial match is now complete}
              i := i + 1;
              if i > wlength then
                begin
                  read(post);
                  if (not (pre in alphabet)) and (not (post in
                  alphabet)) then
                    begin {a word match}
                      nmatches := nmatches + 1;
                    end
                  i := 1;
                  pre := post
                end
            end
          else
            begin {a mismatch}
              pre := chr;
              i := 1
            end
        end;
      readln;
    end
  {assert: nmatches = number of times word found in text}
end
```

Notes on design

1. The dominant instruction for this algorithm will be the comparison of the current text character with the current word character. The number of times this test is made is equal to the number of characters in the text being searched.

2. At the stage in the search when the first j characters have been read and processed all text words that *completely* match the search word in the first j characters will have been counted. After each iteration, the value of the variable i will indicate that the preceding $i-1$ characters in the

text match the first $i-1$ characters in the search word if a partial matching situation prevails. With each iteration, the variable *pre* is assigned to a character that is potentially a preceding character for the next word to be matched. At the completion of the current iteration the variable *post* is either undefined or is assigned to the text character located directly after the current pattern match. The algorithm terminates because with each iteration another character is read and so eventually an end-of-file will be reached.

3. The present algorithm uses a very simple mechanism for the dominant part of the computation.

4. The algorithm can be used to search for prefixes and suffixes of words but it *will not* handle the general pattern searching problem even though it is based on a pattern-match preceding the word match. For example, the present algorithm will not record a match in searching for the pattern *abcabdabc* in the text *abcabcabdabc*.

5. At the cost of specialization, we have developed an algorithm with linear worst-case behavior rather than the quadratic worst-case behavior that is possible for the corresponding pattern matching algorithm.

6. In trying to solve this problem, it is useful to start by considering the smallest problem, that of searching a single word of text. In the implementation we have relied upon the fact that Pascal returns a blank when an end-of-line character is encountered.

7. It is possible to implement significantly more efficient algorithms for solving both the current problem and also the more general pattern matching problem.

Applications

Limited text searching.

Supplementary problems

6.3.1   Modify this algorithm so that it will terminate on finding the first complete word-match.

6.3.2   Design and implement a word-searching algorithm that on finding a mismatch with the current word simply reads characters to the start of the next word before attempting a match again.

6.3.3   Design and implement an algorithm that searches a text and *saves* the *word* that provides the best partial match (other than a complete match) with the search word.

6.3.4   Design and implement an algorithm that prints a list of all words in the text that contain the search word as a prefix.

Algorithm 6.4
TEXT LINE EDITING

Problem

Design and implement an algorithm that will search a line of text for a particular pattern or substring. Should the pattern be found it is to be replaced by another given pattern.

Algorithm development

The need to replace one string by another occurs very frequently in program and documentation preparation. Viewed at its simplest level, the underlying task is to replace *all* occurrences on a line of a particular pattern by another pattern. The mechanism for the hand solution to such a problem is very straightforward, i.e. suppose we want to replace *wrong* by *right* in the line below:

> the two wrongs in this line are wrong   (original)

All we need to do is examine the line, find the pattern *wrong* to be changed and replace it with the new pattern *right*. For our example, we would get:

> the two *right*s in this line are *right*   (edited line)

Our preliminary investigation suggests that there are two phases to the text editing problem. The first stage involves *locating* the pattern to be replaced and the second stage involves the actual *replacement* with the new pattern.

The task should be easier if we take advantage of the natural way the problem divides in designing our algorithm. It is, therefore, probably best to work initially on the search. In our earlier discussion on keyword searching in text the point was made that the searching method we proposed would not handle cases like searching for the pattern *abcabdabc* in the text *abcabcab-dabc*. In our text editing algorithm we want to be able to handle such cases. A good place to start on our algorithm might therefore be with an examination of the problem we have just posed.

We have:

$$abcabdabc \qquad \text{(pattern)}$$
$$abcabcabdabc \qquad \text{(text)}$$
$$\uparrow$$
$$\text{mismatch}$$

Our earlier searching algorithm, when confronted with this problem, would proceed with the match up to the sixth character in the text and pattern. Then, having encountered a mismatch, it would continue by comparing the *seventh* character in the text with the *first* character in the pattern. In adopting this strategy the chance of making a match for our present example is lost. It can be seen that the problem arises because after recovering from the mismatch we have proceeded to compare the first character of the pattern with the seventh character in the text. Had we instead recovered from the mismatch by comparing the first character in the pattern with the *second* character in the text and so on the match we require would not have been missed.

The mechanism we are trying to implement can be thought of *as positioning the start of the pattern at the first character in the text, the second character in the text, and so on.* At each position the degree of match between the pattern and the text must be determined. In this way there will be no risk of missing a match. In our example above there are only four positions at which we can locate the pattern relative to the text. They are:

Positions

	abcabcabdabc	(text)
(1)	abcabdabc	mismatch
(2)	abcabdabc	mismatch
(3)	abcabdabc	mismatch
(4)	abcabdabc	match

The central part of our pattern searching strategy is therefore:

while there are still positions in the text to place the pattern do
(a)   "locate" pattern at next position in text;
(b)   see if there is a complete match at current text position.

From the way the pattern length *patlength* and the text size *textlength* interact we can conclude that there are:

$$textlength - patlength + 1$$

positions at which the pattern can be placed in the text.

Having placed the pattern at a given position i in the text, the next step is to examine the *extent of the match* at the particular text position i. To do this we need to be able to step through the consecutive characters in the pattern and at the same time we need to be able to *look ahead* in the text. To try to establish the required matching mechanism let us return to our earlier example and consider the case where the pattern is positioned starting at the fourth text position. The variable j can be used to characterize the extent of the match.

$$i = 4 \qquad i = 12$$
$$\downarrow \qquad\quad \downarrow$$

abcabcabdabc   (text)
　　abcabdabc   (pattern)
　　↑　　　　↑
$$j = 1 \qquad j = 9$$

In determining the extent of the match at position four we want the text and pattern indices to jointly follow the sequences below:

text	pattern	displacement
4	1	3
5	2	3
6	3	3
⋮	⋮	⋮
12	9	3

As it happens, the sequence for the text is displaced by $i-1$ relative to the pattern sequence. We can accommodate this displacement in our comparison by using:

if $pattern[j] = txt[i+j-1]$ **then** "extend the match"

Incrementing j will serve to extend the match. In fact a loop that extends over the pattern length but will stop on a mismatch will do the job.

We now have a way of making the match between the pattern and the text but as yet we do not have a way of deciding when a complete match has been made or what to do when a mismatch occurs. Referring again to our example, we see that the simplest way to test for a match is to check whether j has advanced *beyond* the pattern length (in our example above, if j were to reach 10 we would know there was a complete match at the current text position). The test we would apply is:

if $j > patlength$ then
　　"a complete match so carry out the edit operation"

The mismatch situation which is likely to be the more common situation clearly does not require that any editing be done. Examination of the first pattern position for our example makes it clear what has to be done in a mismatch situation.

$$i = 1 \quad \text{mismatch}$$
$$\downarrow \qquad \downarrow$$

abcabcabdabc   (text)
abcabdabc   (pattern)
　　　　↑
$$j = 6$$

In this example, before we can test for a match with the start of pattern located at position 2 the pointer for the pattern j will need to be reset to one.

This most recent investigation suggests that the matching mechanism is simpler than we had originally supposed. Whenever we compare a text character and a pattern character one of two situations prevails—*the pair of characters either match or there is a mismatch.* If there is a match then we are obliged to make an additional test to see if the complete match situation has been established. Once we see the problem in this light the need for a separate matching loop disappears. Our central searching strategy has now evolved to:

while $i \leqslant textlength - patlength + 1$ do
(a)   if $pattern[j] = txt[i+j-1]$ then
          (a.1)   increase j by one,
          (a.2)   if a complete match then perform edit
          else
          (a'.1)   reset pattern pointer j,
          (a'.2)   move pattern to next text position by incrementing i.

We have now reached the point where we can successfully search for and detect a pattern match in the text. The task that remains is to formulate the editing step.

To start on this problem, let us refer back to our original example in which we replaced *wrong* by *right*. It is apparent that in general the edited line will be made up of some parts in common with the original line. In our example the common parts are underlined.

the two wrongs in this line are wrong   (original)
the two rights in this line are right   (edited)

In the general case, we cannot expect that the input and edited lines will be of the same length because the original pattern and its replacement may be different in length. This suggests that it will probably be easiest to create a new copy of the common parts in producing the edited line. Our editing step will therefore involve a sequence of *copying* and *pattern replacement* steps with replacement taking place when the searching algorithm finds a complete match and copying prevailing otherwise. So in producing the edited line we must either copy from the original line or from the replacement pattern. The copying from the original line will therefore need to proceed hand-in-hand with the search. The question that must be answered is, how can we integrate the copying operation into the search? It is apparent that whenever there is a mismatch and a corresponding shift of pattern relative to the text, copying can take place. In the case where a character match is made, it is not so apparent what should be done. Examining this situation more carefully we see that i will only be increased when a complete match is made and so in the partial-match situation no copying will be needed. A complete-match signals the need to copy not from the original line but instead from the substitute pattern. So, in fact the two copying situations that we must deal with are well defined:

(a)   When a mismatch copy from the original line.
(b)   When a complete match copy from new pattern.

Let us consider the mismatch copy first. One proposal for the copy might be:

$$newtext[i] := txt[i]$$

This, however, does not take into account that the new line will grow at a different rate if the old and new patterns are different in length. The pattern position variable i will still be appropriate but a new variable k which can grow at a different rate will be needed for the edited line. The copy in the mismatch situation will then be of the form:

$$newtext[k] := txt[i]$$

When we encounter a complete match we need to copy in a complete pattern rather than a single character as this corresponds to the edit situation. The new pattern $newpattern$ must be inserted *directly after* where the last character has been inserted in the edited line of text (i.e. after position k). Since a number of characters need to be copied, the best way to do it will be with a loop. That is,

```
for l := 1 to newpatlength do
   begin
      k := k+1;
      newtext[k] := newpattern[l]
   end
```

Once the pattern is copied, we will need to *move past* the text positions occupied by the old pattern. We can do this by incrementing i by the old pattern length

$$i := i+patlength$$

At this point we will also need to reset the pointer for the search pattern.

We have now established an editing mechanism that will replace a pattern located anywhere and any number of times in the line to be edited. We have also set up a mechanism to copy from the original text line. Examining this mechanism closely we see that it can fail to copy the last few characters from the text because of the smaller value of the positioning index relative to the number of characters in the original text. We must, therefore, insert steps to copy these "leftover" characters. That is,

```
while i≤textlength do
  begin
    k := k+1;
    nextext[k] := txt[i];
    i := i+1
  end
```

Once these editing requirements are incorporated into our pattern searching scheme we will have the complete algorithm.

Algorithm description

1. Establish the textline, the search pattern, and the replacement pattern and their associated lengths in characters.
2. Set initial values for the position in the old text, the new text, and the search pattern.
3. While all pattern positions in the text have not been examined do
   (a)   if current text and pattern characters match then
      (a.1)   extend indices to next pattern/text character pair,
      (a.2)   if a complete match then
         (2.a)   copy new pattern into current position in edited line,
         (2.b)   move past old pattern in text,
         (2.c)   reset pointer for search pattern
      else
      (a'.1)   copy current text character to next position in edited text,
      (a'.2)   reset search pattern pointer,
      (a'.3)   move pattern to next text position.
4. Copy the leftover characters in the original text line.
5. Return the edited line of text.

Pascal implementation

```
procedure textedit (var text,newtext: nchars; var pattern,newpattern:
nchars; var newtextlength: integer; textlength,patlength,newpatlength:
integer);
var i {position of start of search pattern in text};
    j {pointer for search pattern and displacement for current text
    position},
    k {current number of characters in the edited text line},
    l {index for newpattern}: integer;

begin {searches for and replaces pattern by newpattern in text
returning edited line newtext}
```

```
{assert: textlength,patlength,newtextlength,newpatlength >0}
i := 1; j := 1; k := 0;
{invariant: i =<j =<patlength + 1 ∧ newtext[1..k] established ∧
((j =<patlength ∧ last j − 1 characters in text match pattern[1..j − 1])
∨ (j = 1 ∧ text[i..i + patlength] replaced by newpattern in newtext))}
while i <= textlength − patlength + 1 do
   begin
      if text[i + j − 1] = pattern[j] then
         begin{a pattern and text character match}
            j := j + 1;
            if j > patlength then
               begin {a complete pattern match has been made}
                  for l := 1 to newpatlength do
                     begin {copy new pattern to edited line}
                        k := k + 1;
                        newtext[k] := newpattern[l]
                     end;
                  i := i + patlength;
                  j := 1
               end
         end
      else
         begin {a mismatch so copy current text character to edited
         line and reset}
            k := k + 1;
            nextext[k] := text[i];
            i := i + 1;
            j := 1
         end
   end;
while i <= textlength do
   begin {copy left over characters from text to edited line}
      k := k + 1;
      newtext[k] := text[i];
      i := i + 1
   end;
{assert: newtext[1..k] represents edited text with all
non-overlapping occurrences of pattern replaced by newpattern}
newtextlength := k
end
```

Notes on design

1. The dominant instruction in this algorithm is the comparison of the
    current text character with the current pattern character. The pattern
    searching algorithm *by itself* has potentially quadratic worst-case
    behavior since the number of comparisons is slightly less than the
    product of the pattern and text lengths. The present algorithm makes
    considerably fewer comparisons because of the shift made when a
    pattern match is established. The worst-case situation for a given

pattern length is when there are no complete matches but a maximum number of partial matches (e.g. suppose we were searching for *aaab* in the text *aaaaaaaaaaaa*...). The average behavior of the algorithm should be close to linear in the text length.

2. At the stage in the search when the pattern has been placed in the first i positions in the text, all patterns in the text in the first i characters that completely match the search pattern will have been found and replaced by the new pattern. After each iteration the value of the variable j will indicate that the previous $j-1$ characters in the text starting at i match the first $j-1$ characters in the search pattern if either a partial match or a mismatch situation prevails. After an iteration in which a complete match situation exists, j will be set to 1. After each iteration the variable k represents the current number of characters in the edited text line. At the end of each iteration, either i has remained constant and j has increased or i has increased and j has been reset to 1. The variable j can increase under constant i only until it exceeds *patlength* at which time i increases. So, although the loop variable i does not increase with each iteration, there will always only be a finite number (i.e. *patlength*) of non-productive iterations before i is again increased towards the termination limit. It follows that the main loop will terminate as will the two minor copying loops.

3. This algorithm handles the case when the pattern is longer than the text.

4. Viewing the problem as one of placing the pattern at a sequence of text positions simplifies the design.

5. In editing the line of text we have assumed that overlap need not be considered by stepping past matched text when an edit has been performed. In some applications this assumption may not be appropriate.

6. Much more efficient pattern searching algorithms exist as we shall see later in the chapter.

Applications

Limited text editing.

Supplementary problems

6.4.1   Implement a version of the current pattern searching algorithm that counts the number of times a given pattern occurs in a text. Your implementation should accommodate the fact that the search pattern may have repeating subsegments.

6.4.2   Design and implement an algorithm that will remove all occurrences of a particular pattern from a text.

6.4.3   Using English text and patterns determine the average behavior of the pattern searching algorithm in 6.4.1

6.4.4   Try to implement a pattern searching algorithm that has linear rather than quadratic worst-case behavior.

6.4.5   Given two ordered sets of numbers A and B, determine whether or not the set A is contained within the set B.

6.4.6   Implement an algorithm that prints all patterns that are the same length as the search pattern but which may or may not differ from the pattern by one character.

Algorithm 6.5
LINEAR PATTERN SEARCH

Problem

Design and implement a pattern searching algorithm with a performance that is linearly dependent on the length of the string or text being searched. A count should be made of the number of times the search pattern occurs in the string.

Algorithm development

We have already seen a simple pattern matching algorithm used in the text editing problem (algorithm 6.4). The simple algorithm exhibits close to linear behavior for applications like searching English text. That is, the number of character comparisons made is only slightly more than the length of the text. The efficiency of this algorithm can, however, deteriorate seriously in other applications where much *smaller* alphabets are considered. And, in the worst possible case, the number of character comparisons will only be slightly less than the *product* of the string and search-pattern lengths. It is, therefore, desirable to have a pattern searching algorithm with a performance that is always linearly dependent on the string length no matter what alphabet size prevails.

To make a start on the more efficient pattern searching algorithm, let us first examine the simple pattern matching algorithm more closely.

<pre>
        abcabdabc   (search pattern)
        abcabcabdabc...   (string being searched)
            ↑
           mismatch
</pre>

In our example, the match between the pattern and the string proceeds until we get a mismatch with the d and the c in the sixth position. When this happens with the simple pattern matching algorithm, the matching resumes by comparing the *second* character in the string with the first character in the search pattern. In making this step *we need to re-examine characters in the string that we have already looked at before*. It is this repeated re-examination of string characters that contributes to the inefficiency of the simple pattern searching algorithm. Our task is to set up a pattern searching algorithm such that it is never necessary to re-examine earlier characters in the string when a mismatch occurs.

In conducting the simple pattern search, the idea was to "place" the pattern sought at consecutive positions in the text and in each case establish the extent of the match. Referring back to our example, we can see that the problem arises when we get a partial match. If we are not to re-examine any earlier characters in the text we need to find a way of using the information gained in making the mismatch. Let us look again more closely at our example to try to discover if there is an alternative course of action after the mismatch at position 6.

$$abcabdabc \qquad \text{(search pattern)}$$
$$abcabcabdabc... \qquad \text{(string being searched)}$$
$$\uparrow$$
$$\text{mismatch}$$

To explore this we can place the pattern at consecutive positions relative to the string. For example,

Position	mismatch position $\downarrow$	
	abcabc...	(string)
(2)	abcab...	(pattern)
(3)	abca...	(pattern)
(4)	abc...	(pattern)

From the example, for the positions already examined in the partial match at string position one, it can be seen that the second and third positions offer no possibility of a match. The fourth position offers a possibility of a match because the fourth string character matches the first pattern character and so on. Having discovered that the pattern may be able to make a match starting at a position (the fourth) *earlier* than the mismatch position (i.e. the sixth position) we must try to understand what this means. Examining our sample string closely, we see that the reason that a match can start *before* the mismatch position is because the *beginning* of the string is *repeated* before the mismatch. It is this partial match with the repeated part of the pattern that prevents us from resuming the search directly after the mismatch by comparing the first character in the pattern with the seventh character in the string. We must now ask what have we learned from this observation that might allow us not to re-examine any of the earlier string characters?

If we are going to avoid any re-examination of the earlier string characters then, directly after the mismatch at the sixth character, either the sixth or the seventh character will have to be involved. We have also established that it is not appropriate to compare the first pattern character with the seventh string character as this might result in us missing a match. The question now arises, is there any way out of this dilemma? Looking once more at our example with the pattern placed in various positions we see that it would be valid to compare the third character in the pattern with the sixth character in the string as this would introduce no risk of missing a possible match with the pattern positioned starting at the fourth character.

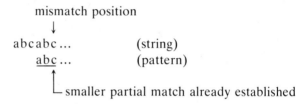

In making this new comparison what we have done is taken note of the *smaller* partial match that exists between the pattern and the string when the mismatch happens at the sixth character in the string. In adopting this strategy, we have been able to avoid looking at any of the characters in the string that precede the mismatch position.

We now know that we can avoid having to step back in the string by taking note of smaller partial matches that may exist at the time when we encounter a mismatch. Our next job is to refine and develop this idea. In our example above, the smaller partial match that exists when the mismatch occurs is *ab*. If we are going to use the idea we have just developed, we need a way of establishing the appropriate smaller partial match (if any) that will exist when a mismatch occurs at *each* possible position in the pattern. Our method for developing this will need to be independent of the string being searched and so we are only left with establishing these partial matches from the pattern itself. To discover this let us look more closely at another pattern.

abcabcacab

If we get a mismatch between the *first* character in the pattern and the current string character, we can compare the *first* character in the pattern with the *next* character in the string (see Fig. 6.1(a)). If, however, the first pattern character matches with the string and it is followed by a mismatch (Fig. 6.1(b)), we can once again compare the first character in the pattern with the next character in the string.

As a further example, suppose the first five characters in the pattern are matched at the current location in the string and there is a mismatch at the sixth character. (See Fig. 6.1(c).)

current situation

```
        abcabcacab        (pattern)
    ...ba...              (string)
        ↑
        mismatch
```

next step

```
        abcabcacab        (pattern shifted forward one place)
    ...ba...              (string)
```

(a) Mismatch at first character in pattern.

current situation

```
        abcabcacab        (pattern)
        a*a...            (string)
        ↑
        mismatch
```

(where "*" is any character other than "b")

next step

```
         abcabcacab       (pattern)
        a*a...            (string)
```

(b) Mismatch at second character in pattern.

current situation

```
        abcabcacab        (pattern)
    ...abcab*...          (string)
             ↑
             mismatch
```

(where "*" is any character other than "c")

next step

```
          abcabcacab      (pattern)
    ...abcab*...          (string)
```

(c) Mismatch at sixth character in pattern.

Fig. 6.1

In this latest situation, after taking into account the mismatch at the sixth character, the extent of the match may actually be *two* because of the way in which *ab* is repeated in the pattern. It follows that we can continue the match by comparing the *third* character in the pattern with the *sixth* character (as shown) in the string. Notice in this case we have *not* advanced in the string at the time of making the next comparison.

Table 6.1 gives the smaller partial matches that will exist when the current mismatch occurs.

Table 6.1   Smaller partial match table

Mismatch position	1	2	3	4	5	6	7	8	9	10
Pattern	a	b	c	a	b	c	a	c	a	b
Smaller partial match	0	0	0	1	2	3	4	0	1	2

To establish these smaller partial matches needed to recover from a mismatch situation, we need to model the process we have just developed by hand. This amounts to taking one copy of the pattern and considering it as a fixed string. The other copy of the pattern is then located at positions relative to the first copy. Whenever a partial match is established (as for example, starting at the fourth position), the positions that are part of the partial match (i.e. 5, 6, and 7 in our example) are then not considered as positions to look for partial matches. The reason for this is that they could only potentially provide smaller partial matches than the one that has already been established. A little thought reveals that we need to always consider the *largest* partial matches to avoid missing complete matches when recovering from mismatches.

We can summarize the procedure for establishing all the partial matches as follows:

while all partial matches for the pattern have yet to be established do
(a)   continue the match from the current starting position and save partial match details along the way until a mismatch occurs;
(b)   if a mismatch has occurred then
    (b.1)   record zero partial match for the current position,
    (b.2)   reset count to consider partial match at the next position.

Having worked out how to derive the partial match information needed for our linear search algorithm, let us try to develop a searching algorithm that uses it.

At the outset it seems fairly clear that we will need to handle the match and mismatch situations between the pattern and the string differently.

Basically, what we must do is consider "placing" the pattern relative to the string as dictated by the partial matches, complete matches, and mismatches that occur. Our basic strategy might be:

while all potential match positions not considered do
(a)   if current string and pattern characters match then
      (a.1)   extend partial match
      else
      (a'.1)   deal with mismatch situation,

To extend the partial match we will need a mechanism that moves to the next positions in both the *string* and *pattern*. Accompanying this increase we will need a test for complete matches. This can simply be a test of the form:

if partial match index exceeds pattern length then
   "a complete match is established".

Whenever this condition is satisfied we will need to count the match. There is also the question of how to "recover" from a complete match. We have so far only considered how to recover from mismatches. Studying the table for our earlier example, we see that the extent of the *partial match* will be *ab*... or in other words the first two characters of the pattern when the complete match is established. It follows that the recovery from the complete match will not need to be handled differently from mismatch recoveries.

Now comes the question of how we are to use the partial match table to recover from a mismatch. In our preliminary discussion on deriving the partial matches, we found that not all mismatch situations were treated identically. They divide into two types, those where the earlier *partial match is zero*, and those where there is a *finite partial match* when the mismatch occurs. In the latter case there is no movement forward in the string when the rematch commences whereas in the zero partial match situation it is simply a matter of advancing one character in the string and comparing it with the first character in the search pattern. The zero partial match is indicated in the table directly by a zero element and so this situation is easy to detect. To decide on the details of the mechanism needed to recover from a mismatch when we have a non-zero partial match to continue with let us consider a specific case.

Suppose that we wish to recover from a mismatch at the seventh character with our pattern used earlier. In this case the partial match on recovery is *abc* and so the *fourth* character in the pattern will need to be compared with the current string character at the next step. Examining Table 6.1, we can see that the value at the *sixth* position (the one *directly before* the mismatch) provides us with the recovery partial match. If the partial match table is called *recover* and the variable *match* gives the position in the pattern when the mismatch occurs then the statement below gives us the new position in the pattern.

$$match := recover[match-1]+1$$

The "1" needs to be added to the recovery value because it is the *next* character in the pattern beyond the current partial match that should be compared with the current string character. The mechanism needed to handle the mismatch condition is therefore:

if zero partial match then
(a)   move to next character in string
(b)   and reset pattern pointer to beginning
else
   $match := recover[match-1]+1.$

Recovery from the complete match is handled similarly. In the implementation a separate procedure can be used for the recovery.

In setting up the partial match table the first position is not set as it corresponds to zero displacement. The index of the recovery can assume values of zero as well as one and so *both* these positions should have a zero value recorded.

We are now in a position to describe in detail the algorithms for setting up the *recover* table and conducting the linear search.

Algorithm description

Description for both the search algorithm and the recovery setup algorithm are given in this section.

(1)   The partial-match table setup algorithm

1.   Establish the search pattern.
2.   Set initial displacement between the pattern and itself to one.
3.   Initialize the zero and first positions in the partial match array to zero.
4.   While all positions of pattern relative to itself not considered do
     (a)   if current pattern and displaced pattern character pairs match then
           (a.1)   save current degree of partial match,
           (a.2)   move to next position in pattern and the displaced pattern
     else
           (a'.1)   a mismatch so set partial match to zero,

(a'.2)   reset pointer to start of displaced pattern,

(a'.3)   move the start of the displaced pattern to the next available position.

5. Return the partial match table.

(2)   The linear pattern searching algorithm

1. Establish the pattern to be searched for and the string in which it is to be sought together with the lengths of the pattern and the string.

2. Set initial values for start of pattern and string and zero the match count.

3. While all appropriate pattern positions in the string have not been examined do

(a)   if current string and pattern characters match then

(a.1)   extend indices to next pattern/string pair,

(a.2)   if a complete match then

(2.a)   update complete match count,

(2.b)   reset recovery position from the partial match table

else

(a'.1)   reset recovery position from the partial match table.

4. Return count of the number of complete matches of the pattern in the string.

(3)   The procedure for recovering from mismatches and complete matches

1. Establish the partial match table, the current position in string and position in pattern.

2. If no smaller partial match then

(a)   move to next position in string,

(b)   return to start of pattern

else

(a')   recover from mismatch or complete match by using table to set new smaller partial match for current position in string.

3. Return smaller partial match and current pattern position.

Pascal implementation

```
procedure kmpsearch (pattern: nchars; string: nchars; var recover:
ntchars; var nmatches; integer; patlength, slength: integer);
var position {current position in string},
    match {one more than extent of current partial match}: integer;

procedure restart (recover: ntchars; var match, position: integer);
```

```
begin {uses partial match table to recover from mismatches and
complete matches}
   {assert: mismatch or complete match ∧ match = position in pattern
   ∧ position = position in string}
   match := recover[match − 1] + 1;
   if match = 1 then
      {no smaller partial match so move to next position and restart}
      position := position + 1
      {assert: (match − 1) = smaller partial match ∧ match = position in
      pattern ∧ position = position in string}
end;



procedure partialmatch (pattern: nchars; var recover: ntchars;
patlength: integer);
var position {current starting position of displaced pattern},
   match {one more than extent of current partial match}: integer;



begin {sets up partial match table used by linear pattern search}
   {assert: patlength > 0}
   position := 2; match := 1;
   recover[0] := 0; recover[1] := 0;
   {invariant: pattern[1..match − 1] matches pattern [position − match
   + 1..position − 1] ∧ recover[position − 1] = match − 1 ∧
   position = < patlength + 1}
   while position < = patlength do
      begin
         if pattern[position] = pattern[match] then
            begin
               recover[position] := match;
               match := match + 1;
               position := position + 1
            end
         else
            begin
               recover[position] := 0;
               match := 1;
               position := position + 1
            end
      end
   {assert: complete partial match table recover[0..patlength]
   constructed}
end;



begin {pattern search algorithm − uses partial match table to achieve
linearity}
   partialmatch (pattern, recover, patlength);
   {assert: partial match table constructed ∧ patlength, slength > 0}
   position := 1; match := 1;
```

          (a'.2)   reset pointer to start of displaced pattern,

          (a'.3)   move the start of the displaced pattern to the next available position.

5.   Return the partial match table.

(2)   The linear pattern searching algorithm

1.   Establish the pattern to be searched for and the string in which it is to be sought together with the lengths of the pattern and the string.

2.   Set initial values for start of pattern and string and zero the match count.

3.   While all appropriate pattern positions in the string have not been examined do

    (a)   if current string and pattern characters match then

          (a.1)   extend indices to next pattern/string pair,

          (a.2)   if a complete match then

               (2.a)   update complete match count,

               (2.b)   reset recovery position from the partial match table

    else

          (a'.1)   reset recovery position from the partial match table.

4.   Return count of the number of complete matches of the pattern in the string.

(3)   The procedure for recovering from mismatches and complete matches

1.   Establish the partial match table, the current position in string and position in pattern.

2.   If no smaller partial match then

    (a)   move to next position in string,

    (b)   return to start of pattern

    else

    (a')   recover from mismatch or complete match by using table to set new smaller partial match for current position in string.

3.   Return smaller partial match and current pattern position.

Pascal implementation

```
procedure kmpsearch (pattern: nchars; string: nchars; var recover:
ntchars; var nmatches; integer; patlength, slength: integer);
var position {current position in string},
    match {one more than extent of current partial match}: integer;

procedure restart (recover: ntchars; var match, position: integer);
```

begin {*uses partial match table to recover from mismatches and complete matches*}
    {**assert**: *mismatch or complete match* $\wedge$ *match* = *position in pattern* $\wedge$ *position* = *position in string*}
    match := *recover*[*match* − 1] + 1;
    if *match* = 1 **then**
        {*no smaller partial match so move to next position and restart*}
        position := *position* + 1
        {**assert**: (*match* − 1) = *smaller partial match* $\wedge$ *match* = *position in pattern* $\wedge$ *position* = *position in string*}
end;

procedure *partialmatch* (*pattern*: *nchars*; **var** *recover*: *ntchars*; *patlength*: **integer**);
var *position* {*current starting position of displaced pattern*},
    match {*one more than extent of current partial match*}: **integer**;

begin {*sets up partial match table used by linear pattern search*}
    {**assert**: *patlength* > 0}
    position := 2; *match* := 1;
    recover[0] := 0; *recover*[1] := 0;
    {**invariant**: *pattern*[1..*match* − 1] *matches pattern* [*position* − *match* + 1..*position* − 1] $\wedge$ *recover*[*position* − 1] = *match* − 1 $\wedge$ *position* = < *patlength* + 1}
    while *position* < = *patlength* **do**
      begin
        if *pattern*[*position*] = *pattern*[*match*] **then**
          begin
            recover[*position*] := *match*;
            match := *match* + 1;
            position := *position* + 1
          end
        else
          begin
            recover[*position*] := 0;
            match := 1;
            position := *position* + 1
          end
      end
    {**assert**: *complete partial match table recover*[0..*patlength*] *constructed*}
end;

begin {*pattern search algorithm* − *uses partial match table to achieve linearity*}
    partialmatch (*pattern*,*recover*,*patlength*);
    {**assert**: *partial match table constructed* $\wedge$ *patlength, slength* > 0}
    position := 1; *match* := 1;

{*invariant*: (*match* =<*patlength* ∧ *string*[*position* −*match*
+1..*position* − 1] *matches pattern*[1..*match* − 1]) ∨ (*a pattern match*
∧ *nmatches* =*number of overlapping matches in first position* − 1
characters of string)}
while *position* <=*slength* **do**
  begin {*see if current partial match can be extended*}
    if *pattern*[*match*] = *string*[*position*] **then**
      begin {*extend match and test for complete match*}
        match := *match* +1;
        position := *position* +1;
        if *match* >*patlength* **then**
          begin {*count and recover from complete match*}
            nmatches := *nmatches* +1;
            restart (*recover, match, position*)
          end
      end
    else {*recover from mismatch*}
      restart (*recover, match, position*)
  end
  {*assert*: *nmatches* =*number of times pattern found in string*}
end

Notes on design

1. In the algorithm for constructing the partial match table, the dominant step is the character comparison between the pattern and the displaced pattern. This is executed only $(m-1)$ times for a pattern of length m. The algorithm is therefore linearly dependent on the length of the pattern.

    With the searching algorithm, once again the character comparison step dominates. The number of times it is executed is determined by the rate at which *match* and *position* increase towards the string end. Since for a string of length n there can be at most n shifts forward made either by the pattern or in the string, then at most $2n$ comparisons could be made. The search algorithm therefore has linear or $O(n)$ performance.

2. For the partial match procedure, after the iteration for a given value of *position* the smaller partial matches for the first (*position* −1) values in the *recover* table will be established. On termination when *position* exceeds *patlength* the complete *recover* table will have been built. Also after the iteration with the current value of *position* the first (*position* −1) characters will have been compared with the displaced pattern.

    After the iteration with the current value of *match* it will remain invariant that the first (*match* −1) characters of the displaced pattern match the fixed pattern, starting at (*position* −1) in the fixed pattern and extending backwards (*match* −1) positions. The algorithm terminates because with each iteration *position* is advanced by one and so eventually it will exceed *patlength*.

In the search algorithm, at the point when the first *position* characters have been considered, all patterns in the string in the first *position* characters that completely match the search pattern will have been counted. This will be reflected by the value of *nmatches*. The same argument that was applied to *match* in the partial match algorithm is relevant for the search algorithm. The argument in note 1 confirms that the algorithm will terminate after at most 2*n* steps for a string of length *n*.

3. Specific examples have been very helpful in uncovering the rather elusive and subtle observations needed to solve this problem.

4. The algorithm performs correctly for patterns of length one.

5. Even in our algorithm as it stands, we have let a number of inefficiencies creep in for the sake of clarity and simplicity. For example, the *recover* table should have the "+1" built directly into it.

6. The recovery function we have developed, although probably the easiest to understand, is not one that minimizes the number of comparisons made by the algorithm. For example, notice when we have:

$$abcabc\ldots$$

and a mismatch occurs at the sixth position, there is no point "recovering" at the third position as this also is destined to give a mismatch.

7. It is possible by constructing an appropriate finite state machine to develop a version of this algorithm that examines each string character only *once*.

8. The algorithm we have implemented is a variation on the algorithm due to Knuth, Morris and Pratt (see D. E. Knuth, J. H. Morris and V. R. Pratt, "Fast pattern matching in strings", *SIAM J. Computing*, **6**, 323–50 (1977)).

9. Aho and Corasick give a very elegant application and implementation of the Knuth, Morris and Pratt algorithm (see A. V. Aho and M. J. Corasick, "Efficient string matching: an aid to bibliographic search", *Comm. ACM.*, **18**, 333–40 (1975)).

10. Bailey and Dromey give a sublinear pattern searching algorithm for strings from small alphabets (see T. A. Bailey and R. G. Dromey "Fast string searching by finding subkeys in subtext", *Inf. Proc. Letts.*, **11**, 130–3 (1980)).

Applications

Pattern searching in small alphabet systems and multiple keyword searching in text.

Supplementary problems

6.5.1   In many applications failure to match with the first character in the pattern will dominate. Try to restructure the algorithm so that it can take advantage of this fact.

6.5.2   Try to construct a better recovery function based on the observation in note 6.

6.5.3   It is possible to implement a much cleaner and more efficient version of the algorithm that does not need to distinguish between zero-match and partial-match recovery states. To do this, a second table *delta* made up of zeroes and ones appropriately placed can be used. The variable *position* will then be updated using

$$position := position + delta[match-1]$$

Modify the partial match algorithm so that it appropriately generates the *delta* table and make changes to the search algorithm so that it takes advantage of the *delta* table.

6.5.4   Using the ideas present in the linear search algorithm, try to develop a sublinear search algorithm that is dominated by a mechanism that needs to examine only every k^{th} character in the string. The value of k should be considerably less than half the search pattern length. (See T. A. Bailey and R. G. Dromey, "Fast string searching by finding subkeys in subtext," *Inf. Proc. Letts.*, **11**, 130–3 (1980).)

Algorithm 6.6
SUBLINEAR PATTERN SEARCH

Problem

Design and implement an algorithm that will efficiently search a given text for a particular keyword or *pattern* and record the number of times the keyword or pattern is found.

Algorithm development

In looking for the keyword SENTENCE in the text

THIS IS A RATHER SLOW ATTACK AT TEXT...

one approach that we can take may proceed as follows. Test if the first character in the word matches the first character in the text (e.g. compare S and T). If they do not match, compare the first character in the word with the second character in the text (e.g. compare S and H) and so on. When the first character in the word matches the current character in text (e.g. S of SENTENCE matches S of SLOW) we then compare the *second* character in the word with the next character in the text (in this case E with L) and so on. It is straightforward to see how this idea can be extended to give complete-word matches. The question we need to ask at this stage is "is there a better way of implementing a text searching algorithm?" In the method described we appear to be doing a lot of unnecessary work but at the same time it is difficult to see that there might be other alternatives.

In the example above we started off by seeing if the word SENTENCE could start at the first character in the text, that is,

```
T H I S   I S   A   R A T H E R   S L OW...    (text)
S E N T E N C E                                (word)
```

If the word SENTENCE were to start at the first character in the text then the first character would have had to be an S. In addition the second character would have had to be an E, ..., and the eight character an E.

Since the word SENTENCE does not start at the first character in the text we may ask "where next could the word SENTENCE start?" Looking carefully at the structure of the word and the text we conclude that it could not possibly start until *after* the eighth character. This is so because the eighth character is a blank and *there is no blank in the word SENTENCE* (see Fig. 6.2).

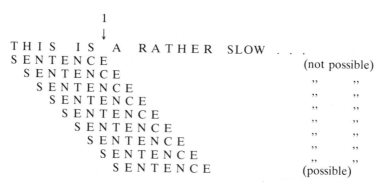

Fig. 6.2 Next starting positions of pattern SENTENCE for given text.

We could just as easily have established that SENTENCE did not start in character position 1 by comparing first the last character in the word against the eighth character in the text. In doing so we would have encountered the blank character which is not in the word SENTENCE. Since a

We can conclude from the above discussion that one of three basic situations applies when we are at any location in the text:

1. the text character hit is *not present* in the keyword;
2. the character hit *is present* in the keyword;
3. the character hit is the *same* as the last character in the keyword.

We have already dealt with the first situation, so let us examine the other two cases in more detail.

Consider that we are searching for the pattern SEPTEMBER and that we have just hit the text character T.

For example:

```
S E P T E M B E R     (pattern)
? ? ? T ? ? ? ? ?     (text)
      └───────┘
          5
```

Examination of SEPTEMBER tells us that we can safely make a jump of five characters past T without risk. If an R is not found with the latest jump then T cannot have been part of the ..T....R fragment of SEPTEMBER. Therefore, skipping could continue in accordance with the identity of the new character encountered. Similarly we can arrive at the following skip list:

```
encounter   S then skip 8
    ,,      E   ,,    ,,  (7, 4, or 1)?
    ,,      P   ,,    ,,  6
    ,,      T   ,,    ,,  5
    ,,      M   ,,    ,,  3
    ,,      B   ,,    ,,  2
    ,,      R   ,,    ,,  0?
```

At this stage there is a problem about what to do when we hit an E or an R. We see that there are three possible skips associated with E.

For example,

```
        S E P T E M B E R
```

We must therefore decide whether a jump of 7, 4, or 1 is appropriate. The situation we have is:

```
    ? ? E ? ? ? . . . X        (text)
S E P T E M B E R           case (1)   skip 1
    S E P T E M B E R       case (2)   skip 4
        S E P T E M B E R   case (3)   skip 7
```

Now if we skipped 7 and really case (1) applied when we encountered an X which is not in SEPTEMBER we would continue. Remembering that we want no risk of missing a keyword match we must conclude that the following rule should apply. When a character in the text is encountered that occurs multiply in the keyword always make the *smallest* skip associated with that character—this guarantees there will be no chance of missing a keyword match (in the example above on encountering an E a skip of 1 would be made).

The other situation that we must consider is what to do when we encounter a text character that is the same as the last character in the keyword? There is no way we can skip forward without risking missing a match. Our only alternative is to start matching backwards until we match the keyword or until we get a mismatch. After the backward matching has terminated we need to again resume forward matching.

If the last character occurs only once in the keyword, then a skip can be made equivalent to the length of the word. If the last character occurs more than once in the keyword as in the word SESSIONS then a skip from the latest occurrence of the multiple character (in this case 4) must always be made.

We can now be specific about the skips associated with all the letters in SEPTEMBER.

For example,

$$8\ 1\ 6\ 5\ 1\ 3\ 2\ 1\ 9 \quad - \quad \text{skips}$$
$$\text{S\ E\ P\ T\ E\ M\ B\ E\ R} \quad - \quad \text{characters}$$

To be able to use this skip information in a search we need to be able to access it quickly. That is, whenever we see an E we want to know immediately that the length of the skip we can make is 1. One way to do this would be to have an array with 26 slots with slot 1 corresponding to the skip for A, slot 2 corresponding to the skip for B, and so on. The procedure would then be that whenever we encountered a B we would look in slot 2 and get the skip associated with B and so on. An even better way to do this is to use the numeric value of each character directly as an index into the array that contains the skip values (e.g. using the ascii character set for our example above, location 65 (i.e. A) would contain 9, location 66 would contain 2, and so on).

To derive the skip table we can start by filling all locations with a skip equal to the keyword length. We can then proceed to modify the table for those characters contained in the keyword by starting at the leftmost character and moving right. In this case we place, at the array location corresponding to the key value, the skip required to reach the last character in the keyword. This can be implemented in the following way if the array *word* contains the keyword characters.

```
for i := 1 to wlength−1 do
   begin
      p := ord(word[i]);
      skip[p] := wlength−i
   end;
p := ord(word[wlength]);
skip[p] := −skip[p]
```

Notice that any multiple characters will get the *smallest* skip associated with that character in the word. The skip associated with the last character in the word is made negative to make it easy to detect when a backward match needs to be pursued.

Our next consideration is to establish how the skip table is to be used in conducting the search. We know the process starts by examining the character at location *wlength* in the text (e.g. suppose $i = wlength$). The next step has to be to identify the numeric value of the text character at position i. To do this we can use:

$$nxt := ord(txt[i])$$

The value *nxt* then becomes the index to the skip table. If the corresponding skip table value is positive, we are not at the end of the word, so we can move on to the character at position

$$i := i+skip[nxt]$$

Otherwise if the skip table value is negative, we have hit the last character and so we must do some "backmatching".

The actual matching process needs only to be a straightforward character by character process. We can now summarize the steps in the algorithm.

Algorithm description

1. Establish the word and text to be searched.
2. Set up the skip table.
3. Set keyword match count to zero.
4. Set character position i to keyword length.
5. While current character position < textlength do
   (a) get numeric value *nxt* of current character at position i,
   (b) index into skip table at position *nxt*,
   (c) if skip value for current character is greater than 0, then
       (c.1) increase current position by skip value
       else
       (c'.1) backwards-match text and word,
       (c'.2) if match made update match count,

(c'.3)   recover from mismatch.
6.   Return match count.

Pascal implementation

```
procedure quicksearch (text,word: tc; tlength, wlength: integer; var
nmatches: integer);
const asize = 127;
type
ascii = array[0..127] of integer;
var i {index for text search},
  j {index for matching backwards in text},
  k {index for matching backwards in word},
  nxt {ordinal value of current character}: integer;
  match {if true when k = 0 then a word match}: boolean;
  skip: ascii;

begin {set up skip table}
  {assert: wlength > 0 ∧ tlength > 0 ∧ wlength = <tlength ∧ text and
  pattern ascii}
  setskips (word, skip, wlength, asize);
  {assert: skip table established for the search pattern word}
  nmatches := 0;
  i := wlength;
  {invariant: i points to next place where pattern word could end ∧
  wlength = < i = < tlength + wlength ∧ nmatches = number of times
  word matched in first i characters}
  while i <=tlength do
    begin {use skip table to drive search for pattern}
      nxt := ord(text[i]);
      if skip[nxt] > 0 then
        i := i + skip[nxt]
      else
        begin {maybe at end of word so match backwards}
          {assert: last character in word found in text}
          j := i − 1
          k := wlength − 1
          match := true;
          {invariant: word[k + 1..wlength] matches text[j + 1..i] ∧
          k >= 0 ∧ j >= 0 ∧ i = <tlength}
          while (k > 0) and (match = true) do
            begin
              if text[j] = word[k] then
                begin {move back one character in word and text}
                  j := j − 1;
                  k := k − 1
                end
              else
                match := false
            end;
```

```
        {assert: (k = 0 ∧ match = true) ∨ (k > 0 ∧ match = false}
        if match = true then nmatches := nmatches + 1;
        {recover allowing for negative skips}
        i := i − skip[nxt]
    end
  end
  {assert: nmatches = number of times word found in text}
end

procedure setskips (word: tc; var skip: ascii; wlength, asize: integer);
var i {index for skip table array},
    j {index for characters in search word},
    p {ascii value of current character in word}: integer;

begin {set skips associated with all characters in alphabet}
  {assert: wlength > 0}
  for i := 0 to asize do
    skip[i] := wlength;
  {assert: j = 0 ∧ all ascii characters given skip length of wlength}
  {invariant: skip table adjusted according to first j characters in
  word}
  for j := 1 to wlength −1 do
    begin {use ascii as index for skip table}
      p := ord(word[j]);
      skip[p] := wlength −j
    end;
  {assign negative skip to last character to differentiate from others}
  p := ord(word[wlength]);
  skip[p] := −skip[p]
end
```

Notes on design

1. Calculating the average case behavior for this algorithm is difficult because of its dependence on the probability distributions of the text and the word or pattern sought. In the best case when none of the characters in the pattern of length m are in the text of length n we can expect n/m character comparisons. This is the lower bound on the number of comparisons. Because of the way in which the matching backwards has been implemented in the worst case we would expect $O(nm)$ comparisons. We can compute the expected number of comparisons for a search in a given text if we know the probabilities of all characters in the alphabet used in text. In this instance we have:

$$\text{No. of comparisons} = \frac{n}{\sum s_j \times p_j}$$

where s_j is the skip associated with the jth alphabetic character for the given pattern or word being sought and p_j is its probability of occurrence. This estimation can be corrected further by multiplying the number of comparisons by the probability of the *last* character in the word. This gives a *first order* correction for the number of backward matches. With the inclusion of this correction we find that the above formula gives very accurate results for English text. In most cases it is relatively close to n/m.

2. For the searching algorithm, after the ith character has been examined all *complete* matches of the pattern with the text will have been established and *nmatches* will represent the count of such matches at all times. The *skip* associated with the ith character will be greater than zero if the ith character is not the last character in the word. If the *last* occurrence of the ith text character is at the kth position in the search pattern of length m then a skip of $(m-k)$ will be made. If at the ith text character a match is made with the *last* pattern character then while the word and text characters match a move backwards of *one* character in both is made. The algorithm terminates because with each iteration of the outermost loop a positive step through the text is made. The inner matching loop also terminates because with each iteration progress is made toward either establishing a match or a mismatch.

3. In the algorithm an attempt is made to make the best use of the information gained at each step. (We could, however, make better use of the backmatching.)

4. What seems the obvious way to tackle the problem (i.e. by matching the first characters first) can only lead to an inefficient algorithm.

5. Table-driven algorithms (as in this case) are often very efficient.

6. The algorithm is more general than a word matching algorithm. It may be more correctly classified as a pattern matching algorithm.

7. The algorithm is only set to work with ascii characters of the case of the input keyword.

Applications

Text editors, pattern matching, keyword searching.

Supplementary problems

6.6.1   Design a main program that calls the procedure *quicksearch*. The main program should be able to read and search successive blocks of text.

6.6.2   Test out the above procedure by counting the number of comparisons it has to make for words of various lengths (try lengths of 5, 10, 15).

6.6.3   Modify the procedure *quicksearch* so that the table indexing on characters is replaced by the use of sets.

6.6.4   A different approach to fast text searching is to step through the text in skips equal to the word length. As soon as we get a mismatch in trying to match the word sought we skip to the start of the next word. To do this it is necessary to build the "skip-to-the-next-word" links into the text. For example,

<u>11</u>THIS   IS   A<u>16</u>SENTENCE   TO   BE<u>6</u>SKIP<u>0</u>SEARCHED

A "0" is used to indicate an end of line. In conducting this preprocessing it is often prudent to skip over small words (which we are usually not interested in searching for). When words of three characters or less are ignored it is only necessary to examine about 10–20% of the text characters in conducting a search. The performance of this new algorithm will therefore frequently compare very favorably with the algorithm we have just developed.

Design the necessary preprocessing and searching algorithms.

6.6.5   Another fast text searching algorithm involves stepping through the text and examining only every m^{th} character (where m is the search pattern length) and then taking appropriate action to confirm the match when text characters are encountered that belong to the pattern. (See C. Lakos and A. Sale, "Is disciplined programming transferrable?", *Aust. Comp. J.*, **10**, 87–93 (1978).)

Implement this algorithm.

BIBLIOGRAPHY

Wirth (1973) provides one of the few introductory treatments of text processing. Aho *et al.* (1974) gives a more advanced treatment. The other references cover variations on the pattern searching algorithms at the end of the chapter.

1.   Aho, A. V., J. E. Hopcroft and J. D. Ullman, *The Design and Analysis of Computer Algorithms*, chapter 9, Addison–Wesley, Reading, Mass., 1974.
2.   Aho, A. V. and M. J. Corasick, "Efficient string matching: an aid to bibliographic search", *Comm. ACM*, **18**, 333–40 (1975).
3.   Bailey, T. A. and R. G. Dromey, "Fast string searching by finding subkeys in subtext", *Inf. Proc. Letts.*, **11**, 130–3 (1980).
4.   Boyer, R. S. and J. S. Moore, "A fast string searching algorithm", *Comm. ACM*, **20**, 762–72 (1977).
5.   Knuth, D. E., J. H. Morris and V. R. Pratt, "Fast pattern matching in strings", *SIAM J. Comp.*, **6**, 322–50 (1977).
6.   Lakos, C. and A. Sale, "Is disciplined programming transferrable?" *Aust. Comp J.*, **10**, 87–93 (1978).
7.   Wirth, N., *Systematic Programming: An Introduction*, chapter 14, Prentice-Hall, Englewood Cliffs, N.J. 1973.

Chapter 7
DYNAMIC DATA STRUCTURE ALGORITHMS

INTRODUCTION

The need for flexible and efficient methods for storing, manipulating and accessing large amounts of information is central in computing science. To meet this demand a variety of very powerful methods for storing information have evolved. These various *data structures* or *information structures* are accompanied by a set of equally powerful algorithms that can be used for their access and manipulation.

Up until now the only data structure we have been concerned with has been the array. The data structures we will now consider are different in that they use storage or memory *dynamically*. The amount of storage used at any time is therefore *directly proportional* to the amount of information stored at that stage of the computation. With these structures it becomes possible to allocate new storage when it is needed and to discard old storage when it is not needed during the progress of a computation. In contrast, with arrays, a fixed amount of storage must be preallocated and remain throughout the execution of the program. An array is therefore described as a *static* data structure. The *set* and *record* data structures as used in Pascal also come under the heading of static data structures. As we will see these static data structures have a role to play in the creation of dynamic data structures. Typically a record, set or array forms the basic *unit of storage* for a dynamic data structure. These basic units of storage are usually referred to as *nodes* (or elements or items) of the data structure. These nodes are interrelated or linked in some way to form the data structure. The linkage information for a particular node is contained within that node. It is the structure imposed on the data by the linkages which characterizes a given data structure. The possibilities for linkage fall into three classes, linear, hierarchical or tree-like, and network (or graph-like in a mathematical sense) structures. The linkages are referred to as links, pointers, or references.

The simplest of these classes is the *linear* class. For members of this class, there is usually only *one* link associated with each node (end nodes have a *nil* link). This link relates the current node to the next node in the list. The result is a chain-like structure with each node consisting of data and link fields. For example,

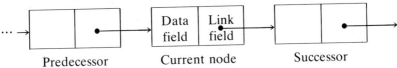

Members within this class are distinguished by the restrictions that they place on the insertion and deletion of nodes or elements. The most important members of this class are *stacks*, *queues* and ordered *linked lists*.

With stacks and queues it is predefined where insertions and deletions take place. For a stack all insertions are made onto the top of the stack and all deletions are similarly made from the top (or *same* end) of the stack. A queue, in contrast to this, allows insertions at one end and deletions at the *other* end. With a linked list, the point at which an insertion or deletion is made depends on the particular item being considered and its relation to the list. A search of the list is therefore usually necessary before an insertion or deletion is made.

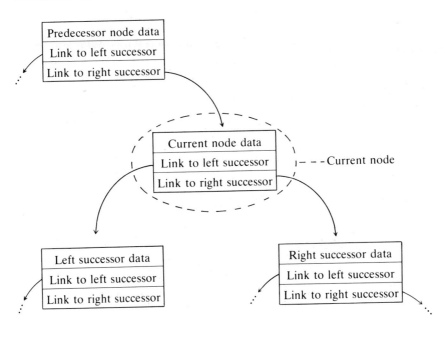

Fig. 7.1 Linked structure for an ordered binary tree.

Among the hierarchical class of dynamic data structures, probably the most widely used structure is the *ordered binary tree* structure. This structure differs from the linear structures in that although nodes can have one predecessor (or ancestor, if we refer to the family tree analogy) they may have as many as *two* successors. Thus each node contains data and the links to its two successors (see Fig. 7.1). The binary tree structure is a *recursive*[†] data structure. What this means is that it is possible to define a tree of a given size in terms of two smaller trees which exhibit the tree-like property. This recursive nature of trees has important implications in relation to the algorithms that are used to process trees. Frequently, recursive algorithms are naturally suited for processing recursively defined tree structures. A feature of the tree data structure is that it allows very fast access of information and efficient insertions and deletions. As with the linked lists, a search of the tree nodes is usually necessary before an insertion or deletion can be made.

The most complicated of the three classes of data structures that we have mentioned are the networks or, as they are more commonly called, the graphs. A *graph* is really a generalization of the tree structure which allows loops. The difference comes about because each node of a graph may have more than one predecessor and more than one successor (in some cases, no distinction is made between predecessors and successors). The operations of searching, insertion and deletion are not usually so important for graphs. Instead, with graphs, we are usually concerned with constructing paths through the graph that link the nodes in some special way. With graphs it is possible for there to be a "distance" associated with the links between pairs of nodes. In the present chapter we will concern ourselves only with linked lists, stacks, queues and binary trees. The various algorithms associated with graphs have their place in the company of a more advanced study.

Algorithm 7.1
STACK OPERATIONS

Problem

Implement two procedures, one for adding items to a stack and the second for removing items from a stack.

---

† See Chapter 8.

Algorithm development

Most of us are familiar with the way some office work-piles operate. As items of work are received they are stacked *on top* of one another on a desk. Then, as time permits, a member of the office staff removes the item that is currently on top of the stack and attends to it. The two possible operations on the office stack are illustrated in Figs. 7.2 and 7.3.

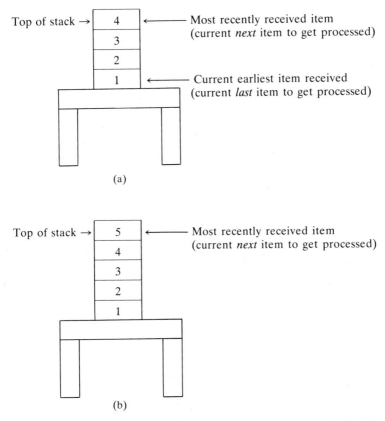

(a)

(b)

Fig. 7.2   Adding to a stack (pushing): (a) Before pushing item 5; (b) After pushing item 5.

In computing science there are many instances (e.g. handling procedure calls, recursion, compiling) where we need to model mechanisms that function in a very similar manner to our office work-pile. A *stack* in computing is considered to be an ordered list of zero or more elements which allows insertions and deletions at only one end called the *top*. A stack pointer is used to record, at all times, the location of the top of the stack. (A deletion cannot be made from an *empty* stack.)

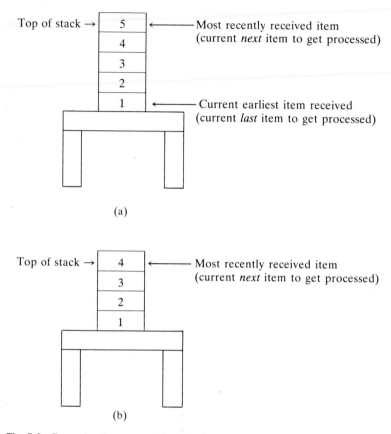

Fig. 7.3 Removing from a stack (popping): (a) Before popping item 5; (b) After popping item 5.

From the description given, an array seems well suited to model the stack mechanisms. Consider how we might use an array to model a stack.

Pushing an item onto the stack is going to correspond to adding another element to the array. For the sake of simplicity let us consider that we want to create a stack of integers.

The *push* will involve:

stackpointer := *stackpointer*+1;
stack[*stackpointer*] := *item*

In making the push we have neglected a check to see whether or not the stack has room for another item. After incorporating this check, the Pascal implementation of a stack push will be as described below (we have neglected a written description for this procedure and those that follow because of the simplicity of the steps involved).

```
procedure push (var stack:nelements; var stackpointer:integer;
    item,maxsize:integer);
begin {pushes items onto an array stack}
    if stackpointer<maxsize then
        begin {push item onto stack}
            stackpointer := stackpointer+1;
            stack[stackpointer] := item
        end
    else
        writeln('stack overflow')
end
```

Popping an item off the top of the stack is handled just as simply as the push. It amounts to removing an element from the array. The central steps are:

```
item := stack[stackpointer];
stackpointer := stackpointer−1
```

This time we do not need a check to see if there is overflow but rather a test must be made to see if there is an item on the stack that can be removed. A zero value for the *stackpointer* will signal this *underflow* if our array *stack* has the range [1..*maxsize*]. The Pascal implementation for *popping* from a stack is therefore as described below.

```
procedure pop (var stack:nelements; var item,stackpointer:integer);
begin {pops items from an array stack}
    if stackpointer>0 then
        begin {pop item off top of stack}
            item := stack[stackpointer];
            stackpointer := stackpointer−1
        end
    else
        writeln('stack underflow')
end
```

We notice in this procedure that when an item is "removed" from the top of the stack it still remains in the array. However, because of the way in which the stack pointer is used, it is no longer part of the current stack. These observations highlight a weakness in using an array to implement a stack. Typically in the way in which stacks are used, they may grow and shrink rather dramatically during the course of execution of a program. Furthermore, it is sometimes necessary to store large amounts of information in each stack element. As a consequence, stacks can potentially use up large amounts of storage.

With the array implementation of a stack it is necessary to preallocate the maximum stack size at the time of implementing the program. A much more desirable way to use a stack would be to have it only take up as much space as there were items on the stack at each point in time during the execution. A number of programming languages, including Pascal, can accommodate this type of dynamic storage allocation. In adopting this latter approach, we are implementing the stack in a way that naturally takes advantage of its dynamic nature.

To proceed with the dynamic stack implementation we will need to take advantage of language dependent facilities for handling dynamic storage allocation. In Pascal, this amounts to using the *pointer* mechanism coupled with a linked list structure. To do this we can set up a chain of records. Each record will need an information storage part *info* and a linkage part *link* that points back to its predecessor in the chain. The structure will be:

$$pointer \rightarrow \boxed{info.n \mid link.n} \rightarrow \boxed{info.n-1 \mid link.n-1} \rightarrow \cdots \rightarrow \boxed{info.1 \mid nil}$$

The type declarations that will be needed to implement this data structure are:

```
type stackpointer = ↑stackelement;
     stackelement = record
                      info : integer;
                      link : stackpointer
                    end
```

The inclusion of the pointer field of type *stackpointer* in each record of type *stackelement* allows us to set up a linked list of records. The other declaration needed is the pointer variable *pointer* which must be of type *stackpointer*. This can be set up by a standard variable declaration in the calling procedure.

In principle, the new mechanisms for pushing and popping elements on and off the stack are like the array versions but now extra steps are needed to maintain the linkage and create and remove records.

To try to understand the linkage procedure let us examine what happens as the first several items are pushed onto the stack. Initially, before any items have been pushed onto the stack, the pointer will not be pointing to anything. This case can be signalled explicitly by the initialization:

$$pointer := nil$$

This will be the value of the pointer before the first record is pushed. When the first record is created, it will include the first link component of the stack. We must decide how this link is assigned to maintain the stack. Now that we have a record on the stack, the pointer will need to point to this record and the record itself (which is the *bottom* of the stack) will point "nowhere".

We will have:

$$pointer \rightarrow \boxed{\text{first} \mid nil}$$

When a second item is pushed on the stack we will get:

$$pointer \rightarrow \boxed{\text{second} \mid \quad} \longrightarrow \boxed{\text{first} \mid nil}$$

So, as each new component is pushed onto the stack, the *pointer* will need to be updated to point to it and the *link* for the new component will need to point to what was previously the top of the stack. The assignments will be:

> *link* := *pointer*
> *pointer* := *newelement*

To actually create the new component a call will need to be made to the Pascal procedure *new*. The clearest way to make references to the new component is via Pascal's **with** statement.

To pop an element off the top of the stack we must essentially "reverse" the process we have just described.

We start out with:

$$pointer \rightarrow \boxed{\text{second} \mid \quad} \longrightarrow \boxed{\text{first} \mid nil}$$

and want to end up with:

$$pointer \rightarrow \boxed{\text{first} \mid nil}$$

This involves resetting the pointer to the top of the stack so that it points to *the element pointed to by the element on top of the stack*. The data on top of the stack must also be collected and the top element removed using Pascal's *dispose* function. The assignment to update the pointer will be:

$$pointer := link$$

Once again the implementation can be done using a **with** statement. To test for an empty stack we will now need to check for a *nil* pointer. The detailed descriptions of the linked list implementations of the push and pop operations can now be given.

Algorithm description

(1) Pushing an item onto a stack

1. Establish data to be pushed onto stack.

2. Create new record and store data.
3. Establish link from new element back to its successor.
4. Update pointer to top of stack.

(2)   Popping an item off top of a stack

1. If stack not empty then
   (a) get pointer to top element,
   (b) retrieve data from top of stack,
   (c) reset top of stack pointer to successor of top element,
   (d) remove top element from stack
   else
   (a') write stack underflow.
2. Return data from top of stack.

Pascal implementation[†]

```
procedure push (data: integer; var pointer: stackpointer);
var newelement {pointer to new element created}: stackpointer;

begin {pushes data onto top of stack}
  {assert: pointer points to top of stack}
  new(newelement);
  with newelement↑ do
    begin
      info := data;
      link := pointer
    end;
  pointer := newelement
  {assert: newelement pushed onto stack ∧ pointer points to top of
  stack}
end
```

```
procedure pop(var data: integer; var pointer: stackpointer);
var topelement {pointer to pop element on stack}: stackpointer;

begin {pops data off top of stack}
  {assert: pointer points to top of stack}
  if pointer<>nil then
    begin
      topelement := pointer;
      with topelement↑ do
```

---

† It is assumed that *stackpointer* and *pointer* have been declared as described in the
discussion.

```
            begin
                data := info;
                pointer := link
            end;
        dispose(topelement)
    end
    {assert: top element removed from stack ∧ pointer points to new
    top of stack}
    else
        writeln('stack underflow')
end
```

Notes on design

1. Stack operations involve essentially one compound step and as such their time complexity is of little interest. With regard to storage efficiency the linked implementation is better because it only uses as much storage as there are elements on the stack. In contrast to the array implementation, storage for the maximum anticipated stack size is committed *throughout* execution of the program.
2. The condition that remains invariant for both the *push* and *pop* operations is that after a transaction the stackpointer is adjusted so that it once again points to the top of the stack.
3. The linked implementation of the stack operations is more in keeping with the dynamic nature of the stack.
4. No upper limit on stack size needs to be explicitly defined in the linked implementation although it is conceivable that the stack size allocated by the system could overflow.

Applications

Parameter tracking and passing with procedure calls, compilers, recursion.

Supplementary problems

7.1.1   Implement the main program that would supply and receive data from the *push* and *pop* procedures.

7.1.2   Design and implement a procedure that accepts as input a character string that represents an arithmetic expression, for example,

$$y := (a+b))*(c+d)/((x*y)/(w+z)$$

and determines whether or not it is well-formed. By well-formed it is meant that the parentheses should be properly balanced according to standard algebraic conventions (note that the expression above has an equal number of left and right parentheses but it is not well-formed).

7.1.3   It is sometimes necessary to perform stack operations with variable length strings. Implement *push* and *pop* procedures that manipulate such strings stored on a stack consisting of a fixed length character array.

7.1.4   Design and implement procedures that maintain two stacks within one array.

Algorithm 7.2
QUEUE ADDITION AND DELETION

Problem

Design and implement procedures that maintain a queue that can be subject to insertions and deletions.

Algorithm development

We often need to model processes similar to what we observe in a canteen queue. In this queue, when someone gets served everyone moves up one place. Newcomers always take their place at the rear of the queue. For example, the job scheduler in an operating system needs to maintain a queue of program requests.

Before starting on the design for this problem we need a clear idea of what is meant by a *queue* in the computing science context. A *queue* is defined to be a linear list in which all insertions are made at one end (the rear) and all deletions are made at the other end (the front). Queues are therefore used to store data that needs to be processed in the order of its arrival.

Schematically, we have:

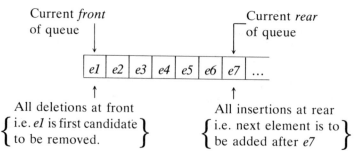

To model a queue in a computer we will need a suitable data structure. The definition and example suggest that an array may be what we need. Let us explore this idea with another example. We will start out with an empty queue which corresponds to an array with no active elements.

1	2	3	4	5	6	7	8	9

Empty queue ≡ empty array

The obvious place to add the first queue element *e1* is in the first array location.

1	2	3	4	5	6	7	8	9
e1								

The second element *e2* (providing *e1* has not been deleted) can go in the second array location.

1	2	3	4	5	6	7	8	9
e1	*e2*							

In adding elements to the rear of the queue what we are concerned with is knowing at each stage *where* the next element must be added. One way to do this would be to start at the front of the queue and step through the elements until we find an empty location. As the queue gets longer, this process becomes more and more inefficient. A closer examination of the problem reveals that we can keep track of where the end of the queue is by simply employing a variable whose value always marks the rear of the queue. With this suggestion, inserting an element at the end of the queue involves two steps:

1. updating the rear marker;
2. placing the new element in the location pointed to by the rear marker.

Our ideas on queue insertion seem practical so let us move on and see how queue deletion should be treated. If we start with the configuration below:

				rear		
1	2	3	4	5	↓	
e1	*e2*	*e3*	*e4*	*e5*	*e6*	

then the first element to be deleted will be *e1*. We can achieve this deletion by moving each element one position closer to the front and adjusting the rear. That is,

1	2	3	4	5	...		
e2	e3	e4	e5	e6	e6		

↑
rear

With this mechanism we are going to need to change the position of *every* remaining element in the queue each time the first element is deleted. As the queue gets longer this will become a relatively costly step. We might therefore ask, is there another less costly approach? In posing this question what we are really asking is whether there is a way of maintaining a queue *without* having to move all the elements each time the front element is removed.

After examining our example closely, we see that if the elements themselves are not to be moved then the only other alternative is to move the *front of the queue*. A variable with a complementary role to that of *rear* will do the job. So, for our example, after deletion of the first element, we would have:

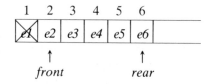

1	2	3	4	5	6	
e1	e2	e3	e4	e5	e6	

↑   ↑
front   *rear*

We now have mechanisms for queue insertion and deletion. As more insertions and deletions are made the current queue entries are going to be displaced further and further to the right (towards the high suffix end) of the array. To give an example, initially we might have the following queue parameters:

$front = 1$
$rear = 25$
$qlength = 25$ $(qlength = rear - front + 1)$

and some considerable time later after a number of insertions and deletions:

$front = 87$
$rear = 102$
$qlength = 16$

These examples imply that over a long period of time we may be faced with a very high storage cost. This excessive use of storage is obviously going to make our current proposal unacceptable for practical use. Ideally it would be desirable to have to commit only an amount of storage equal to the maximum anticipated queue length. This goal seems reasonable since in many applications, because of the way insertions and deletions compete, the queue length is relatively stable. From our earlier example it is clear that a queue can be maintained within an array greater than or equal to its maximum length by shifting the elements as we had originally proposed. The question that remains is, can we do it without having to move all the elements after each deletion? One idea might be to wait until *rear* reaches the end of the array and then move all elements as far to the front as possible. This is certainly a lot better than the previous proposal of shifting every time. Before the shift we might have:

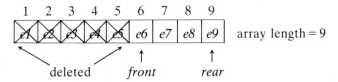

With this configuration there is no more room for insertions at the end of the array but now the first 5 locations have become free. We can, therefore, shift *e6* to position 1, *e7* to position 2 and so on. The problem with this is that it still involves a lot of shifting. So, now we need to ask the question once again, are there any better alternatives? Since the space at the front of the array is now free we could certainly store *e10* in position 1, but what impact would this have on maintaining continuity of our queue? If we were to do this it would mean that the rear was *in front of* the front of the queue. That is,

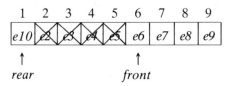

This arrangement seems rather peculiar. Let us see what happens when we try to insert another element, *e11*. Applying our earlier idea for insertion we get:

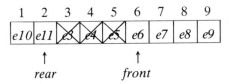

Peculiar as our arrangement seems, it appears to be allowing us to maintain a queue provided we take the end of the array into account properly. We see that eventually, after more insertions and deletions, we will get the configuration again where the front is no longer *behind* the rear:

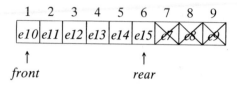

And so what we have is a queue that can *wrap-around* in an array. It is referred to as a *circular queue*. The process is stable for insertions and deletions as long as the queue size never exceeds the array size chosen to maintain the queue. To maintain our queue every time we make either an insertion or deletion we will need to check whether the *rear* or *front* markers are going to exceed the array size. Whenever this happens the corresponding marker will need to be reset to 1.

Having worked out our basic mechanism for maintaining a queue in an array, our next task is to take a closer look at the design of the insertion and deletion algorithms. Examining our queue data structure carefully we see that a number of conditions can apply when we want to make the next insertion:

1.   the queue can be empty;
2.   the queue can be already full;
3.   the end of the array has been reached prior to the insertion;
4.   none of the above conditions apply (the most likely case).

We might anticipate that at least some of these cases will involve other than direct insertion in the next location. An important case that we must detect is when an attempt is made to insert into a *full* queue. From our previous examples it would seem that the easiest way to do this would be to check if the *front* and *rear* markers are equal. However, as soon as we start to think about implementing this we realize that there is going to be a whole range of situations where the queue only contains *one* element which will have the condition *front = rear*. For example,

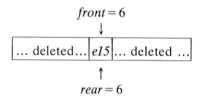

We are therefore going to need some other way of distinguishing between a queue with one element and a full queue. To make the problem simpler and easier to understand let us look at the smallest queue array (i.e. the queue has maximum length 1) to see if we can distinguish between it being full or empty. The difference between the two situations involves only one element so it may be easier to see what is happening.

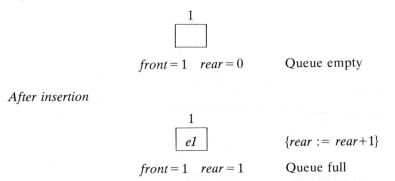

1

Queue array of length 1

front = ? *rear* = ?

Normally when an insertion is made *rear* is increased by one and the element is placed in the queue. If we were to apply this rule in the present case *rear* would need to have been initially set to zero. There is then the question of what to do about the *front* initially and after deletion. Only two possibilities exist for our one element array. The marker *front* can only be either 0 or 1 before the insertion. If we choose *front* = 1 initially we have:

Before insertion

1

front = 1   *rear* = 0   Queue empty

After insertion

1

e1   {*rear* := *rear*+1}

front = 1   *rear* = 1   Queue full

At this point we have distinguished between full and empty. Let us see what happens now when we delete an element. This involves increasing *front* by one but since it takes us *beyond* the end of the array it must be reset to the start of the array. There is a problem here because the start and end of the array are at the same position and so once again, on deletion in this way, we would end up with

After deletion

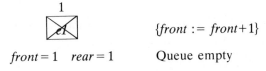

1

{*front* := *front*+1}

front = 1   *rear* = 1   Queue empty

This contradicts the earlier situation. Because of this problem let us look at the other alternative starting out with *front* = 0.

Before insertion

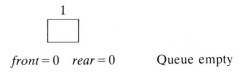

1

front = 0   *rear* = 0   Queue empty

After insertion

1

| *e1* |

$\{rear := rear+1\}$

$front = 0$ $rear = 1$ Queue full

Now let us once again try to do a deletion.

After deletion

1

$\{front := front+1\}$

$front = 1$ $rear = 1$ Queue empty

The *empty* state after deletion is now *different* from the full state. Also in comparing the empty case *after deletion* with the empty case *before insertion* we see that in *both* cases when the queue is empty the front and the rear are equal. Now that we have a mechanism that will work for queues of maximum length one, our next task is to see if we can generalize it to work for potentially larger queues.

As a first step in this direction, consider the case where we have only a *single* element left in the array of length greater than 1.

Before deletion

1	5	9
deleted	*e15*	deleted

Queue not empty

After the deletion (which will include $front := front+1$) we want the relation $front = rear$ to hold to indicate that the queue is empty. So, if before the deletion we have:

$$front = 4 \quad \text{and} \quad rear = 5$$

we will obtain the desired condition on deletion. This is analogous to the situation for our array of length 1.

After deletion

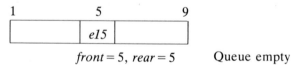

1	5	9
	e15	

$front = 5, rear = 5$ Queue empty

With this configuration, if we try to make another deletion we will know that we must not do so because $front = rear$.

The steps for deletion will be:

if *front* = *rear* then
   "queue is empty so cannot delete"
else
   "advance front ensuring it stays within array bounds"

To ensure *front* stays within bounds as soon as it exceeds *arraylength* it should be reset to one. That is,

$$front := front+1;$$
    if $front > arraylength$ **then**
      $front := 1$

We now have to investigate whether or not the *full* case can be generalized in a similar manner. Our conditions for specifying an empty queue require that *front* is one step before the first element in the queue and the *rear* marks the last element in the queue. Consider the full queue below, where we have applied these criteria:

1	2	3	4	5	6	7	8	9
e5	e6	e7	e8	e9	e1	e2	e3	e4

Queue full

$$front = 5, \ rear = 5$$

We again run into problems because *front* and *rear* are equal. This corresponds to the condition we have been trying to use to signal an empty queue. Also, if we apply the mechanism of queue addition with this configuration we will overwrite the first queue element. What we want is for the *front* and *rear* not to be equal when the queue is full. That is, *rear* would have to be 4 when the queue was full. That is,

1	2	3	4	5	6	7	8	9
e5	e6	e7	e8	e9	e1	e2	e3	e4

Queue full?

$$rear = 4 \qquad front = 5$$

If this configuration is to correspond to a "full" queue then we will only be able to store 8 elements in 9 positions. Now when we have the configuration below:

1	2	3	4	5	6	7	8	9
e5	e6	e7	e8		e1	e2	e3	e4

Queue full

$$rear = 4 \qquad front = 5$$

and we try to add another element we first extend the rear by one and then test to see if the queue is full. Under these conditions *front = rear* will indicate the queue is full.

The steps for adding an element to the rear of the queue will therefore be:

1. Advance *rear* ensuring it does not go out of array bounds
2. If *front = rear* then
   (2.a)   queue full so take appropriate action
   else
   (2'.a)   add new element to rear of queue.

We can ensure that *rear* stays within the array bounds by using a similar mechanism to that required for confining *front*. If the queue is full, *rear* should be reset to its former value so as not to confuse the full and empty states. In making this adjustment we need to take into account the array bounds. That is,

if queue full then
(a)   write message queue full;
(b)   *rear := rear*−1;
(c)   if *rear* = 0 then *rear := arraylength*.

The step (c) is needed to handle the case below:

*Before readjustment
of rear*

1	2	3	4	5	6	7	8	9
	e1	e2	e3	e4	e5	e6	e7	e8

Queue full

front = 1   *rear* = 1

*After readjustment
of rear*

1	2	3	4	5	6	7	8	9
	e1	e2	e3	e4	e5	e6	e7	e8

Queue full

front = 1   *rear* = 9

The descriptions for queue insertion and deletion will now be outlined. It will be assumed that *front* and *rear* are both one when the queue is initially empty.

Algorithm descriptions

(1) Queue insertion
1. Establish the queue, data for insertion, array length, *front*, and *rear*.
2. Advance the rear according to mechanism for keeping it within array bounds.
3. If *front* not equal to *rear* then
    (3.a)   insert data at next available position in queue
    else
    (3.a')   queue is full so write out full signal,
    (3.b')   restore *rear* marker to its previous value taking into account array bounds.
4. Return updated queue and its adjusted *rear* pointer.

(2) Queue deletion
1. Establish queue, arraylength, front and rear markers.
2. If front not equal to rear then
    (2.a)   advance front according to mechanism for keeping it within array bounds,
    (2.b)   remove element from front of queue
    else
    (2.a')   queue empty so write out empty message.
3. Return updated queue, the element off the front of the queue and the adjusted front marker.

Pascal implementation

```
procedure qinsert (var queue: nelements; var rear: integer;
data,arraylength,front: integer);

begin {inserts data at rear of circular queue—rear points to last
element}
    {assert: rear points to end of queue ∧ 1=<rear=<arraylength}
    rear := rear + 1;
    if rear >arraylength then
        rear := 1;
    if front <>rear then
        queue[rear] := data
        {assert: element added to rear of queue ∧ rear points to end of
        queue ∧ 1=<rear=<arraylength}
    else
        begin {queue full so signal and readjust rear to previous value}
            writeln('queue full—cannot insert');
            rear := rear -1;
```

```
            if rear = 0 then
                rear := arraylength
          end
      end


      procedure qdelete (var queue: nelements; var data,front: integer;
      arraylength,rear: integer);

      begin {deletes elements from front of queue—front precedes first
      element}
          {assert: front pointer precedes first element ∧
          1 =<front =<arraylength}
          if front <>rear then
            begin {remove front element}
                front := front +1;
                if front >arraylength then
                  front := 1;
                data := queue[front]
            end
            {assert: element removed from front of queue ∧ front pointer
            precedes first element ∧ 1 =<front =<arraylength}
          else
              writeln('queue empty—cannot delete')
      end
```

Notes on design

1. Queue operations involve essentially one compound step and so their time complexity is of little interest.

2. The condition that remains invariant for both queue insertion and deletion operations is that after a transaction the *rear* marker again points to the last element in the queue and the *front* marker points to the position just preceding the first queue element. If the queue is empty this condition is still signalled by *front* equals *rear* after an attempted deletion. Also, if the queue is full this condition is still signalled by *front* and *rear* after an attempted insertion.

3. With the present implementation one array location must always be kept free (e.g. only a maximum of 9 queue elements can be maintained in an array size of 10). It is possible to implement algorithms for queue insertion and deletion that allow *all* elements of the array to be occupied when the queue-full condition applies. The penalty for this is extra tests during insertion and deletion.

4. As we have observed in note 3, we can often trade storage for a more efficient implementation.

5. Consideration of the smallest queue problem gives us some useful insights for solving the general problem.

6. An alternative way to keep *front* and *rear* within the array bounds
    would be to use an increment of the form

$$front := (front+1) \ mod \ arraylength$$

7. In the present discussion we have not considered the linked list
    implementation of a queue. In some applications this implementation
    would be appropriate. In principle it is also simpler to utilize. This
    implementation is left as an exercise for the reader.

Applications

Simulation problems, job scheduling.

Supplementary problems

7.2.1   Modify the present algorithm so that the *mod* function is used to
        keep *front* and *rear* within the array bounds. Care should be taken in
        specifying the array bounds for this implementation (see note 6).
7.2.2   Design and implement queue insertion and deletion algorithms that
        allow all array elements to be occupied when the queue.is full (see
        note 3).
7.2.3   Choose a queue of initial size n, then use a random number gen-
        erator to simulate insertions and deletions (e.g. $0<0.5 \Rightarrow$ addition,
        $0.5 \leqslant 1.0 \Rightarrow$ deletion) and determine what is the minimum array size
        that will support this queue without causing overflow.
7.2.4   A dequeue is a linear list that allows insertions and deletions at *both*
        ends. Implement procedures for maintaining a dequeue.
7.2.5   Implement a queue as a linked linear list such that it only occupies
        an amount of space proportional to the current queue size. (See
        algorithms 7.1, 7.3 and 7.4.)

Algorithm 7.3
LINKED LIST SEARCH

Problem

Design and implement an algorithm to search a linear ordered linked list for
a given alphabetic key or name.

Algorithm development

With the stack and queue data structures it is always clear in advance exactly where the current item should be retrieved from or inserted. This favorable situation does not prevail when it is necessary to perform insertions and deletions on linear linked lists. Before we can carry out such operations with an ordered linked list we must first carry out a *search* of the list to establish the position where the change must be made. It is this problem that we wish to consider in the present discussion. We will need such a search algorithm later when we come to discuss linked list insertion and deletion operations.

Before starting on the algorithm design let us consider an example that defines the problem we wish to solve. Suppose we have a long alphabetically ordered list of names as shown in Table 7.1 and that we wish to insert the name DAVID.

Table 7.1 Insertion into an alphabetically ordered list.

Location	Name		
1	AARONS		
2	ADAMS		
3	DANIEL	←	DAVID needs to be
4	DROVER		inserted here.
5	ENGEL		
6	FRY		
7	GRAY		
⋮	⋮		

The task that must be performed before the insertion can be made is to locate exactly *where* DAVID should be inserted. After examining the names' list above we quickly respond that DAVID needs to be inserted *between* DANIEL and DROVER. At this point, we will not concern ourselves with how the insertion (or deletion) is made but rather we will concentrate on developing the accompanying search algorithm for a linked list structure. In deciding where DAVID should be inserted, what we have had to do is search the list until we have either found a name that comes alphabetically later (in the insertion case) or until we have found a matching name (in the deletion case). On the assumption that the list is ordered there will be no need to search further in either case. The central part of our search algorithm will therefore be:

1. While current search name comes alphabetically after current list name do
   (a) move to next name in the list.

This algorithm does not take into account that the search name may come *after* the last name in the list and as such it is potentially infinite—we will need to take this into account later. Our development so far has been straightforward and the problem would be almost solved if we only had to search a linear list rather than a linked linear list.

The motivation for maintaining an ordered set of names as a linked list arises because it allows for efficient insertion and deletion of names while still retaining the alphabetical order. As we will see later this is certainly not true for a list of names stored as a linear array.

At this point, we are ready to consider the linked list representation of an ordered list and the accompanying search algorithm. In the linked list data structure each record or name has an appended pointer field that points to the location of the *next* record in logical (usually alphabetical) order in the list. From this definition we can see that there no longer has to be a direct correspondence between the way the names are arranged physically and their logical order. It is this relaxation of the relationship between physical and logical order that makes it possible to do efficient insertions and deletions. The difference is illustrated in Fig. 7.4.

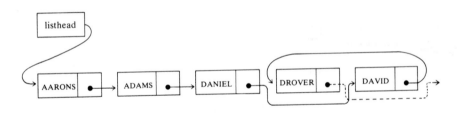

Physical order—left to right
Logical order—as indicated by pointers or links

Fig. 7.4   Difference between physical and logical order for a linked list.

In conducting a search of a linked list we must follow the logical order rather than the physical order. The search of an ordered list like the one we have just described must begin at the *first* list element in logicial order. If all list nodes have the structure:

> *listnode* = **record**
> 　　　　　*listname* : *nameformat*;
> 　　　　　*next* : *listpointer*
> 　　　**end**

then we will need to use the linkage information *next* to proceed along the list (i.e. if the search cannot be terminated at the first element). This will simply amount to assigning the pointer value *next* in the current node to the current node pointer, i.e.

$$current := next$$

If we step through the logical order of the list in this manner we will eventually arrive at the desired position corresponding to the place where the search name either exists or is able to be inserted. Assuming the search has terminated we must now ask what information must be passed back to the calling procedure to allow an amendment to the list or to indicate whether the name is present or not? A Boolean variable *notfound* which is set to *true* when the search procedure is called and which may subsequently be set to *false* can be used to terminate the search. In our search, at the time of termination, we will have a pointer to the current node. That is,

The insertion situation:
   (to insert DAVID)

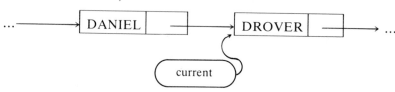

The match or deletion situation:
   (to match or delete DAVID)

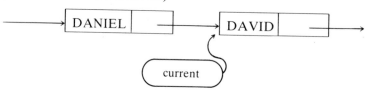

In both situations, the pointer to the current node is actually the information stored in the "DANIEL node". To make either an insertion or a deletion the pointer information stored in the "DANIEL node" is going to have to be changed (i.e. in the insertion case DANIEL's pointer would have to point to the DAVID node rather than the DROVER node). Our search mechanism should therefore always keep around the pointer to the previous node which can be returned to the calling procedure when the search terminates. This can be done (assuming the **with** statement is used) using the following steps at each node before moving on to the next node:

$$previous := current;$$
$$current := next$$

The only other consideration that must be made relates to the termination problem that we had mentioned earlier. Our search mechanism needs to be able to handle the case where the name we are searching for is alphabetically beyond the end of the list (e.g. the last name in the list might be WILSON and the search name ZELMAN). Since the last name in the list has no successor its pointer points to "nowhere". This situation is signalled by setting the pointer field to *nil*. If WILSON were the last name in the list we would have:

The search loop should therefore terminate either on reaching the search name's position (virtual or real) or on encountering a *nil* pointer. A special pointer to the start of the list *listhead* will need to be supplied to the search procedure. To accommodate the case where the search name occurs *before* the first name in the list the pointer to the previous node will need to be initialized to *nil*. Our algorithm can now be detailed.

Algorithm description

1. Establish search name, and the pointer to the start of the list.
2. Initialize previous node pointer to *nil* and set flag for continuing the search to *true* and current pointer to start of list.
3. While search can logically proceed and not at end of list do
    (a) if search name alphabetically less than current list name then
        (a.1) set condition for terminating search
        else
        (a'.1) set previous node pointer to current node pointer,
        (a'.2) adjust current node pointer so that it points to next node.
4. Establish whether or not search name found.
5. Return previous and current node pointers and found status.

Pascal implementation

Before giving the search procedure the type declarations needed in the calling procedure will be given. It will be assumed that names are no more than 20 characters. The declarations are:

```
const namesize = 20;
type nameformat = packed array[1..namesize] of char;
     listpointer = ↑listnode;
     listnode = record
                    listname : nameformat;
                    next : listpointer
                end;
```

```
procedure listsearch(searchname: nameformat; var current,previous:
listpointer; listhead: listpointer; var found: boolean);
var notfound {if true indicates next node must be examined}:
boolean;

begin {searches ordered linked list for the presence of searchname}
  {assert: listhead points to head of list}
  previous := nil; notfound := true; current := listhead;
  found := false;
  {invariant: searchname occurs alphabetically after name at.
  previous node if previous node <>nil}
  while notfound and (current <>nil) do
    with current↑ do
      if searchname <=listname then
        notfound := false
      else
        begin {move pointers to next node}
          previous := current;
          current := next
        end;
      {assert: searchname is equal to or occurs before the name
      at current node if it exists}
  if current <>nil then
    if searchname =current↑.listname then found := true
    else found := false
end
```

Notes on design

1. The cost of the ordered list search is proportional to the number of
    nodes that have to be examined before the search terminates. Over a
    large number of trials, if the search has equal probability of stopping at
    each node, then on average half the list will need to be searched. In the
    worst case all nodes will need to be examined. (See analysis in first
    chapter.)

2. At the end of each iteration of the search loop, it will be established
    that all names in nodes *preceding* the current node occur in dictionary
    order *before* the search name. The pointers *previous* and *current* will
    point respectively to the current node and the next node after the
    current iteration. The Boolean variable *notfound* will remain true
    unless the search name has been found or bypassed. The loop will
    terminate because eventually (if not before) the condition *current = nil*
    will be true when the end of the list is reached. The other termination
    condition where the search name matches or occurs alphabetically
    later than the current list name will usually force termination before
    the end of the list is reached.

3. A refinement to the current search algorithm would involve using a
    sentinel to bring about termination of the search when the search name

was beyond the end of the list. This would involve linking the last node to the sentinel which can be set equal to the *searchname*. When this is done the test:

$$current <> nil$$

can be dropped and replaced by a single test *outside* the loop to establish whether the name or the sentinel has been found.

4. The search algorithm we have constructed can be used in conjunction with list insertion and deletion procedures because it establishes the information that is needed for these list amendments.

5. The binary search algorithm *cannot* be used to search the linked list even though it is ordered because the correspondence between physical and logical order does not exist. It follows that the linked list structure commits us to a sequential search. Other storage alternatives (i.e. trees) should be considered if it is anticipated that the list will be very long.

Applications

Maintaining short linked lists.

Supplementary problems

7.3.1 Modify the list searching algorithm so that it will search a list that cannot be assumed to be ordered.

7.3.2 Design a list searching algorithm that incorporates a sentinel (see note 3).

7.3.3 Design and implement a list searching algorithm that uses arrays for both the names and the pointers.

7.3.4 Design and implement an algorithm that accepts as input an *ordered* list of search names. The task required is to establish and report the absence or presence of these search names in a second much longer ordered list.

Algorithm 7.4
LINKED LIST INSERTION AND DELETION

Problem

Design and implement procedures for inserting and deleting elements from a linear ordered linked list.

Algorithm development

We have already encountered the idea (in the preceding algorithm) that linked lists are efficient for maintaining the logical order of data sets that are subject to frequent insertions and deletions. Let us try to understand why linked lists exhibit this efficiency before proceeding with the insertion and deletion algorithms.

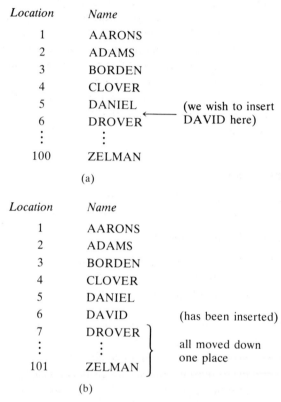

Fig. 7.5   Inserting an element into an ordered list: (a) Before insertion of DAVID; (b) After insertion of DAVID.

As an example of the type of problem that we are likely to encounter, suppose that we have an alphabetically ordered list of surnames. The tasks that we need to consider are inserting an element into this list in a way that preserves the order and deleting an element from the list. For example, suppose that we wish to insert DAVID into the list shown in Fig. 7.5(a). We could represent this list in the computer by using an array of names. We see in Fig. 7.5(b) that to insert DAVID into this array *all* elements occurring alphabetically "later" than DAVID would need to be moved down one place in the array. For an array of names, the amount of data needing to be moved quickly becomes excessive as the size of the list grows. It follows that use of an array in this way is obviously *not* suitable for maintaining a list of names that is subject to frequent insertions and deletions. On average with such an arrangement, we could expect to have to shift *half* the elements in the list with each amendment.

Physical Location	Name	Link	(physical location of logical successor)
1	AARONS	2	
2	ADAMS	3	
3	BORDEN	4	
4	CLOVER	5	
5	DANIEL	6	← previous node
6	DROVER	7	← current node (where logical search stops)
⋮	⋮	⋮	
100	ZELMAN	?	*nil*
101	DAVID	?	logical successor of DANIEL

(a)

Physical Location	Name	Link	(physical location of logical successor)
1	AARONS	2	
2	ADAMS	3	
3	BORDEN	4	
4	CLOVER	5	
5	DANIEL	101	
6	DROVER	7	
⋮	⋮	⋮	
100	ZELMAN	*nil*	
101	DAVID	6	

(b)

Fig. 7.6 Inserting an element into a linked ordered list: (a) Physical insertion of DAVID; (b) Logical insertion of DAVID.

Clearly if we are to maintain an ordered list that is subject to frequent insertions and deletions we need to minimize the amount of data movement. The most desirable situation in this context would be not to move *any* of the names at all when a name is either inserted or deleted. We can certainly store DAVID after ZELMAN at the end of the list without having to move any of the other list members. If we do this, however, the list is no longer in alphabetical order. What we are looking for at this point is a mechanism that allows us to physically place inserted items at the *end* of the list while at the same time retaining the logical order of the list. A way we can do this is to associate with each name a link field which at all times points to the physical location of its logical successor in the list. Once this is done the physical order loses its relevance. If we start out with the configuration in Fig. 7.6(a) then the steps to logically insert DAVID are shown in Fig. 7.6(b).

After the logical insertion of DAVID we see that DANIEL's link points to the physical location of DAVID and DAVID's link points to the physical location of DROVER. The insertion of a new element has only involved a very small change to the existing list structure. A linked structure therefore allows insertions and deletions at low cost.

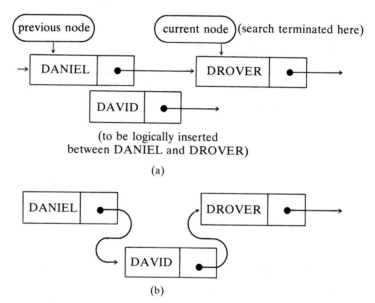

(a)

(b)

Fig. 7.7   Inserting an element into the middle of a linked list: (a) Before insertion; (b) After insertion.

We could use arrays to implement the linked list data structure but it turns out to be more practical and economical in the use of storage to use records and pointers. With the latter approach, it is only necessary to commit as much storage as there are nodes presently in the list, whereas with the array implementation we need to preallocate a fixed amount of storage.

Our task now is to consider the insertion and deletion mechanism using pointers. As we have already seen, before we can make a change (insertion or deletion) to a list we have to find the appropriate place in the list where the changes are needed. The list searching procedure in algorithm 7.3 can be used to find the place where either the insertion or the deletion is needed.

There are therefore two steps to insert (or delete) an element:

1. Search the list in logical order until a name is found that does not come before (in dictionary order) the name to be inserted.
2. Insert the name (or delete it).

The search has been considered before, so we can proceed with the development of the insertion and deletion mechanisms.

To avoid confusion we can consider the list insertion process first. Using our previous example, the list structure before and after insertion of DAVID is given in Figs. 7.7(a) and (b) respectively. To make the insertion, the previous node's pointer (DANIEL's) must be amended to point to the inserted node (DAVID) and the inserted node's pointer must point to what was the node at the time when the search for DAVID's place of insertion terminated. The pointer changes are therefore:

previous node pointer := inserted node location
inserted node pointer := current node location

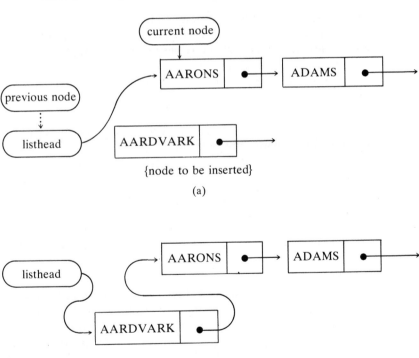

Fig. 7.8 Inserting an element before the first element in a linked list: (a)Before insertion; (b) After insertion.

These steps will need to be preceded by the creation of a node. This can be done using Pascal's *new* function. When we check this mechanism on some examples we see that it works correctly in the general case. We need to be sure also that it will work correctly when an item is inserted *before* the first element, *after* the last element and as the first element in the list.

The case where the inserted node is to be placed *before* the first element in the list is given in Fig. 7.8. We see that insertion before the first node requires that the *listhead* pointer has to be updated since there is no previous node pointer. Insertion in front of the first node will therefore need to be treated specially. To do this we must detect when such an insertion is required. Our list searching algorithm should somehow supply the information we need. When we terminate the search at the first node we see that the current node pointer will be pointing to the listhead. We can therefore employ the following test and pointer update:

if previous node pointer is equal to *nil* then
(a)   adjust listhead to point to newly inserted node.

The inserted node's pointer will point to its successor as in the usual case. Having dealt with this special case we should also look at the other two special cases mentioned above. When we do this with examples and diagrams we discover that they fit within the pattern of the general mechanism.

The steps for updating the pointers when a new node is inserted (taking into account the special case) are therefore:

1.   Adjust pointer of inserted node so that it points to its successor.
2.   If previous node pointer not pointing to listhead then
     (a)   adjust previous node's pointer so that it points to the inserted node
     else
     (a′)   adjust listhead to point to newly inserted node.

We are now ready to fully describe the search and insertion steps but we will postpone this description until we have considered the case of deleting an element from the list.

In principle we might imagine that the same sort of adjustments are needed for deletion as for insertion. To try to discover what is involved let us consider some specific examples of deletion. Suppose that we wish to delete DAVID from the list. Referring to Fig. 7.9 we see that the previous node's pointer (DANIEL's) must be amended to point to the successor of the node being deleted, that is,

previous node pointer := *deleted node's pointer*

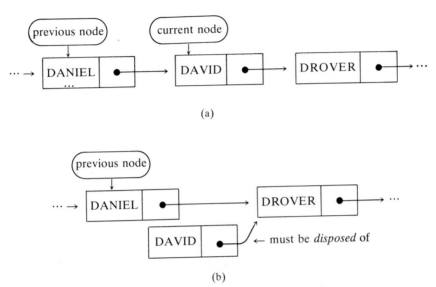

(a)

(b)

Fig. 7.9   Deleting an element from the middle of a linked list: (a) Before deletion; (b) After deletion.

There will also need to be a step to reclaim the storage occupied by the deleted node. Pascal's *dispose* function can be used for this purpose.

As with the insertion we should also consider the unusual cases of deletion, i.e. deletion of the first element, deletion of the last element and deletion from a single element list. The diagrams relevant for deleting the first element are given in Fig. 7.10.

In this special case it is the *listhead* pointer that must be updated rather than the previous node pointer. This case must therefore be detected as special and treated accordingly, that is,

1. If previous node pointer not pointing to *nil* then
    (a)   adjust previous node's pointer so that it points to successor of deleted node

    else

    (a′) adjust listhead to point to successor of the deleted node (i.e. the new first node of list).

Investigation of the other two unusual cases indicates that they do not need to be treated specially.

We are now ready for the complete descriptions of the insertion and deletion procedures.

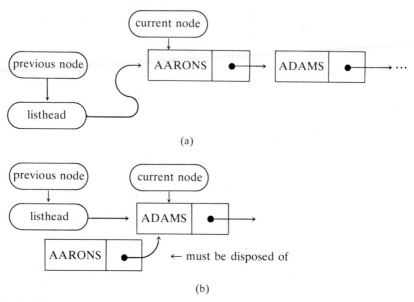

Fig. 7.10   Deleting the first element from a linked list: (a) Before deletion; (b) After deletion.

Algorithm descriptions

(1)   Linked list insertion

1.   Establish the name to be inserted and the pointer to the head of the list.
2.   Initialize previous node to *nil* and current node pointer to head of list.
3.   Search list for the insertion position of the name to be inserted and return pointers to their logical predecessor and successor nodes.
4.   Create new node.
5.   Store the name to be inserted in the new-node (inserted node).
6.   Adjust inserted node's pointer so that it points to its logical successor.
7.   If not inserting new name at front of list then
     (a)   adjust previous node's pointer so it points to inserted node.
     else
     (a')   adjust head of list pointer so that it points to inserted node at head of list.
8.   Return updated list and listhead.

(2) Linked list deletion

1. Establish the name to be deleted and the pointer to the head of the list.
2. Initialize the previous node pointer to *nil* and the current node pointer to the head of the list.
3. Search list for name to be deleted and return pointers to their logical predecessor and the node itself (if found).
4. If name to be deleted found then
   (a)   if node to be deleted not head of list then
          (a.1)   set previous node's pointer to point to the successor of the node to be deleted
        else
          (a'.1)   set listhead pointer to point to the successor of the node to be deleted;
   (b)   dispose of the node to be deleted
      else
   (a')   write out that the name cannot be deleted.
5. Return updated list and listhead.

Pascal implementation

The **record** description needed in the calling procedure is:

```
const namesize = 20;
type nameformat = packed array[1..namesize] of char;
     listpointer = ↑listnode;
     listnode = record
                    listname : nameformat;
                    next : listpointer
                end;
```

(1) Linked list insertion

```
procedure listinsert (newname: nameformat; var listhead:
listpointer);
var previous {pointer to previous node},
    current {pointer to current node},
    newnode {pointer to new node to be inserted}: listpointer;
    found: boolean; {true if newname found}

begin
    {assert: listhead points to head of list}
    previous := nil; current := listhead;
    listsearch (newname, current, previous, listhead, found);
```

```
{assert: newname occurs alphabetically earlier than name at
current node if list not empty}
new(newnode);
newnode↑.listname := newname;
if previous <>nil then
    begin
        newnode↑.next := previous↑.next;
        previous↑.next := newnode
    end
else
    begin
        newnode↑.next := listhead;
        listhead := newnode
    end
    {assert: node containing newname inserted in list in alphabetical
    order}
end
```

(2)   Linked list deletion

```
procedure listdelete (oldname: nameformat; var listhead: listpointer);
var previous {pointer to previous node},
    current {pointer to current node}: listpointer;
    found {true if name for deletion (oldname) found}: boolean;

begin
    {assert: listhead points to head of list}
    previous := nil; current := listhead;
    listsearch (oldname, current, previous, listhead, found);
    {assert: oldname is equal to or occurs before name at current node
    if a name present}
    if found then
        begin
            if previous <>nil then
                previous↑.next := current↑.next
            else
                listhead := current↑.next;
            dispose(current)
        end
        {assert: node containing oldname removed from list and links
        restored}
    else
        writeln('not present—cannot delete', oldname)
end
```

Notes on design

1. The linked list insertion and deletion algorithms are dominated by the
    list search. The cost of the search is proportional to the list length
    requiring half the list to be searched on average and a complete list
    search in the worst case.

2. The correctness of these algorithms rests on the correctness of the search algorithm. Both the insertion and deletion algorithms perform operations on lists that maintain the logical order of the list as determined by the associated pointer set.

Applications

Maintaining relatively small ordered lists that are subject to frequent insertions and deletions.

Supplementary problems

7.4.1   Design and implement an algorithm that inserts items on the end of a list. Your algorithm should not have to search the list to perform the insertion.

7.4.2   Design and implement list insertion and deletion algorithms that use arrays to store both the names and the pointers. Unused (either initially unused or deleted) storage should be maintained as a free list. That is, all unused storage should be *linked* together in a list. When a new item is deleted it is placed on the end of the freelist and when a new item is inserted the space should be taken from the end of the freelist.

7.4.3   Design and implement an algorithm that will merge two ordered linked lists.

7.4.4   In some applications, particular information needs to be retrieved from a list with a much higher frequency than other information. Under these conditions the best way to arrange the list is to put the most frequently retrieved item at the head of the list, the second most frequently retrieved item in the second position and so on. The appropriate order is often not known in advance. To make a list progress towards the appropriate order whenever an item is retrieved it can be exchanged with its predecessor. Under this scheme the most frequently retrieved items eventually migrate to the front of the list. Design algorithms that search and maintain such a linked list.

7.4.5   Another way of performing the task described in 7.4.4 is to always move an item to the head of the list after it is retrieved. Design and implement algorithms that search and maintain a linked list in this form.

7.4.6   Following the theme of the previous two problems include a frequency of retrieval parameter in each node and only shift an item higher in the list when it has a higher frequency of retrieval than its predecessor. The retrieval parameter should be kept up to date.

7.4.7   Design and implement an algorithm that performs insertions and deletions on a doubly linked list. In a doubly linked list each node has *two* pointers (except at the head and tail), one to its successor and one to its predecessor. (This allows for list traversal in both backward and forward directions.)

Algorithm 7.5
BINARY TREE SEARCH

Problem

Design and implement an algorithm to search an ordered binary tree for a given alphabetic key or name.

Algorithm development

We have seen previously in discussing the binary search algorithm (algorithm 5.7) how information can be very efficiently retrieved from an ordered array. The only difficulty with such a data structure is that it is very costly to maintain if insertions and deletions need to be made frequently. The linked list data structure (algorithms 7.3 and 7.4) avoids this difficulty but, in doing so, it will only allow a sequential search rather than the much more efficient binary search. Since sequential searching is costly, particularly for long lists, it is highly desirable to have a data structure which allows efficient insertions and deletions but which also can be searched very efficiently. Fortunately, there is a linked data structure that enables us to do this.

We saw previously that the binary search algorithm (algorithm 5.7) was very efficient in searching an ordered array because the search mechanism treated the ordered data as though it were organized as a binary tree. In this context, an ordered array with n elements translates into a search in which at most $\lfloor \log_2 n \rfloor$ elements must be examined to locate any element. That is, the search mechanism superimposes an imaginary tree on the ordered file. The alternative to this arrangement is to explicitly construct the tree using a set of links or pointers. See Fig. 7.11.

To *explicitly* construct the data structure corresponding to the superimposed binary search tree we can see that each node in the tree will need to have two links or pointers associated with it, one pointing to the root of its left subtree and the second pointing to the root of its right subtree. This is shown in Fig. 7.12.

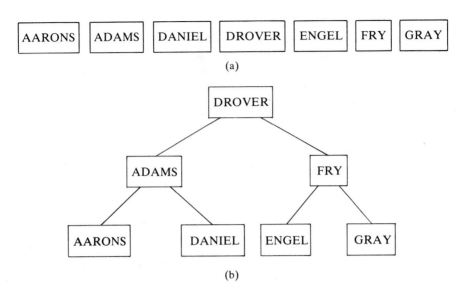

(a)

(b)

Fig. 7.11   (a) Ordered data; (b) Corresponding binary search tree.

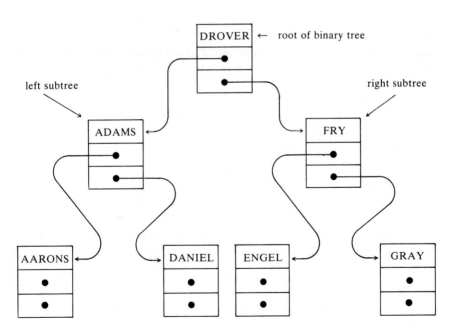

Fig. 7.12   An ordered binary tree with associated pointers.

The tree structure we have created is an *ordered binary tree*. At this point it is worth defining an ordered binary tree. An *ordered binary tree* is a finite set of nodes which is either empty or consists of a root node as the ancestor of two disjoint binary trees called the *left subtree* and the *right subtree* of the root. Any node of the left subtree when compared with any node of the right subtree satisfies the ordering relation (e.g. alphabetical or numerical) of the tree. The left or right subtree at any level may be empty.

We might ask, what can be gained by representing the data in this way? Before trying to answer this we should think back to the linked list structure. There we saw that the advantage of the linked structure over the ordered structure was that it allowed easy insertion and deletion with only small changes to the data structure. As we will see later, insertions and deletions using an ordered binary tree are also efficient and relatively straightforward to perform.

Our present concern is with developing an algorithm that will search the linked binary tree representation we have just described. Suppose that we wish to search the ordered binary tree for the name DANIEL.

We might expect there would be considerable similarities between the binary search algorithm for an ordered data set and the search of a linked binary tree. If we were to binary search our ordered set of names for the name DANIEL we would start by comparing the middle name in the set DROVER with DANIEL. With regard to our ordered binary tree, this is equivalent to comparing the search name DANIEL with the name at the *root* of the binary tree. The comparison of the two names in the binary search case tells us that DANIEL must be in the *first half* of the list of names. The middle name ADAMS in the first half of the list is therefore examined next. Equivalently, with our ordered binary tree, we must examine the name ADAMS at the root of the left subtree. To locate this name instead of using a computation (as in the binary search) we employ the left pointer stored in root node since it points to the root of the left subtree. Assuming the appropriate node definition has been made and that we are within the bounds of a **with** statement the step will involve:

$$current := left$$

The steps in our search for DANIEL are:

DANIEL < DROVER ⇒ move to left subtree (root ADAMS)
DANIEL > ADAMS ⇒ move to right subtree (root DANIEL)
DANIEL = DANIEL ⇒ terminate search

Whether we branch into the left or right subtree at any point in the search will depend on the name stored at the current node and the name being searched for; that is,

if name in node comes alphabetically after search name then
(a)   move to root of left subtree
else
(a′)   move to root of right subtree.

These steps give us a way of traversing the tree in the desired manner but they do not give us any way of stopping either when the name sought has been located or when the search has been unsuccessful. It follows that the compound statement above should only be executed when it is established that there is no match at the current node.

We will then have:

if match at current node then
(a)   terminate search
else·
(a′)   move to appropriate left or right subtree.

We also need to allow for the case where the search is unsuccessful. To see what must be done in this case, consider that we were searching for DAVID which is not stored in our tree. Following the links through for DAVID, we see that we would eventually get to the name DANIEL, at which point we would decide that DAVID was in DANIEL's right subtree. However, DANIEL has no right subtree. For nodes that have no successor a *nil* is placed in the pointer field and is used to indicate that a node does not have a successor. The search must therefore continue until we find a match with the search name or until we encounter a node with a *nil* pointer on the linked path we are pursuing.

Because we intend to use our tree search algorithm as part of tree insertion and deletion algorithms, we should also maintain a pointer to the previous node. The reason for this will become clearer later on, but for now it will suffice to say that these operations are similar to the list insertion and deletion operations which required a pointer to the previous node to be kept. A statement of the form:

$$previous := current$$

that is performed *before* the current node variable is updated will save the required information. We have now established how the information needed for insertion and deletion can be obtained. The one remaining task is to establish whether or not the search key was found.

We have already seen that there are two ways in which our search loop can terminate, either by finding a match or by coming to the end of a path in the tree. Our task is, therefore, to determine the way the search terminated in the current instance. This brings us back to the question of how to terminate when a match is made. Until a match has been made the search remains in a "not found" state which suggests we should continue if there is still an allowable path to follow. However, as soon as a match is made, the search reverts to a "found" state. We can capture this mechanism by using a *notfound* Boolean variable which remains true until a match is made. A test of the status of this variable *after* the search has terminated will enable us to determine whether or not the search has been successful. We can use:

$$found := \mathbf{not}(notfound)$$

The development of the ordered binary tree search is now complete.

Algorithm description

1. Establish the search key and the pointer to the root of the tree.
2. Set the not found state and make the current node pointer point to the root and the previous node pointer to *nil*.
3. While search key not found and there is still a valid path to follow in the tree do
    -   (a)   if search key is not found at the current node then
        -   (a.1)   save pointer to current node in previous node pointer,
        -   (a.2)   if search key is in the left subtree then
            -   (2.a)   adjust current node pointer to point to the root of left subtree

            else
            -   (2'.a)   adjust current node pointer to point to the root of the right subtree

        else
        -   (a'.1)   make the not found condition false to signal termination of the search.
4. Establish whether or not search key found.
5. Return pointers to the previous node, the current node, and a variable indicating whether or not the search was successful.

Pascal implementation

The **record** declaration needed in the calling procedure is

```
const namesize = 20;
type nameformat = packed array[1..namesize] of char;
     treepointer = ↑treenode;
```

```
treenode = record
              treename : nameformat;
              left : treepointer;
              right : treepointer
           end;
```

```
procedure treesearch (searchname: nameformat; var current,
previous: treepointer; root: treepointer; var found: boolean);
var notfound {if false indicates search must terminate}: boolean;

begin {searches an ordered linked binary tree for the presence of
searchname}
    {assert: root points to root of tree}
    previous := nil; current := root; notfound := true;
    {invariant: after current iteration if searchname were (or is) present
    it would be in subtree with root current node and predecessor
    previous node}
    while notfound and (current <> nil) do
      with current↑ do
        if searchname <> treename then
          begin {save previous node and proceed to appropriate
          subtree}
            previous := current;
            if treename > searchname then
              current := left
            else
              current := right
          end
        else
          notfound := false;
    {assert: searchname found at current node V could be inserted in
    subtree of previous node}
    found := not notfound
end
```

Notes on design

1. The cost of the ordered binary tree search is proportional to the
    number of nodes that have to be examined before the search termi-
    nates. The number of nodes that need to be searched depends on the
    structure of the tree. In the worst possible case (where only all right
    pointers were linked or all left pointers were linked) the tree structure
    can degenerate into a linked linear list then on average half the nodes
    would need to be examined. What is of more interest to us is the search
    length for an "average" tree structure. One way to determine this
    parameter is to consider trees that have been formed from randomly

arranged data of size n. It is then necessary to average the search for all data items over the resulting $n!$ trees. The analysis is rather involved but it leads to the prediction that on average slightly less than $2 \log_e n$ nodes will need to be examined. This compares with the $\lfloor \log_2 n \rfloor$ in the binary search and perfectly balanced tree cases.

2. At the end of each iteration of the search loop it will be established that the search name is at the *current* node (if it is present) or it is in the subtree whose root is the *current* node. The pointer *current* will point to the *next* node to be examined and the pointer *previous* will point to the node that has most recently been examined. The Boolean variable *notfound* will remain true after each iteration unless the *searchname* is found. The loop will terminate because eventually (if not before) the condition *current* = *nil* will be true when there are no further branches in the tree to follow. The other termination condition where the *searchname* matches the *treename* may force an earlier termination of the loop.

3. In structure this algorithm has similarities with the linked list search and the binary search algorithm.

4. The search algorithm we have constructed can be used in conjunction with tree insertion and tree deletion procedures.

5. A refinement similar to that suggested for the list search can slightly improve the efficiency of the search. This would involve creating a sentinel node and ensuring that all nodes are linked to this node when their paths terminate. For most applications such a refinement is hardly worthwhile.

6. Various methods for traversing an ordered binary tree will be discussed in the next chapter on recursion.

Applications

Maintaining a large file of items that is subject to frequent searches, insertions and deletions.

Supplementary problems

7.5.1   Design and implement a tree searching algorithm that uses arrays for the names and the left and right pointer sets.

7.5.2   Implement a tree search algorithm that employs a sentinel as described in note 5. Assume that the tree has been set up so that the sentinel node exists but has not been set.

7.5.3   Design a tree search algorithm that adds one to a counter stored in each node as it is encountered during a search.

7.5.4   Design and implement an algorithm that will search a tree structure
that may have more than two nodes emanating from each node. As
part of the design it will be necessary to construct a suitable data
structure for storing such trees.

Algorithm 7.6
BINARY TREE INSERTION AND DELETION

Problem

Design and implement procedures for inserting and deleting elements from
a linked ordered binary tree.

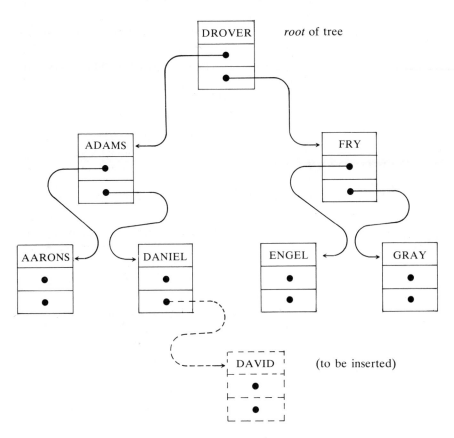

Fig. 7.13   Insertion into an ordered binary tree.

Algorithm development

After having considered the insertion and deletion procedures for linked lists we may anticipate that the corresponding binary tree operations will have a similar flavor. That is, we might expect to have to first do a search and then adjust some pointers to perform either an insertion or a deletion. The nature of the tree structure is, however, likely to stop the algorithms from being the same as the list algorithms.

As we did with the list problem let us first deal with the tree insertion mechanism. To make a start on this, consider the situation where we wish to insert the name DAVID in the ordered binary tree shown in Fig. 7.13.

The first question we must answer before we can do the insertion is *where* in the tree should DAVID be placed? We could arbitrarily place it in different positions and test if the relation for an ordered binary tree was satisfied. This approach seems rather arbitrary and likely to be time consuming. We might, therefore, anticipate that there is a better way to tackle the problem. Our experience with ordered binary trees up to date has involved searching for a name *already present* in the tree. That is, we know how to search a binary tree to either locate a name or establish that it is not present. Our next question might be, can this help us in any way? We could certainly search the tree for DAVID, but how would this help? When we do this our search follows the pattern:

DAVID < DROVER   move to left subtree (root ADAMS)
DAVID > ADAMS   move to right subtree (root DANIEL)
DAVID > DANIEL   move to right subtree (root *nil* so terminate)

In this case our search terminates unsuccessfully because DAVID is not present but if DAVID had been positioned at the root of DANIEL's right subtree then the search would have been successful. Thus indirectly the search has answered our question about where to place DAVID—that is, the inserted item must be placed in the position where the tree search algorithm would expect to find it if it were present. Therefore, the first part of the tree insertion involves a search to find where in the tree the new item is to be inserted. Referring back to our tree searching algorithm, we see that for our example, the pointer *previous* will be pointing to DANIEL's node and the *current* value will be *nil* when the search terminates. That is,

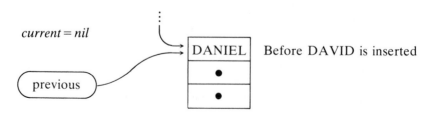

Before DAVID is inserted

To insert DAVID it will need to be placed at the root of DANIEL's *right* subtree. This will involve setting the *previous* node's (i.e. DANIEL's) right pointer so that it points to the new DAVID node. That is,

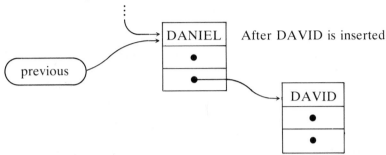

At this point we are ready to summarize the basic steps in the mechanism:

1. find where new name is to be placed in tree by searching for it,
2. create a new node and store in it the name to be inserted. Since it has no subtrees its left and right pointers will be *nil*;
3. adjust the previous node's pointer so that it points to the node to be inserted.

The search mechanism has been discussed in detail before and so we do not need to consider it further other than to assume that the *treesearch* procedure developed in algorithm 7.5 can be used. Creation of the new node and the storage mechanism is also straightforward. We are, therefore, only left with the problem of adjusting the previous node's pointer. Examining our searching mechanism again we see that at the point when the search terminates (assuming the name is not already present) the only information we have is a pointer to the previous node and a current node value of *nil*. Before we can make the insertion we need to know whether the new node is to be inserted in the previous node's left or right subtree. However, the information has been lost during the search. That is, for our example we are effectively at the previous node DANIEL and we must decide whether DAVID should be placed in its left or right subtree. A simple order test using the previous node's name and the name to be inserted will resolve the situation and allow us to update the appropriate pointer, i.e. within the context of the previous node we can apply the step:

if treename>newname then
(a)   insert newname in left subtree by updating left pointer of previous node
else
(a')   insert in right subtree by updating right pointer of previous node.

In the situation where the tree is initially empty we *do not* apply these steps but instead we must update the root pointer so that it points to the newly inserted node.

We can now give a full description of our tree insertion algorithm. Before moving on to this description we will consider in detail the tree deletion algorithm.

The fact that a node to be deleted from a binary tree may be linked to left and right subtrees suggests that the deletion mechanism may be more complicated than insertion. At the outset we should therefore take the trouble to consider *all* environments in which deletion of a node might be required. These are shown in Fig. 7.14, where in each case the node to be deleted is marked with an asterisk (*).

If we have to treat the seemingly large number of environments for deletion as *all* special cases our algorithm is going to be very complex. Our goal in this context must therefore be a general algorithm for deletion in which there are as *few* special cases as possible. We must therefore begin to look for *similarities* rather than differences among the various cases (e.g. cases (a), (b), (c) and (d) of Fig. 7.14 all involve deletion of the root node).

One approach we could take would be to try to deal with the simplest cases first and attempt to group them together. This may work but it is usually easier to design an algorithm that will handle the most complex case in the hope that this will encompass the simpler cases. For this reason, let us start by examining case (l) where we intend to delete the node marked with a 12. As a first step in this direction, let us remove all links involving node 12. We are left with:

⑧Predecessor of deleted node

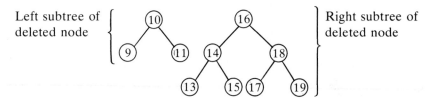

Left subtree of deleted node   Right subtree of deleted node

Our tree is now broken into three subtrees. What we must decide is how these subtrees can be linked together in a way that allows the new tree to conform to the definition of an ordered binary tree. When dealing with ordered linked lists it was simply a matter of linking the predecessor of the deleted node to its successor. In the binary tree case, there is one "predecessor" (or ancestor) node (i.e. ⑧ in our example) as with the lists but now there are *two* successor nodes (i.e. ⑩ and ⑯). After examining the situation we see that both the subtree with root ⑩ and the subtree with root ⑯ are candidates for being the new right subtree of ⑧. At this point it does not seem to matter which of these subtrees we link to ⑧. Let us, therefore, link ⑧ to ⑯.

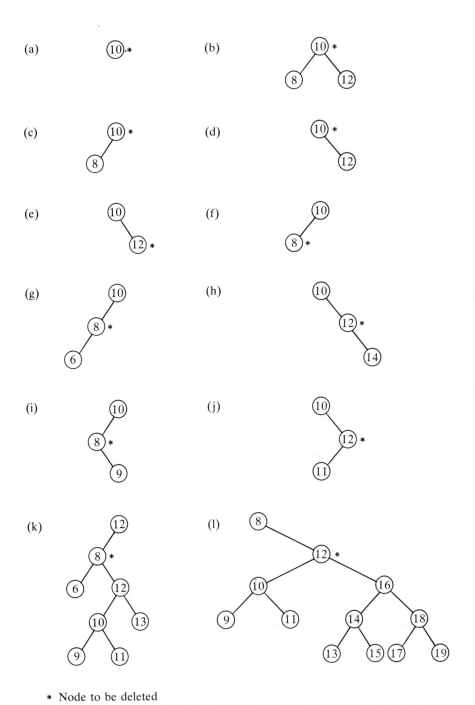

* Node to be deleted

Fig. 7.14   Cases for tree deletion.

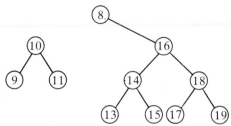

Now comes the question of what to do with the subtree whose root is 10 . It cannot take up the position as left subtree of⑧ as this violates the definition of an ordered binary tree (see algorithm 7.5 for the definition). The only possible nodes left to attach this subtree to are therefore ⑬, ⑮, ⑰, and ⑲. An examination of all these possibilities reveals that the only suitable role for this subtree will be as the left subtree of node ⑬. All the other possibilities violate the definition of an ordered binary tree. The new tree after deletion of node ⑫ therefore, should have the form:

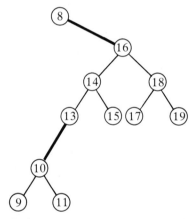

The two linkages needed to restore the tree are marked with heavy lines.

What we must now try to do is extract some *generality* from this example. To do this we must compare the tree before and after deletion of node ⑫. From this comparison we can conclude that the following steps must take place:

if a node in a right subtree has to be deleted then
(a)   link the predecessor node of the deleted node to the right subtree of the deleted node;
(b)   link the left subtree of the deleted node to the *leftmost* node in the subtree resulting from step (a).

The *leftmost* position mentioned in step (b) is the only place to put the left subtree of the deleted node that does not violate the definition of an ordered binary tree. This is shown in block diagram form in Fig. 7.15.

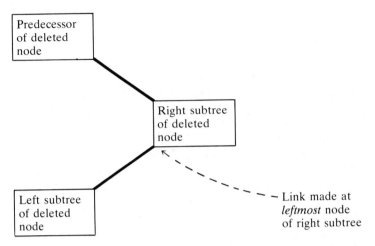

Fig. 7.15 Schematic representation of deletion of a node from a right subtree.

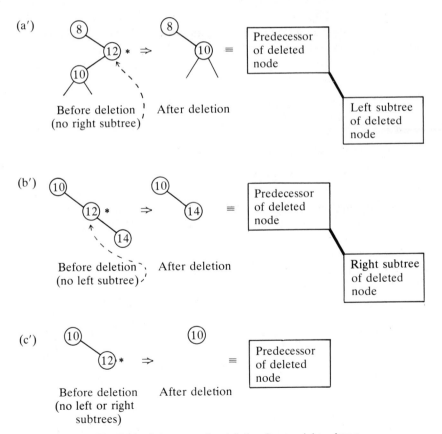

Fig. 7.16 Other cases for deletion from a right subtree.

Looking back to our set of diagrams we see that the variations on the current scheme for deleting from the right subtree are:

(a')   The deleted node may have no right subtree.
(b')   The deleted node may have no left subtree.
(c')   The deleted node may have no left or right subtrees.

The corresponding diagrams for these cases are given in Fig. 7.16. Note that in case (c') the right link of (10) will need to have the value *nil* on termination.

Case (a') looks as though it may cause problems. We will postpone this consideration until a little later when we have worked out the details for the more general case where there are left and right subtrees of the deleted node.

To begin working on the deletion mechanism let us reconsider our situation at the time when the node to be deleted has been located by the *treesearch* procedure. At that point the only information we have is a pair of pointers to the *previous* node and the *current* node (i.e. the one to be deleted). We must now ask, is this all the information needed to put the tree back together after deletion of the current node? After studying our previous example we see that we have enough information to link the predecessor of the deleted node to the right subtree of the deleted node (if it exists). The statement:

> **if** *previous* < > *nil* **then**
>   *previous↑.right* := *current↑.right*
> **else**
>   *root* := *current↑.right*

will enable us to perform this task allowing for *root* = *current*. Figure 7.17 shows this in terms of pointers. We do not at this stage, however, have enough information to link the left subtree of the deleted node to the *leftmost* node of the right subtree of the deleted node (refer to situation (l) in the aforementioned set of examples). The thing that stops us from making this link directly is that we do not know the identity of the leftmost node in the right subtree of the deleted node. Referring to our earlier example we have:

Our task is to find the *leftmost* node in this right subtree of the node to be deleted. To move into this right subtree a statement of the following form is needed:

$$newcurrent := current \uparrow .right$$

After this assignment *newcurrent* will point to the *root* of the right subtree.

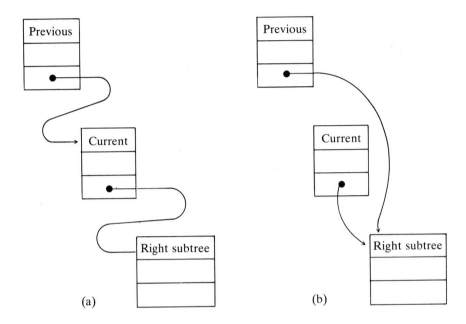

Fig. 7.17 (a) Before deletion; (b) After deletion.

To actually find the leftmost node of this subtree, we can start at the root and follow down the successive left links until we encounter a node with a *nil* left link—this is the *leftmost* node in the right subtree (i.e. ⑬ in our example). The steps we will need to perform the search for the leftmost node in the right subtree are:

1. Get pointer to root of right subtree and save it.
2. While current pointer not *nil* do
   (a) save current pointer,
   (b) set current pointer to its left link.

We need to save the current pointer *before* resetting it to prevent the pointer to the leftmost node from being set to *nil* when the search loop terminates. Our procedure will also need to take into account that the loop may not be executed at all (i.e. the node to be deleted may not have a right subtree).

Once we have a pointer to the leftmost node of the right subtree it is simply a matter of linking this node's left pointer to the root of the left subtree of the deleted node, i.e. if *newprevious* points to the leftmost node in the right subtree we will have (provided *current* node is not the *root* node in which case *root* := *current↑.left*)

$$newprevious\uparrow.left := current\uparrow.left$$

We discovered earlier when considering case (a') that the step we have just described *should not* be performed when the deleted node has no right subtree. This situation can be detected by a check whether *current↑.right* is *nil*. When this situation prevails we need to place the left subtree of the deleted node as the right subtree of the node preceding the deleted node. We can do this using

$$previous\uparrow.right := current\uparrow.left$$

provided *current* is not *root* in which case *root* becomes *current↑.left*. Refer back to case (a') for the appropriate diagram.

We have now established a mechanism to delete a node from a right subtree. Our mechanism will account for the case where the node for deletion has no right subtree and where it has both left and right subtrees. It is a simple task to establish that the other cases fit within our general framework.

Having considered all the possibilities for deleting a node from a right subtree, our next task is to consider all the cases for deleting a node from a left subtree. In starting to consider this new problem, we soon come to realize that it can be treated as the "mirror image" of the problem we have just solved. Some further deliberation reveals that simply replacing *right* by *left* and vice versa everywhere in our previous discussion will give us a mechanism for deleting an element from a left subtree.

We now have mechanisms for deleting elements from either right or left subtrees. The only task remaining is to specify the procedure that allows us to first find the node to be deleted and then appropriately call either the procedure for deleting an element from a left or right subtree. The algorithm follows directly from this description.

We are now at a stage where we can fully describe all the procedures that we have developed in this discussion.

Algorithm description

(1)   Binary tree insertion

    1.   Establish the name to be inserted and the pointer to the root of the tree.

    2.   Find where new name is to be placed in tree using *treesearch*.

3.   Create a new node and store in it the name to be inserted. At the time of insertion this new node will have no subtrees so its left and right pointers must be set to *nil*.

4.   If tree is not initially empty then
      (a)   if tree name comes alphabetically later than newname then
           (a.1)   adjust previous node's left pointer so that it points to the new node
      else
           (a'.1)   adjust previous node's right pointer so that it points to the new node,
      else
      (a')   adjust root pointer to point to new node.

5.   Return the updated tree and its root pointer.

(2)   Binary tree deletion

1.   Establish the name to be deleted and the pointer to the root of the tree.

2.   Search tree for name to be deleted and return pointers to the name to be deleted and its predecessor if it is present.

3.   If node to be deleted is found then
      (a)   if node to be deleted is in the left subtree then
           (a.1)   invoke procedure for deleting node from left subtree
      else
           (a'.1)   invoke procedure for deleting node from right subtree,
      else
      (a')   report name to be deleted was not present.

4.   Return tree from which node has been deleted (if present).

(3)   Deletion from right subtree[†]

1.   Establish pointers to the current node to be deleted, its predecessor (or ancestor), and the root of the tree.

2.   Link the predecessor node of the current node to its right subtree.

3.   Get pointer to the root of the right subtree of the current node and set it as the new current node pointer.

4.   Find leftmost node in right subtree by following down a set of left links until a *nil* is encountered.

[†]   Deletion from the left subtree is identical to the above procedure if the words left and right are interchanged in the description above.

5. If the node to be deleted has a right subtree then
    (a) make the left subtree of·the node to be deleted into the left subtree of the leftmost node in the right subtree and adjust root if necessary

    else
    (a') make the left subtree of the node to be deleted become the right subtree of the predecessor of the node to be deleted and adjust root if necessary.
6. Dispose of the deleted node.
7. Return the tree from which the node has been deleted (if present).

Pascal implementation

(1) Binary tree insertion

```
procedure treeinsert(newname: nameformat; var root: treepointer);
var current {pointer to current node},
    previous {pointer to node above current node},
    newnode {pointer to newly inserted node}: treepointer;

    found {if true means name already present so no insertion}:
    boolean;

begin
  {assert: root points to root of tree}
  treesearch (newname, current, previous, root, found);
  if not (found) then
    begin
      {assert: previous node is predecessor node for newname to be
      inserted if tree not empty}
      new(newnode);
      with newnode↑ do
        begin
          treename := newname;
          left := nil;
          right := nil
        end;
      if root <>nil then
        with previous↑ do
          if treename >newname then
            left := newnode
          else
            right := newnode
      else
        root := newnode
    end
    {assert: previous node linked to newnode containing inserted
    newname maintaining ordered binary tree}
  else
    writeln('The name ', newname, ' is already present')
end
```

(2) Binary tree deletion

```
procedure treedelete (oldname: nameformat; var root: treepointer);
var current {pointer to the node to be deleted},
    previous {pointer to the ancestor of node to be deleted}:
    treepointer;
    found {true if name to be deleted is in tree}: boolean;

begin
    {assert: root points to root of tree}
    treesearch (oldname, current, previous, root, found);
    if found then
    {assert: current node points to node containing oldname}
        if previous <>nil then
            if oldname <previous↑.treename then
                leftsubtree(current,previous,root)
            else
                rightsubtree(current,previous,root)
        else
            rightsubtree(current,previous,root)
        {assert: oldname removed from tree and links restored to
        maintain ordered binary tree}
    else
        writeln ('The name', oldname, 'is not present in tree')
end
```

(3) Deletion from right subtree[†]

```
procedure rightsubtree (current,previous: treepointer; var root:
treepointer);
var newcurrent {pointer to leftmost node examined so far in right
subtree},
    newprevious {finally contains pointer to leftmost node in right
    subtree}: treepointer;

begin {removes current node from binary tree—current node has a
"smaller" ancestor}
    {assert: root points to root of tree}
    newprevious := previous;
    newcurrent := current↑.right;
    {link predecessor node of the current node to its right subtree}
    if previous <>nil then
        previous↑.right := current↑.right
    else
        root := current↑.right;
    {assert: newcurrent points to root of right subtree of current node}
    {invariant: newcurrent points to leftmost node examined so far in
    right subtree of current node ∧ newprevious points to its
    predecessor}
```

---

†   The procedure for deletion from the left subtree has exactly the same form as the
procedure *rightsubtree*. To convert this procedure to the procedure left subtree the
roles of *left* and *right* must be exchanged.

```
while newcurrent <>nil do
    begin {find leftmost node in right subtree of predecessor node}
        newprevious := newcurrent;
        newcurrent := newcurrent↑.left
    end;
if current↑.right <>nil then
    {left subtree of current node becomes left subtree of leftmost
    node in right subtree}
    if newprevious <>nil then
        newprevious↑.left := current↑.left
    else
        root := current↑.left
else
    {no right subtree so left subtree becomes right subtree of
    predecessor node}
    if previous <>nil then
        previous↑.right := current↑.left
    else
        root := current↑.left;
dispose(current)
{assert: current node removed and links restored to maintain
ordered binary tree}
end
```

Notes on design

1. The cost of ordered binary tree insertion and deletion is proportional to the number of nodes that need to be examined before the insertion or deletion can be made. It follows that the discussion of performance will take the same path as that given in note 1 of the *treesearch* algorithm (algorithm 7.5). We might therefore expect on average for a randomly constructed tree with n nodes that approximately $2 \log_e n$ nodes will need to be examined.

2. In the discussion of the behavior of the tree insertion and tree deletion algorithms, we will not consider the treesearch algorithm since its behavior has been characterized in algorithm 7.5. The adjustments to the tree made by the tree insertion algorithm depend on the pointer *previous* passed to this procedure by the *treesearch* procedure. If the tree is empty before insertion then the root is set to point to the newly inserted node. If the tree is not initially empty then the procedure will use the information stored in the would-be ancestor of the new node to decide whether the new node should be placed in either the left or right subtree of its ancestor. The changes made to the tree made by the *rightsubtree* deletion algorithm depend on the values of the *previous* and *current* pointers returned by the *treesearch* procedure. We can

characterize the behavior of the iterative process used in this procedure in the following way. After each iteration, the pointer *newprevious* will point to the leftmost node in the right subtree of the node to be deleted that has been examined so far. The pointer *newcurrent* will point to the node at the root of the left subtree of the node pointed to by *newprevious*. On termination *newprevious* will point to the leftmost node in the right subtree of the node to be deleted.

On termination of the algorithm if the tree only contained the node to be deleted then the *root* pointer will be set to *nil*. If the *root* node has been deleted then the new *root* of the tree will be the root of the right subtree. If a leaf node has been deleted (i.e. a node with *nil* left and right subtrees) then the predecessor node will have a *nil* pointer where it previously had a pointer to the leaf node that was deleted. If an internal node has been deleted (i.e. a node with left and right subtrees) then the right pointer of the predecessor will be changed to point to the root of the right subtree of the deleted node. The left subtree of the deleted node will become the left subtree of the leftmost node in the right subtree of the deleted node. If the deleted node has no right subtree then the left subtree of the deleted node will assume the role of the right subtree of the predecessor of the deleted node. The behavior of the *leftsubtree* procedure can be described similarly to the *rightsubtree* procedure.

The behavior of the *treedelete* procedure is governed by the behavior of the *treesearch* and *leftsubtree* and *rightsubtree* procedures.

The *treeinsert* procedure terminates because the *treesearch* procedure terminates. It consists of a linear sequence of steps and so it must terminate. The *treedelete* and *leftsubtree* and *rightsubtree* procedures terminate for similar reasons. The loop in *rightsubtree* terminates because with each iteration a new node is examined and so because the tree is finite eventually a node will be found that has a *nil* pointer. This will force termination of the loop.

3. In the preceding discussion we have considered one insertion and one deletion algorithm for ordered binary trees. Also we have only considered one possible representation for ordered binary trees. As we might expect there are a number of other algorithms and representations that can be used for these operations. We will cover some of these other algorithms in the notes on design and supplementary problems.

4. In the present algorithm for tree deletion we have tried to take advantage of the symmetry in the problem. As a result we have ended up with separate procedures for deleting nodes from left and right subtrees. The limitations of Pascal and the data structure chosen do not make it

very easy to pass information in such a way as to use the *same* procedure for left and right subtree deletions. Most other algorithms for deletion exhibit asymmetry with respect to deletion from left and right subtrees. This difference in operation can over a period of time introduce additional asymmetry into the existing tree structure which is usually undesirable.

5. A separate procedure has been used for locating the position of insertion and the node to be deleted. Because the insertion and deletion processes *both* involve an initial search phase which is separate to the manipulation of the tree nodes, it is therefore reasonable to use a separate procedure for the search.

6. The tree insertion and deletion algorithms can be implemented quite elegantly using recursion. The recursive algorithms do, however, tend to hide (from the beginner, at least) some of the subtleties of the mechanisms of tree insertion and deletion (see Chapter 8 for a discussion on recursion).

7. The algorithm for tree insertion can be used for sorting of data. To actually retrieve the items from the tree in "sorted" order it is necessary to traverse the tree in a particular order. What is called an *Inorder* traversal of the tree is necessary to retrieve the items from an ordered binary tree in sorted order. Tree traversal algorithms (including inorder traversal) are discussed in the next chapter on recursion.

8. There is a risk with the tree insertion and deletion algorithms described that the tree will have a depth considerably greater than $\log_2 n$ for n nodes stored. To avoid this risk tree insertion and deletion algorithms that incorporate a balancing mechanism have been developed. These mechanisms which are the logical extension of the insertion and deletion algorithms we have described allow insertion and deletion with $O(\log_2 n)$ steps even in the worst case. The basic idea behind balancing is to ensure for every node that the height of its left and right subtrees differ by at most one.

Applications

To maintain large amounts of information which must be able to be changed easily and searched quickly—e.g. airline reservations.

Supplementary problems

7.6.1 Design and implement tree insertion and deletion algorithms that use arrays for the names and left and right pointer sets. A linked free list should be used to keep track of unused storage. You should be able to design your algorithm such that *only one* procedure is

needed to perform the role of the *leftsubtree* and *rightsubtree* procedures described above.

7.6.2   Design a tree deletion algorithm that handles left and right subtrees
similarly. A variation on the *rightsubtree* procedure should be used
to also delete nodes in left subtrees. Figure 7.18 illustrates how your
procedure should handle deletion of node ⑪.

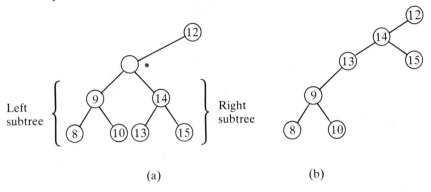

(a)   (b)

Fig. 7.18   (a) Before deletion; (b) After deletion.

7.6.3   Another deletion algorithm involves searching the right subtree for
its leftmost node. This leftmost node is then moved to the position of
the deleted node and the leftmost node is replaced by its right
subtree. This rearrangement mechanism is useful because it does
not change the average length of the tree. Figure 7.19, in which
node ⑩ is to be deleted, explains the mechanism. Implement this
mechanism.

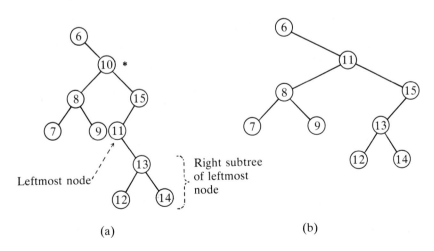

(a)   (b)

Fig. 7.19   (a) Before deletion; (b) After deletion.

7.6.4 Design and implement an algorithm that will convert a general multiway tree (each node may have more than two successors) to the corresponding ordered binary tree.

BIBLIOGRAPHY

There are numerous excellent texts on data structures. Wirth (1976), Gotlieb (1978) and Hoare (1972) provide important treatments of the subject as does Knuth (1973).

1. Berztiss, A. T., *Data Structures: Theory and Practice*, Academic Press, N.Y. 1975.
2. D'Imperio, M. E., "Data structures and their representation in storage", *Ann. Rev. in Automatic Programming*, **5**, 1–75 (1969).
3. Gotlieb, C. C. and L. R. Gotlieb, *Data Types and Structures*, Prentice-Hall, Englewood Cliffs, N.J., 1978.
4. Hoare, C. A. R., "Notes on data structuring" in O.-J. Dahl, E. W. Dijkstra and C. A. R. Hoare, *Structured Programming*, Academic Press, N.Y., 1972.
5. Horowitz, E. and S. Sahni, *Fundamentals of Data Structures*, Comp. Sci. Press, Woodland Hills, Calif., 1976.
6. Knuth, D. E., *The Art of Computer Programming*, Vol. 1: *Fundamental Algorithms*, 2nd ed., Addison–Wesley, Reading, Mass., 1969.
7. Knuth, D. E., *The Art of Computer Programming*, Vol. 3: *Sorting and Searching*, Addison–Wesley, Reading, Mass., 1973.
8. Lewis, T. G. and M. Z. Smith, *Applying Data Structures*, Houghton Mifflin, Boston, Mass., 1976.
9. Nievergelt, J., "Binary search trees and file organizations", *Comp. Surv.*, **6**, 195–207 (1974).
10. Page, E. S. and L. B. Wilson, *Information Representation and Manipulation in a Computer*, Cambridge University Press, London, 1973.
11. Tremblay, J. P. and P. C. Sorensen, *An Introduction to Data Structures with Applications*, McGraw–Hill, N.Y., 1976.
12. Wirth, N., *Algorithms + Data Structures = Programs*, Prentice-Hall, Englewood Cliffs, N.J., 1976.

Chapter 8
RECURSIVE ALGORITHMS

INTRODUCTION

Recursion is a programming technique with a completely different flavor to the methods we have encountered in earlier discussions. In a number of the problems we have discussed in previous chapters, we have found it useful to call other procedure(s) or function(s) within the *body* of the main procedure. For example,

> **procedure** *external*(...)
> :
> **begin**
> :
>   *internal*(...) ← Call to a second procedure *internal* within the
> :   body of procedure *external* (note that proce-
> **end**   dure *internal* may itself call other procedures
>   and so on)

Under these conditions the statements in procedure *external* are executed according to the flow of control in the procedure as influenced by the input conditions or data. At the point in procedure *external* where the call to procedure *internal* is encountered, execution of procedure *external* is *suspended*. As soon as procedure *external* is suspended, procedure *internal* starts to execute. Procedure *internal* continues until it *terminates*. Directly after termination of procedure *internal*, procedure *external resumes* execution where it left off, taking into account any changes to its variables that the call to *internal* may have brought about. Even if procedure *internal* itself calls another procedure *innermost* within the body of its statements, the sequence of execution of the whole process involving the three "nested" procedures follows in a natural order, i.e. for this new example:

1. *external* executes until a call to *internal* is encountered at which point procedure *external* suspends execution.

2. With *external* suspended, procedure *internal* starts to execute and continues until it encounters a call to procedure *innermost* at which point *internal* also suspends execution (i.e. now *both external* and *internal* are suspended).

3. With both *external* and *internal* suspended, procedure *innermost* begins to execute and continues execution until it reaches termination.

4. At the point when *innermost* terminates, the procedure *internal* resumes where it left off. (At this stage *innermost* has terminated and *external* is still suspended.) Procedure *internal* then continues until it comes to termination.

5. With both *innermost* and *internal* terminated, the main procedure resumes from where it left off at the call to *internal* and proceeds until it too comes to termination at which point the whole process comes to termination.

The whole process we have described is relatively straightforward and easy to use. Another rather simplified way to view the complete process is to imagine that *each* procedure call is replaced by the set of statements that make up the procedure. The result is an expanded version of the main procedure in which the called procedures appear to form a nested structure. For our previous example, the "imagined" expansion of procedure *external* would take the form shown in Fig. 8.1.

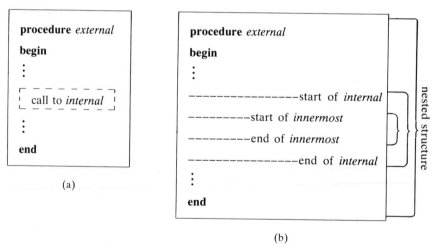

Fig. 8.1 (a) Original main procedure; (b) Expanded view.

We have now laid the foundations we need to allow us to introduce the ideas of recursion and recursive procedures (and recursive functions).

A special case of one procedure calling another procedure (or function) is where the original procedure calls *itself* rather than some other procedure. Algorithms that are implemented in this way are said to be *recursive*. It is possible to break up the class of recursive algorithms into several important subclasses as described below.

Linear recursion

The simplest type of recursive algorithm is that in which only *one* internal recursive call is made within the body of the procedure (or function). Recursive algorithms of this type are said to be *linear*. Many linear recursive algorithms fit within the following general framework (although the order of the steps may change).

```
procedure linear( ... )
begin
    if "termination condition satisfied" then
        (a)   return some value(s)
    else
        begin
        (a')   perform some action(s)
        (b')   make a further recursive call to linear
        end
end
```

For this type of procedure, the *last* recursive call made *before* the termination condition is met is the *earliest* call to terminate. The following mechanism tree illustrates this idea. The nodes refer to recursive calls.

Linear recursion

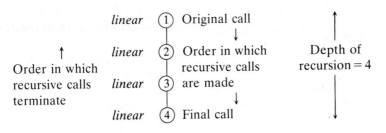

Probably the simplest and most often quoted examples involving linear recursion are the factorial and greatest common divisor computations. Linear recursive algorithms follow directly from their recursive definitions. Several possible implementations are:

```
function nfactorial(n:integer):integer;
begin
  if n = 0 then
    nfactorial := 1
  else
    nfactorial := n * nfactorial(n-1)
end


procedure fact(n:integer; var nfactorial:integer);
var t : integer;
begin
  if n = 0 then
    nfactorial := 1
  else
    begin
      fact(n-1, t);
      nfactorial := n * t
    end
end

function gcd(n, m:integer):integer;
begin
  if m = 0 then
    gcd := n
  else
    gcd := gcd(m, n mod m)
end
```

As we have seen in earlier chapters, both the factorial and greatest common divisor computations have simple efficient iterative solutions. We will therefore not dwell on these examples. To be sure that the examples are understood, the reader should carry out the hand calculations for these functions for several specific inputs.

A final remark is in order regarding linear recursion. With linear recursive algorithms, there is usually a much greater risk of incurring a large depth of recursion (e.g. copying a long list recursively). *Each* recursive call requires the saving of an additional set of parameters, local variables, and links. Therefore, potentially, a linear recursive algorithm can be much more expensive in its use of memory than simple iterative solutions. This overhead tends to also make linear recursive algorithms slower than their slightly less concise iterative counterparts. When we move away from linear recursion the space–cost argument against recursion usually becomes much less relevant.

Binary recursion

The next increase in sophistication with the use of recursion is found in the mechanism called *binary recursion*. Binary recursion is a special case of the more general *non-linear recursion*. Because of its wide application and importance in computing science, it is relevant to discuss binary recursion separately. An algorithm that makes *two* internal recursive calls to itself is said to employ *binary recursion*. Many problems in computing science fit within this framework. A problem is solved by first breaking it down into *two* smaller problems that are each in turn solved by being broken into two still smaller problems, and so on recursively. A number of problems that involve recursively defined data structures (e.g. binary trees) are solved most simply and naturally using binary recursion. In the first half of this chapter, we will consider in detail several algorithms involving binary recursion. A commonly used structure for algorithms employing binary recursion is given below. For a given implementation the order of the various steps and details may change.

> **procedure** *binary*(...)
> **begin**
>   **if** termination condition met **then**
>   (a)   perform some action(s) and/or return some value
>   **else**
>   **begin**
>   (a′)   perform some action(s)
>   (b′)   make a recursive call to *binary* that solves one of the two smaller problems
>   (c′)   make another recursive call to *binary* to solve the other smaller problem
>   **end**
> **end**

A very simple example of binary recursion involves recursive computation of the Fibonacci sequence. As for our linear examples, the iterative solution is simpler and more efficient. However, as we will see later, iterative solutions to solve problems involving binary recursion are often *much* more complicated and require the use of stacks. We will also see later that it is usually easiest to interpret binary recursion in terms of a binary mechanism tree.

Non-linear recursion

Non-linear recursion is widely used in computing science. When an algorithm uses a number of internal recursive calls within the body of the procedure then the procedure is said to involve *non-linear recursion*. In these systems, multiple internal recursive calls are usually generated by placing a *single* recursive call within a loop. In the second half of this chapter we will discuss in detail several non-linear recursive algorithms. A general framework is given below which fits many non-linear recursive algorithms.

```
procedure nonlinear( ... )
begin
  for j := k to n do
    begin
    (a)   perform some action(s)
    (b)   if "termination condition not met" then
          (b.1)   make a further recursive call to nonlinear
          else
          (b'.1)   "perform some action(s)
    end
end
```

As for binary recursion, these mechanisms are best understood in terms of tree-like structures.

Mutual recursion

Yet another more unusual type of recursion is called *mutual recursion*. With this type of recursion, a procedure calls itself *indirectly* via another procedure that calls itself indirectly via the first procedure. In a sense the two (or more) procedures are *interlocked* together. A simple but typical model for mutual recursion is given below.

```
procedure mutual( ... )
begin
  ⋮
    internal call to another
  ⋮
end
procedure another( ... )
begin
  ⋮
    internal call to mutual
  ⋮
end
```

There are many variations on this basic theme; Pascal compilers use recursive descent which is a form of mutual recursion. We will choose not to consider mutual recursion further in this chapter.

What we are likely to discover in our first encounter with recursion, is that the difficulty in understanding it lies in trying to get, at one time, an overall picture of what is happening and in what order it is happening. Once we can overcome this with diagrams etc. the whole concept becomes a lot clearer and easier to use. We will not deal with all aspects of recursion but rather we will concentrate on simpler and related examples in an effort to bring home the more fundamental aspects of the topic.

Problems like factorial and the gcd algorithm are not considered in detail (although they are often used as examples elsewhere) because they do little to convey the real flavor and power of recursion.

Algorithm 8.1
BINARY TREE TRAVERSAL

Problem

Design recursive procedures for *inorder*, *preorder*, and *postorder* traversal of an ordered binary tree.

Algorithm development

There are many ways in which we can systematically examine all the nodes of an ordered binary tree exactly once. Several of these methods of traversal are important because of the order that they superimpose on the data stored in the tree. In an earlier discussion (Chapter 7) we saw a way for storing a set of names in a binary tree such that any given name could be retrieved in $O(\log_2 n)$ steps on average. A task that we may often wish to perform with this data would be to print out the names in alphabetical or lexical order. To try to understand how we might do this let us consider the example shown in Fig. 8.2. The lexical order for this set of names is:

AARONS, ADAMS, DANIEL, DROVER, ENGEL, FRY, GRAY.

When the names stored in an ordered binary tree are printed in lexical order it is said that an *inorder traversal* of the nodes of the tree has been performed.

The information that we have on hand *before* beginning to print out the names is just a pointer to the root node (i.e. the node containing DROVER). At this point we have a dilemma because DROVER obviously cannot be printed first. Our only alternative since we cannot print this node initially is to "save" it (or a pointer to it) to avoid having to consider the root node again (remember our earlier restriction of wishing to examine each node in the tree *only once*). After examining our tree diagram we see that *all* the

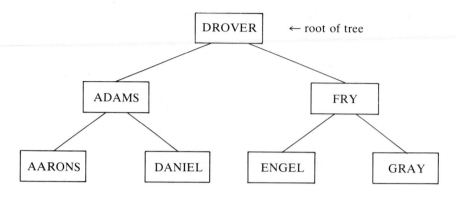

Fig. 8.2   An ordered binary tree.

names that come alphabetically *after* DROVER are in its right subtree. The basic situation that we have is shown in Fig. 8.3. From this, we can infer that *all* the nodes in the left subtree will have to be printed *before* printing the root name. All nodes in the right subtree will need to be printed *after* the root name. The printing order is therefore:

1. Print all names in left subtree of root.
2. Print the name at the root.
3. Print all names in right subtree of root.

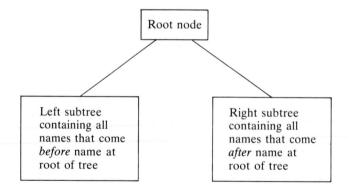

Fig. 8.3   Schematic subtree representation of an ordered binary tree.

Referring back to our example, we discover that when we move to the left subtree of the root we encounter a node with the name ADAMS which still cannot be printed first. The name ADAMS should however be printed before the root name DROVER. The question that now arises is what should we do on encountering a second name ADAMS which should not be printed yet? Our only alternative once again is to store it and look in the left subtree whose root is ADAMS. Examining this situation more carefully we discover that what we should do (as far as printing is concerned) when we are at the node containing ADAMS is essentially the *same* as what we needed to do when we were at DROVER. That is, when we arrive at the node containing ADAMS we must go through the process of printing all the members of its left subtree, then ADAMS, and then all members of ADAMS' right subtree. *This sequence of steps suggests that recursion can be used to perform the task* since as we move from the root to the left subtree and so on we are actually applying the *same* process over and over. If we can formulate the problem recursively, we should be able to avoid having to explicitly save names that we encounter before it is their turn to be printed.

In our earlier discussion, we found that the steps involved in printing the names in lexical order were:

1.   Traverse and print all names in left subtree;
2.   Print name at root of tree;
3.   Traverse and print all names in right subtree.

To construct our recursive procedure we will need to refine steps (1) and (3) and to work out the conditions for termination of a recursive call. To begin the printing process by considering the left subtree we can make the sub-tree's root the root of the tree to which we again apply steps (1) through (3). This amounts to making a recursive call to our original 3-step procedure. If our recursive procedure is called *inorder* then a recursive call of the form:

$$inorder(current\uparrow.left)$$

will allow us to descend to the root of the left subtree. Similarly, a recursive call of the form:

$$inorder(current\uparrow.right)$$

will allow us to descend to the root of the right subtree of the current node. The steps that we have in our recursive call to *inorder* are:

1.   *inorder(current↑.left)*;
2.   write name at current node;
3.   *inorder(current↑.right)*.

We can see that a series of recursive calls must be made to take us down the left subtree until we encounter the name AARONS—the first name to be printed. When we reach the node containing AARONS and try to apply the three steps:

1.   Traverse and print the names in AARONS' left subtree;
2.   Print the name AARONS;
3.   Traverse and print the names in AARONS' right subtree,

we find that the node containing AARONS has no left subtree because its left pointer is *nil*. It follows that whenever we try to process a tree (or subtree) whose root is *nil* the recursive process must terminate. Taking into account that the root of AARONS' right subtree is also *nil* we see that all that should happen when we try to process the subtree with root AARONS is:

1.   No left subtree so terminate recursion in left branch.
2.   Print the root of the subtree AARONS.
3.   No right subtree so terminate recursion in right branch.

The overall result of visiting the node containing AARONS is simply to print the name AARONS as we require. The three steps in the recursive procedure can therefore be guarded with a statement of the form:

if root of current subtree not *nil* then
(a)   proceed with recursive 3-step procedure.

We now have a complete formulation of our recursive procedure for printing the names of an ordered binary tree in lexical or alphabetical order. This corresponds to an *inorder* traversal of the nodes of the tree.

Before we are completely satisfied that we have formulated our algorithm correctly, we should trace through a small example very carefully. The result of doing this trace for the example we considered earlier at the start of the discussion is shown in Fig. 8.4.

In implementing recursive algorithms we should always pay attention to the potential depth of recursion for our problem. If it is possible that the depth of recursion can be large in relation to the problem size then we should look for an iterative solution to the problem or try to change the recursive implementation to reduce the upper bound on the depth of recursion. The reason for this is that there can be costly storage overhead when dealing with large problems. For our present problem, provided care has been taken in building the tree, the depth of recursion should only be of the order $\log_2 n$ for a tree with n nodes.

Before giving the complete description for the *inorder* traversal method, we need to consider the *preorder* and *postorder* traversal methods.

The two other methods for binary tree traversal that we wish to consider differ in the order in which they visit the root node and its left and right subtrees.

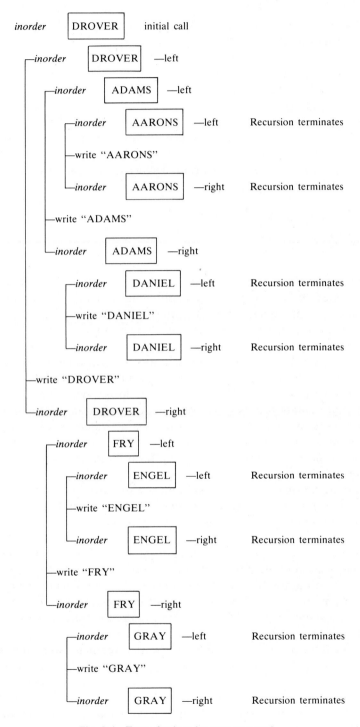

Fig. 8.4 Trace for inorder tree traversal.

For *preorder* traversal, the order in which the root node and its left and right subtrees are visited is:

1. Visit root and print name.
2. Visit left subtree.
3. Visit right subtree.

Like the *inorder* traversal, this process and the *postorder* traversal below are both recursive.

For *postorder* traversal, the order in which the root node and its left and right subtrees are visited is:

1. Visit left subtree.
2. Visit right subtree.
3. Visit root and print name.

Both the *preorder* and *postorder* traversals are important in relation to the computer evaluation of arithmetic expressions which can be considered to have the form of a binary tree. The internal or branch nodes of the binary tree contain the operators and the leaf nodes contain the variables and constants.

Traversing the binary tree representation of an arithmetic expression in postorder results in a representation of the expression (called *reverse polish* or *postfix* notation) in which each operator follows its pair of operands. The latter representation is very convenient for evaluating such expressions using a stack. We will not pursue further the development of the *preorder* and *postorder* procedures since their recursive implementations follow directly from the definitions and have a form that is closely similar to the *inorder* procedure.

Before leaving off this discussion, it is instructive to compare the three methods of traversal we have considered to be sure that we have a firm understanding of their differences. If we look back at our binary tree of names, we see *inorder* traversal corresponds to the order in which we encounter the nodes when we move from left to right across the page. Another way to think about this and the other methods of traversal is to imagine that the tree is a solid structure and that we start at the root and make a traversal around the perimeter of the tree moving first to the left subtree as shown in Fig. 8.5. (The path followed is marked with a dashed line.)

Now if we imagine that *each* node in the tree may have three spokes (two horizontal and one vertically down) protruding from it as indicated in Fig. 8.6, then we have a very easy way of seeing the difference between *inorder*, *preorder* and *postorder* traversals. The order in which our dashed path *crosses* the *vertical* spoke of each node corresponds to *inorder* traversal.

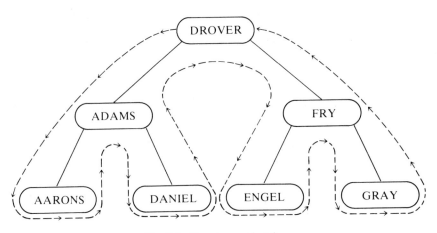

Fig. 8.5   Tree traversal path.

Similarly, the order in which the dashed path crosses the *left* spoke of each node corresponds to *preorder* traversal, and the order in which the path crosses the right spoke of each node gives us *postorder* traversal.

The three different orders for the set of names in our original example are shown below:

Inorder traversal:
AARONS, ADAMS, DANIEL, DROVER, ENGEL, FRY, GRAY

Preorder traversal:
DROVER, ADAMS, AARONS, DANIEL, FRY, ENGEL, GRAY

Postorder traversal:
AARONS, DANIEL, ADAMS, ENGEL, GRAY, FRY, DROVER.

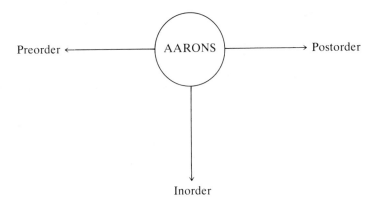

Fig. 8.6   Scheme for distinguishing among preorder, inorder and postorder traversal.

Algorithm description

(1)   Procedure for inorder traversal of an ordered binary tree[†]

1. Establish current node (initially the root of the tree).
2. If current node not *nil* then
   (a) recursively do an inorder traversal of the left subtree of the current node;
   (b) print the name at the current node;
   (c) recursively do an inorder traversal of the right subtree of the current node.

Pascal implementation

(1)   Inorder traversal

```
procedure inorder(current: treepointer);
begin
  if current <> nil then
    begin
      inorder(current↑.left);
      {assert: names in all nodes in left subtree of current node have
      been printed in lexical order}
      writeln(current↑.treename);
      {assert: name in current node printed}
      inorder(current↑.right)
      {assert: names in all nodes in right subtree of current node
      have been printed in lexical order}
    end
end
```

(2)   Preorder traversal

```
procedure preorder(current: treepointer);
begin
  if current <> nil then
    begin
      writeln(current↑.treename);
      {assert: name in current node printed}
      preorder(current↑.left);
      {assert: names in all nodes in left subtree of current node have
      been printed in preorder order}
      preorder(current↑.right)
      {assert: names in all nodes in right subtree of current node
      have been printed in preorder order}
    end
end
```

† The descriptions for the *preorder* and *postorder* traversals differ from the current procedure only in their arrangement of (a), (b) and (c) in step 2 above. They have therefore not been included.

(3)   Postorder traversal

```
procedure postorder(current: treepointer);
begin
  if current <> nil then
    begin
      postorder(current↑.left);
      {assert: names in all nodes in left subtree of current node have
      been printed in postorder order}
      postorder(current↑.right);
      {assert: names in all nodes in right subtree of current node
      have been printed in postorder order}
      writeln(current↑.treename)
      {assert: name in current node printed}
    end
end
```

Notes on design

1. The performance of the inorder, preorder and postorder traversal algorithms is directly proportional to the number of nodes in the tree. The number of recursive calls made is probably the best measure to use. For an ordered binary tree with n nodes there will be $(2n+1)$ calls to each of the recursive procedures with the present implementation.

2. With the *inorder* procedure, it is necessary to establish that it prints first all names in the left subtree, then the name at the current node and then all elements in the right subtree. To try to characterize the behavior of this procedure, let us consider the case where the current call to *inorder* does not invoke any further *internal* recursive calls to *inorder*. This implies that we are dealing with a leaf node since only when *current↑.left* and *current↑.right* are *nil* will there be no internal recursion. In this case, the two internal calls to *inorder* will have no effect. As a result, the current name (i.e. the name at the leaf node) will be printed as required. Now if we assume that the internal calls to *inorder* result in the names in the left and right subtrees being printed correctly, then the current call to *inorder* will result in all names being printed correctly in the left subtree, then the name at the current node being printed, and then the names in the right subtree being correctly printed. Therefore the tree that encompasses the left and right subtrees will also be correctly printed. This argument can form the basis for a formal inductive proof of the procedure. Each recursive call to *inorder* results in a move to a lower level of the tree and since we know that recursion always terminates at the leaf nodes we may loosely conclude that the algorithm will terminate. The *preorder* and *postorder* procedures may be considered similarly.

3. If non-recursive implementations for these traversal algorithms were

to be made then it would be necessary to explicitly save on a stack information relating to nodes that have been visited but not printed. The result is a seemingly much more complex and less transparent implementation in each case.

4. In situations where a stack is needed it is usually better to use a recursive implementation for the problem.

5. We notice in the present implementation that there are always *two* fruitless procedure calls on each leaf node. This can be costly since there are *always more leaf nodes than internal nodes*. We can avoid these redundant calls by stopping the recursion one step earlier. To do this we must include an explicit, but computationally cheap, test for leaf nodes. The changes will be:

```
          ⋮
begin
    notleaf := (current↑.left <> nil) or (current↑.right <> nil)
    if notleaf then
        begin
            if (current↑.left <> nil) then inorder(current↑.left);
            writeln(current↑.treename);
            if (current↑.right <> nil) then inorder(current↑.right)
        end
    else
        writeln(current↑.treename)
end
```

If we use this implementation, a separate test *outside* the procedure will be needed to be sure that the procedure is not called to print a tree with no nodes.

6. We have used binary recursion to solve this problem.

Applications

Maintenance of large stores of information, evaluation of arithmetic expressions.

Supplementary problems

8.1.1 Design a non-recursive algorithm for inorder traversal of an ordered binary tree.

8.1.2 Design a recursive procedure for counting the number of nodes in an ordered binary tree.

8.1.3 Design a recursive procedure that counts the number of leaf nodes in an ordered binary tree.

8.1.4   Design and implement recursive tree insertion and tree deletion algorithms.

8.1.5   Design an algorithm that uses an ordered binary tree to sort a set of names. Once the tree has been created, print out the sorted result.

8.1.6   A binary tree can be traversed without either directly using a stack or employing recursion. This can be done by traversing the tree in *triple order* which is defined by the following steps (each node is visited 3 times):

> *Triple order mechanism*
> 1. visit current node
> 2. traverse its left subtree
> 3. visit current node
> 4. traverse its right subtree
> 5. visit current node.

If we ensure each *nil* pointer is replaced by a reflexive pointer to the node itself the pointer adjustments given below can be used in a simple iterative scheme to traverse the tree in triple order. The algorithm can terminate when *current = nil*.

> *Pointer adjustments for triple order traversal*
> $next := current\uparrow.left$;
> $current\uparrow.left := current\uparrow.right$;
> $current\uparrow.right := previous$;
> $previous := current$;
> $current := next$.

Implement this method of tree traversal (see B. Dwyer, "Simple algorithms for traversing a tree without an auxiliary stack", *Inf. Proc. Letts.*, **2**, 143–5 (1974)).

Algorithm 8.2
RECURSIVE QUICKSORT

Problem

Design and implement a recursive version of the quicksort sorting algorithm.

Algorithm development

We have already seen in our earlier discussion of the quicksort algorithm (algorithm 5.6) that it uses a divide-and-conquer strategy. The original set of data is first separated into two "partitions" as shown in Fig. 8.7.   After the separation, *all* elements in the first (*rightlower*−1) positions (left partition) will be less than or equal to all elements in positions (*leftupper*+1) through *n* (the right partition). After this first step, the *same* partitioning mechanism is then applied to *both* of the smaller partitions (i.e. a[1..*leftupper*] and a[*right-lower*..*n*]. The partitioning of smaller and smaller segments continues until we end up with segments of size *one*. At this point, following from our earlier discussion of quicksort, the array will be completely sorted.

What we recognize in this mechanism is that essentially the *same* process is being repeatedly applied to smaller and smaller problems. The mechanism is therefore recursive in nature. Having made this observation, let us write down the basic steps that are being repeated and then try to develop a recursive algorithm for the problem. The basic steps are:

1.   Partition the data into *left* and *right* partitions provided there is more than one element in the current set.
2.   Repeat the partitioning process for the *left* partition.
3.   Repeat the partitioning process for the *right* partition.

To construct our recursive procedure, we must refine these steps and work out details on how the recursion can be terminated.

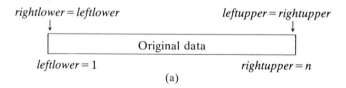

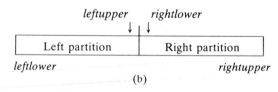

Fig. 8.7   (a) Before separation; (b) After separation.

With regard to the partitioning mechanism, we can use the partitioning method described in algorithm 5.6. The first step in our recursive quicksort can therefore be a procedure call of the form:

partition(a, *leftlower*, *rightupper*, *leftupper*, *rightlower*)

We will not discuss the partitioning mechanism further here other than to say that *rightlower* and *leftupper* will define the limits of the right and left segments after the *partition* call. The values of *leftlower*, *leftupper*, *right-lower* and *rightupper* follow from our original algorithm.

Now let us consider steps (2) and (3). To repeat the partitioning process for the left partition we can make a recursive call to our original 3-step procedure. If our recursive procedure is called *quicksort2* then a call of the form:

$$quicksort2(a, leftlower, leftupper)$$

will allow us to sort the left partition. Similarly, a recursive call of the form

$$quicksort2(a, rightlower, rightupper)$$

will allow us to sort the right partition.

The task that remains is to work out the condition for termination. We would expect termination to be related to the smallest segment that needs to be partitioned. If recursive calls to *quicksort2* are made with smaller and smaller partitions, eventually a call will be made with a segment of size one.

From our earlier discussion on partitioning we recognize that it is not meaningful to try to partition a one-element segment. Furthermore, at this stage, there is no point in making new recursive calls to *quicksort2* since there will no longer be any left and right partitions to operate on. We can therefore conclude that a call to a one-element segment should result in termination of the recursion. The body of the recursive process should be guarded by a test to see if the current segment contains more than one element. Since in the call to *quicksort2* the lower and upper limits of the segment are defined we can use the test:

if "segment contains more than one element" then
(a)   partition into left and right partitions,
(b)   *quicksort2* left partition,
(c)   *quicksort2* right partition.

Because *rightupper* will be greater than *leftlower* when a segment contains more than one element the test can take the form:

if *leftlower*<*rightupper* then
(a)   continue with body of recursive procedure

The detailed Pascal implementation of our *quicksort2* algorithm follows directly from our discussion:

```
procedure quicksort2(var a:nelements; leftlower,
    rightupper:integer);
var leftupper {upper limit of left segment},
    rightlower {lower limit of right segment}:integer;
```

begin
  if *leftlower<rightupper* **then**
    begin
      partition(a, leftlower, rightupper, leftupper, rightlower);
      quicksort2(a, leftlower, leftupper);
      quicksort2(a, rightlower, rightupper)
    end
  end

Once again we have used binary recursion to solve a problem. At this point it is worth tracing through a small example, Fig. 8.8, to be sure that we fully understand the mechanism and are convinced that it is correct. The partition being operated on in the current call to *quicksort2* is "boxed". The two partitions generated from the current call to *partition* are underlined. Each call is parenthesized with three linked bars. Note that because partitioning stops on the partitioning element 18 in the first instance it can be excluded because it is already in place.

We notice from this example that there is a considerable build up of partitions to be sorted later. We should, therefore, investigate what is the maximum possible depth of recursion as it may result in a very large storage overhead. In the worst possible case, each call to *partition* with a segment of n elements will result in a left partition of $(n-1)$ and a right partition of *one* which is saved away to be dealt with later. As a result of this, the depth of recursion can grow to size $(n-1)$. This will result in a very considerable storage overhead for large n. In our stack implementation of the algorithm we got around this problem by always sorting the smaller partition first. The maximum size for the stack was then only $\log_2 n$ when n elements were to be sorted. This follows since the *biggest smaller problem* with each successive call is $\frac{1}{2}n$. There can be at most $\log_2 n$ calls before the stack again decreases. We should be able to carry this idea across to our recursive implementtion to limit the depth of recursion to $\log_2 n$. There are only two situations that we have to deal with:

1. The left partition is smaller than the right partition in which case it should be sorted first.
2. The right partition is equal to or smaller than the left partition in which case *it* should be sorted first.

These two situations can be accommodated by preceding the recursive calls with a test that decides the order in which the left and right partitions should be sorted. That is,

if left partition smaller than right partition then
(a)   sort left partition first,

(b)   then sort right partition
else
(a′)   sort right partition first,
(b′)   then sort left partition

quicksort2($\boxed{20 \quad 35 \quad 8 \quad 18 \quad 14 \quad 41 \quad 3 \quad 39}$)   Initial call

  ([$\underline{3 \quad 14 \quad 8}$] 18 [$\underline{35 \quad 41 \quad 20 \quad 39}$])   Result of first call to *partition*
┌*quicksort2*($\boxed{3 \quad 14 \quad 8}$ 18 [35 41 20 29])
│ ┌([$\underline{3 \quad 8}$][$\underline{14}$] 18 [35 41 20 39])   Result of second call to *partition*
│ ├*quicksort2*([3 8] $\boxed{14}$ 18 [35 41 20 39])   Recursion
│ │   terminates
│ └*quicksort2*($\boxed{3 \quad 8}$ 14 18 [35 41 20 39])
│   ┌([$\underline{3}$][$\underline{8}$] 14 18 [35 41 20 39])
│   ├*quicksort2*([3]$\boxed{8}$ 14 18 [35 41 20 39])   Recursion
│   │   terminates
│   └*quicksort2*($\boxed{3}$ 8 14 18 [35 41 20 39])   Recursion
│   terminates
└*quicksort2*(3 8 14 18 $\boxed{35 \quad 41 \quad 20 \quad 39}$)
   ┌(3 8 14 18 [$\underline{35 \quad 39 \quad 20}$] [$\underline{41}$])
   ├*quicksort2*(3 8 14 18 [35 39 20] $\boxed{41}$)   Recursion terminates
   └*quicksort2*(3 8 14 18 $\boxed{35 \quad 39 \quad 20}$ 41)
      ┌(3 8 14 18 [$\underline{35 \quad 20}$] [$\underline{39}$] 41)
      ├*quicksort2*(3 8 14 18 [35 20] $\boxed{39}$ 41)   Recursion
      │   terminates
      └*quicksort2*(3 8 14 18 $\boxed{35 \quad 20}$ 39 41)   Recursion
                                                                       terminates
         ┌(3 8 14 18 [$\underline{20}$] [$\underline{35}$] 39 41)
         ├*quicksort2*(3 8 14 18 [20] $\boxed{35}$ 39 41)   Recursion
         │   terminates
         └*quicksort2*(3 8 14 18 $\boxed{20}$ 35 39 41)   Recursion
                                                                       terminates

Fig. 8.8 Trace for recursive quicksort.

The complete description of our recursive implementation of *quicksort2* can now be given.

Algorithm description

1. Establish the array of elements to be sorted and the upper and lower limits for the current segment to be sorted.
2. If the current segment contains more than one element then
    (a)   partition the current segment into two smaller segments such that all elements in the left segment are less than or equal to all elements in the right segment;
    (b)   if left segment smaller than the right segment then
          (b.1)   recursively *quicksort2* the smaller left segment,
          (b.2)   recursively *quicksort2* the larger right segment
          else
          (b'.1)   recursively *quicksort2* the smaller right segment,
          (b'.2)   recursively *quicksort2* the larger left segment.

Pascal implementation

```
procedure partition (var a: nelements; l,u: integer; var j,i: integer);
var k {index of partitioning element},
    t {temporary variable for exchange},
    x {guess at median – used for partitioning}: integer;

begin {partition segment a[l..u] into segments a[l..j] and a[i..u]
about x}
  {assert: l =<u}
  k := (l +u) div 2;
  x := a[k];
  i := l;
  j := u;
  while a[i]<x do i := i +1;
  while x <a[j] do j := j –1;
  {invariant: l =<i ∧ all a[l..i –1]=<x ∧ j =<u ∧ x =<all a[j +1..u]}
  while i <j –1 do
    begin {exchange wrongly partitioned pair and then extend both
    partitions}
      t := a[i];
      a[i] := a[j];
      a[j] := t;
      i := i +1;
      j := j –1;
      while a[i]<x do i := i +1;
      while x <a[j] do j := j –1
    end;
  if i <=j then
    begin
      if i <j then
```

```
          begin
            t := a[i];
            a[i] := a[j];
            a[j] := t
          end;
        i := i + 1;
        j := j - 1
      end
      {assert: j < i ∧ all a[l..i − 1] = < all a[j + 1..u]}
  end


  procedure quicksort2 (var a: nelements; leftlower, rightupper:
  integer);
  var leftupper, {upper limit of left segment}
      rightlower {lower limit of right segment}: integer;

  begin {proceed with sort if segment contains more than one
  element}
    if leftlower < rightupper then
      begin {partition current into two smaller segments}
        partition (a, leftlower, rightupper, leftupper, rightlower);
        {assert: leftlower < rightlower ∧ all a[leftlower ..
        leftupper] = < all a[rightlower .. rightupper]}
        if (leftupper − leftlower) < (rightupper − rightlower) then
          begin {sort the smaller left segment first}
            quicksort2 (a, leftlower, leftupper);
            {assert: a[leftlower .. leftupper] sorted in non-descending
            order}
            quicksort2 (a, righlower, rightupper)
            {assert: a[rightlower .. rightupper] sorted in non-descending
            order}
          end
        else
          begin {sort smaller right segment first}
            quicksort2 (a, righlower, rightupper);
            {assert: a[rightlower .. rightupper] sorted in
            non-descending order}
            quicksort2 (a, leftlower, leftupper)
            {assert: a[leftlower .. leftupper] sorted in non-descending
            order}
          end
      end
  end
```

Notes on design

1. In terms of comparisons and exchanges, the performance of the recursive implementation of quicksort is the same as the stack implementation. (See discussion with algorithm 5.6.) In the worst case, of the order

of n^2 comparisons will be required for the sort whereas in the average case of the order of $n \log_2 n$ comparisons will be required.

2. For the procedure *quicksort2* it is necessary to establish that, after completion of execution, the array elements are in non-descending order (ascending order if they are unique). The behavior of the algorithm must be characterized in terms of the boundaries of the left and right partitions. If the present call to *quicksort2* results in a call to *partition* then the latter function will return two parameters *leftupper* and *rightlower*. It will also permute the elements between *leftlower* and *rightupper* in such a way that all elements in the left partition will be less than or equal to all elements in the right partition. That is,

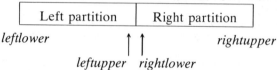

and so a partial ordering exists. Now if we assume that the two recursive calls to *quicksort2* function correctly then the result will be to have sorted all elements between *leftlower* and *rightupper* correctly as we originally required. The algorithm terminates because with each call to *quicksort2* two *smaller* segments are considered for sorting. Eventually the segments required for sorting will all reduce to the size one where recursion always terminates.

3. With this problem we have seen the importance of paying attention to the depth of recursion. Where a problem divides into two smaller problems and recursion is involved it is usually best to deal with the smaller problem first.

4. The recursive implementation of quicksort is conceptually the simplest, the most natural and also the easiest to program. For practical applications, however, where sorting time is of the highest priority, it is not recommended that the recursive implementation be used because of the overhead the recursive procedure calls incur.

5. The condition for termination of recursion follows naturally from consideration of the smallest sorting problem.

6. Once again we have seen how binary recursion can be used to implement an important algorithm.

Applications

Demonstration of the recursive nature of the quicksort algorithm.

Supplementary problems

8.2.1   Implement the two recursive versions of quicksort given and compare the maximum depth of recursion they require for random data.

8.2.2   Compare the execution time differences for the two recursive implementations for:

(a)   a data set yielding worst-case performance,
(b)   random data.

8.2.3   Compare the execution time differences for the better recursive and stack implementations of quicksort on your particular computer.

8.2.4   Modify the *quicksort2* algorithm so that it generates a histogram of the frequency of calls made for segment sizes in the range 1 to n. What conclusions can you draw from this profile?

8.2.5   A modified recursive quicksort can be implemented based on the final partitioning mechanism used in algorithm 4.6. This partitioning mechanism at each call breaks a segment into three parts as shown below:

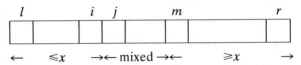

The basic structure of the algorithm is:

```
procedure threesort (var a: nelements; l, r: integer);
    ⋮
    if l<r then
      begin
        partition (a, l, r, i, j, m);
        threesort (a, l, i);
        threesort (a, j, m−1);
        threesort (a, m, r);
        threemerge (a, l, i, j, m, r)
      end
    ⋮
```

where the procedure *threemerge* merges the three segments after they have been sorted. Implement this algorithm.

Algorithm 8.3
TOWERS OF HANOI PROBLEM

Problem

Design and implement a recursive algorithm to solve the Towers of Hanoi problem for one or more disks.

Algorithm development

An ancient Brahmin tale has it that the life of the universe is defined in terms of the time it will take a group of monks (working continuously) to move a set of 64 gold disks, all of *different* diameters, from one pole to another. There are specific rules about how the transfer should be done. These rules make the project far from trivial and also a very "long-term" project, to put it mildly. The rules are:

1.   Only one disk may be moved at a time.
2.   A third pole may be used for temporary storage of disks.
3.   No disk should ever be placed on top of a disk of smaller diameter.
4.   The disks are arranged on the original pole initially with the largest disk on the bottom, the second largest disk on top of it, and so on. The smallest disk ends up being on top of the stack.

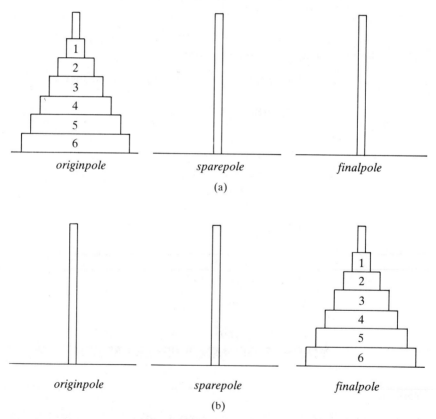

Fig. 8.9   A six disk Tower of Hanoi problem: (a) Initial configuration; (b) Required final configuration.

The problem as defined is known as the Towers of Hanoi problem (see Fig. 8.9).

When we start to play around with this problem, we soon realize that it is far from easy even for the case where only 6 disks have to be moved from the *originpole* to the *finalpole* (in fact this case requires at least 63 disk transfers). If you have not at this stage attempted to solve the problem even for as few as 4 disks, it is instructive to do so just to get some feel for what is involved.

After having made these preliminary explorations with the problem, we are usually left with the feeling that it is difficult to explain, to say the least. A computer solution to the problem seems to be a long way off. The other response we are likely to have to the problem is that we suspect that there must be a systematic way to solve it. Our task therefore, is to try to discover a systematic method for specifying how the disk transfers should be made. To do this we will consider the case where 6 disks have to be moved from the *originpole* to the *finalpole*.

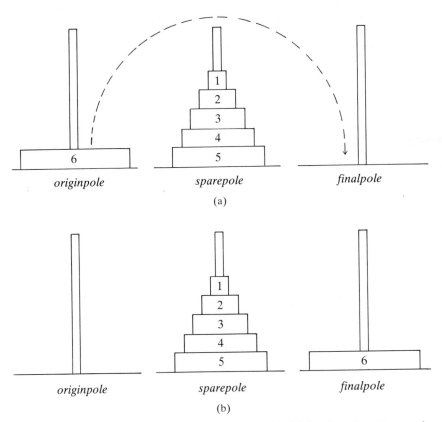

Fig. 8.10 (a) Configuration before transfer of biggest disk; (b) Configuration after transfer of biggest disk.

Our earlier experience with the problem has probably been that it is very easy to get bogged down in detail and lose sight of a possible mechanism. With this in mind, we might ask the question, what would constitute real progress towards our final goal? A response might be that we would have progressed if we could get a configuration where the largest disk (6, as numbered here) had been moved to the *finalpole*. Before we would be able to do this we would need to remove *all* the other disks! This prompts a second question—where could the disks on top of the largest disk be placed without breaking the rules given? They obviously cannot be distributed between the *sparepole* and the *finalpole* and they cannot all be on the *finalpole*. The only place for them *all* would be on the *sparepole*.

The corresponding configuration is shown in Fig. 8.10(a). Only when this configuration prevails can we transfer the biggest disk from the *originpole* to the *finalpole*. (Figure 8.10(b)).

If we can find a way of legally moving the five smallest disks to the *sparepole* then we will be able to transfer the biggest disk from the *originpole* to the *finalpole*. Let us now reassess this new situation. We have made some progress (with assumptions) in that the biggest disk is where we want it but there are still 5 other disks in the wrong place.

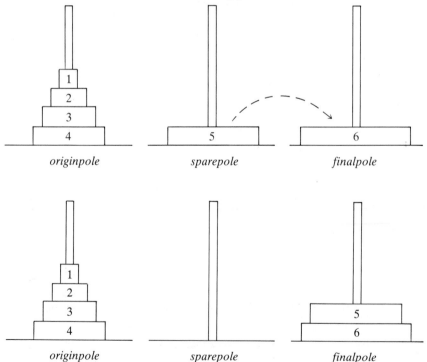

Fig. 8.11   Transfer of second biggest disk to *finalpole*.

To make further progress the second largest disk (disk 5) which is currently at the *bottom* of the *sparepole* will need to be placed on top of the largest disk on the *finalpole*. Following the same line of reasoning as we used before, the four smallest disks on top of disk 5 will need to be moved temporarily onto the *originpole*. When this has been done disk 5 can be moved from the *sparepole* to the *finalpole*. This second step again rests on the assumption that we have a way to transfer the four smallest disks from the *sparepole* to the *originpole*. The steps involved are shown in Fig. 8.11.

Reassessing the situation again, we see that now the two largest disks are where we want them and the four others are on the *originpole*. After studying this most recent configuration carefully, we recognize that it corresponds to essentially the same problem we started out with. The only difference is that now 4 rather than 6 disks need to be moved from the initial to the *finalpole*. The observation we can make at this point is that a basic mechanism is being applied to smaller and smaller subproblems of the original problem. This suggests that we may be able to solve the problem recursively. The assumptions (e.g. that at the first step we can get the 5 smallest disks onto the *sparepole*) may end up "being taken care of" in the recursion.

In a recursive solution to a problem, we often expect to be able to apply the *same* procedure to a problem *one size* smaller. For our situation, the problem of size 4 is similar to the problem of size 6. We seem to somehow have bypassed the problem of size 5, or have we? Let us take another closer look at the problem of size 5. What we recognize on looking back at the latter step is that it too is really *analogous* to the problem of size 6. The only difference is that the roles of the *sparepole* and the *originpole* have been interchanged. This is encouraging because we are now beginning to see the relationship between a problem of a given size and the problem of the next size down. It is this relationship we will need to fully understand if we are going to be able to construct a recursive algorithm for the problem.

At this point, let us try to apply what we have learned to write down the basic steps of the algorithm in terms of the same problem that is one size smaller.

If, in general, there are *ndisks* to be transferred then our initial problem is to:

> transfer *ndisks* from the *originpole* to the *finalpole*

In terms of a problem with (*ndisks*−1) disks the mechanism will involve the steps shown in Fig. 8.12. (Compare with Fig. 8.10 which relates the problem of size 6 to the problem of size 5.)

What we recognize from this description is that *both* steps (a) and (c) involve the solution of problems *one* smaller in size than the original problem. We might ask how should these two smaller problems be solved? Our

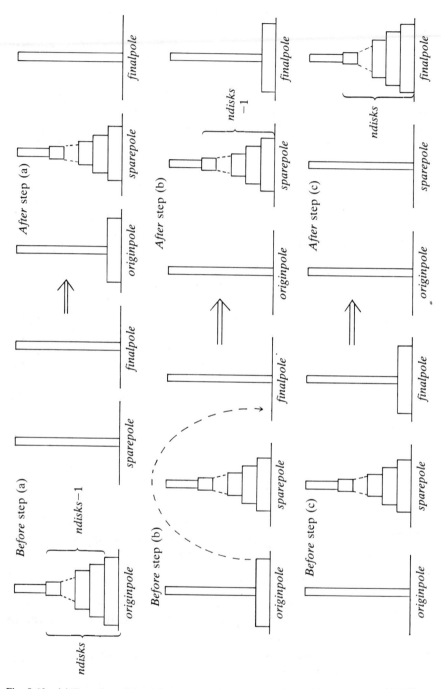

Fig. 8.12   (a) Transfer *ndisks*–1 from the *originpole* to the *sparepole*; (b) Transfer the one remaining disk from the *originpole* to the *finalpole*; (c) Transfer the *ndisks*–1 from the *sparepole* to the *finalpole*.

response to this might be that there does not seem to be anything inherently different in solving *each* of these problems in terms of yet two other problems one smaller in size. It is in this way that recursion can come into the mechanism.

When we have progressed this far with the development of a mechanism and there are still some lingering uncertainties in our mind as to whether the mechanism will solve the problem, we can resort to a diagram. In fact, it is always good practice when developing recursive algorithms to try to draw a diagram to explain the mechanism. Examining our earlier examples, we see that a model that naturally describes our recursive procedure is a *binary* tree. Once again we are dealing with binary recursion. Consider the tree for solving the problem of size 4 shown in Fig. 8.13. The problem of size 4 splits into two problems of size 3, which in turn each split into two problems of size 2, etc.

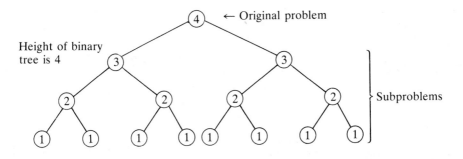

Fig. 8.13   Binary tree illustrating mechanism for solving a Towers of Hanoi problem of size 4.

The root of the tree corresponds to the original problem that must be solved. We can imagine that at *each* node a transfer is made. For a given node, the *left subtree* represents transferring all the smaller disks from on top of it. The *right subtree* represents transferring all the smaller disks back on top of the current disk *after* it has itself been transferred. (For example, the left subtree of node 4 represents the mechanism for transferring the 3, 2, and 1 disks *off* disk 4, and the right subtree of 4 represents transferring the *same* disks *back onto* disk 4 *after* it has been moved to the *final pole*). The *leaves* of the tree all correspond to problems of size one. It is not possible to meaningfully split a problem of size one into two smaller problems. This gives us a clue as to how the recursion should be terminated. We will come back to the problem of termination a little later.

From the preceding discussion we can see that recursion provides us with a way of *postponing* the solution to a large problem until smaller and easier problems are solved. At each stage of the solution, the simple transfer step builds the solution towards its final goal. The network of parameter passing ensures that each smaller problem is properly related to the bigger problems that must be solved, and ultimately to the original problem we set out to solve.

Our binary tree diagram actually tells us all we need to know about the *order* in which transfers are *made* as well as the order in which they are *proposed*. The order in which transfers are made is exactly the same as the order in which nodes are printed in the *inorder* traversal of a binary tree (see algorithm 8.1). In fact, it is easiest to think of the Towers of Hanoi problem as *inorder traversal* of an ordered binary tree. When all the details are stripped away the underlying mechanisms are the same.

Consideration of the tree model for the mechanism has given us a better insight into the nature of the problem and also a clue as to how we might handle termination. The task that remains is to refine the recursive mechanism we have proposed and to incorporate the termination condition.

In setting up the procedure calls for the recursive procedure what is important is going to be the order in which the parameters identifying the three poles are specified. The order is important because within the subproblems we have seen that the *originpole*, *sparepole*, and *finalpole* play different roles to that defined by the original problem.

Let us start by defining the original procedure call. If the recursive procedure is called *towershanoi* and the number of disks to be transferred is *ndisks* then the call can have the form:

towershanoi(ndisks, originpole, sparepole, finalpole)

We can now establish the procedure calls for the subproblems with reference to the original procedure call.

The first recursive call in the body of the procedure involves transferring (*ndisks*−1) disks from the *originpole* to the *sparepole*. For this problem, the role of the *finalpole* and the *sparepole* are interchanged. Noting this fact the procedure call for step (a) will be:

towershanoi(ndisks−1, originpole, finalpole, sparepole)

Step (b) which involves the transfer of a single disk from the current *originpole* to the current *finalpole* can be handled by a call to a procedure named *transferdisk* that accepts as input two parameters, *originpole* and *finalpole*. The call can take the form:

transferdisk(originpole, finalpole)

We will postpone the discussion on this procedure until after consideration of the second internal recursive call to *towershanoi*. Referring back to our diagrams and to our description of step (c) we observe that what remains to be done to solve the problem of size *ndisks* is to transfer (*ndisks*−1) disks from the *sparepole* to the *finalpole*. This time the roles of the *originpole* and the *sparepole* are interchanged. The procedure call will therefore have the form:

towershanoi(ndisks−1, *sparepole, originpole, finalpole)*

The *transferdisk* procedure has two input parameters, the *originpole* and the *finalpole* both of which can assume *three* possible labels. The easiest way to define these labels is to declare a *pole* data type, for example,

type *pole* = (*origin, spare, final*)

The *transferdisk* procedure then only needs two case statements, one to identify and print out the *originpole* label and a second to identify and print out the *finalpole* label. The constructs can have the form:

```
case originpole of
    origin : write('origin-pole to');
    spare : write('spare-pole to');
    ⋮
```

The only consideration left to deal with relates to termination. We saw earlier in our discussion with the tree model for the problem that recursion proceeds until we get to a problem of size 1 which involves a direct transfer. If recursion were to proceed further, it would imply that a problem with *zero* disks were to be solved. We can therefore proceed with recursion until a problem of size zero occurs. The body of the recursive procedure can be guarded by a statement of the form:

```
if ndisks>0 then
    "proceed with recursion"
```

The Pascal implementation may then be:

```
procedure towershanoi(ndisks:integer; originpole, sparepole, final-
            pole:pole);
begin
    if ndisks>0 then
        begin
            towershanoi(ndisks−1, originpole, finalpole, sparepole);
            transferdisk(originpole, finalpole);
            towershanoi(ndisks−1, sparepole, originpole, finalpole)
        end
end
```

We notice when the problem reduces to size 1 there are two internal calls to *towershanoi* that achieve nothing. Because there will usually be a large number of problems of size 1 involved in any Towers of Hanoi problem it is a better strategy to halt the recursion *one step* earlier. To do this the guard will need to be changed to:

> **if** *ndisks*>1 **then**
> "proceed with recursion"

With this change the direct transfer for the problem of size 1 will need to be handled separately. That is,

> **if** *ndisks*>1 **then**
> "proceed with recursion"
> **else**
> *transferdisk*(*originpole*, *finalpole*)

This modification eliminates the redundant calls for problems of size 1. A complete description of the algorithm can now be given.

Algorithm description

(1) Towers of Hanoi procedure
1. Establish the number of disks to be transferred, the *originpole*, the *sparepole*, and the *finalpole*.
2. If current problem involves transfer of more than one disk then
   (a) recursively call function to transfer all disks except the bottom disk from the current *originpole* to the *sparepole*,
   (b) transfer the bottom disk from the *originpole* to the *finalpole*,
   (c) recursively call function to transfer all disks' from the *sparepole* to the *finalpole*
   else
   (a′) transfer current disk from the *originpole* to the *finalpole*.

(2) Transfer disk procedure
1. Establish the current *originpole* and *finalpole* labels.
2. Determine the identity of the current *originpole* label.
3. Write out the label for the current *originpole*.
4. Determine the identity of the current *finalpole* label.
5. Write out the label for the current *finalpole* indicating that the transfer has been made *to* this pole.

Pascal implementation†

```
procedure towers(ndisks: integer);
type pole = (origin,spare,final);
```

> † The calling procedure should also check to see that *ndisks* is *at least* one to avoid infinite recursion.

```
procedure transferdisk(originpole, finalpole: pole);
begin {simulate transfer of disk from current originpole to current
finalpole}
    case originpole of
        origin: write('origin-pole to ');
        spare: write('spare-pole to ');
        final: write('final-pole to ')
    end;

    case finalpole of
        origin: writeln('origin-pole');
        spare: writeln('spare-pole');
        final: writeln('final-pole')
    end
end;

procedure towershanoi(ndisks: integer; originpole, sparepole,
finalpole: pole);
begin {solves the towers of hanoi for ndisks disks}
    if ndisks >1 then
        begin {solve current problem by first solving next smallest
        problem}
            towershanoi(ndisks −1, originpole, finalpole, sparepole);
            {assert: (ndisks −1) transferred from originpole to sparepole
            according to rules}
            transferdisk(originpole, finalpole);
            {assert: disk transferred from originpole to finalpole}
            towershanoi(ndisks −1, sparepole, originpole, finalpole)
            {assert: (ndisks −1) transferred from sparepole to finalpole}
        end
    else
        transferdisk(originpole, finalpole)
        {assert: disk transferred from originpole to finalpole}
end;

begin {towers}
    towershanoi(ndisks,origin,spare,final)
end
```

Notes on design

1. The performance of the *towershanoi* procedure can be measured in
    terms of the number of transfers needed to move all disks from the
    originpole to the *finalpole*. The easiest way to count these transfers is to
    refer to our tree model for the algorithm. The number of transfers
    needed to solve a given problem corresponds to the number of nodes in
    the appropriate complete ordered binary tree. A problem with n disks
    corresponds to a tree of height n (where n is the number of levels in the
    tree). A tree of height n has $2^n - 1$ nodes. It follows that the number of

transfers required is an exponential function of the number of disks to be transferred. It is interesting to refer back to the task to be carried out by the monks. Their job was to transfer 64 disks. The number of transfers for them is $2^{64} - 1$ which is 18,446,744,073,709,551,615 — a task that is sure to take a long time at any rate of progress.

2. The characterization of the behavior of the *towershanoi* procedure can be done in terms very similar to that used to describe the *inorder* tree traversal algorithm (algorithm 8.1) as it too involves binary recursion. The only real difference is that instead of printing names at each node as during inorder traversal, a disk transfer is made. The reader is therefore referred to the Notes on design section of algorithm 8.1

3. In developing this algorithm, we have seen how looking at partial solutions to a problem can guide us to a simple but powerful general solution. Looking at what would constitute the smallest amount of positive progress to solving a problem is often useful.

4. In solving this problem we have done so by decomposing the original problem into two smaller problems which are solved recursively and then combined to solve the original problem. This problem-solving strategy which is known as the decomposition principle is widely used for solving combinatorial problems.

5. Another way of looking at this problem is to say that recursion has allowed us to *postpone* the solution of a large problem until a group of other smaller problems has been solved.

6. We have seen how it is often useful to construct a diagram to model our algorithm's behavior. In this example it has told us a lot about the mechanism and also about termination of the algorithm.

7. With recursion, we usually have several choices for termination. Compare the two Pascal implementations given in terms of the procedure calls they make. This is left as an exercise for the reader.

8. This example helped us to discover the underlying relationship between the Towers of Hanoi algorithm and inorder tree traversal.

9. This algorithm does not in itself have a practical application other than perhaps measuring the life of the universe. It does, however, provide us with an important illustration of how recursion can be used to make a seemingly otherwise difficult problem easy to solve. (It so happens that there is also a simple iterative solution—see P. Buneman and L. Levy, "The Towers of Hanoi Problem", *Inf. Proc. Letts.* **10**, 243 (1980)).

10. The depth of recursion is at most n for solving a problem that involves the transfer of n disks.

11. Notice that every *alternate* move consists of a transfer of the smallest disk from one pole to another. If we imagine the three poles to be in a

circle, and that they are numbered, smallest to largest as 1, 2, 3, ..., n then all those disks with odd numbers rotate in one direction and all even-numbered disks rotate in the other direction. This observation can form the basis of an iterative solution.

Supplementary problems

8.3.1   Implement a version of the *towershanoi* procedure that uses three arrays each of n elements to solve the problem for n disks. If the disks are labelled 1 through n with the largest diameter disks being n, the contents of the three arrays after each transfer should reflect the corresponding status of the 3 poles. Incorporate a suitable printout that reflects the status of the poles after each transfer.

8.3.2   Incorporate a rectangle (or disk) plotting routine into the algorithm so that the disks and poles are suitably printed after each transfer. A typical plot might be

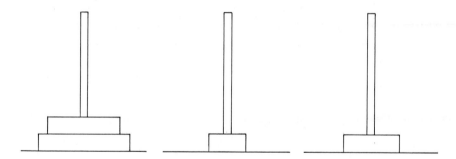

8.3.3   Design an algorithm for solving the Towers of Hanoi problem that does not employ recursion (see notes 9 and 11).

8.3.4   Design an algorithm that solves the Towers of Hanoi problem where there are n disks and $k = \lceil \sqrt{(2n)} \rceil$ poles. For this configuration your algorithm should exhibit *linear* rather than exponential behavior. Recursion is not necessary to solve this problem.

Reference

W. W. R. Ball, *Mathematical Recreations and Essays* (11th edn), Macmillan, N.Y., 1967.

Algorithm 8.4
SAMPLE GENERATION

Problem

Design an algorithm that generates all permutations of the first n integers taken r at a time and allowing unrestricted repetitions. This is sometimes referred to as sample generation. The values of n and r must be greater than zero.

Algorithm development

The problem of generating permutations with unrestricted repetitions is probably the simplest of the combinatorial problems. Our interest in the problem arises not because of the combinatorics involved but because it represents a problem that does not have a simple *obvious* general iterative solution. An example will make this clear. Suppose n refers to the first 5 integers and they are to be sampled 3 at a time (i.e. $r = 3$). The first few, and last unrestricted permutations of this set, are listed in Fig. 8.14.

As an aside, it is worth noting that if the integers are restricted to 0 and 1, then for a given r the set of permutations with restricted repetitions will correspond to the r-bit *binary* representations of the first 2^r integers (including zero).

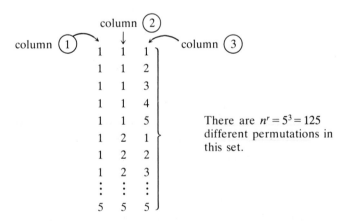

Fig. 8.14   Permutations with unrestricted repetitions for $n = 5$ and $r = 3$.

After studying Fig. 8.14 carefully, we see that each of the three (r) columns can assume *all* of the 5 (n) values. Furthermore, since the values in the third column extend over their complete range for each change in the second column, we can conclude that this *particular* problem could be solved with three nested loops of the form:

    ⋮

```
for i := 1 to 5 do
   for j := 1 to 5 do
      for k := 1 to 5 do
         "write out i, j and k values";
```

    ⋮

A check of this mechanism confirms that it will solve our particular problem. However, if we wished to generate an unrestricted repetition permutation set of different size (i.e. of different r value) we would be in trouble. It is easy to see that the number of nested loops must be equal to the r value. This creates a problem if we are to construct a general algorithm that will work for any r value. The reason there is a problem is because our programming languages do not allow us to easily write programs that have a variable number of nested loops. Simply executing one loop that encloses another loop does not look promising. If we are to make any progress with the problem we will need to look to some other mechanism for generating this permutation set. Somehow we will need to focus on the loop count variables.

Before starting on an alternative approach, let us examine more carefully the proposed solution to the specific problem that we discussed earlier. There are several things that this proposed solution suggests. Firstly, the role of each of the nested loops appears to be the *same*. All each loop must do is generate an index in the range 1 to 5 (in the general case, the range would be 1 to n). Secondly, a new permutation is available only after a change of index has been made in the *innermost* loop. For example, the first permutation is available only after we have moved from the outermost loop to the innermost loop. Each loop contributes a *single* integer to the first permutation and also to all the other permutations. What we see happening is that the solution to a large problem is being built up by solving and combining a set of solutions to other smaller problems each of which can be solved in a similar way.

To try to make some headway with this problem, let us concentrate on solving first the *smallest* problem—that of generating the set of values in the first column of the set. A simple loop ranging from 1 to n will solve this problem. The first step towards a solution to the general problem might therefore take the form:

```
for i := 1 to n do
   begin
      "solve the remaining smaller problems in a similar fashion"
   end
```

To generate the integers for the second column, we again need a loop that extends over the range 1 to n. To solve our particular problem it must extend over the range 1 to n for *each* value of the first loop. Therefore, for each iteration of the *first* loop we must solve a problem that is essentially the *same* as that for the first loop. It is at this point that we must recognize that the process we have described is really a recursive process. If the original process calls *itself once* with each iteration we will have solved our permutation generation problem for two columns. In a similar manner if *each* of the secondary calls initiates another set of calls we will have solved the problem for three columns. It is easy to see that this mechanism will allow us to deal with the general case of r columns. Basic steps in our mechanism might therefore be:

while all indices for current column not generated do
(a)   generate next index for current column,
(b)   repeat the same index generation process for the *next* column.

These steps seem to embody much of what we need to solve our problem recursively. Our mechanism as it stands includes no details relating to termination and output of the permutations.

Output was brought about in our original mechanism by simply printing the current loop indices after each change in the innermost loop. A similar approach with our recursive algorithm does not seem possible because of the localized influence of loop variables. What, therefore, is an alternative that will allow us to pass information about the status of the computation to the other column values? Our only choice must be to store the column values in an array. There is then the question of how the array should be used to store the column values. Our response will probably be that the only practical solution is to associate each array element with one column of the permutation set. So now, instead of generating loop indices, we will need to keep our array elements appropriately updated. To ensure that the array element associated with the kth column *column*[k] takes on its appropriate set of values we can insert the following statement in the main loop of our mechanism:

$$column[k] := column[k]+1$$

Before entering the loop *column*[k] will need to be initialized to zero. If we give our recursive procedure the name *sample* and include the refinements suggested above we will have:

```
procedure sample( ? )
   ⋮
begin
```

```
column[k] := 0;
while column[k]<n do
  begin
    column[k] := column[k]+1;
    sample( ? )
      ⋮
  end
end
```

We are now left with the task of deciding what parameters should be passed to our procedure both externally and in the recursive call. Also, we need to establish the mechanism for termination and the point at which a new permutation is available for printing. A study of the mechanism we have created suggests that k must play a role as a parameter because it identifies the current column that is being updated. The variable k can therefore be included in the original parameter list for the procedure. The internal recursive call to *sample* is intended to deal with the *next* column. In terms of k this is the $(k+1)^{th}$ column. Therefore, $k+1$ can be a parameter for the internal call. The parameters n and r do not change so they can be stored in the calling procedure. It will also be easiest to store the array in the calling procedure.

To try to work out the details about when each new permutation is available and when termination should be enforced, let us first return to our original nested-loop algorithm. If we can work out the details from it about when each combination is available, we may be able to carry this over to the equivalent situation for the recursive algorithm. We see that with the iterative solution, a new permutation is available only after the rightmost (innermost) loop or r^{th} column of the permutation set has been updated. We must now ask, what is the equivalent situation for our recursive algorithm? Our recursive algorithm can only make updates to the rth column when

$$k = r$$

This suggests that when k is equal to r we should be able to output the first r elements of the *column* array as the current permutation. If we are a little uncertain about this we should attempt to draw a diagram that tries to capture the mechanism we have outlined. To do this we can refer to the $^5U_3$ problem discussed earlier. (U stands for permutation with unrestricted repetitions.) The first call to our procedure for this problem generates *five* first column values. Associated with *each* of these first column values is a set of five second column values. And, in turn, associated with each second column value is a set of five third column values. This suggests a tree-like structure. Part of our mechanism tree for the $^5U_3$ problem is shown in Fig. 8.15. Each of the permutations with unrestricted repetitions can be found by

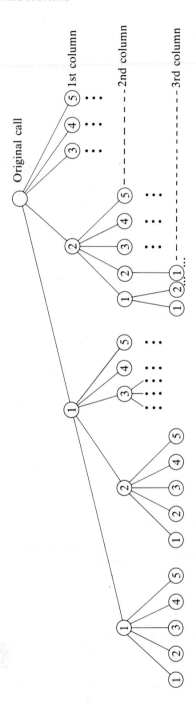

Fig. 8.15 Part of mechanism tree for $^5U_3$ problem.

tracing a path from the root down through the tree to the leaf nodes. This diagram confirms that when we are at the rth column (i.e. at the 3rd column or leaf node, in this case) a new permutation will be available. Our algorithm can be imagined to make an *inorder* traversal of the nodes of this tree (see the discussion in algorithm 8.1 for an explanation of tree traversal).

Our discussion suggests that whenever $k = r$ we will be able to print the next permutation. We can therefore insert the following statements in the loop of our procedure after updating the *column*[k] value:

> **if** $k = r$ **then**
> **begin**
> **for** $j := 1$ **to** r **do**
> *write(column[j])*;
> *writeln*
> **end**

We are now only left with the problem of termination. In the general case, we only need to generate permutations of values for r columns. Our recursive algorithm is structured such that while it is generating the values for the current column it initiates calls to the procedure to generate the values for the next column. It follows that when we are at the rth column (i.e. when $k = r$) there are no further columns to consider and so there should be no further calls to greater depths of recursion. This ties in nicely with our printing of permutations whenever $k = r$. In fact, when $k = r$, *instead* of doing a further recursive call at the next level we can simply output the current permutation.

To reinforce our understanding of this algorithm, we can work through the first few cycles for the $^5U_3$ problem. It is useful to relate these steps to the mechanism tree. (See Figs. 8.15 and 8.16.)

The procedure can be started with $k = 1$ and all elements of the *column* array should be set to zero. The complete description of the algorithm is given below.

Algorithm description

1. Establish positive non-zero set size, permutation size, and array for storing permutations. Also establish index to current column of permutaion set.
2. Initialize current column value to zero.
3. While current column index less than set size do
   (a) increase current column value by one,
   (b) if current column index not at final column then
       (b.1) recursively call procedure to generate all the next column values associated with current column value
       else
       (b'.1) new permutation available in array so write it out.

—*sample* $(k=1$ $\boxed{0\ 0\ 0}$ $)$ First level-one call

$(k=1$ $\boxed{1\ 0\ 0}$ $)$

—*sample* $(k=2$ $\boxed{1\ 0\ 0}$ $)$ First level-two call

$(k=2$ $\boxed{1\ 1\ 0}$ $)$

—*sample* $(k=3$ $\boxed{1\ 1\ 0}$ $)$ First level-three call

$(k=3$ $\boxed{1\ 1\ 1}$ $)$ 1st permutation printed

$(k=3$ $\boxed{1\ 1\ 2}$ $)$ 2nd permutation printed

$(k=3$ $\boxed{1\ 1\ 3}$ $)$ 3rd permutation printed

$(k=3$ $\boxed{1\ 1\ 4}$ $)$ 4th permutation printed

$(k=3$ $\boxed{1\ 1\ 5}$ $)$ 5th permutation printed

—*sample* $(k=2$ $\boxed{1\ 1\ 5}$ $)$ Second level-two call

$(k=2$ $\boxed{1\ 2\ 5}$ $)$

sample $(k=3$ $\boxed{1\ 2\ 5}$ $)$ Second level-three call

$(k=3$ $\boxed{1\ 2\ 1}$ $)$ 6th permutation printed

$(k=3$ $\boxed{1\ 2\ 2}$ $)$ 7th permutation printed

$(k=3$ $\boxed{1\ 2\ 3}$ $)$ 8th permutation printed

$(k=3$ $\boxed{1\ 2\ 4}$ $)$ 9th permutation printed

$(k=3$ $\boxed{1\ 2\ 5}$ $)$ 10th permutation printed

—*sample* $(k=2$ $\boxed{1\ 2\ 5}$ $)$ Third level-two call

$(k=2$ $\boxed{1\ 3\ 5}$ $)$

⋮   ⋮   ⋮   ⋮   ⋮

⋮   ⋮

Fig. 8.16 Trace for sample set generation for $^5U_3$ problem.

Pascal implementation

```
procedure sampleset(n,r: integer);
var column: array[1..20] of integer;
    k:integer;

procedure sample(k: integer);
var j {index for printing permutations}: integer;
begin {recursively generates all permutations with unrestricted
repetitions for the first n integers taken r at a time. The permutations
are generated in lexical order}
    {assert: n>0 ∧ r>0 ∧ r=<n ∧ 1=<k=<r}
    column[k] := 0;
    {invariant: after ith iteration column[1..k-1]=c1, c2, ..
    column[k]=i ∧ columns column[k+1..r] have assumed all possible
    values [1..n] with unrestricted repetitions and been printed when
    k=r ∧ i=<n ∧ all column values in [1..n] ∧ 1=<k=<r}
    while column[k]<n do
        begin {generate next value for current column}
            column[k] := column[k]+1;
            if k<r then
                {generate subsequent column values associated with current
                column value}
                sample(k+1)
            else
                begin {next permutation available – write it out}
                    for j := 1 to r do
                        write(column[j]);
                    writeln
                end
        end
    {assert: all permutations beginning with c1, c2, ... , c(k-1) have
    been generated}
end;

begin {sampleset}
    k := 1;
    sample(k)
end
```

Notes on design

1. The number of times the conditional test in the loop is executed gives
    us a measure of the time complexity of this algorithm (this is equal to
    the number of nodes in our mechanism tree). For our particular
    example when $n = 5$ and $r = 3$ there were 5 choices for the first column.
    Associated with *each* of these 5 choices there were 5 choices for the

second column which comes to n^2 values for the first two columns. In general, when there are r columns the conditional test will be executed n^r times. The algorithm therefore exhibits exponential behavior. The depth of recursion is r.

2.   To characterize the behavior of this procedure involving non-linear recursion, let us consider first the case where the call is made to *sample*$(k+1)$. If we assume that this call does not alter the elements in the first k columns and that it generates all appropriate permutations for *column*$[k+1]$ through r, then we can consider in detail the case where the call is made to *sample*(k). When the current call to *sample* does not invoke any further internal recursive calls, our assumptions must be correct. In the general case, where the call is made to *sample*(k), admitting the assumptions associated with the call to *sample*$(k+1)$, the present call will leave the elements in *column*$[1..k-1]$ untouched since they are not referenced in the body of the procedure. Furthermore, the present call ensures that all permutations of *column*$[k..n]$ are produced correctly because all possible choices of *column*$[k]$ are made. After each choice, a recursive call to *sample*$(k+1)$ is invoked. This argument can form the basis of a formal inductive proof of the procedure. Each recursive call to *sample* results in a move to a higher column and it terminates at $k=r$ in each case. We can therefore loosely conclude that the algorithm terminates.

3.   Notice with this algorithm how the solution to a large problem is built up by solving a succession of smaller inter-related problems.

4.   The impractical iterative solution to a specific problem was helpful in guiding us to a general recursive solution to the problem. To get a better understanding of what is needed for a recursive solution, it is often useful to explore an impractical iterative solution as a preliminary step. From such explorations, one can often discover details about termination, loop limits and the depth of recursion required.

5.   When a solution to a problem appears to demand a variable number of nested loops, it is usually advisable to see if it is possible to solve the problem using non-linear recursion. Using the approach we have described, a set of r nested loops has been replaced by a recursive procedure that calls itself r times. Many problems can be solved in this way.

6.   In the procedure *sample*, we have chosen to include only the variable k as a parameter for reasons of efficiency. To handle the details of the initialization, *sample* has been embedded in another procedure. It allows a simpler procedure call by the user. This practice has been adopted for the remaining algorithms in the chapter which suffer from the same problem.

Applications

Combinatorics, generation of sequences of numbers with a given base, simulations.

Supplementary problems

8.4.1   Implement a recursive algorithm that generates the ^nU_r permutations with unrestricted repetitions in *reverse* lexical order.

8.4.2   As it happens in this particular problem, it is possible to construct a *simple* iterative solution if one adopts the mechanism for converting numbers from base 10 to base r. Try to implement this simple iterative solution to the problem.

8.4.3   Another simple (although not so efficient) way to generate these permutations in lexical order is to start with the permutations $\{1, 1, 1, ..., 1\}$. The next permutation in each case is generated by scanning the current permutation from right to left until we encounter an element that has *not* attained its maximum value. This element is incremented by one, and all elements to the right of it are reset to their lowest allowable values and so the process repeats. Implement this algorithm.

8.4.4   Design an algorithm that accepts as input a given permutation of the ^nU_r set and returns as output

     (a)   the permutation that directly precedes it,
     (b)   the permutation that directly follows it in lexical order.

8.4.5   Make a modification to the permutation generation algorithm so that it only prints those permutations that add up to a given value 5. A separate loop to do the summing should *not* be used.

8.4.6   When our algorithm is used to generate the first 2^n binary integers we notice that much of the time more than one binary digit must be changed in going from one integer to the next. Another approach to generating this set (not in lexical order) is to arrange the computation so that *only one* binary digit is changed in going from one representation to the next. The way this is done is as follows. The digit that must be changed to generate the kth binary representation from the $(k-1)$th representation is equal to one plus the *power* of the largest power of 2 that *exactly* divides k. The algorithm should start with all binary digits set to zero. Implement this algorithm. These representations are called gray codes.

Algorithm 8.5
COMBINATION GENERATION

Problem

Design an algorithm that generates all combinations of the first n integers taken r at a time where n and r are greater than or equal to 1.

Algorithm development

There are many occasions in computing science and probability theory applications where we want to know the number of possible ways (written ^nC_r) for choosing a subset of r objects from a set of n objects. In other instances, we want to explicitly identify each of these combinations. We will concern ourselves with the latter problem. The algorithm we will *develop* is useful in solving a variety of other problems. To simplify the argument let us concentrate on developing an algorithm that will generate all combinations of the first n integers taken r at a time.

To get a feel for what is involved let us consider a specific example, perhaps that of generating all combinations of size 3 using the first 5 integers. Note that when dealing with combinations (as opposed to permutations) of objects, order plays no part. For example, the sequences {1, 2, 3}, {2, 1, 3} and {3, 1, 2} all represent a single combination. To avoid unnecessary computation it will be highly desirable that we generate *only one* representation of each combination. It is not very difficult to show that the ten combinations of the first five integers taken three at a time are:

$$
\begin{array}{cccccccccc}
1 & 1 & 1 & 1 & 1 & 1 & 2 & 2 & 2 & 3 \\
2 & 2 & 2 & 3 & 3 & 4 & 3 & 3 & 4 & 4 \\
3 & 4 & 5 & 4 & 5 & 5 & 4 & 5 & 5 & 5
\end{array}
$$

After studying this example carefully, we may conclude that the set of combinations can be generated using three nested loops. The outermost loop will handle the first column of integers, the middle loop the middle column and the innermost loop the righthand column. We can get the limits for each loop by observing the starting and ending integer in each column.

The central part of our algorithm for generating combinations of size 3 from the first 5 integers may therefore have the form:

```
for a := 1 to 3 do
  for b := 2 to 4 do
    for c := 3 to 5 do
      writeln(a,b,c);
```

When we check out this mechanism we discover that our *lower* loop limits are not correct (e.g. one of the "combinations" generated would be {3, 2, 3}). After studying our example again more carefully we conclude that the "*b*-loop" must always start at *one more* than the current *a*-value. Similarly, the "*c*-loop" must always start at *one more* than the current *b*-value. With these changes we get:

```
for a := 1 to 3 do
   for b := a+1 to 4 do
      for c := b+1 to 5 do
         writeln(a,b,c);
```

A check of this mechanism confirms that it solves the $^5C_3$ problem. Unfortunately, the mechanism we have created solves *only one* particular problem. For example, to solve the problem $^6C_4$ we would need *four* nested loops (one for each column) and a different set of loop limits. Implementation of a program with a *variable* number of nested loops would seem to be impractical just as we had found with the previous algorithm. We must therefore ask, is there any other path open to us?

Before trying to embark on a new path, let us examine the mechanism we have proposed to see if there is anything we can learn from it. One thing we notice is that it is only after a change is made in the innermost loop that a new combination is written out. For each value of *a* the variables *b* and *c* take on a range of values. Similarly, for each combination of *a* and *b* the variable *c* takes on a range of values.

What this mechanism suggests is that a solution to a large problem is created by solving a succession of smaller problems in such a way that the solution of each of the smaller problems depends on its predecessor. In our search for a more practical combination-generation algorithm let us concentrate first on the smallest problem—that of generating the elements in the first column for the general case. The initial thing that we must establish is the range of values for the first column. From our previous example and other simple examples, we can establish that in general the first column can assume $(n-r+1)$ values. We can write down a loop to generate these values as before. The inner loops have been replaced by a general statement.

```
for a := 1 to n−r+1 do
   begin
      "solve the remaining smaller problems in a similar manner"
   end.
```

The question that this raises is, how can we solve "the remaining smaller problems in a similar manner"? To generate the range of values in the second column, we need a loop that generates integers in the range 2 to $n-r+2$. As we discovered earlier in the $^5C_3$ example, it is not simply a matter of generating integers in this range. The key to solving the problem must lie in the way the numbers in the second column are related to the numbers in the first column. Studying our earlier example, we see that for *each* value of the first column, the numbers in the second column *always* start at one more than this value and extend to their upper limit. From this we can conclude that the values in the second column could be generated by a loop similar to our original loop but with the upper limit increased by one and the lower limit always starting at *one more* than the current value for the first column. The problem for the second column can therefore be solved in a similar way to the first column. Combining the results for the first and second columns will take us a step closer to solving the general problem. It is this similarity of each of the smaller problems to one another that suggests that it might be fruitful to use recursion.

Originally, we had proposed that each new nested loop would look after the generation of another column of the values required for the combination set. Viewing the problem as a recursive one, we might anticipate that a recursive call in the body of the main loop could achieve the same effect. If our original procedure is called *combinations* then we might have:

```
procedure combinations(lowervalue, upperlimit)
begin
  for a := lowervalue to upperlimit do
    combinations(a + 1, upperlimit + 1)
    ⋮
end.
```

This skeleton recursive procedure seems to embody much of what we need to solve our problem recursively. It does not, however, address the problems of termination and output of combinations. In our original mechanism, we used loop indices to give us the combinations we were seeking. It would appear that this is not possible with our recursive algorithm because of the localized effect of the loop variables. Our only choice must be to store the column values in an array as we did in the previous algorithm. These values can then be accessed by *any* recursive call. Again we can associate each array element with *one* column of the combination set. If we adopt this strategy, our task then becomes one of ensuring that at each step in the computation, all the array elements are appropriately assigned and updated. Provided this is done correctly, it will then be only a matter of printing out the array elements as each new combination is generated.

At this point, as well as introducing an array, we will need to express our algorithm somehow in terms of the n and r values used to define the combination set we are seeking.

Reassessing the situation, the lower limit for the loop will now be determined by the *current value* of the array element corresponding to the *preceding column*. If the array *column* is used to store column values of the column set then the starting value for the kth column in the current situation will be:

$$column[k] := column[k-1]+1$$

Having established and related the lower limit of *column[k]* to the current value in the previous column, we are then free to increment *column[k]* to its upper limit. Our earlier discussion showed that the upper limit for the first column was $n-r+1$. Further examination of our earlier example and other examples shows that the upper limit for the second column will be $n-r+2$, the upper limit for the third column will be $n-r+3$ and so on. Generalizing this, we would expect that the upper limit for the kth column is:

$$n-r+k$$

We have now defined the upper and lower limits for the kth column. The lower limit has been properly related to the current value of the previous column and the upper limit has been related to n and r. Our next task is to try to build these ideas into our basic recursive framework.

The role of our original loop mechanism was to ensure that the current column (i.e. loop index) value took on the appropriate range of values. In the present context, this translates into the current array value assuming the appropriate set of values. To increment the value of the kth column we can use:

$$column[k] := column[k]+1$$

Using this idea and relating the lower limit to the previous column, the loop written generally will have the form:

```
procedure combinations( ? )
    ⋮
begin
    column[k] := column[k-1];
    while column[k]<n-r+k do
        begin
            column[k] := column[k]+1;
            combinations( ? )
            ⋮
        end
end
```

We must now decide what parameters should be passed to our procedure. Studying the text of our procedure, it becomes clear that the variable k must play an important part as it defines the column we are currently operating on, k, and the column we must operate on next, i.e. column $(k+1)$.

This suggests that our original procedure call should be in terms of k and the recursive procedure call should involve $(k+1)$. The other variables, n, r, and the array *column* can be referenced from the calling procedure.

Having settled most of the details of the recursive aspects of the mechanism we are left with the problems of termination and output of combinations.

Using a line of reasoning similar to that used in the previous algorithm, we see that our recursive algorithm only makes an update to the rth column when:

$$k = r$$

This suggests that when k is equal to r we should be able to output the first r elements of the *column* array as the current combination. Referring to the $^5C_3$ problem discussed earlier, the first call to our procedure for this problem generates *three* first column values. Associated with *each* of these first column values is a set of second column values. And, in turn, associated with each second column value, is a set of third column values. This suggests a tree-like structure. Following this line of reasoning through, the mechanism tree for the $^5C_3$ problem will have the form shown in Fig. 8.17. Each of the combinations can be found to be tracing a path from the root down through the tree to the leaf nodes. This diagram confirms that whenever we are at the rth column (i.e. at the 3rd column or leaf nodes in this case) a new combination will be available. Our algorithm essentially makes an *inorder* traversal of the tree (see the discussion in algorithm 8.1 for explanation of tree traversal).

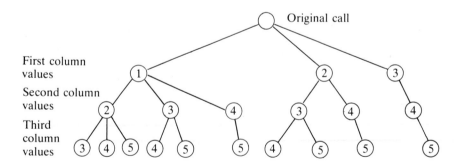

Fig. 8.17   Mechanism tree for the $^5C_3$ problem.

Our preceding discussion has led us to the conclusion that whenever $k = r$ a new combination will be available for printing. To print the current combination we can use:

```
if k = r then
  begin
    for j := 1 to r do
      write(column[j]);
    writeln
  end
```

These steps can be inserted directly after the point where the kth column is updated.

Our only concern now is to deal with the problem of termination. In the general case, we only need to generate combinations of values for r columns. Our recursive algorithm is structured such that while it is generating the values for the current column it initiates calls to the procedure to generate the corresponding values for the *next* column. It follows that when we are at the rth column (i.e. when $k = r$) there are no further columns to consider and so there should be no further calls to greater depths of recursion. This ties in nicely with our output of combinations when $k = r$. In fact when $k = r$, instead of doing a further recursive call at the next level we simply output the current combination. Compare this with the previous algorithm.

The whole recursive process can be started by a call to the procedure with k set to 1. When $k = 1$ the *column*[0] element is referenced. This element should be initialized to zero. The complete description for the algorithm can now be given.

Algorithm description

1. Establish positive non-zero set size, combination size, and array for storing combinations. Also establish index to current column of combination set.
2. Initialize current column value to current value of previous column.
3. While current column value is less than its upper limit do
   (a) increase current column value by one;
   (b) if current column not final column then
       (b.1) recursively call procedure to generate all the next column values associated with the current column value
       else
       (b'.1) new combination available in array so write it out.

Pascal implementation

```
procedure combinationset(n,r: integer);
var column: array[0 .. 20] of integer;
    k: integer;
```

```
procedure combinations(k: integer);
var j {index for printing combinations}: integer;
begin {recursively generates all combinations of first n integers r at a
time in lexical order}
   {assert: n>0 ∧ r>0 ∧ r=<n ∧ 1=<k=<r ∧ column[0]=0}
   column[k] := column[k−1];
   {invariant: after the ith iteration column[1 .. k−1]=c1, c2, ...,
   c(k−1) ∧ c1<c2 .. <column[k] ∧ column[k]=column[k−1]+i ∧
   column[k]=<n−r+k ∧ column[k+1 .. r] have assumed all
   possible values in [column[k]+1 .. n] such that column[k]<
   column[k+1]<.. column[r]}
   while column[k]<n−r+k do
      begin {generate next value for the current column}
         column[k] := column[k]+1;
         if k<r then
            {generate subsequent column values associated with the
            current column}
            combinations(k+1)
         else
            begin {next combination available − write it out}
               for j := 1 to r do
                  write(column[j]);
               writeln
            end
      end
   {assert: all combinations beginning with c1, c2, ..., c(k−1) have
   been generated}
end;

begin {combinationset}
   column[0] := 0;
   k := 1;
   combinations(k)
end
```

Notes on design

1. The number of times the conditional test in the loop is executed gives
    us a measure of the time complexity of this algorithm (this is equal to
    the number of nodes in our mechanism tree). Referring to the tree for
    our $^5C_3$ example, we see that there are $^5C_1$ leaf nodes, $^4C_2$ nodes the
    next level up and only $^3C_1$ nodes at the top level. In this case, there are
    therefore $^5C_3 + ^4C_2 + ^3C_1 = 19$ nodes. In the general case, there will be

    $$\sum_{i=1}^{r} {}^{n-i+1}C_{r-i+1} \text{ nodes.}$$

    The depth of recursion is r.

2. To characterize the behavior of this non-linear recursive procedure, let us consider first the case where the call is made to *combinations*($k+1$). If we assume that this call does not alter the elements in the first k columns and that it generates all appropriate combinations for columns $k+1$ through r then we can consider the case where the call is made to *combinations*(k). When the current call to *combinations* does not invoke any further internal recursive calls our assumptions must be correct. In the general case, where the call is made to *combinations*(k), admitting the assumptions associated with the call to *combinations*($k+1$), the present call will leave the elements in *column*$[0..k-1]$ untouched since they are not referenced in the body of the procedure. Furthermore, the present call ensures that all combinations of *column*$[k..n]$ are produced correctly because all possible choices of *column*$[k]$ are made. After each choice a recursive call to *combinations*($k+1$) is invoked. This argument can form the basis of a formal inductive proof of the procedure. Each recursive call to *combinations* results in a move to a higher column and it terminates at $k=r$ in each case. We can loosely conclude that the algorithm terminates.

3. Notice with this algorithm, like the preceding one, how the solution to a larger problem is built up by solving a succession of inter-related smaller problems.

4. The impractical iterative solution to a specific problem was helpful in guiding us to a general recursive solution to the problem.

5. A set of r nested loops can be replaced by a recursive procedure that calls itself r times. Many problems can be solved in this way.

6. In the implementation, we have chosen to include only the variable k as a parameter for reasons of efficiency.

Applications

Combinatorics, applications of probability theory.

Supplementary problems

8.5.1   Modify the given algorithm so that it prints out all combinations *up to* r at a time in lexical order.

8.5.2   Implement a recursive algorithm that generates the ^nC_r combinations in reverse lexical order.

8.5.3   Design a combination generation algorithm that accepts as input a set of n characters and produces as output all combinations of size r of these characters.

8.5.4   Another simple way to generate combinations in lexical order is to start with the combination $\{1, 2, 3, ..., r\}$. The next combination in each case is generated by scanning the current combination from right to left until we encounter an element that has *not* attained its maximum value. This element is incremented by one, and all elements to the right of it are set to their lowest *allowable* values and so the process repeats. Implement this combination generation algorithm and compare its performance with our original algorithm.

8.5.5   Design an algorithm that accepts as input a given combination of the ^nC_r set and returns as output the next combination in lexical order.

8.5.6   In many instances, the algorithm we have produced must change more than one element in going from one combination to the next. Try to design a combination generation algorithm that only needs to make one change in going from one combination to the next. (Ref. P. J. Chase, "Combinations of *m* out of *n* objects", *Comm. ACM*, **13**, 368 (1970).)

Algorithm 8.6
PERMUTATION GENERATION

Problem

Design an algorithm that generates all permutations of the first n integers taken r at a time where n and r are greater than or equal to 1.

Algorithm development

As we shall see, the problem of permutation generation shares some of the characteristics of the last two problems. It also possesses other aspects which should help to deepen our understanding of recursion. As with our previous two problems, we will concentrate on dealing with the problem expressed in terms of integers. Related problems for other than integers can be handled similarly.

To make a start with the problem we can consider a specific example involving the generation of all permutations of the first 5 integers taken 3 at a time. Unlike the combinations' situation, order is important and so sequences like $\{1, 2, 3\}$, $\{2, 1, 3\}$ and $\{3, 1, 2\}$ all represent *distinct* permutations.

Some of the permutations of the first 5 integers taken 3 at a time are:

$$
\begin{array}{ccccccccc}
1 & 1 & 1 & 1 & 1 & 1 & \ldots & 5 & 5 \\
2 & 2 & 2 & 3 & 3 & 3 & \ldots & 4 & 4 \\
3 & 4 & 5 & 2 & 4 & 5 & \ldots & 2 & 3
\end{array}
$$

Studying our example carefully, we see that each of the three (r) columns can assume *all* of the 5 (n) values as in algorithm 8.4. However, within a given permutation, no value may occur in more than one column (i.e. no repetitions are allowed). In the combination generation problem too, no repetitions were allowed. We should therefore see if this approach can be used here.

Unfortunately, when we try to solve the permutation generation problem in the same way as the combination generation problem we run into trouble. The problem arises because the integers within a given permutation need not be ordered. (For example, {1, 3, 2} is a perfectly acceptable permutation.

It may be worthwhile trying to phrase the problem in terms of a simple but impractical nested loop structure. Such an exploration may provide us with the clues we need to solve the problem. At this point there are three things we have discovered about permutation sets. Firstly, *each* column must be able to take on *all* of the first n integer values. Secondly, the integers in a permutation need not be ordered and, thirdly, there must be *no* repetitions within a given permutation. Our work in algorithm 8.4 gave us a simple nested-loop structure for ensuring that each column assumed all the values in the range 1 to n. Three loops were needed to solve the $^5U_3$ problem. We therefore might expect to be able to use three loops to solve the $^5P_3$ problem. If we were to do this we would need some method for deciding that no integer was repeated in each permutation printed. Applying this restriction, the algorithm needed to solve the $^5P_3$ problem might be:

```
    ⋮
for i := 1 to 5 do
  for j := 1 to 5 do
    for k := 1 to 5 do
      if "there are no duplicates among i, j, and k" then
         "print out i, j, and k as next permutation"
```

Our experience with the last two algorithms has shown us that a set of r nested loops can often be replaced by a recursive procedure that calls itself to depth r. We might therefore be encouraged to try to formulate a recursive solution to the present problem. The explorations we have made so far suggest that we may tentatively describe the required algorithm as follows:

```
for i := 1 to n do
    begin
        "solve the remaining smaller problems similarly ensuring that
        there are no duplicates."
    end
```

This mechanism will handle the generation of the values in the first column. To generate the range of values in the second column, we once again need a loop that generates integers in the range 1 to n. The generation of integers for the second column is accompanied by a *restriction. No second column value can be the same as its first column value*. Extending this argument to the third column we see that although all integers in the range 1 to n are potential candidates, no third column value can be equal to either the first or second column values of the current permutation. The same argument applies to subsequent columns. We must now face up to the problem of generating these restricted column values. We might envisage using a collection of complicated **if**-statements or a loop to do the job but these methods look as though they will be unwieldy. We therefore need to look for a simple way of *remembering* what the current situation is in the columns that precede the current column. What would be preferable is a *single* test to see if the current integer is eligible for use in the current column. The question that remains is, can we construct a one step test to decide the eligibility of the current integer in the permutation being generated? Since the test must not involve a series of comparisons the issue is, in what other way can we *remember* what integers have been used already? Our only alternative seems to be to use an array to store those integers that have been used. The question now is, can an array be compatible with making a single eligiblity test? Our answer to this must be yes, provided we make the test by *indexing*. This will involve several things. When integer i has been employed in a column we will need to mark accordingly the ith position in our "remembering" array as it is used. At any given time we can then test if a given integer k has already been used by seeing if the array location at k has been marked. A Boolean array can be used for this purpose.

Having overcome the problem of deciding what integers are eligible for a particular column, we see that the problem that remains to be solved is almost the same as that for generating permutations with unrestricted repetitions (algorithm 8.4). We can therefore summarize our progress with the following outline for a permutation generation algorithm:

```
for i := 1 to n do
    if integer i is eligible for the current column k then
    (a)  mark ith integer as no longer eligible for subsequent columns,
    (b)  save i as current column value,
```

(c)   recursively generate values for the remaining columns for the current permutation.

Studying this mechanism carefully, we see that it has a flaw because as soon as the first permutation has been generated *all* of the first n integers will have been marked as ineligible. To try to work out how to correct this, let us consider a specific example. Suppose the first permutation generated for $n = 4$ is:

$$1 \quad 2 \quad 3 \quad 4$$

The next permutation will be:

$$1 \quad 2 \quad 4 \quad 3$$

To derive the second permutation from the first, both the 3rd and 4th column values need to be changed with the third column value being changed *first*. If this is to work out the 4 must be eligible for selection as the third column value. This can only happen if it has previously been *removed* from the not-eligible set. We must work out how to incorporate this removal operation into our algorithm. Studying our algorithm, we see that the value of the loop index is marked as "not eligible" *before* the recursive call is made because this information must be carried through to *later* calls for the *current* permutation. It follows that after the recursive step has terminated, the current loop index is no longer needed in the "not eligible" set. At this point the index value needs to be *removed* so that it may be eligible for use in a later (or earlier) column for the next permutation. With this addition to our algorithm it should function correctly. The step to be added to the loop is:

(d)   remove current index i from the "not eligible" set

The Boolean values *true* and *false* can be used to mark and remove values from the not-eligible set.

At this point we have done enough development to be able to describe our algorithm. We will give the Pascal implementation as we might already have some reservations about the efficiency of the algorithm we have produced because with each recursive call the range 1 to n must be considered.

```
procedure lperm(var k:integer);
var i:integer;
begin
   for i := 1 to n do
      if available[i] then
         begin
            column[k] := i;
            available[i] := false;
```

```
        if k<r then
            lperm(k+1)
        else                '
            "write out current permutation";
            available[i] := true
        end
    end
```

The permutations are stored in the array *column* and the Boolean array *available* is used to mark which integers are no longer available. They must all be made available initially. The algorithm we have constructed produces the permutation set in lexical order. Studying this mechanism carefully, we observe that the dominant instruction is the test to see if the integer i is currently available for selection. The test will have to be made n^r times which is usually *much* greater than the number of permutations in the set, ^nP_r.

From the observations we have just made, we are led to the question, how can we improve the performance of our algorithm? What we need to do is find a way of reducing the cost of generating each new permutation. To try to discover a method let us again focus on the steps for going from the first to the second permutation for $n = 4$

$$
\begin{array}{llll}
1 & 2 & 3 & 4 \\
1 & 2 & 4 & 3
\end{array}
\qquad
\begin{array}{l}
\text{(first permutation)} \\
\text{(second permutation)}
\end{array}
$$

These two permutations only differ in the order of their last two elements. Our present algorithm must execute the test

if *available[i]* **then** ...

four times to go from the first to the second permutation.

This seems rather excessive since the two permutations only differ in the order of their last two elements. We might therefore ask, is there a simpler mechanism that would allow us to go from the first to the second permutation? The answer is yes, all we need to do is *exchange* the last two elements of the first permutation.

We also see from this example that exchanging any pair of elements in the set will give us another permutation. This suggests that we may be able to construct a more efficient permutation generation algorithm that is based on exchanging pairs of elements. If we are to base our algorithm on exchanging pairs of elements, we will need to do it systematically to avoid missing any permutations and also to avoid generating duplicates.

The question that we must face up to is, how can we systematically generate permutations using exchanges? Our earlier experience for related problems suggests that a good way to proceed might be by building up the solution column by column. We might therefore be hopeful of constructing an algorithm with at least some of the framework of our earlier proposal. We know, for example, that the first column must assume all values in the range 1 to n. Once the first column value is chosen we are left with only $n-1$ choices for the second column value. Furthermore, once the first and second column values are chosen we are left with only $n-2$ choices for the third column and so on.

For example, for the $^5P_3$ case when we have the first two columns set as below:

$$\boxed{3 \mid 1}$$

then the possible choices for the *third* column are:

$$\{2, 4, 5\}$$

That is, we could have:

$$
\begin{array}{ccc}
3 & 1 & 2 \\
3 & 1 & 4 \\
3 & 1 & 5
\end{array}
$$

This example suggests that at any given time our n integers are divided into *two* sets, the set that has been already *chosen* and the current *unchosen* set. Our earlier algorithm used a Boolean array to distinguish between the chosen and unchosen sets. What we are now seeking is a more efficient way to distinguish between these two sets. If we can find a more efficient way of maintaining the two sets we should end up with a more efficient algorithm. Some thought reveals that one possibility would be to simply keep the k chosen values in the first k locations of the array and the remaining $n-k$ values in the remaining $n-k$ locations. Our task, then, to generate a new permutation will involve exchanging values back and forth between the chosen and unchosen sets, i.e. schematically our mechanism will involve

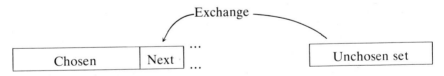

Having progressed this far, let us again try to write the simple but impractical nested loop structure for the $^5P_3$ problem and then try to proceed from there. Our discussion suggests that three nested loops will be needed to generate a three-column permutation set. In choosing the values for a given column, probably the best way to do it systematically is to choose them *consecutively* from the unchosen set. Having established these choices we might propose the following loop structure:

```
for i := 1 to 5 do
  for j := 2 to 5 do
    for k := 3 to 5 do
      begin
        column[1] := column [i];
        column[2] := column [j];
        column[3] := column [k];
      end
```

Studying this mechanism we discover that while it might at first glance appear to do the job we want, it has some flaws and inefficiencies. While *column*[1] can take on *all* its values, *column*[2] and *column*[3] are prevented from assuming *all* values. For example, suppose we start out with 1, 2, ..., 5 in the first five array locations when *column*[1] assumes the value 2 our mechanism *does not* place the 1 into the unchosen set. At this point our mechanism produces:

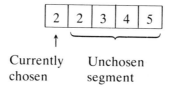

2	2	3	4	5

Currently   Unchosen
chosen   segment

which means that *column*[2] is prevented from assuming the value 1. Instead, at this point we want the configuration below.

2	1	3	4	5

How can we achieve this configuration? A straightforward approach is to *exchange* the first column value with the ith column value. Extending this idea we see that the second column value should be exchanged with the jth column value and so on. Furthermore, since i does not change in the two innermost loops, the exchange between *column*[1] and *column*[i] should take place *outside* these two loops.

In our earlier implementation, we found that it was necessary to reverse the process of eligibility. We might expect a similar situation to apply with our new algorithm. Once a value has been selected and finished with for a given column, it needs to be returned to its original position so that it can be selected for other columns. It follows that the exchange process must be *reversed*. Our nested-loop solution for the $^5P_3$ problem will therefore have the form:

```
for i := 1 to 5 do
(a)   exchange the 1st and ith column values,
(b)   for j := 2 to 5 do
```

(b.1)   exchange the 2nd and j^{th} column values,
(b.2)   for $k := 3$ to 5 do
        (2.a)   exchange the 3rd and k^{th} column values,
        (2.b)   write out current permutation,
        (2.c)   exchange the kth and 3rd column values,
(b.3)   exchange the jth and 2nd column values,
(c)   exchange the ith and 1st column values.

A check of this mechanism confirms that it will perform the task we require. Our next task is therefore to formulate it as a general recursive algorithm. Studying our nested-loop mechanism we see that essentially the same process is repeated with each loop. The common steps associated with *each* loop are:

1.   While all *available* values for current column not selected do
   (a)   exchange j^{th} available value with current column value,
   (b)   repeat the process for the remaining columns,
   (c)   exchange the current column value with the jth available value.

If we regard step (b) of this mechanism as a recursive step, then these steps embody much of what is needed to solve the problem recursively. We now must address the problems of termination and output of the permutations.

Further investigation of our mechanism confirms that it is structurally similar to our original proposal and so termination and output of permutations can be handled similarly. The marking of eligibility and non-eligibility of a given integer has been replaced by an exchange and its reversal. The test for eligibility has been replaced by adjusting the loop index so that it will always select from the currently *unchosen* or eligible set.

With the addition of the termination and output steps, formulation of our new algorithm is complete and so it can be described in detail.

Algorithm description

1.   Establish set size, permutation size, and array for storing permutations (it must be equal in length to the set size rather than the permutation size). Also establish index to current column of permutation set.
2.   While all available values for current column not selected do
   (a)   exchange j^{th} value from unchosen set with current column value,
   (b)   if current column index not at final column then
       (b.1)   recursively call procedure to generate all the next column values associated with the current representation for all columns up to the current column,

else

(b'.1)   new permutation available so write it out,

(c)   reverse the exchange made in step (a).

Pascal implementation

```
procedure permutationset(n,r: integer);
var column: array[1..20] of integer;
    k:integer;

procedure permutations(k: integer);
var i {index for printing permutations},
    j {index for selecting values from the unchosen set},
    temp {temporary variable used in exchange}: integer;
begin {recursively generates all permutations of the first n integers
taken r at a time. The permutations are not in lexical order}
    {assert: n>0 ∧ r>0 ∧ r=<n ∧ 1=<k=<r ∧
    column[1..n]=c1,c2,...c(n) ∧ c1,c2,.. all in [1..n]}
    {invariant: after jth iteration column[1.. k−1]=c1,c2,...,c(k−1)
    where c1,c2,... uniquely chosen from set [1 .. n] leaving n−k+1
    unchosen values in column[k .. n] ∧ all permutations of column
    [k .. n] generated in which column[k]=c(j) ∧ k=<j=<n}
    for j := k to n do
        begin {select all available values for the current column}
            temp := column[k];
            column[k] := column[j];
            column[j] := temp;
            if k<r then
            {generate subsequent column values}
            permutations(k+1)
            else
                begin {next permutation available – write it out}
                    for i := 1 to r do
                        write(column[i]);
                    writeln
                end;
            temp := column[k];
            column[k] := column[j];
            column[j] := temp
        end
    {assert: all permutations beginning with c1,c2,...,c(k−1) have
    been generated}
end;

begin{permutationset}
    for k := 1 to n do
        column[k] := k;
    k := 1;
    permutations(k)
end
```

Notes on design

1. When we study the mechanism tree for this algorithm we see that its time complexity is proportional to $n!/(n-r)!$. The tree for $^4P_3$ has the form given in Fig. 8.18. The number of leaf nodes is $4 \times 3 \times 2 = 24$ which corresponds to the number of permutations of 4 elements taken 3 at a time.

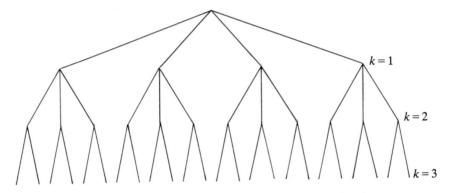

$k = 1$

$k = 2$

$k = 3$

Fig. 8.18 Mechanism tree for the $^4P_3$ problem.

2. We can characterize the behavior of this algorithm using arguments very similar to those used in characterizing the previous two algorithms. This is left as an exercise for the reader.

3. In studying our final implementation we notice that it has some built-in inefficiencies. Notice that the *first* time through the loop at each level $k = j$ and so making an exchange is unnecessary. Also setting *temp := column[k] inside* the loop is redundant because k *does not* change within the loop.

4. A common problem involving permutations is to generate all permutations of n objects taken n at a time. When our algorithm is applied to this problem, we see that it will make some unnecessary steps because it proceeds to the situation where $k = r = n$. We only really need to proceed to the situation where $k = n-1$ because after the first $n-1$ elements have been chosen, the nth element is completely determined.

5. Our final implementation, although more efficient than our earlier proposal, has only been able to gain this efficiency by sacrificing lexical output of the permutations. It may be added that there are currently about forty different algorithms that have been proposed for generating permutations. Our proposal is certainly not the most efficient but it does illustrate a rather general computational structure that can be applied to a wide range of problems.

6. Note that algorithms for generating permutations in lexical order are inherently less efficient than other algorithms because they must often use more than one exchange to go from one permutation to the next.

7. In solving this problem once again we have seen how the final solution has been built from the solution of simpler problems. Starting with the simplest problem leads us in a natural way to the idea of using *chosen* and *unchosen* sets. Once we have made this discovery it is then only a matter of working out the mechanics for maintaining these two sets. The simple nested loop model was helpful in this regard.

8. With our final algorithm, there are *two* exchanges in the body of the loop. We might suspect that it is possible to formulate an algorithm that requires *only one* exchange in the body of the loop. In fact we can make a simple change to our algorithm to produce a more efficient implementation for computing the $n!$ permutations of the first n integers. All we need do is include a test before the recursive call that will allow us to exchange the jth and k^{th} elements if $(n-k)$ is odd or exchange the nth and k^{th} elements if $(n-k)$ is even.

Applications

Combinatorial problems, simulation.

Supplementary problems

8.6.1   Modify the algorithm given to incorporate the improvements suggested in note 3.

8.6.2   Implement a recursive algorithm to compute the $n!$ permutations of the first n integers. In your implementation, the internal recursive call should be of the form *permutations(n−1)* rather than *permutations(k+1)* as we have used in the present algorithm.

8.6.3   Design an algorithm that accepts as input a given permutation of the ten digits and returns as output the *next* permutation in the set in lexical order. As an example, if we have:

current permutation is: 7 9 0 1 6 3 8 5 4 2
then the next permutation is: 7 9 0 1 6 4 2 3 5 8

As a hint, note that the last four digits in the current permutation are in *descending* order.

8.6.4   Design a recursive algorithm for generating permutations in lexical order that is based on the mechanism used to solve problem 8.6.3.

8.6.5   Implement the suggestion made in note 8 and compare the number of exchanges for this new implementation with the original and the results from problem 8.6.3.

BIBLIOGRAPHY

Rohl (1979) provides one of the best introductory treatments of recursion. Rohl's other papers and Wirth (1976) give a detailed introduction to recursion. Sedgewick (1977) gives a comprehensive survey of permutation generation methods.

1.   Alagic, S. and M. A. Arbib, *The Design of Well-Structured and Correct Programs*, Springer-Verlag, N.Y., 1978.
2.   Barron, D. W., *Recursive Techniques in Programming*, American Elsevier, N.Y., 1968.
3.   Buneman, P. and L. Levy, "The Towers of Hanoi Problem", *Inf. Proc. Letts.*, **10**, 243–4 (1980).
4.   Hayes, P. J., "A note on the Towers of Hanoi Problem", *Comp. J.* **20**, 282–5 (1977).
5.   Rohl, J. S. in "Why Recursion?" in *Proceedings of the Symposium on Language Design and Programming Methodology* (Sydney), ed. J. Tobias, 71–83, 1979.
6.   Rohl, J. S., "Recursion as an alternative to back-tracking and non-deterministic programming", pp.177–89 in *Programming Language Systems*, eds. M. C. Newey, R. B. Stanton and G. C. Wolfendale, A.N.U. Press, Canberra, 1978.
7.   Rohl, J. S., "Programming improvements to Fike's algorithm for generating permutations", *Comp. J.*, **19**, 150–9 (1976).
8.   Sedgewick, R., "Permutation generation methods", *Comp. Surv.*, **9**, 137–64 (1977).
9.   Wirth, N., *Algorithms + Data Structures = Programs*, Prentice-Hall, Englewood Cliffs, N.J., 1976.

INDEX

435